Pvt. Ltd.

Decentralised Governance *and* Planning in India

(Essays in Honor of Prof Abdul Aziz)

Editors

Gayithri Karnam

N. Sivanna

M. Devendra Babu

2020

Studium Press (India) Pvt. Ltd.

Decentralised Governance *and* Planning in India

(Essays in Honor of Prof Abdul Aziz)

ISBN: 978-93-85046-61-2

Published by:

Studium Press (India) Pvt. Ltd.
4735 / 22, 2nd Floor, Prakash Deep Building
(Near Delhi Medical Association)
Ansari Road, Darya Ganj, New Delhi-110 002
Tel.: + 91-11-43240200-15 (15 lines); Fax: 91-11-43240215
E-mail: pubdir@studiumpress.in

Printed at India

Foreword

It is not easy to write about a friend whom one has known for nearly six decades. I would like to start with a story Professor Aziz narrated years ago. It made a deep impact on me and even today I recall it vividly. The story deals with an issue which is important in our academic and social context. Also it gives an insight into Aziz's personality. In his younger days, recalls Aziz, he realized the importance of being proficient in English. He must have been more than competent in writing because his school record was outstanding but perhaps he felt the need to hone his oral communication skills. The solution he found is interesting. He and some friends in the Muslim hostel in Mysuru made a pact among themselves to speak only in English. Any lapse meant a penalty of 25 paise. And this was adhered to strictly. Anyone who listens to Aziz today will hardly believe that he ever had problems using English. This is a first rate illustration of his discipline and commitment and above all that will to excel. This is interesting because there is a view that those who do not use English at home and are educated in rural and often non-English medium schools find English difficult to learn. And Aziz typifies all the disadvantages listed above. I should also add that he communicates with felicity in Kannada, oral as well as written. The story I have narrated brings out the quintessential Aziz, never willing to rest on his laurels, confident but not oversure of himself and always trying to reach greater heights. It demonstrates how his success is very largely the result of his own effort and owes little to advantages accruing by dint of other reasons.

We met in 1956 as students in the economics honours course in Maharaja's College in Mysuru. He had migrated from Kolar district, his early college education was in Kolar. He recalled to me once how a certain gentleman in his native town, Taikal, was responsible for inducing his father to send him to Kolar to pursue his studies in college. Interestingly the gentleman was no relative of the Aziz family; indeed he was not even a co-religionist. The rest, as they say is history. It came as no great surprise when, in a batch of very talented students in the honours, he topped the list in the final honours and won the gold medal. He kept up his track record with a high first in the master's and then turned to research. His first love was labour economics but in a few years he turned to decentralization and today is recognized as a specialist of distinction in this field.

Aziz and I worked together in the Institute of Correspondence Course and Continuing Education in the University of Mysore; it was the forerunner of the present Karnataka State Open University. Along with his work in the Institute Aziz kept himself busy as a researcher. After a few years he made a decision, in my view rightly and wisely, to seek fresh pastures and joined ISEC. This is where his research abilities found full expression. Aziz has contributed in terms of extensive research particularly relating to decentralization and local government institutions and equally by initiating and organizing training programmes for elected members of Panchayat Raj Institutions. In addition he was a member of the State Finance Commission and the High Power Committee for the redressal of regional imbalances, popularly known as the D.M. Nanjundappa committee. It would not be an exaggeration to state that Aziz's works in these areas are almost pioneering. Also I know from personal experience what a role model and healthy influence he is on the younger faculty and researchers in ISEC.

A matter that has puzzled me, and I have shared this with Aziz, is that he appears never to have showed the slightest inclination to become a Vice-Chancellor. With his academic record such a position ought to have been well within his reach. Let alone seeking the position, that he would never do, he seems to have expressed no interest in it. The loss is not his; the academic world could do with a scholar and morally upright person like Aziz. This testifies to another important facet of his character, namely, a high sense of morality and scrupulous avoidance of pursuing office. It is another matter that in this instance the 'ambition' would have been wholly justified.

Let me turn now to the volume of papers brought out in his honour. Knowing Aziz as I do nothing would please him more than an academic honour such as this book of papers. They centre on a theme which is close to him, decentralization/devolution. It is in this sphere that he has made a mark as a scholar and also a firm advocate of devolution. The felicitation volume is a good blend of the different dimensions which we encounter within devolution and the practice of decentralized governance. The principal aspects discussed in this selection are the following.

There is an evolutionary narrative (M. Umapathy) which presents the manner in which institutions of local government have evolved in the country and in Karnataka. This historical perspective sets the stage as it were for the discussion in the papers that follow which deal with specific issues such as, for instance, the financial relations between the union/centre and the states. One paper traces the changing nexus of centre-state relations (Sreekantaradhya). This helps situate decentralization in the larger context of centre-state relations and with particular reference to the thorny question of sharing of resources. The paper focuses attention on the landmark changes which have taken place in this contentious area. A knotty problem in this area relates to centrally sponsored schemes. There is a complaint from the states, quite often justified, that through this route the autonomy of the states is adversely affected. There is a paper which should be read in conjunction with the one on centre-state relations. It examines centrally sponsored schemes (Shailendra and Rajput) and suggests, by implication at least, some problems requiring further inquiry. For instance is it politically easier for an authority at a distance like the union government to implement decisions which are likely to be electorally unpopular? At the same time how justified is it to bypass state governments in a federal or quasi-federal set up? While no simple answers are provided for these questions the papers help focus the light on their importance.

Regional imbalance within the state of Karnataka is discussed in a paper exclusively devoted to the theme (Seshadri). The paper remarks perceptively that presently the state displays 'united existence and divided development'. It also points out that the problem is a long standing one. There are questions which this analysis suggests. For instance is there a growing awareness in the relatively more backward areas of imbalances? Does this awareness itself hint at some progress having been made in regard to development? What is the degree to which imbalances are influenced by developments at the national level such as for example the withdrawal of the state from some spheres of activity and the corresponding increase in reliance on market forces? Possibly a contribution focusing on this dimension would have rounded off this aspect of the discussion. However a paper on what state initiative can achieve makes valuable reading. This is the paper by G. Palanithurai on habitat planning which brings home the point that a well conceived and properly implemented intervention by the state can result in positive outcomes. What good governance consists of is adumbrated in some detail by S.N. Sangita. The paper speaks of the perennial problem of the unwillingness of higher tiers/levels of governance to share power with the lower ones. This is seen as a serious constraint in the way of successful devolution. Here again a question that leaps up is, which are the factors that make for that elusive entity called 'political will' and what can be done to promote it. Perhaps a discussion of the constellation of circumstances which led to the failure of Rajiv Gandhi's government to push through the 64th constitutional amendment bill—largely the precursor of the 73rd amendment — would have presented the issue within a wider perspective.

The implications of decentralised governance for development and the absence of strict demarcation between state governments and panchayats regarding functions is dealt with in three papers (N. Sivanna, Devendra Babu, Gopinath Reddy). Babu's paper is an addition to the literature on the evolution of decentralised planning for development in India. Reddy situates his analysis in the specific context of Telengana and regards both this state and unified Andhra Pradesh as 'decentralisation deficit' states.

An interesting presentation is the analysis of the Lambani Thandas with reference to what the author (Pradeep Ramavath) calls 'dysfunctional school development'. A matter which should have captured attention but does not appear to have is how the status of the Lambanis within the SC category (in Karnataka they are regarded as a touchable SC), impacts upon their lives. The empirical part of the volume is represented by a study (Billava and Kulkarni) on the functioning of the Gram Sabha. As might be expected the findings are not flattering to the institution of Gram Sabha. Sivanna expresses a similar view in his paper already referred to.

The papers in this felicitation volume are a fitting tribute to a fine scholar, a committed researcher and a model worthy of emulation, a true exemplar. This is to wish Abdul Aziz many more years of creative work and happiness with Mrs. Zeenat Aziz, the inspiration and support behind his achievement.

Prof. V K Natraj
Board Member, ISEC
Former Director of MIDS, Chennai

About the Editors

Gayithri Karnam is a Professor of Economics in the Center for Economic Studies and Policy at the Institute for Social and Economic Change, Bangalore. She specializes in the area of Public Economics, Industrial Economics and Public policy studies. She has conducted extensive research in the area of state fiscal studies, public expenditure planning and management, Budget reforms. She has served as an advisor on a number of state government committees and as consultant to international donor agencies like USAID and DFID in state level fiscal studies. She has been a recipient of Shastri Indo Canadian faculty research fellowship twice to undertake comparative fiscal studies at the Carleton University, Canada. She has undergone training at the Duke Center for International development, Duke University on aspects relating to 'public budgeting and financial management'. She has also participated in the executive education program on 'Public financial management in a changing world' at the John F Kennedy School of government at the Harvard University, Boston.

Dr. N. Sivanna (retired from service as Professor at ISEC, Bengaluru) currently working as Chief Executive Officer, Karnataka Panchayat Parishath, Bengaluru and also as Hon. Professor, Karnataka State Rural Development and Panchayat Raj University, Gadag. He is a development practitioner, researcher, consultant and trainer with special interest in decentralization and its process. In a career, spanning more than 30 years, he has the working experience of conducting independent research in the areas of political and administrative decentralization, guided nine PhD students and one Post-Doctoral fellow, handled projects, sponsored by the World Bank, Ford Foundation, IDPAD and Governments of India and Karnataka, conducted training programs to functionaries of local government institutions like Panchayati Raj Institutions, urban local bodies and engaging as resource person to both government and non-government organizations. He has authored four books, six monographs, nine working papers and more than fifty research articles published in various research journals.

Dr. M Devendra Babu, Ph. D in Economics from Bangalore University is currently Honorary Professor, Karnataka State Rural Development and Panchayat Raj University, Gadag. Prior to this he served in Institute for Social and Economic Change (ISEC), Bangalore for about 33 years and retired as Professor and Head, Centre for Decentralisation and Development. His research area includes rural decentralisation, rural development and public economics. In his long service in the Institute carried out quite a large number of research projects for Karnataka government and for international organisations. He has quite a large number of publications to his credit, both in national and international journals, published books and Monographs, presented papers in national and international seminars and conferences. He was also consultant to World Bank, India.

Acknowledgements

The editors would like to acknowledge the initiative of Prof S. Japhet, National Law School of India University, in conceiving the idea of a book in honor of Prof Abdul Aziz, when he was bestowed with Karnataka Rajyotsava award by the Government of Karnataka. A special word of thanks is due to Prof Venkata Rao, Vice Chancellor, National Law School of India University to have facilitated the felicitation function and a seminar in honor of Prof Abdul Aziz.Prof M.G. Chandrakanth, Director. Institute for Social and Economic Change played a key role in the felicitation and seminar and we thank him for the same. Our thanks are also due to Prof Babu Mathew and Prof Sony Pellissery who took the lead in coordinating the program along with Prof Gayithri, Prof Devendra Babu and Prof Sivanna. This book would not have happened but for the cooperation of the paper contributors who responded to the deadlines and made their presentations at the seminar. We thank each one of them.We acknowledge the critical input of all the resource persons who participated in the seminar and gave their valuable comments on the papers presented.We are thankful to Prof V.K.Nataraj, who participated in the seminar and also has written foreword for this volume. Most importantly we thank Prof Abdul Aziz for having inspired a number of scholars to conduct research on decentralization theme and also trained them. A special word of thanks to Studium Press and in particular to Dr Govil for the professional manner in which they have executed publication of this volume.

Table of Contents

1

Introduction and Overview

K. Gayithri[1], N. Sivanna[1] and M. Devendra Babu[1]

The major justification for decentralization is derived from the fact that it is said to take Government and administration closer to people, involve people in decision-making process and ensure administrative transparency and accountability of the functionaries to people; effectively mobilize local resources for development; ensure fulfillment of the felt needs and aspirations of the people; and facilitate cost effective planning and implementation of local development projects using local resources and local wisdom. The rationale of decentralization is derived from the failure of national and state level governance in some areas and the ability of decentralized governments to start from where the former has left.

The failure of macro plans (resource allocation decision-making) at the macro and meso (state) levels to reach benefits of development to backward regions, weaker sections and traditional sectors had set in motion some effort to explore new planning strategies. Decentralized planning which emerged as a new planning strategy was expected to take care of the local development needs with focus chiefly on weaker sections, backward sub-state regions and traditional sectors. A good measure of theoretical literature which emerged from the various schools of thought (such as public choice, public administration, public finance and political economy schools) built up a strong theoretical base for decentralized resource allocation decision-making.

In India, decentralized planning, though was talked about as far back as the Fourth Five-Year Plan, picked up momentum after the 73rd

[1] This volume is an outcome of a seminar organized to felicitate Prof. Abdul Aziz who was conferred the Karnataka Rajyotsava award for his academic excellence by the Government of Karnataka.

and 74th Amendment to the Constitution in 1992. The state legislation which followed soon thereafter created the institutional structures required for planning and implementation of local development projects.

It is customary to trace the history of decentralization in India to ancient times referring to the little village republics which were administered by the *panch*- the five village headmen. The British are credited to have revived decentralized governance system by establishing Panchayats and municipalities for rural and urban governance respectively.

Failure of the centralized system of governance and planning to resolve local problems and to promote local level development has led to an upsurge of interest in local governance in recent years. However, it must be recognized that the local governance system will not provide answers to local problems and development imperatives unless such a system is responsive to these problems, effective and efficient in its reach.

NORMATIVE MODEL OF LOCAL GOVERNANCE

There is a general consensus in the country about the principles which should govern local governance system if it were to be responsive and efficient. Based on such consensus, a summary of a normative model was attempted elsewhere by Aziz (1993 and 1994). It may be worth starting by summarizing the main constituents of such a model. It is generally agreed that any local governance system should (a) Have an appropriate institutional structure, and (b) The latter should have a conducive environment in which it functions. The institutional structures needed are:

1. Decentralized political institution to identify and articulate people's felt needs and aspirations.
2. Decentralized administrative structure to formulate and implement the local level plans keeping in view the felt needs of the people; and
3. Decentralized data collection machinery to collect and supply the required data to the plan formulating agency.

The environment required should have the following attributes:

i) Representation in the governance system to various interest groups such that decision-making power is equitably distributed and well represented;

ii) People's participation in planning and implementation of development programs so that local interest and initiative are encouraged;

iii) Political and financial autonomy to the local governance system to ensure that these bodies function independently of higher level governments;

iv) Presence of experts, planners and data collecting personnel to facilitate formulation of technically competent and feasible plans;

v) Integration of the local level political institutions into a system of state and union government; and

vi) A close working relationship between local governments and people's organizations/NGOs.

Keeping these parameters we may now review the evolution of governance system to see how far the latter has moved towards the normative goal.

The paper *by* S.S. Meenakshisundaram, Panchayati Raj in India: A vision and roadmap for the future, takes a close look at the journey of PRIs for the last 25 years. In doing so, the author observes that since the theoretical and empirical realities throws genuine doubts about the capacity and accountability of these grassroot level institutions, what needs to be done to bring the practice in line with the theory? In the light of the experience gained during the last 25 years, what should be our vision for the future of panchayats and what could be an ideal roadmap to realize that vision? This paper makes an attempt to answer these questions. The paper looks into both positive and negative aspects of panchayats functioning and observes that panchayats, based on reports, are not functioning in most parts of the country, they appear strong in structure but weak in delivery and on an average, decentralization of governance in India has been poorly implemented with wide variation among States. The key deficiencies identified are. poor response to the grama sabhas across states with their meetings not taking place regularly; lack of operational linkages between different tiers of local governance at district, intermediate and village levels preventing efficient service delivery; lack of devolution of functions, funds and functionaries; the fragmentation of central and state programmes and funding streams; the retention of decision making power in the state and central levels through parallel bodies and sectoral bureaucracy and poor accountability.

In spite of the above-mentioned shortcomings, certain achievements and positive features of the Panchayati Raj system have also come to notice such as, improvement in attendance of school teachers and medical staff, increase in revenue from assets transferred to the Panchayats, significant public awareness of the welfare programmes implemented at different levels, better communication between the people and the government, early warning system for disaster management etc. Political will and public demand are however required to build on these positive features and overcome the shortcomings.

Keeping in view the above negative and positive aspects of Panchayats functioning, Meenakshisundaram provides a vision for Panchayati Raj governance over the next ten to fifteen years. To start with, the basic vision should be to ensure that the Panchayats function as Institutions of Self-Government as envisaged under Articles 40 and 243 (G) of the constitution. Gandhiji's dream and the constitutional mandate empowering people to achieve good governance through democratic decentralization have to be realized without any further delay. Strengthening, catalyzing and facilitating panchayats to improve the quality of life and infrastructural amenities for their citizens by adopting good and responsive governance practices should be the immediate vision for Panchayats. Strengthening democracy at the grass roots levels through peoples' organizations such as the Self-Help Groups (SHG), Watershed Development Committees (WDCs), School Development and Management Committees (SDMCs) etc., below the GP level and integrating these with the Grama Sabha/GP to attain decentralized and participatory local governance through such institutions should also have to be achieved.

Strategies to strengthen decentralization in rural India have to be evolved keeping in mind two distinct scenarios. First is to accept the existing design (of having a uniform three tier system in the larger states) and propose strategies for achieving the vision envisaged. The second is to take a critical look at the existing structure itself and then determine whether the structure needs to be redesigned to ensure better governance at the local level. In making a case for alternative institutional structure for local governance in India, he proposes a single local governance structure covering both rural urban institutions. A single local government at the district level can perhaps look after the needs of its urban and rural components with a set of safeguards built into it so as to ensure just development of the entire area. Such a district government can also plan for the entire district obviating the need to have a separate DPC to coordinate action by various implementing agencies at the district level, including the ZP and city/town municipalities. The district government will be the first level of decentralization below the state and will provide the necessary link between the state and the local governments either directly or through its units/offices spread across the district. Reorganizing the PRIs as indicated above requires a lot of debate and discussions among the different stakeholders and ultimately another constitution amendment perhaps!

The paper *by* M. Umapathi provides a kaleidoscopic view of the history of local governments in India in general and Karnataka in particular covering, ancient, medieval, British rule and post- independence. Using this historical perspective, the author analyses the evolution of local governments, their present predicament and offers policy-oriented suggestions, based on the learnings of their functioning, for strengthening the functioning of present-day local government institutions. The author traces and argues that the earliest local governments were found to be 'really local' with the status of sovereign and self- governments. They were even called 'republics'. As higher-level governments emerged, the local governments came under their supervision, subordination and control. Modern local governments, especially in India, have become statutory, regulated and weak 'local bodies' or 'token bodies'.

Today, with the burgeoning population, ever expanding territorial size, the challenges of economic development and frequently faced grim ecological crises have put local governance in doldrums. Argued in this backdrop, the author observes that local governments are crying for reforms. The 73rd and 74th Constitutional Amendments have in a way improved to some extent their status, stability, representation and financial resources. But they have fallen short of in improving their political, administrative, financial and technical capabilities for solving both their organisational and institutional problems. Notwithstanding, the local governments in India demand a second tranche of constitutional reforms to provide them capable structures, better resources and powers to function autonomously from the state governments. Bold democratic, managerial and technocratic designs and solutions are called for and are needed to be well defined.

As reform measures, the paper suggests for establishing *Keri*/street panchayats to take decentralization to where people really live and help build 'local communities' and to protect 'commons'; provision for directly elected presidents and mayors to promote a strong, stable and institutionalized local leadership; provision for cabinet form of local governments for integrated and accountable governance; providing for 'specialised' managerial' and 'technical' services at the local government level to free them from the domination of the 'generalist' state civil services and; for making governance- local and national- to move ultimately towards capable governments from *Keri*/street level to the national level.

In making a case for decentralisation, governance and inclusive development, the paper *by* Satyanarayana Sangita, Democratic Decentralisation, Good Governance and Inclusive Development in India, argues that Decentralised Governments (DGs), along with central and state governments, promote good governance and inclusive development in a diverse society like India. Unlike higher level governments, he further argues that DGs facilitate for the participation and representation of the socially disadvantaged groups and minorities to exercise control over the governance of the local area for promoting their development in particular and others in general. More significantly, the author observes that the decentralised governments enable the local people to formulate, implement, supervise and monitor development programmes and schemes and ensure accountability of leaders and administrators to deliver services efficiently, effectively and see that the benefits of development are equitably distributed to all sections of the society. These issues and concerns are analysed on the basis of India's experience with the rural decentralised governments *viz.*, Panchayat Raj Institutions.

In concluding the discussion, the author observes that democratic decentralization promotes good governance and inclusive development by enabling minorities and disadvantaged groups to share power in the governance of the country. People's participation promotes trust in the decentralised government, since they got opportunity to select their own governments and policies. The representation also enables the people to trust their government. The decentralised government enables to formulate policies reflecting the needs and aspiration of the people and also promotes accountability and there by reduces wastages and corruption. In spite of these advantages the decentralised governments are not able to function as an autonomous institution due to political, administrative and financial interference from the higher level governments. However, the author strongly feels that committed 'political' will of the higher-level governments is seen as the main constraint for effective functioning of decentralised governments.

Forging a strong link between the Centrally Sponsored Schemes (CSSs) and Panchayat Raj Institutions (PRIs) is seen as a solution which can both help CSSs to shed their top-down character for better outcomes, and enable PRIs to emerge as institutions of real self-governance. In this context this paper looks at the emerging experiences and challenges focusing on six major CSSs. Eight major states representing four broad geographical regions of India were selected for the study. Data were collected at four levels for each scheme: State, Zilla Panchayat (ZP), Intermediate (Block) Panchayat (IP), and Village Panchayat (VP). A relatively backward district was selected in each state to examine the role being played by PRIs at the three levels. The paper by Shylendra and Rajput makes an attempt to capture for each programme the underlying processes and outcomes of involving of PRIs in planning, implementation and monitoring.

The study reveals that the thrust for actual linkage comes mainly from attaining programme specific goals than the aim of deepening the devolution process. As a result neither the goal of improving grassroots delivery of CSSs nor the cause of empowering Panchayats is addressed fully. The study observed wide variations across schemes and states in the involvement of PRIs. Overall, the PRIs are found involved largely in some aspect of programme implementation and monitoring.

The study has identified systemic and programmatic hurdles that limit an effective linkage between CSSs and PRIs. Systemically, inadequate and slow progress towards devolution is a major constraint. The continued top-down nature of CSSs is a programmatic constraint which affects the potential role of PRIs. What is needed for a meaningful linkage is restructuring of CSSs to come out of their top-down mould and enabling the states to deepen the decentralisation process.

India adopted Five Year Plans to accelerate economic growth and at the same time to reduce poverty, unemployment, inequalities and regional disparities. Centralised planning (top-down approach) was practiced at the national and state levels. Macro planning undertaken in the country from 1951 had succeeded in promoting growth of Gross Domestic Product (GDP), but the country could not overcome the problems of poverty, social and economic inequalities even after decades of planning. Though the need for decentralised planning was highlighted in the First Five Year Plan (1951–56) and in the subsequent plans no concrete shape emerged towards this policy change. Meanwhile an upsurge of interest is witnessed towards decentralization in the last three decades in the third world countries. India also adopted decentralization policies and reforms through amending the Constitution (73rd and 74th) in the year 1992. The constitution places emphasis on decentralised planning and towards this end incorporated many provisions in the 73rd Amendment relating to Panchayats such as Article 243G – powers and functions, 243H- fiscal powers, 243I – constitution of finance commission by the states, 243ZD of 74th amendment for constitution of planning committee at the district level. Many of the states have by and large incorporated the above-mentioned provisions in their Panchayat Raj Acts.

In this background the paper *by* M. Devendra Babu critically evaluates the status of decentralised planning in India. The grass-root level planning, by and large, has not moved forward in an intended manner and speed. Only two or three states in India (Kerala, Karnataka and Maharashtra) realistically initiated planning from below. Though the then planning commission made a policy shift of preparing plans from below *i.e.,* through Panchayats and urban bodies for the eleventh plan synchronising with that of state and central plans. This attempt too failed. Though the states prepared the 11th Five Year Plan for the districts through grassroot level elected governments, they have not been implemented for various reasons.

B.S. Sreekantaradhya's paper discusses some landmark developments in the evolution of India's federal finances. The recent years have witnessed a few landmark developments in India's federal financial relations. First, there has been a fundamental shift in the structure of financial transfers from the centre to the sub-national governments. The Constitution (Eightieth Amendment) Act 2000 facilitated augmentation of the centre's resources available for transfers by including the proceeds of all central taxes in the divisible pool. Further, the successive Finance Commissions of India increased the percentage share of the states from the divisible pool. The recommendation of the Fourteenth Finance Commission, in particular, is very significant in this regard. Its recommendation to increase the share of the states to 42 percent of the divisible pool was a landmark decision as it contributed to higher empowerment and enhancement of the autonomy of the states with the availability of more untied transfers.

Second, the landmark 73rd and 74th Amendments to the Indian constitution provided impetus to the decentralisation process. After these amendments, it is mandatory on the part of the Central Finance Commission (CFC) under Article 280bb and 280c to recommend measures needed to augment the consolidated fund of a state to supplement the resources of Panchayats and urban local bodies. The CFC recommends a certain percentage of the divisible pool of central taxes (over and above the share of the states) and converts this into grants-in-aid under Article 275 and this amount is distributed among the local bodies as per the criteria recommended by the Finance Commission. This arrangement augments the financial resources of the local bodies very significantly enabling them to carry out the responsibilities entrusted to them more effectively.

Third, restructuring of the Centrally Sponsored Schemes (CSSs) under the NITI Aayog regime to remove several of their defects about which states were constantly complaining is another landmark development in India's federal financial relations. The new approach to non-statutory transfers marks a great departure from the past. The number of CSSs has been greatly reduced. One-size-fits-all approach of the past has been given up and the states have been given greater autonomy to meet state-specific needs. Transfers to the states for these schemes are based on the criteria evolved by a committee and the discretionary powers of the Ministries of the Government of India in this regard have been dispensed with. These changes have contributed to the strengthening the autonomy of the state's leading to meaningful cooperative federalism.

In her paper on Fiscal Dependence of Local Bodies, Gayithri analyses the sources of finances of the local bodies. The paper observes that local governments in India in general and Karnataka in particular have depicted a large-scale dependence on state government financial support in discharging their functions and provision of services. It is argued that the excessive dependence of the local bodies on transfers leads to a situation where in the decentralization process tends to get vitiated and the performance of local bodies becomes vulnerable to any adverse changes in the resource transfer. Further the extent and nature of transfers is largely dependent on the fiscal capacity of the state government supporting the local bodies even while providing adequate resources for the state's own commitments.

The paper observes that devolution to local bodies is observed to be highly vulnerable to state's overall fiscal position creating uncertainty in the flow of funds. This phenomenon is reported to be more predominant for the PRIs as the share of ULBs is observed to be by and large on the increase albeit it's smaller share in total. This is more with reference to plan/development funding than the non-plan funding which largely is towards salary. Uncertainty/unpredictability of fund support and hamper the developmental activities of the local bodies.

There has been a sharp decline in plan funding from the state's plan outlay from both the state and center sources reiterating the fact that while development funding is receiving a setback, the salary component continues to be on the rise. The support provided by the centre and states are not complementing each other rather they are substituting for one another, which once again raises the issue of predictability of assured funding.

Decentralized governance in India has effectively begun with the 73rd Amendment to the Constitution, which opened a new era in the history of Panchayati Raj. Set in this context, N. Sivanna in this paper attempts to look at the journey of decentralization in the state of Karnataka over the last two decades. The author analysis this Karnataka's journey keeping in view the processes involved in decentralizing the power and authority and their implications on the development outcomes. The paper reveals that the Karnataka has been a progressive state in empowering the three-tier Panchayats and has been steadily evolving with the government putting constant and meaningful efforts to enable Panchayats to function as 'Institutions of Self-Government', as visualised in Constitutional 73rd Amendment, and thereby making them to function as instruments of rural development. In support of this the author makes a point that in Karnataka, more and more government programmes and schemes are being implemented through Panchayats with a clear budgetary allocation for district sector to improve the development process. Notwithstanding, the well institutionalised processes of decentralized governance, there are certain structural and social constraints that often come in the way of Panchayats from delivering the development outcomes at the local level. It has been a long journey for the Panchayats to transform from traditional role of maintaining community affairs at the local level in attaining the constitutional status as "Institutions of Self-Government". The failure of centralized planning in post second world war most of the developing countries have initiated decentralized reforms with an intent of involving people in decision-making thereby improving the effectiveness of delivery of public services at the local level. In India, Panchayat Raj system has started in 1959 with an understanding that Panchayats can deliver better services compared to state or union governments. Karnataka state is one of the progressive states as far as implementing the decentralized governance reform is concerned; Successive amendments in the Panchayat Raj Act indicates the will of state governments to devolve tho 'power to the people'.

The paper narrates the various processes involved in decentralizing the power and authority to the local government institutions and more so to rural areas. Initiatives such as decentralized planning through people participation at the local level is relatively successful in institutionalizing the bottom-up planning. Thereby we can witness a considerable change in the priorities of local development shifting from infrastructure to rural employment and social sectors. However, the development outcomes are not satisfactory in the ground. This can be attributed to the factors such as low people's participation especially by the women, SCs/STs and youth in the Grama Sabha meetings. It has serious implications on the efficacy of Grama Sabha and its role in enabling decentralised planning process for the development.

An important observation is that even now the basic services such as education and health are delivered through respective departments. Although these subjects are enumerated in Eleventh Schedule (Article 243G) and has to be devolved to PRIs, sadly Grama Panchayats have a least role in the implementation of education and health related programs/schemes. Structural barriers such as influence of dominant castes and their role in dictating the agenda of Grama Sabha, in the selection of beneficiaries especially for the housing schemes, practices of untouchability, not heeding the voices of disadvantaged sections of the society all these impede the deepening of democracy thereby altering the development priorities.

The gradual increase in the budgetary allocations to rural development, social infrastructure and welfare of women, SCs/STs indicates the financial commitment to attain the better outcomes of social well being. However, providing functional and financial allocations are not sufficient for the successful decentralized governance. It also requires adequate human and institutional capacities. The recent amendment in PR Act of 2015, the Karnataka state government has promulgated a separate cadre for the Panchayats *i.e.*, Karnataka Panchayat Administrative Services (KPAS). This may bring the required human personnel to enable Panchayats for better function to cater the needs of rural people and development. Heavy reliance of Panchayats for the funds is still a serious concern. Revenue generation by Panchayats is very weak.

Addressing the above mentioned human and institutional concerns may pave the way for better prospects for the decentralised governance. Once the system in place with necessary provisions such as staff, capacity building of the elected representatives, local bureaucracy and most importantly the citizens, then one can expect the desired changes in the societal development. Achieving rural development through Panchayats remains as a slogan if people do not perceive the system as their own and is there for their well being.

The paper *by* M. Gopinath Reddy, on decentralized governance process in Telangana state and its implications for development, while setting a tone for decentralization states that in recent times there is an increasing realization that genuine decentralization leads to development. It is also felt that decentralization of power to the local units of government and management is one of the best ways of empowering people, promoting public participation and increasing efficiency. It is also often argued that decentralization is a more effective and efficient framework for delivering pro-poor programmes. Set in this theoretical and normative framework of decentralization the paper takes a critical look at the experience of Telangana state (TS) in decentralized process and governance for ameliorating the living conditions of rural people in particular and rural society in general.

However, the author observes that not much has happened to decentralized governance in the new state of Telangana since it is still in the process of making. As it emanated from the discussion above that the United Andhra Pradesh always remained a 'decentralization deficit' state. Unfortunately, the new state Telangana is in the same order at the moment. Thus decentralization deficit status has serious implications for local development. The inadequate devolution of 'Three Fs (Funds and Functionaries, Functions)' has serious implications in developing overall basic infrastructure by the PRIs. Secondly, strengthening PESA is of utmost importance in the 5th scheduled areas of Telangana. The planning apparatus of the District Planning Committees is yet to emerge as serious planning units for decentralized planning of rural and urban areas. The new state of Telangana has a task cut out with regard to strengthening decentralization ecosystem and come out of a decentralization deficit status. It is hoped that the recent reforms ushered by TS Government will bring in desirable changes in the ecosystem of democratic decentralization status of Telangana state.

A key concern in the context of development has been the regional imbalances which has almost been integral and inseparable part of the development process. India in general and Karnataka state in particular have been suffering regional imbalances, despite the planned development initiatives under various five year plans. In fact, it is popularly believed that the overall development of the state of Karnataka is pulled down by the backwardness of certain pockets, especially that of the North Karnataka.

The paper *by* Seshadri on "Redressal of Regional Imbalances in Karnataka" is an excellent contribution to a theoretical understanding of regional imbalances and an empirical verification of regional imbalances in Karnataka. The paper carefully tracks the historical circumstances in which regional imbalances have emerged in the state of Karnataka and their threats to the overall state's development. The paper argues that regional imbalances are congenital to the state of Karnataka since 1956, the formation of state of Karnataka with the merger of lagging districts of Bombay- Karnataka, Hyderabad-Karnataka, Madras Presidency and the 'C' state of Coorg with the relatively developed old Mysore state. The author further argues that, what is achieved is significant, but what remains to be achieved is more significant. The paper argues that by way of remedial measures, government needs to put in a well defined and flexible regional policy. The current practice of thinly spreading resources should be stopped and adequate funds released fully and on time which further get completely utilised in time will help in redressing the regional disparities.

Grama Sabha (GS) is the door to see the entire democratic India, and it is an essential component for rural development which can change the fortune of the nation through decision in its meetings. It is a political forum for people (all adults whose names are registered in the village voters list) to meet and discuss their problems. The 73rd Constitution Amendment (1992) mandates GS as the constitutionally recognized institution below the village/grama Panchayat. With regard to the functioning of this institution the studies revealed that they have not been found successful in various states.

In the above context, the paper *by* Narayana Billava and Arun Kumar Kulkarni tries to present the process and extent of people's participation in Grama Sabha (GS), decision making, actual role of GS in decentralized governance affairs, and discuss the ways for strengthening this people's institution in the future. The paper is based on the information collected on Grama Sabha in four selected Grama Panchayats in Dharwad district of Karnataka. The paper reveals that the participation of citizens in the GS in general is very less at 35 percent. The participation of weaker sections such as scheduled castes and scheduled tribes and women in GS meetings are far from satisfactory. Most of the people (60 percent) who attended GSs were not satisfied with the way they are functioning. In particular they are not happy with regard to preparation of developmental plans for the village, selection of beneficiaries, time and date of GS meetings, poor implementation and monitoring of welfare schemes. It is also pitiable to note that the officials and members of Grama Panchayats lack knowledge about conducting GS meetings. Further the study found that for effective functioning of Grama Sabha the leadership of President (Adhyaksha) of Grama Panchayat is important. There is also need for creation of awareness among the people about the importance of their participation in GS meetings. The functionaries of Grama Panchayats have to hold GS meetings convenient to people and officials of various local level departments. Grama Sabha should become a forum where quick decisions are taken on the problems and demands of the people which ultimately leads to transparency in the governance affairs of Grama Panchayat. If these are ensured then the GS would see its worth existence.

The Tamil Nadu state in India is known for its pro-poor policies, schemes and programmes right from 1960s. The political parties in the state which have been in power evolved a pro-poor development perspective. Some of the schemes designed and implemented in the state have been replicated by other states in India. The concern for the poor has deepened among the regimes on quite a competitive mode after 1967. Among the pro-poor schemes in the state the 'THAI' (Tamil Nadu Village Habitations Improvement) programme is the one with most significant intent and impact. The AIADMK government launched this programme in 2012 keeping in view the non availability of basic services and infrastructure such as drinking water, street lights, electricity in the houses, roads in rural small hamlets and habitations and in particular the localities where the dalits (scheduled castes) and the other marginalized sections live. The formulation and implementation of plans under the THAI programme is entrusted to Grama Panchayats the lowest tier in the Panchayat structure. From 2011–12 to 2015–16 Rs. 3,400 Crore has been spent under the programme through 12,524 Grama Panchayats.

In the above context this paper on Habitation Level People's Plan and its Significance in Tamil Nadu *by* Palanithurai makes an attempt to critically evaluate the objectives of the programme, planning and implementation process, the impact created on the lives of the people. The methodology followed for the study include: interaction with officials and the elected representatives of the rural local bodies, focus group discussion with the beneficiaries of the programme, verification of the records/documents at Grama Panchayats, physical verification of the infrastructure created. For this purpose a sample of three districts covering Twelve Panchayat Unions (Intermediate Panchayat) and within these twelve Grama Panchayats were selected.

The study reveals that for the first time in Tamil Nadu, after Independence the remote and neglected hamlets and habitations have benefitted greatly through the THAI programme. Now these villages and in particular the dalit localities have been provided with regular drinking water supply, electricity connection to the houses, streetlights, cement roads, water, shelter and approach roads to burial grounds. The programme has led to the adoption of innovative processes in the planning and implementation. The people belonging to dalits and other marginalised sections have been participating in the Grama Sabha meetings in a large number. The study suggests that the innovative ideas adopted need to be sustained, fine-tuned and institutionalized. Funds are channelized to rural local bodies for development through a host of schemes and programmes, the experiences of THAI programme should be guiding spirit.

China and India have pursued decentralization policies to promote school education; but, the approaches followed and outcomes of school education differed across the countries. Against this background, the paper *by* Rajasekhar D. aims to: (i) Provide an overview of the decentralization approaches followed in the two countries, and (ii) Discuss the outcomes of school education with the help of review of existing literature. The experiences of China and India with decentralization in education reaffirm the mixed outcomes emanating from implementation of decentralized practices emphasised in the literature. In China, the decentralization reforms succeeded in resource mobilisation at the local level, improved enrolment rates and reduced student-teacher ratios. However, over devolution of expenditure responsibilities has led to insufficient financing, inadequate provision of educational services and growing inequality.

In India, different states have adopted different approaches regarding the management and governance of education as provincial governments were provided with powers to decide what needs to be decentralized in their provinces. The most notable approach is the constitution of parents' committees for facilitating the participation of people in the planning, implementation and monitoring of provision of school education. The educational outcomes differed across the states due to differences in the functioning of peoples' organisations. As far as the outcomes are concerned, there has been good progress in the enrolment rates (especially among girls) in the last two decades – after the introduction of decentralization reforms. But, much of this progress is to be attributed to government programmes and schemes such District Primary Education Programme (DPEP), mid-day meal, Education for All Movement and Right to Education Act which not only ensured that there are adequate resources for the development of primary education but were also instrumental in strengthening the decentralization reforms in India.

The experiences of these countries offer some lessons that may be taken into consideration while formulating and implementing decentralization policies for the education sector in China and India: (1) Decentralization leads to the improved outcomes through improved governance processes, (2) Accountability is a key mechanism to ensure the quantitative and qualitative reforms regarding education, (3) Accountability is greatly affected by participation and awareness levels of population which in turn is dependent on distribution of literacy and community's socio-economic characteristics. Educational decentralization policies should therefore be preceded by or concomitant to the policies aiming at ensuring the above, (4) Sufficient resources at the disposal of local implementing authorities and financial autonomy are crucial for implementing the reforms, and (5) A clear statement and division of responsibilities is important to avoid later confusions among different levels in the implementation.

Community participation through democratic decentralization is suggested as it brings in qualitative governance processes. The theoretical linkages between decentralization and poverty reduction have been well established in the literature. On this theoretical premise, the paper *by* Manjula R. explores the links between poverty reduction and the implementation of public works programme (Mahatma Gandhi National Rural Employment Guarantee Scheme – (MGNREGS) through decentralised government. MGNREGS, which is being implemented by the Grama Panchayats, is expected to provide better livelihood security to the rural households especially those who are dependent on wage labour. With the help of primary data collected from the sample households spread across several Grama Panchayats from developed and backward taluks of Ballari district in Karnataka, the paper has analysed the impact of MGNREGS on poverty reduction.

The paper finds that the proportion of households crossing poverty line with MGNREGS earnings was only 5.1 percent in Ballari Taluk and 3.8 percent in Kudligi Taluk. This shows that the impact was low in general, but comparatively lower in the backward Taluk of Kudligi. This negates the general expectation that the decentralized governance will be more effective in backward region. Secondly, although MGNREGS did contribute to the poverty reduction, the contribution is not sufficient to lift the ultra poor households above the poverty line. However, there was a positive impact on those households who are bordering on poverty line. If notional income from MGNREGS, with an assumption that the households obtained full employment of 100 days, is included in the monthly per capita income of the poor households, one can see a considerable decline in the proportion of poor among sample households. The paper concludes that if MGNREGS was properly implemented more number of poor households would have come out of the poverty.

Pradeep Ramavat attempts a critical appraisal of School Development and Monitoring Committees in Lambani Thandas of Karnataka. National policy on education of 1986 visualized direct community involvement in the management and monitoring of school development activities through decentralized educational governance framework. Article 21A of Indian constitution mandates state to guarantee 'elementary education' as an important fundamental socio-cultural right of children aged between 6–14 years. This important constitutional responsibility when read along with Article 273G and eleventh schedule visualizes maneuvering decentralized governance mechanism in elementary education through Grama Panchayats. Systematic co-option efforts to create parallel institutions in 'Decentralized Governance Framework' with the establishment of school development and monitoring committees by centralized executive order is an unintended effort by educational bureaucracy to delink Panchayats from mandated constitutional responsibility. Unplanned fund disbursal by *Sarva Shiksha Abhiyan* and recent confusions created by 'Right to Education Act of 2009' on the roles and responsibilities of individuals, authorities, institutions etc., are seen as some of the common reasons for dysfunctioning of school development and monitoring committees in Lambani Thandas of Karnataka. Critical appraisal of these committees using institutional ethnography has helped to probe more on the inability of these badly engineered '*pseudo decentralized structures*' in performing the roles and responsibilities prescribed to them by educational bureaucracy.

The present effort is to disseminate the recent decentralization experiences for wider audience. However, we do not make tall claims about capturing all the issues in this volume which would be a herculean task. Nevertheless, the contributions in the present volume are hoped to serve the student and research community in understanding the working of the decentralization initiatives. The policy insights of the contributions in the volume are expected to be pointers to the corrective measures needed in toning up local governance and in this sense, it could be of immense value to the state and central level policy makers. The book is a tribute to Prof. Abdul Aziz who has contributed extensively to research on decentralization and local government institutions and to training programmes for elected members of Panchayati Raj Institutions. He also had the distinction of serving the first State Finance Commission of Karnataka.

2

Panchayati Raj in India: A Vision and A Roadmap for the Future

S.S. MEENAKSHISUNDARAM[2]*

ABSTRACT

The paper attempts a close look at the journey of PRIs for the last 25 years. In the context of the poor capacity and accountability of these grassroot level institutions, the paper attempts to address issues such as what needs to be done to bring the practice in line with the theory? In the light of the experience gained during the last 25 years, what should be our vision for the future of Panchayats and what could be an ideal roadmap to realize that vision. The paper looks into both positive and negative aspects of Panchayats functioning and observes that Panchayats, based on reports, are not functioning in most parts of the country, they appear strong in structure but weak in delivery and on an average, decentralization of governance in India has been poorly implemented with wide variation among states. The key deficiencies identified are: poor response to the Grama Sabhas across states with their meetings not taking place regularly; lack of operational linkages between different tiers of local governance at district, intermediate and village levels preventing efficient service delivery; lack of devolution of functions, funds and functionaries; the fragmentation of central and state programmes and funding streams; the retention of decision making power in the state and central levels through parallel bodies and sectoral bureaucracy and poor accountability.

2.1. INTRODUCTION

The Constitution 73rd Amendment inserting Part IX on the Panchayats to the Constitution of India is now 25 years old. Since the subject of

[2] Visiting Professor, National Institute of Advanced Studies, Bengaluru, Karnataka 560012.

**Corresponding author:* E-mail: meenakshi54@hotmail.com

local government is listed under the State list of the Seventh Schedule of the Constitution, the States are responsible for the implementation of the Panchayati Raj system through their own Acts enacted in accordance with the Constitution Amendment. During the last two decades, almost all mandatory provisions of the Amendment have been complied with by the States. All States have held elections to constitute Panchayats at the appropriate levels. The reservation provisions have also been faithfully implemented. However, the implementation of the decentralization process has not been uniform across the States. Devolution of the 3 Fs *viz.* Functions, Finances and Functionaries by the States is highly uneven. While across the key sectors, the State Panchayat laws mandate a role for the Panchayats, in most cases, the law is ambiguous enough to allow for both decentralized and centralized modes of programme management/service delivery to co-exist. In some cases, where the States have devolved such responsibilities to the Panchayats, these are either still largely being provided in a top-down manner through the State civil service machinery or the ability of panchayats to deliver these is limited because of the deficient financial and administrative powers and, therefore these services do not reach the needy.

Some of my colleagues not only in the Indian Administrative Service but also from technical services strongly believe that elected local governments are a dispensable part of the democratic process, that it belongs to a specifically English political culture and that it is unreasonable to transplant it to a developing country. In my view, certain basic political mechanisms dictate themselves by their own logic. They are not culture specific. An elected local government appears to be one such. We seek to achieve four things in a local government through the mechanism of local participation. First, the ordinary local citizen should feel that he is not just an inert subject of an arbitrary government far removed from him, but a person whose views must be considered since the local government belongs to him and the ruler exists for his benefit and not the other way round. Second, the choice as to who rules them should be made by the local people themselves, as they are likely to choose the one who cares for their interests. Third, the local ruler should bear in mind the need to be sensitive to the local needs and articulate their needs so that he may continue to enjoy their local support. Fourthly, the local participation should provide the momentum for faster development through the harnessing of local resources. None of these benefits can be attributed either to a nominated local government or to the bureaucracy representing a distant government.

Local governments, though popular, may not always produce the results that the national leaders were hoping for. Elected councilors could be ignorant and self-seeking, lacking a sense of responsibility to their electors. They may usually concentrate on expanding the social services to the neglect of investments in productivity. The local government bureaucracy may be of poor quality, frequently losing control over their own accounting system. Local autonomy may lead to multiple frictions between the centre and the local body. But, with these and other possible shortcomings, the mere existence of local democratic structure can be a contribution; people generally prefer them to direct administration, even where the elections only give power to existing local leaders. The central legislature in any country, however popularly constituted, can never replace the local genius of the people as an agency of devising local solutions to local problems. Locally elected councils can exercise greater surveillance over local officials than that exercised by the central legislature over the Central Government officials. A guarded optimism on the utility of the decentralization in developing countries stands theoretically justified.

If the theory demands decentralization, particularly in a large democracy like India and the practical status throws genuine doubts about the capacity and accountability of the Panchayati Raj Institutions (PRIs), what needs to be done to bring the practice in line with the theory? In the light of the experience gained during the last 25 years, what should be our vision for the future of Panchayats and what could be an ideal roadmap to realize that vision? This paper attempts to answer these questions. Since articulating a vision should necessarily follow the genesis of the system and an analysis of the current status, the rest of this paper is divided into four sections. The first provides a brief history of panchayats in India leading to the Constitution Amendment and the second an analysis of the current status, which is followed by an achievable vision in the third. Strategies to achieve that vision are narrated in the next section. The paper ends with a concluding section summarizing the key action points.

2.2. THE HISTORY

Village communities common to most agrarian economies have been in existence in India for over centuries. They were called "Panchayats" — councils of five persons, one in every village. Jawaharlal Nehru points out in *The Discovery of India* that "in olden days the village Panchayat or elected council had large powers both executive and judicial and its members were treated with the greatest of respect by the king's officers. Lands were distributed by this Panchayat which also collected taxes out of the produce and paid the government's share on behalf of the village. Over a number of these village councils there was a larger Panchayat or council to supervise and interfere if necessary. Sir Charles Metcalfe, a British Governor in India during the 19th century, called them "little republics having nearly everything they want within themselves and almost independent of foreign relations. They seem to last where nothing else lasts". During the British Raj, with its central focus on control and command and little concern for service delivery, the system of local governance received a setback. Powers were centralized and loyalty to the British regime was rewarded with land grants, leading to the creation of a class of feudal aristocrats who dominated the local political scene wielding power on behalf of the British Government.

During the independence movement, Gandhiji propagated strongly the idea of 'gram swaraj' and wanted to revive the Panchayats with adequate powers given to them so that village would become 'a self-sufficient independent entity for its own vital needs, yet inter-dependent for many others'. However, there was a strong opposition in the Constituent Assembly to recognize village as the basic unit of administration, as some members considered village as 'a sink of localism, a den of ignorance, narrow mindedness and communalism'. To pacify Gandhiji an Article was introduced in the Directive Principles of State Policy ordaining the State to "organize village panchayats and endow them with such powers and authority as may be necessary to enable them to function as units of self-government". This provision was however not acted upon by any State until the Balwantrai Mehta Committee constituted to study the Community Development and National Extension Service programmes came up with a recommendation for establishing a three tier Panchayati Raj system to secure people's participation in their own development. The first phase of decentralization in India thus emerged in the late 1950s, was essentially to deliver development benefits to the people through an institutional structure with the Grama Panchayat (GP) as its base.

Unfortunately due to a number of reasons including absence of regular elections, prolonged super-cessions, poor representation of the Scheduled Castes, Scheduled Tribes and Women and inadequate devolution of powers and financial resources, the Panchayats did not acquire the status and dignity of viable and responsive people's bodies over a period of time. The phase of decline which started in late 1960s continued for over two decades which compelled the Government of India to bring in two Constitution Amendment Bills in 1992 to formally introduce a third tier in the administration of the country through local governments in the rural and urban parts of India.

2.3. THE CURRENT STATUS

Part IX of the Constitution now provides among other things, Grama Sabha in a village or group of villages; Panchayats at village, intermediate and district levels; direct elections to all seats in Panchayats, to be conducted by a State Election Commission; reservation of seats for the scheduled castes and scheduled tribes in proportion to their population for membership of Panchayats as well as office of Chairpersons in the Panchayats; reservation of not less than one-third of the seats/chairpersons for women; fixing a tenure of 5 years for Panchayats and holding elections within a period of 6 months in the event of super-cession of any Panchayat; devolution by the State Legislature of funds, powers and responsibilities upon the Panchayats with respect to the preparation of plans for economic development and social justice and for the implementation of development schemes; setting up of a Finance Commission within one year of the proposed amendment and thereafter every 5 years to review the financial position of Panchayats and recommend measures to improve the same; regular auditing of accounts of the Panchayats; etc.

Since the provisions of this Amendment could not apply to certain predominantly tribal areas listed in the Fifth Schedule of the Constitution (In ten States outside the north-eastern part of India), the Panchayats (Extension to scheduled areas) Act (PESA) was passed in 1996 extending Part IX of the Constitution to those areas subject to certain exceptions and modifications. The provisions of the Constitution 73rd Amendment did not also apply to the States of Nagaland, Meghalaya, Mizoram and the hilly areas of Manipur which are included in the Sixth Schedule as "Tribal Areas" in the North-East region as well as to the hill areas of Darjeeling District in West Bengal, duly acknowledging the traditional system of local governance already in existence in those areas. The Table 2.1 sums up the local government systems now in position in rural India.

Table 2.1: Rural local government system in India.

Panchayats (Constitution 73rd Amendment)	*Fifth schedule areas*	*Sixth schedule areas (Traditional systems)*	*Other systems established through state laws*
• 25 States, • 6 Union territories	Spread over 10 States (PESA) • Andhra Pradesh • Telangana • Chhattisgarh • Madhya Pradesh • Rajasthan • Himachal Pradesh • Jharkhand • Maharashtra • Gujarat • Orissa	Areas of • Assam, • Meghalaya • Mizoram, • Tripura	• Hill areas of Manipur, • Nagaland, • Darjeeling Gorkha Hill Council; (Exempt from having ZPs) • Jammu and Kashmir

Decentralized planning is the core function of local self-governance envisaged by the Constitution. Article 243G enjoins the Panchayats to 'prepare plans for economic development and social justice'. By asking the panchayats to plan programmes for their jurisdictions, the Constitution has underscored the democratic, inclusive and instrumental value of the local governments. The local governments are to prepare the plans while the District Planning Committees (DPCs) are to 'consolidate' the plans and make 'draft development plan for the district'. The erstwhile Planning Commission has given the roadmap for decentralized planning by providing Guidelines for District Planning (2006) and a District Planning Manual (2008) for bottom-up planning. However, these guidelines have not been translated into action in most States and the planning process continues to be top-down.

Several Commissions and Expert Committees have critically reviewed the progress in the implementation of various facets of the Panchayati Raj system during the last two decades. The National Commission headed by Justice M.N.Venkatachaliah to review the working of the Constitution set up during 2000, the Expert Group under the Chairmanship of V. Ramachandran appointed in 2005, by the Ministry of Panchayati Raj to study and make recommendations on the issue of planning at the grassroots level, the Second Administrative Reforms Commission appointed by the President of India in 2006 under the Chairmanship of Veerappa Moily and the Punchhi Commission on Centre State Relations appointed in April 2007 have all inter-alia made several recommendations to improve the functioning of the Panchayats.

All these reports have brought out one common concern namely the Panchayats are not functioning in most parts of the country. They appear strong in structure but weak in delivery. On average, decentralization of governance in India has been poorly implemented with wide variation among States. The key deficiencies identified are: poor response to the Grama Sabhas across States with their meetings not taking place regularly; lack of operational linkages between different tiers of local governance at district, intermediate and village levels preventing efficient service delivery;lack of devolution of functions, funds and functionaries; the fragmentation of Central and State programmes and funding streams; the retention of decision making power in the State and Central levels through parallel bodies and sectoral bureaucracy and poor accountability.

In spite of the above mentioned shortcomings, certain achievements and positive features of the Panchayati Raj system have also come to notice such as, improvement in attendance of school teachers and medical staff, increase in revenue from assets transferred to the Panchayats, significant public awareness of the welfare programmes implemented at different levels, better communication between the people and the Government, early warning system for Disaster Management etc. Political will and public demand are however required to build on these positive features and overcome the shortcomings.

2.4. VISION

A recent study by the National Council of Applied Economic Research, based on a unique data set and an intense six year research effort, has come to some interesting conclusions. In their opinion "despite operating in a very poor system, local governments have been able to make significant contributions to the provision of basic services. Even though the expenditures of the Panchayats on water, health and education may be small, they did have a positive and significant impact on the quantity and quality of these services. Second, the improvement in the quality of services is partly a consequence of improved resolution of service problems at the local levels. Third, the study finds a variety of formal and informal mechanisms which are effective in reducing service gaps across gender and economic classes which no doubt exists. These include the reservation of the Panchayat Chairperson's position to women and members from SCs/STs, participation in the Grama Sabha, discussions of service delivery issues in the Grama Sabha, establishment of and participation in Village Education and Water Users' Committees, etc. This leaves one with the thought that if the PRI system, even when it is poorly implemented, can have beneficial impacts, won't it do much better if it is adequately empowered, funded and staffed".

Pursuing this thought, what should be the vision for Panchayati Raj governance over the next ten to fifteen years? To start with, the basic vision should be to ensure that the Panchayats function as Institutions of Self-Government as envisaged under Articles 40 and 243G of the Constitution. Gandhiji's dream and the Constitutional mandate empowering people to achieve good governance through democratic decentralization have to be realized without any further delay. Strengthening, catalyzing and facilitating panchayats to improve the quality of life and infrastructural amenities for their citizens by adopting good and responsive governance practices should be the immediate vision for panchayats. Strengthening democracy at the grass roots levels through peoples' organizations such as the Self-Help Groups (SHG), Watershed Development Committees (WDC), School Development and Management Committees (SDMC) etc., below the GP level and integrating these with the Grama Sabha/GP to attain decentralized and participatory local governance through such institutions should also have to be achieved.

While that should be our immediate vision, a long term vision for a local government has to be to deal with not only market failures but also with government failures. This role requires the Panchayats to operate as purchasers of local services, facilitators of networks of government providers and entities beyond government, and gatekeeper and overseer of State and National governments in areas of shared rule. Panchayats will then play a mediator's role among various entities and networks to foster greater synergy and harness the untapped energies of the broader community for improving the quality of life of citizens. Globalization and the information revolution also reinforce these conceptual perspectives on a catalytic role for local governments. The new vision of local governance should aim at a leadership role for local governments in the multi-centered and multi-level system obtaining in India. Table 2.2 sums up the existing situation and the proposed new vision of local governance in rural India.

In brief the GPs in the near future will have to be the proverbial last mile in the provision of services now planned and delivered by the

Table 2.2: Role of local government under the new vision of local governance.

20th century: Old view	*21st century: New view*
Is based on the principle of residuality and local governments as wards of the state	Is based on the principle ofc subsidiarity and home rule
Is focused on government	Is focused on citizen-centered governance
Is agent of the central government	Is the primary agent for the citizens and leader and gatekeeper for shared rule
Is responsive and accountable to higher-level governments	Is responsive and accountable to local voters; assumes leadership role in improving local governance
Is direct provider of local services	Is purchaser of local services
Is focused on in-house provision	Is facilitator of network mechanisms of local governance, coordinator of government providers and entities beyond government, mediator of conflicts, and developer of social capital
Depends on central directives	Is autonomous in taxing, spending, regulatory, and administrative decisions
Is rules driven	Has managerial flexibility and accountability for results
Is bureaucratic and technocratic	Is participatory; works to strengthen citizen voice and exit options through direct democracy provisions, citizens'charters, and performance budgeting
Is fiscally irresponsible	Is fiscally prudent; works better and costs less
Is exclusive with elite capture	Is inclusive and participatory
Is boxed in a centralized system	Is connected in a globalized and localized world.

Central and State Governments. The beneficiary/ community will look upon the GPs to provide all services, without knocking at the doors of the Government departments as at present. It is for the GPs to link themselves with the line-departments and procure services for their citizens. In the long run, the GPs will graduate themselves to purchase those services either from the Government or from the open market and will have the capacity to negotiate and obtain what is best for their citizens. How they will get that capacity depends on the capacity building strategies that have to be designed over the next few years.

2.5. STRATEGIES

Strategies to strengthen decentralization in rural India have to be evolved keeping in mind two distinct scenarios. First is to accept the existing design (of having a uniform three tier system in the larger States) and propose strategies for achieving the vision envisaged. The second is to take a critical look at the existing structure itself and then determine whether the structure needs to be redesigned to ensure better governance at the local level. We shall look at both these options.

Presuming that the Constitutional pattern of the Centre having laid down some broad mandates and the scope and ambit of LGs being largely determined by States cannot be changed, our approach would largely be to consider what improvements can be made within the existing framework. In that scenario, if the GP has to become the last mile in the process of governance and development, there has to be an active interface between the GP and the citizens living in their jurisdiction. The citizens should look upon the GP as the provider of basic services and also the implementer of all the schemes meant for their welfare. The GP should also be able to provide up to date market information on the key produce the local farmers are interested in. This requires each GP to have an office equipped with necessary staff and facilities to discharge these functions. While the intermediate and district Panchayats as of now have most of these facilities which can be upgraded as and when required, several GPs even today do not have their own offices, dedicated staff and supporting facilities. The first step would therefore be to provide them uniformly throughout the country so that the citizens can approach them without any difficulty.

To strengthen the Panchayati Raj Institutions (PRIs) to truly become institutions of self-governance at the local level the following areas need to be specifically looked at:

Past experience shows that programmes in health and education, and many types of rural development initiatives including the national rural employment guarantee programme, rural housing, rural drinking water, watershed management, etc., are most effective when there is active involvement of the local community. The Fourteenth Finance Commission has recommended substantial grants to the GPs with the stipulation that they should be spent only for basic services and functions assigned to them under the relevant State legislations. The GPs will now be getting a total grant of over rupees two lakh crores during 2015–2020. In addition, the GPs are also getting substantial funds allocated to them under several centrally sponsored schemes. No doubt the other tiers of the Panchayati Raj tier structure should also be supported with adequate funds for the discharge of functions assigned to them in the respective States. That has to be achieved by providing substantial funds to them through the State budgets. Mobilization of own resources, including borrowing strategies for development by the PRIs have to be encouraged.

Like Union Finance Commission, the recommendations of the State Finance Commission (SFC) are recommendatory and not mandatory in nature, but unlike Union Finance Commission, SFC's recommendations are being given cold shoulders. In fact, many States are making a mockery of the constitutional provision. On the one hand, they constitute a body with people of smattering knowledge; on the other hand, they do not even consider their report. If the report is considered, very few recommendations are accepted. In the process, the crucial ones are rejected without assigning reasons. In the action taken report, only numbers are mentioned. In this number game, sometime the most crucial recommendations are found rejected surreptitiously. At the top of it, many times, the accepted recommendations are not implemented. Sometime, money was not released even though actions on these recommendations were notified. The story becomes more interesting given the fact that a State Government took two and half years to only consider the report of the SFC. Government of India in this unhealthy scenario has to step in with necessary guidelines on the Constitution of SFCs and a workable timetable for submission of their recommendations and the consideration and acceptance (or otherwise) of each one of the recommendations by the State Governments.

Devolution of funds to Panchayats must be accompanied by greater accountability. Social mobilization of people and community involvement at ground level is important. Transparency can be a very effective tool to increase accountability and the Right to Information Act enacted in 2005 is a major step in this direction. Strengthening the Grama Sabha is crucial. Taking government closer to the people, we have to ensure that the Grama Sabha serves as the empowered and proximate forum for local democracy. Steps have to be taken to ensure that the Grama Sabhas meet regularly and take decisions transparently. Only then we can hope for better accountability at the GP level.

Social audits have already been introduced for selected programmes in the States to initiate public dialogue and scrutiny. This has to be extended to all activities undertaken by the PRIs. There is however a need to make social audits more inclusive by enabling the community, the beneficiaries and other disadvantaged sections to play an active role, lest there is scope for manipulation by the facilitating agencies. Apart from ensuring credibility and legitimacy of social audit forums, the capacities of all concerned agencies need to be built. Strengthening direct civic action is another measure required in making social audits relevant and effective.

Empowering Panchayats with adequate devolution of powers to play a more autonomous role is urgently required to improve the capacity of the PRIs to deliver services/ programmes. Unfortunately, a significant proportion of funds are now being spent through structures that are alternatives to PRIs. These comprise line departments, so-called autonomous societies and 'missions', typically arranged around the district administration, which consists of a small group of official and political personalities. Parallel bodies are set up as directed by the State or Central governments to plan and execute development projects in areas that are in the functional domain of PRIs, using funds provided by the State or Central governments or donors. They are called parallel because they have a separate system of decision-making on resource allocation and execution of projects, which is independent and removed from the Panchayati Raj set up. These parallel bodies have considerable autonomy and provide places to bureaucrats, elected representatives, non-officials and community representatives in their governing structure. Examples of parallel bodies include District Rural Development Agency (DRDAs), Forest and Watershed Development agencies and societies set up for implementing specific programmes such as the Sarva ShikshaAbhiyan, National Rural Health Mission and National Horticultural Mission.

While the parallel bodies established below the level of the GP serve the purpose of deepening democracy in most cases, the parallel bodies at other levels do not add any specific value, except perhaps the involvement of technical experts and interested citizens in decision making. While it is necessary to disband these bodies, it may not be possible in the near future in view of the possible commitments made to the international donors in some cases. Hence, the best way to empower the PRIs in the discharge of their legitimate functions relating to those subjects appears to be: (i) to direct the parallel bodies functioning at the village level to report their activities regularly to the concerned Grama Sabha (which incidentally will also help in enhancing the status of the Grama Sabha) and (ii) to bring all the parallel bodies at the intermediate and district levels within the ambit of the Panchayats at that level which can be achieved either by bringing them under the administrative control of the Panchayat concerned or by making them as Sub-Committees of those Panchayats.

To have effective devolution of functions, responsibility mapping among the different tiers of Panchayats is a must. This requires the subjects/sectors to be unbundled and assigned to different levels of PRIs on the basis of clear principles of public finance and public accountability as well as the principle of subsidiarity to provide clarity to the citizens on who does what and also to avoid duplication of efforts. Though this task has already begun in several States, it needs to be completed without any further delay.

It is essential to provide competent and willing functionaries to work with the PRIs. While establishing a Panchayati Raj service commission to recruit personnel for the PRIs should be the ultimate objective, evolving a system of transferring the State/Scheme officials to the PRIs for effective implementation of schemes has to be the short-term strategy. The system adopted for the deputation of All India Service officers from the State Cadres to the Centre can be adopted in the reverse direction *i.e.,* from the State to the PRIs. Deputations have to be need based, for a specific tenure, without affecting the career opportunities available to the deputed individuals.

There is a great need for capacity building of the elected representatives as well as the functionaries of the PRIs to ensure that plans evolved at the ground level are technically viable and the delivery of services meet the requirements of the people. There is, therefore, a need to earmark substantial funds for capacity building. Active involvement of NGOs assisting the PRIs has proved to be very effective in many States in capacity building. Current approaches to capacity building and training are supply driven. Training of PRIs is generally spasmodic, slow to implement, has poor coverage and the quality of assimilation is unmonitored. While detailed frameworks for training and capacity building have been formulated, these have not been implemented fully because of delays in procuring hardware, the lack of an adequate number of high-quality face-to-face trainers and the lack of content tailored for rapid up-scaling. This results in a glaring paradox; even when efforts are on to providing funds for implementing such strategies in full, the available funds for training lapse. Simply put, there is no capacity to create capacity.

Answer to this paradox lies in changing the whole paradigm of local government capacity building, from being low-value and supply-driven to an effective, adaptive and demand-driven knowledge-support. Only then can we rapidly reach out to large numbers of elected representatives, who need information and guidance, by using a carefully designed basket of technologies aimed at user friendliness and easy recognition and retention. This can be made available both online and offline. Modules have to be prepared for PRI representatives that encourage and enable them to learn just about everything they need on their own. Packaging such learning in the style that is most sensitive and responsive to their needs is what is sorely needed, not expensive, cascading lecture sessions. The rapidly growing electronic connectivity in the country is an opportunity that is pregnant with possibilities. Social networking and new media over the internet can work as a significant enabler for an effective knowledge support system for the elected representatives. As stated earlier, there is no clearly discernible functional space for PRIs and that the government system is unable to satisfactorily respond to the huge demand for knowledge support. It is necessary to realize that devolution by itself will accelerate capacity building by making it demand-driven. If one really gives PRIs clear roles and holds them accountable for these, they will have an incentive to seek out the capacity support they need.

Gender gap in development remains a major issue. In spite of several obstacles, both institutional and social, the participation of elected woman representatives has no doubt resulted in both developmental and empowerment outcomes. Women have initiated work on plans to bring piped water in the village and also to build schools as against other infrastructural development favoured by men. Results from a nationwide survey of women's participation in Panchayats suggest that a majority of the elected women representatives reported an enhancement in their personal effectiveness and image after being elected. They also reported a reduction in household responsibilities. Specific programmes for capacity building of women representatives will further enhance the quality of their participation. Many States carry out training and capacity building activity to mostly the chairpersons of the Panchayats rather than to all the elected representatives. Building the capacities of the elected women, scheduled caste and scheduled tribe representatives will certainly make them more effective and ensure social justice at the local levels.

DPCs as mandated by the Constitution have to be established throughout the country. The Grama Panchayat Development Plans (GPDPs) covering the functions devolved to the GP should be prepared at the GP level with the approval of the Grama Sabhas and these plans must be consolidated by the DPC into a district level plan taking into account of the availability of funds from the devolution of State plan resources and the earmarked funds flowing from various central schemes.

Panchayats (Extension to the Scheduled Areas) Act played a major role in the development of PRIs in those areas. PESA attempts to vest legislative powers in the Grama Sabha, specifically in matters relating to development planning, management of natural resources and adjudication of disputes in accordance with prevalent traditions and customs. This significant legislation was expected to have far reaching consequences in the social, economic and cultural life of tribal people in the scheduled areas. The Grama Sabha has been made the soul of PESA, the palladium of tribal identity, traditional customs and practices, and community assets, and in resolving local disputes. The distinctive premise is that a small group affords great scope for face-to-face democracy and participation will be effective if the community and the beneficiary organizations in particular, are institutionally and statutorily involved in managing their own affairs and decision-making processes. This Act envisages the transformation of the tribals from being targets/objects to participants/actors in the democratic process pertaining to their lives and development.

Serious gaps in implementation of PESA however remain. Information dissemination and subsequent awareness about their roles in determining their destiny were crucial in the process of empowering the tribals. This ignorance was one of the main reasons for the low turnout of tribals for the activities associated with this decentralization reform. The awareness level in the Grama Sabha as well as in the Grama Panchayat/other PRIs on ownership, control and management of natural resources in general and the Minor Forest Produces (MFPs) in particular is very low. Organized efforts have to be made by the respective State Governments to inform, educate and organize Grama Sabhas and GPs on ownership over MFPs. While the States have to be persuaded to enact necessary rules to legally fill up the huge gaps noticed in the implementation of PESA, awareness creation process will have to be designed and implemented to enhance the capacity of the tribals to manage their own affairs through the Grama Sabhas.

If the GPs have to play the role of the single point contact for the citizens, then in addition to development functions, the GPs have to perform certain regulatory functions as well. Registration of births and deaths, issue of birth/death/marriage and caste certificates, issuing certified copies of documents relating to land and house properties are some of the functions the States can entrust to the PRIs, by suitably amending the laws relating to these subjects.

In addition, rural safety is another subject that should be entrusted to the GPs. The system of Village Head Man assisted by one or more village watch man for policing self-sufficient ancient villages was in vogue in India for centuries. This system was allowed to fade away and was replaced by a chain of police stations and out posts, after the dawn of independence. Since the beginning of this century all the Police Commissions/Committees set up in India have accepted the impossibility of carrying on an efficient rural policing system by means of official police man and have stressed the need to secure the aid of the village community. The elected representatives of the people who constitute the GPs are the more appropriate instruments of the government for the maintenance of public order and policing in their own areas. The process of democratic decentralization cannot be complete without the gradual transfer of the functions and powers of the village police from the State Government Officials in the villages to the GPs. In most of the developed countries policing is a municipal job and there is no reason why it should not be so in India.

Another area where the GPs need to be empowered is the delivery of justice at the local level. While the Constitution Amendment has delineated the contours of political, administrative and financial decentralization no attempt was made at that time to decentralize the delivery of justice. To ensure speedy and inexpensive justice in civil and criminal matters of a relatively minor nature, Nyaya Panchayats need to be constituted at the GP level to bring the process of justice to the door steps of the citizens. The effectiveness of social sanction; the widespread experience that truth surfaces locally without elaborate evidence; and the salutary effect of shortening the span between crime and punishment, injury and redress need to be utilized in any system of democratic decentralization.

Basic reforms in devolution of power, conduct of business and building transparency are fundamental to the process of strengthening PRIs. Technology is an enabler in the overall process of these reforms. There are a number of areas in which the PRIs can exploit the power of

Information and Communications Technologies (ICTs). The E-Panchayat project which is currently under implementation has great potential to transform PRIs into symbols of modernity, transparency and efficiency. This project well implemented will ensure people's participation in decision making, implementation and delivery. However, there are several GPs which lack in ICT infrastructure and internet connectivity even now. The earlier we fill up these gaps the better will be the delivery of services by the GPs. In addition, capacity building programmes meant for the PRI functionaries should necessarily include a strong component on ICT to facilitate effective implementation.

2.6. INSTITUTIONAL STRUCTURE

Let us now turn to the second option and take a look at the institutional structures established through the Constitution Amendment. A good local governance system has to conform to certain design parameters that create the right incentives for the institutions to function in a responsible and accountable fashion. First, they must be constructed to minimize, or at least discourage, destructive political rivalries between themselves and between them and political representatives of higher levels of government. Second, they must have a clearly defined functional space that is their own, where higher levels of government have little role to play. Third, they must also have a clearly defined fiscal space, created first and foremost by giving them a meaningful tax base, sufficient tax assignments and, if necessary, untied fund transfers to handle specific shortcomings or responsibilities. Fourth, they must have the freedom to secure the capacity that they need, both institutional and for the people who run these governments, from either higher levels of government or from other sources. Last, there must be good systems in place for people to hold their local governments to account-either directly or through recourse to an independent agency empowered to intervene.

Elected local governments are in position throughout India. The structure is well set even though many States have started questioning the need for a three-tier system of elected rural local bodies. While some States like Kerala would like to dispense with the intermediate tier, Tamil Nadu would prefer not to have a district tier at all. Some experts also raise a basic question as to why should a multi-tier system be prescribed for rural governance in India which always had a single-tier of governance in urban areas.

The institutional design for decentralization should take into account not only the developmental thrusts built upon the capabilities at the local levels but also the need to ensure local participation in decision-making. The dynamics of development necessitates that the technical expertise of a high order be made available at levels below the State to sustain the momentum of development which, in many cases, has been already administratively decentralized at the district level. The inescapable conclusion, therefore, is that the district should be the first point of decentralization, under popular supervision, below the State level.

The problem of striking a balance between technological requirements and possibilities for meaningful participation by the people in development management recurs at levels below the district. Since it is extremely difficult to combine representativeness and viability in one level of local government, this problem is sought to be solved by having two or more tiers in such a way that the smaller area one is closer to the people while the larger area one is better financed and technically more powerful.

The question of adequate area for a unit of administration is quite complicated in any given State, owing to unevenness in terms of economic resources, communication facilities, population density, level of social integration, civic commitment, etc. A uniform set of criteria cannot apply, even within a State. It would, therefore, seem appropriate to leave the exact pattern of local government below the district level to the States. The Central Government could at best lay down the general criteria for guidance.

More recently two criteria have been suggested for determining the size of a local government unit. These are access and service. If service is taken as the prime determinant of size, an important consideration has to be the population, because the cost of the service is a function of the population requiring that service, although at some point, when the population reaches a certain level, the unit cost of the service would reduce. It means, therefore, a minimum and a maximum population can be established — a minimum to guarantee that the service is not too expensive and consequently inaccessible to the people and a maximum to ensure quality and promptness in service.

Access to government in terms of influencing public policy decisions and enhancing both responsible and responsive administration is a prime requirement for any democratic government. If access is an important prerequisite of size, then, in addition to population, one has to look at the communication network, level of political awareness, and also the area. While the service criteria will take care of the economic viability and administrative efficiency, the access criteria should serve the political and democratic needs of the people. Should the application of these criteria lead to divergent views, one has to raise the basic query, whether the functions of local government can be or should be performed for profit.

Insisting on viability for local government and not for other levels of government would amount to an obvious discrimination against local government since the local government provides an instrument for democracy or at least provides an extra avenue for democratic participation. The "access" criteria should therefore precede the "service" criteria in determining the structure of PRIs in any State.

It must, however, be added that the lowest tier should not be so small in size as to make it insignificant or incapable of discharging its legitimate duties as a local government. For instance, the GPs in most parts of India, covering a population of about 2,500 or less cannot perform any functions on their own and hence do not command the respect a local government deserves. The Mandal Praja Parishads in Andhra Pradesh, with a population of about 40,000 and the Grama Panchayats in Kerala and West Bengal with a population of around 30,000, appear to satisfy both the access and service criteria and have the potential of becoming the growth centres which can discharge the duties of a local government, closer to the people, fairly effectively. It is obvious that one of the things that must be done immediately is that the size of the GP has to be increased uniformly in several States of India to provide viability as well as to assure public participation in decision making. If for political reasons the GPs cannot be reorganized in the near future, then a few adjoining GPs can be grouped into a 'cluster panchayat' with an office building and an establishment of its own, performing the role of the lowest functional unit of decentralization in that State.

If the lowest tier can satisfactorily meet the criteria of access and service, there may not be any need for an intermediate tier at all between the district and the village. If the physical distance between the district headquarters and the Panchayat is substantial, establishment of deconcentrated offices of the district government under public supervision at convenient locations can bridge that gap and bring the district government nearer to the people.

A closely related question is whether there should be separate urban and rural local governments in India, as has been the practice till now. The rationale for parallel systems of urban and rural local self-governments could be that the character of the two communities being different, the problems to be managed by these local governments are altogether different. The rural areas depend on primary production activities whereas the urban areas thrive on secondary and tertiary activities. The land and resource use issues are entirely different and hence it would be desirable to let each system concentrate on issues specific to the character of the communities they serve. Another argument could be that the fusion of these two types of governments might put rural areas to disadvantage. The low level of education, lack of experience in public affairs, inability to control the mass media, the bureaucratic biases, the difficulties in the way of organization and mobilization of public support scattered in thousands of small village communities and the capabilities of urban representatives to push through large projects with an urban bias may work against the interests of the rural sector. Parallel systems would insulate and protect rural interests against urban influences. The urban areas, being the main contributors of resources for public investment, might feel a similar threat of being overwhelmed by resource-hungry poor majorities from rural areas.

The costs of parallel forms of local government are, however, equally heavy. They have produced artificial resource constraints. Even though urban populations' need for water, land, energy and nutrients is increasing, it has not been able to develop these resources for more equitable sharing simply because these resources are usually located outside their jurisdiction. Nor have the rural areas been able to develop them because of severe financial constraints. Using their control on State power and money power, the urban areas offer attractive prices and facilities for increasing the rate of resource exploitation without incurring the cost of resource replenishment. Over a period of time, the cumulative result of the process of over-exploitation has been the impoverishment of environment from where rural areas could get life supports — free fuel, fodder, fruits, timber, renewal of soil nutrients, unpolluted water, etc. The urban local governments have been reluctant to expand services like water supply, electricity, roads and transport, sewerage, etc., to neighbouring villages because the revenue income from the villages is too small to pay for even a fraction of such services. On the other hand, the land scarcity in urban settlements with severe deficiencies in basic civic amenities, forcing the inhabitants to live in dangerously polluted environments and dilapidated structures.The administrative costs of a dual form of local government are also high. Municipal revenue of small and medium towns is so pitiable that most of them have not been able to meet even the basic needs of their citizens. On the other hand, the existing rural local government has staff resources which, with marginal adjustments, could be used to look after the municipal needs of their headquarters town which can be developed as the growth centre for both the urban and rural communities.

The case for ending the dualism in local government is thus strong. A single local government at the district level can perhaps look after the needs of its urban and rural components with a set of safeguards built into it so as to ensure just development of the entire area. In the current context, a population of one million may be a suitable cut-off; however, exceptions may have to be made in respect of larger-size urban settlements, keeping in view their social and economic settings such as the community identities and the hinterland served by the city. Such a district government can also plan for the entire district obviating the need to have a separate DPC to coordinate action by various implementing agencies at the district level, including the ZPs and city/ town municipalities.

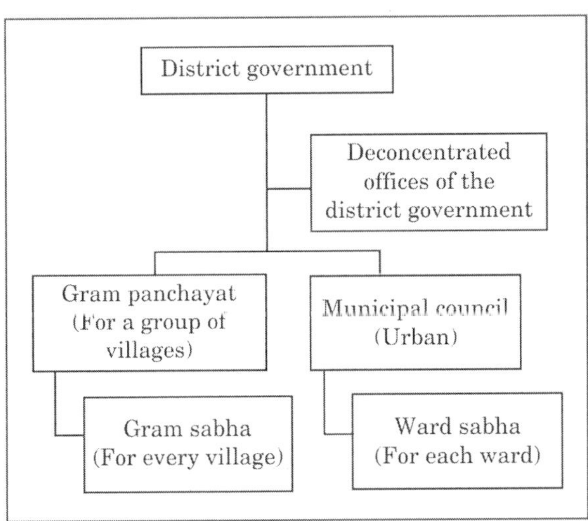

Fig. 2.1: Ideal structure for local governance in India.

This in effect means that every Indian will belong to either a GP or a Municipality and will look upon that as the local government entrusted with the responsibility of providing what all he needs from the entire system of governance. The district government will be the first level of decentralization below the State and will provide the necessary link between the State and the local governments either directly or through its units/offices spread across the district. Reorganizing the PRIs as indicated above requires a lot of debate and discussions among the different stakeholders and ultimately another Constitution Amendment perhaps! The ideal model of local governance in India is depicted in Fig. 2.1.

2.7. CONCLUSIONS

Decentralization whereby local governments are empowered to make all policy and programme decisions on behalf of their resident-voters represents a complex system of political, administrative and fiscal autonomy and associated accountability mechanisms to the electorate. Properly laying out a decentralized system of governance with legal status and institutions is important but not sufficient. Unless the institutions operating in the environment are given real powers, decentralization cannot succeed. A proper stream lining of functions between central, state and local governments is necessary for the local governments to operate effectively. The concept of devolution does not permits concurrent jurisdiction. All tiers of Panchayats are units of local self-government. They are sovereign within their own functional areas and are not subordinate to another tier of Panchayat. To ensure that the devolution is tier- specific there should not be any concurrent jurisdiction over the devolved functions not only among different tiers of the panchayats but also between the local and state governments. Unless the devolved items meant for the PRIs are excluded from the purview of the line departments the devolution would not have any functional meaning.

Fiscal decentralization is crucial to make decentralization an overall success. If local governments are not enabled to raise their own revenues, they cannot perform their functions effectively. Tax decentralization has to be pursued vigorously along with functional and expenditure decentralization assigned to them. The local governments as a policy should not depend on central resources and even when grants are made by the higher level governments, that should be either untied or for specific purposes and formula based.

Capacity building of the PRIs goes a long way in ensuring that they truly constitute the basic tier of governance and development. In order to create responsible, effective and accountable local governments, participation of people in the process of decision making is of paramount importance. Regular conduct of Grama Sabha coupled with social audit can ensure peoples' participation and accountability of the local governments to their electorate.

To sum up, we need to concentrate on activity mapping, untied grants, decentralized planning and capacity building of the elected representatives and the functionaries of the PRIs. All these will pose a lot of challenges and also provide opportunities. The next decade is therefore crucial for the development of the PRIs and also the Indian democracy through them.

REFERENCES

Adamolekun, L., Olowu and Laleye, M. (1988). *Local Government in West Africa since Independence,* University of Lagos Press.

Constituent Assembly Debates (1948).

Gandhiji (1942). *"My Idea of village swaraj", Harijan.*

Imperial Gazetteer of India (1909), 4: 278.

Jain, L.C. (1989). Interview on Panchayati Raj and Decentralization, Kurukshetra.

Meenakshisundaram, S.S. (1994). *Decentralization in Developing Countries,* Concept Publishing Company, New Delhi.

Meenakshisundaram, S.S. (2012). "Decentralized Local Governance and Citizen Participation in South Asia", National Institute of Advanced Studies, Bangalore.

Mukarji Nirmal (1989). "Decentralization below the state level". *Economic and Political Weekly.*

Nagarajan Hari, Binswanger-Mkhize Hans, P. and Meenakshisundaram, S.S. (2014). *Decentralization and Empowerment for Rural Development,* Cambridge University Press, New Delhi, India Private Limited.

Nehru Jawaharlal (1964). *The Discovery of India,* Signet Press, Calcutta, p. 288.

Rondenelli, D.A., Nellis, J.R. and Cheema, G.S. (1984). *Decentralization in Developing Countries,* Washington, World Bank.

3

History of Local Governments in India (With Special Reference to Karnataka) Lessons for Future

M. UMAPATHY[3*]

ABSTRACT

The paper provides a kaleidoscopic view of the history of local governments in India in general and Karnataka in particular covering, ancient, medieval, British rule and post- independence. Using this historical perspective, an analysis of the evolution of local governments is made, their present predicament is discussed and policy-oriented suggestions are made to strengthen the functioning of present-day local government intuitions, based on the learnings of their present functioning. The paper finds that the earliest local governments were found to be 'really local' with the status of sovereign and self-governments. They were even called 'republics'. As higher-level governments emerged, the local governments came under their supervision, subordination and control. Modern local governments, especially in India, have become statutory, regulated and weak 'local bodies' or 'token bodies'.

3.1. INTRODUCTION

Local Government is the oldest type of government. Perhaps, it was the only type of government for most of the time in the ancient period. In other words, the earliest local governments in history were really proximus, fully sovereign and self-governments. Historians naturally termed them as resplendent 'Village Republics'. In course of time as

[3] Retired Professor of Political Science, University of Mysore, 843 "SMITHA" 12th Main, K.H. Road, Saraswathipuram, Mysore - 570009, Karnataka.

Corresponding author: E-mail: umapathy42@gmail.com

monarchies and empires developed they came to experience some weak control, supervision and subordination by higher governments. But, in the modern period, especially, since the 19th and 20th centuries, with modern political ideologies of nationalism, capitalism communism and fascism, as well as the technological instruments of bureaucracy, communication and transportation developing, did the local governments really lose their power and prominence to higher governments. Local governments have become 'statutory', regulated, subordinated and weak 'local bodies' or 'token bodies'.

Today, the nature of localities or local places of peoples' dwellings is fast changing. Bursting population, ever expanding size and increasing complexities of local problems to be handled have put local governance in doldrums. For illustration, if anybody looks at our national capital Delhi with the 2.58 crore population, being the fifth largest city of the world and also the first among the most polluted cities of the world sees an agonizing process of both explosion and implosion of local problems and governance. Our big cities like Bombay, Chennai, Bangalore and Hyderabad, though they are hubs of our fast growing national economy appears to be most chaotically governed. The recent urban floods in these cities held a mocking mirror to the absence of any meaningful local planning and government.

The situation is not different in rural areas. The burgeoning population, increasing communication, raising, awareness and aspiration of the people and the challenges of integrating with fast growing urban and national economies need and demand good local governance.

Local government in India, in general, demands the next generation of reforms. It demands better devolution of functions, finances and functionaries. In this context 'Decentralization' in governance is the *Mantra* needed to make India's democracy and development – both national and local as well as rural and urban – real and full.

This write-up aims at a bird's eye view of the history of local government in India and Karnataka. It is divided into three sections. Section I: discusses on Local Government in ancient and medieval period. Section II: on Local Government under British Rule, and Section III: deals with Local Government after Independence. It ends with some lessons for the future of local governments in India.

I

3.2. LOCAL GOVERNMENT IN ANCIENT AND MEDIEVAL PERIOD

India has a history of six millenniums. India has largely been a land of villages. Village settlements were traced in Balochistan area much before the urbanised Harappa, Mohenjo- daro settlements. In the early or *vedic* period of Aryans "Vedic hymns frequently pray for the prosperity of villages but rarely for that of towns and cities"[1].

Towns and cities have been less in number and importance through history. Harappa. Mohenjo-daro urban settlements were of course the most planned urban centres of the ancient world. Later, some small towns and urban centers such as Hastinapur, Ayodhya, Dwarka, Patliputra and Ujjain did develop. In the Mughal period also Delhi, Allahabad, Ahmedabad, Lucknow were re-knowned urban Centres.

In Karnataka too, villages and Village Panchayats have been more in number and importance. They were resplendent in the period of Chalukya, Vijayanagara and Hoysala Kings. Institutions like *Panchayats, Agraharas, Nadus, Mahanadus*, with many democratic characteristics formed the substance of the golden age of rural self-governments in medieval Karnataka. Aihole and Vijayanagara were exceptional examples of urban administration in ancient and medieval Karnataka.

On the whole, urbanization and urban administration started developing in India only under the British. Increasing trade, communication and industrialization facilitated this. After independence, planned economic development accelerated these trends. Only in the 21st century, however, India has been moving fast towards urbanization leaving the tag of "a land of villages" behind. In this background, in Indian history the village administration in particular and the rural local government in general have been the focal points of administration.

3.2.1. Village Government

The village, called Grama has been the basic unit of rural local government in India. In Karnataka, in addition, a special village or part of a village called *agrahara* has been found since the medieval period[2]. The village government consisted of the village headman, his administrative assistants, a village executive – cum – judicial council and a village assembly.

The head of the village administration has been named variously through history as *Gramani* (vedic period) *gramika* (North India) *Gaonda, Patela, Desai, Heggade, Hebbar, Urodeya, Prabhu* (in Karnataka). He was responsible for the functioning of the village defense, law and order, welfare, revenue collection and chairing the village council and assembly. This was most often a hereditary post and occassionally an elected one (*e.g., Masaveggade* or monthly head in Karnataka)[3].

To assist him there was a village accountant called *Senabova, Shanbhag* or *Kulkarni* and other village servants like *Thoti* and *Talwar*. In addition, in Karnataka, the various socio-economic services for the village were undertaken by 12 village servants called *Ayagars* namely (1) the *talari,* (2) the boatman, (3) the *barika* (watchman) (4) the *totiga* (inferior servant), (5) the stonemason (6) the *Kammar* (iron smith), (7) the *Chamar* (the leather worker), (8) the goldsmith, (9) the carpenter, (10) the barber, (11) the weaver and (12) the astrologer[4].

The village headman and the servants worked generally under the guidance of a) the village Executive-cum-Judicial Council called the Panchayat and b) the village assembly called variously as *grama, Okkalu, Uru, Praje, Halaru, Hadinekentujati*, Samudaya, *Jagat, Janani, Gramacaria, Bhuddivantaru, Mahajana* (Karnataka) Mahatma (Maharastra), *Uru* or *Perumukkal* (Tamil Nadu)[5]. These councils and assemblies gave the village the touch of self-government. Yet, by nature, they were normally a limited gathering of the selected, hereditary, elderly, or only family heads and most often of males only. They were essentially gerontocratic than democratic. Only in some places and times they were elected by 'lot' as in the Chola period in Tamil Nadu[6].

It is interesting to note that bigger villages or agraharas had provided for further decentralized administration. Dikshit notes poignantly in his book Local Self-Government in Medieval Karnataka:

> ".... The bigger *agrahara* and town had their *Puras* or extensions, *Keris* or quarters, *balas* or words. All these had their own components of headmen and assemblies and were to a large extent autonomous. The way in which the *agrahara* of Huli delegated authority to its subordinate assemblies in

its different quarters or *Keris* will provide a few lessons in democratic decentralization even to modern times"[7].

3.2.2. Urban Government

Mohenjo daro – Harappan civilization was known for its urban development. Its town planning, wide and paved streets, granaries, market places, community baths, drainage system testified to the presence of an effective municipal administration. But, little details are known about them. Again, in the post-vedic or epic period and later some famous urban centers like Indraprastha, Ayodhya, Hastinapura, Pataliputra, Takshashila, Nalanda, Ujjaini, Delhi, Lucknow, and in Karnataka Aihole and Vijayanagara emerged. They were termed as Nagra or Pura. They had executives called Purapala, Nagarika, Vara, Kotwala, Mirs and assemblies or committees like Ghoshti, Panchkula and so on. Pataliputra had a well organized city administration during the 3rd and 4th centuries B.C., and the town of Aihole (in Karnataka) had its own corporation. Some cities like Takshashila and Ujjaini even had enjoyed the privilege of issuing their own coins[8].

3.2.3. Above the Village and Town level

Above the villages and towns also there were some units of rural local government. In ancient and medieval India they were known as *Janapada, nadu*, Tehsil, Taluk at the present hobli or taluk level and *Mahanadu, Vishya, Janapada* at the present district level[9].

The *nadu* in Karnataka was a body with a group of villages. It was an intermediary and coordinating body among different constituent villages as well as with higher governments. It had executive heads called *nadagowda* or *nadaprabhu* and accountants called *nadakarni* or *nadasenabhava*. It had an assembly of its own, also called as *nadu*, consisting of *prabhu gowdas* (village headmen), *nadu* officers, *prabhu gowdas* (area representatives) and representatives of merchant guilds and agraharas[10]. The *mahanadu* was an association of *nadus* at the district level. It had an assembly of *nadagaundas* and representatives of professional guilds. It met very occasionally[11].

Further as the medieval period progressed foreign aggressions, frequent wars, rise of despotic kings, sultans, nawabs and Mughal emperors became normal. Administration (especially revenue and police) came to be centralized and were passed on more and more into the hands of the agents of higher government such as Subedars, Amildars,

Talukdars and Zamindars. Local governments at all levels normally became weaker.

3.2.4. In Sum

On the whole, the ancient and medieval periods for a long time were indeed the golden ages of local self-government in its history in India and Karnataka. Non-existence of higher governments or the latter's weaker existence gave the local governments corporate powers and high autonomy. It gave them opportunity to experiment. The local governments in this period were considerably if not completely democratic in character. The various assemblies and councils they had was one evidence. Use of their names like *Urusabhe* (village assembly), *Samastha prajegalu* (all people), *Halaru* (many people), *Prajegaundas* (representatives of people) underlines their representative nature. Also, use of such expressions in their working as *Saravikyamathyavagi* (with the consent of all), *Aikaswamyavagi* (unanimously), *Vadambattu* (consent) indicates that in these institutions there were processes of public presentation, coordination and discussion of issues as well as consent, consensus and unanimity in decision-making. If not everywhere or all the time these democratic aspects prevailed widely[12]. However, we must not forget that in line with the ethics and ethos *i.e.,* the *Yuga Dharma* of those times these assemblies and councils were normally gatherings of selected and hereditary males only. By nature, these were more gerontocratic (rule of the aged) than democratic.

Naturally, there were many ups and downs in the life of these local bodies. Strong central governments as in Mughal period weakened them by centralizing police and revenue functions. Anarchic periods of petty nawabs and *Palegars* (local feudals) helped the village headman or gowdas to become more powerful. Yet, the village panchayats and assemblies played some important role to meet local needs. When British came and started expanding their rule in India they found their role interesting. This explains why Britishers like Elphinstone, Metcalfe, Munro and in the case of Mysore State Mark Wilks who spanned out in the country praised Indian villages as 'republics'[13]. Lt. Col. Mark Wilks, the first British to write a history of Mysore in 1810 concluded:

> "Every Indian village is, and appears always to have been in fact, a separate community or republic"[14].

Perhaps, this was a little too much to say about the local institutions of the early 19th century Karnataka. Indeed, even the little remnants of the good old system were enough to drive the alien white man, who had otherwise assumed all the orientals to be barbaric, to make frenzied statements pricking his own bubble of assumption. But, it did not last long for the British ruler in India to realize that everything was not so good with the local institutions of India. That is why he soon began to introduce legal reforms in this field. Of course, initially these reforms were minimum, highly centralized and were mainly to promote the financial interests of the colonial governments. Only in the 20th century they were guided by a democratic touch to promote local self-government to appease and douse the surging freedom movement.

II

3.3. LOCAL GOVERNMENT UNDER BRITISH RULE

3.3.1. In India

The British colonial government in India was initially mainly interested in establishing its control over the revenue and police administration. Therefore, continuing the pattern of Mughal rulers it introduced reforms in these areas. It introduced the system of *Zamindari, Ryotwari, Mahalwari* system. The purpose was to collect revenue through ruthless agents and at least cost to the administration. In the area of law and order administration it resorted to reform the provincial, district, sub-district, taluk and village level administration. It created powerful institutions of Governors, District Magistrates, sub-divisional Magistrates, Taluk Magistrates and revenue and Police *patels*. Starting from Bengal these reforms spread across the country. Later, they fortified these institutions by creating Indian Civil Service and Indian Police Service. These centralizing reforms not only continued the neglect of local institutions which had begun in the period of Mughals and Nawabs, but even deliberately contributed to their decline. The ruthless revenue collection by *Zamindars* and District Magistrates not only impoverished the rural areas but *Zamindars*, revenue magistrates and *Patels* even supplanted the local self-governments[15].

However, as (1) the British rule in India became expanded and stabilized; (2) the population and the economy started growing; and (3) the port-towns of Calcutta, Madras and Bombay – the hub of British Empire and economy – expanded, the British rulers felt the need to reform the urban local government. This resulted in the establishment of (1) Madras Municipal Corporation in 1687; (2) the Mayor's Court in each of these Presidency towns in 1720; (3) Justices of Peace for

Presidency towns with powers to tax in 1793 and (4) Town committees for sanitary purposes under the Bengal Act of 1842 in Bengal Province[16].

The First war of Independence in 1847 was a turning point. East India Company's rule over India was ended. The British Government came to rule India directly after the Queen Victoria Proclamation in 1858. Attempts to extend reforms in urban government in particular and local governments in general increased. Lord Mayo's Resolution of 1870 emphasizing decentralization from centre to provinces and then to municipalities was the first policy resolve of importance in this regard. Lord Rippon's Resolution of 1882 on local self-government became a famous policy land mark to strengthen local self-government in India even as it was against the strong district administration. But it remained merely on paper as the I.C.S. bureaucrats in India and the colonial controllers above were not interested in it.

Yet, gradually the growing freedom movement in India and the foreign support to it made the British government to move towards promising more self-government at national and local levels. In the 20th Century this resulted in (1) The Royal Commission on Decentralization 1907, (2) The Minto-Morley Reforms of 1909, (3) The Dyarchy of 1919 and (4) The Government of India Act of 1935. These led to more powers to provinces especially with regard to local governments. A plethora of local government legislations were enacted in this period. Local governments widely became statutory bodies. Gradually, more and more local governments were established in both urban and rural areas. Democratic elements started appearing in them. Some District Boards and municipal governments gained noticeable attentions in the period just previous to Independence. However, neither these local government measures were adequate nor the dynamics of Indian politics for freedom allowed them to take roots. Real local government reforms were left to independent India to deal with.

3.3.2. In Karnataka

In Karnataka, the then Princely State of Mysore enthusiastically responded to the British moves on local self-government. It enacted legislations on local government and established statutory local bodies in urban areas from 1850s and in rural areas from 1874 onwards. Municipal councils emerged in Mysore and Bangalore cities in 1850s. City Improvement Trust Boards were added in 1903[17]. Interestingly,

Mysore city was the second city in the whole of India to get a City Improvement Trust Board in 1903. Bombay got it first *i.e.,* in 1887. Delhi got it only in 1911. If Mysore is the cleanest city in India continuously in 2014-15 and 2015-16 the credit goes considerably to this early start for city planning, especially in sanitation.

In rural area the first modern official local government institution was the Local Fund established in 1862. District level Local Fund Committees were established in 1874[18]. Rural local government legislations and statutory local bodies emerged from 1903 onwards. Between 1903 and 1947 the enthusiasm shown for local government reforms in old Mysore state was enormous. The Government of the Maharaja of Mysore had appointed two committees (KantharajeUrs Committee and Srinivasa Iyengar Committee) in 1914 for recommending local government reforms. State level local self-government conferences were held in 1915 and 1926. It is interesting to note that the 1915 conference was at a private initiative and it was perhaps the first of its kind in India[19]. A series of legislations were passed to establish and reform rural local bodies in 1903, 1918 and 1926. Many experiments such as Panchayat Unions (1903), Village Panchayats, Taluk Boards and District Board (a three-tier structure 1918) and village Panchayats and strong District Boards (a two-tier structure in 1926) were undertaken. The District Board was a resplendent institution between 1926–1952[20].

We must also note here without fail the vision and efforts of the Princely State of Mysore (known as a 'model state' and its rulers termed as *Rajarishis* (Sainlty kings) by Mahatma Gandhi) for rural development. These include (1) The Mysore Village Improvement Committees (1914); (2) The Mysore Village Improvement Manual (1917); (3) The Concentrated Propaganda Scheme (1936) aiming at 'model village' (This was equivalent, in advance to the National Extension Scheme of the Post-Independence period); (4) The Rural Development Department (1942); (5) The Hobli Drive Scheme (1942). (This was equivalent to the Block Development Programme after Independence. It operated in selected Hoblies (a group of revenue villages and a unit of revenue administration). This scheme provided for non-official *Grama Sudharakas* (Village Reformers) Advisory Committees and a monthly journal called *Gramodaya* (Village Development); (6) finally, The Rural Development Scheme (1948) with a Rural Development Fund and full-fledged Taluk, District and State level Rural Development Committees[21].

The above trends towards rural development were admirable. But, neither these programmes were well planned and endowed nor were they well integrated with local governments. Indeed, local governments of the pre-independence period were inherently weak, unfit, unprepared and unpermitted for undertaking development programmes.

In sum, the local governments of this period, both in the British provinces and in the princely states like Mysore were (1) statutory, (2) subordinate, (3) dominated by ex-officio and nominated members and presidents, (4) having very limited resources and powers, (5) working always under the Damocles' sword of suspension, dissolution and state takeover of administration. It was natural that under the British colonial rule neither India nor local governments could have real 'self-government'. Independence had to be awaited for this.

III

3.4. AFTER INDEPENDENCE

3.4.1. In India

When India woke up at midnight of 14th – 15th August 1947, to face her 'tryst with destiny' the problems of the country were really nightmarish. The problems of partition, refugees, law and order, integrating the 'princely states' and finalizing a 'Constitution' for this ancient land of extreme plurality were undoubtedly mountainous. The problem of reforming local governments naturally got postponed until after the new Constitution came into force on 26th January 1950. Immediately after this legislation to tune the local governments, with the new Constitution began to appear. The States-Reorganisation' in November 1956 led to integration of local government legislations and further changes in them.

The Constitution of India 1950 set the tone, tenor and boundaries of the democratic and federal governance of the country. The Article 40 of the 'Directive Principles of State Policy' in the Constitution emphasized the promotion of village panchayats as units of local self-government. The Entry 5 in the List II (State List) of the Seventh Schedule, distributing powers between the Union and State Governments, made the State Governments clearly responsible for establishing, regulating and promoting "Local Government" in general as units of "local self-government".

3.4.2. Major Trends and Developments

Over 70 years of India's Independence local governments have been subjected to lots of attention and reforms. These have culminated in the 73rd and 74th Constitutional Amendments made in 1992. Below, we just list the major trends and developments in local government promotion in India.

A. Role of union government

Though 'local government' is a subject in the 'State List', the Union Government has been continuously engaged in promoting local governments on the following lines[22].

1. It has organized periodic all India Conferences of Local Self-Government Ministers, Mayors, Panchayat representatives to generate awareness, discussions, policies, legislations and programs in local government area. The first such conference was held in 1948.
2. It established 'The Central Council of Local Governments' in 1954.
3. It has appointed a number of committees, commissions and study teams from time to time to study problems of local government and to make suitable recommendations for reforms[22].
4. On the basis of such recommendations the Union Government has led and persuaded the state governments to reforms local governments all over the country.
5. It has made attempts to promote integration of 'decentralized planning' with local governments.
6. It has provided planned and unplanned grants to state governments and the local governments to improve the strength and quality of the local governments.
7. Yet, the most epoch making measures taken by the Union Government regarding local governments are the enactment of the 73rd and 74th Constitutional Amendments (1992) to make Panchayat Raj Institutions and Urban Governments respectively a third-tier of governments in the Indian federal system by giving them a clear and detailed position in the Constitution of India. The 73rd Amendment dealing with the rural local government did this by including in the Constitution a new Part IX, new Articles 243 to 243–0 and a new schedule XI. The 74th Amendment did

the same with regard to Urban Local Governments by adding part IX A, Articles 243–P to 247–ZC, and Schedule XII. These Amendments guaranteed autonomous structures, periodic elections and reservations for local governments and the establishment of State Election Commission and Finance Commissions by States for the purpose of promoting local governments' interests[23].

B. Role of state governments

Local government being a subject in 'State List' of the Constitution, State Governments have the primary responsibility to enact legislations and manage local governments. Since Independence some major steps of state governments regarding local governments have been as follows.

1. They first enacted new legislations or amendments to tune the local governments, with the new democratic Constitution of India to make them more and more local "self-governments".
2. After States Reorganization in 1956, they enacted new legislations to integrate and consolidate local government regulations in all the regions of the state.
3. Over time they also had appointed their own committees and commissions to study and recommend local government reforms.
4. The States have cooperated with the Union Government in ushering in local government reforms including the 73rd and 74th Amendments.
5. Some of the State Governments like Karnataka and West Bengal even experimented with some models of local governments which indeed became the basis of the 73rd and 74th Amendments.

3.4.3. In Karnataka

Karnataka state has been one of the most leading States in India in introducing local government reforms in a big way in rural local governments and moderately in urban governments.

1. Even before Independence the Old Mysore State – the core of present Karnataka – had a remarkable history of appointing committees and holding conferences for local government reforms. This trend has continued here even after Independence. Some committee reports on this issue have been brilliant, prescient and prescriptive of reforms required and to take place in India later. Significant in this regard was, first, the D.H. Chandrashekariah

Committee Report of 1954 which foresaw the Balwantray Mehta Report of 1957 in designing rural local governments to accommodate the C.D. and NES schemes of decentralized planned development. Secondly, the Kondajjee Basappa Report of 1964 was prescient about the Ashok Mehta Committee report of 1978 in terms of philosophy and focus on a strong Zilla Parishad, Gram Sabha and Nyaya Panchayat[24].

2. Regarding the models and legislations of Panchayati Raj after State Reorganization of 1956 in Karnataka there have been three of them[25]. First one was "The Mysore Village Panchayats and Local Boards Act 1959". The focal institution in it was the Taluk Development Board. It aimed at integrating the then prevailing Community Development Block (at the Taluk level) with the Panchayat Raj Institution. The Village Panchayats under this Act were too many and too weak. The District Development Council at the district level was an ex-officio and predominantly a bureaucratic and a mere coordinating body.

   In contrast, the second one, "The Karnataka Zilla Parishads, Taluk Panchayat Samithis, Mandal Panchayats and Nyaya Panchayats Act 1983" ushered a fresh air of democratization and decentralization. It was a model based on the Ashok Mehta Committee report 1978. It contained a powerful and elected Zilla Parishad at the district level, a viable unit of Mandal Panchayat as an effective group panchayat, and a Grama Sabha for each Village. The Taluk Panchayat was only a coordinating body. In addition, its provisions for 25% reservation of elected seats for women apart from reservations for S.C., S.T. and OBCs; the provisions for appointing state Finance Commission once in five years; the provision to elevate the status and position of elected representatives and the provision for constituting the State Development Council headed by the Chief Minister to guide the Panchayat Raj System were unique[26].

   The political will and statesmanship shown by the then government of Mr. Ramakrishna Hegde for this was unusual. According to some experts' opinion

   "..... The Panchayat Raj Act of 1983 could be regarded as a landmark in the history of democratic decentralization"[27].

   "its implementation, though short-lived, between1987–1989, drew national and even international attention to the potentialities of PRIs and democratic decentralization.

..............In fact, the Act was so progressive that it became a model which led to the 64th Amendment Bill and its successor, the now famous 73rd Constitutional Amendment Act. The 73rd Amendment Act is indeed a virtual tribute to the 1983 Act of Karnataka and an attempt to universalize it with some marginal changes[28]".

The third PRI model and legislation in Karnataka, which is the one in operation today, is The Karnataka Panchayat Raj Act 1993, which is now rechristened as Karnataka Gram Swaraj and Panchayat Raj Act, 1993. It provides for Grama Sabha, Ward Sabha and Habitation Sabha at the base and a three-tier of Village, Taluk and Zilla Panchayats above them. Regrettably, it is the most regressive legislation on PRIS in Karnataka. It reversed and undid all the gains made under the preceding 1983 Act. The most elevated and powerful decentralized democratic institution of 'Zilla Parishad' was reduced in status and weakened in powers by the 'Zilla Panchayat' which replaced it. The most viable and growth Centre oriented 'Mandal Panchayats' were replaced by too many small and weak 'Village Panchayats'. It overdid the reservations by extending it to chairpersonships weakening the PRI's at all levels. The worst was the recentralization, re-bureaucratization than decentralization and democratization of powers, resources and especially controls over PRIs. Indeed, it was a 'leap backward' as a model[29]. Dissatisfaction with it and the charade of discussions, committee reports and amendments to it continue with it even in 2016.

3. In the area of urban governments after State Reorganization, the Karnataka Municipalities Act 1964 and the Karnataka Municipal Corporation Act 1976 have been enacted and enforced. In addition, legislations to establish many parastatal bodies such as the Urban Development Authorities, Housing Boards, Water and Sewage Boards and Slums Clearance Boards have been in place. After the 74th Amendment Act these Acts, especially the Municipal Acts, have been Amended suitably to conform to it. Since then many urban bodies like Nagar Panchayats, Town and City Municipalities, City Municipal Corporations and a host of Parastatal agencies have been in operation[30].

Today, the democratic character and inclusiveness in the composition of urban local governments have improved. But their "institutional capacity building" has not improved. According to a very senior Secretary level officer of the State Government "..... the parastatal agencies have.............. fallen short of expectations", Karnataka has been hesitant "to implement certain important provisions of at the 74th Amendment Act like the constitution of Ward Committee, District Planning Committee and Metropolitan Planning Committee"[31]. Urban local governments too have been too much government and bureaucracy controlled. Integrated, efficient and effective urban self-government is still a long way. High urbanization and industrialization rates are giving a shaking and testing time to urban governance.

3.5. CONCLUSIONS

Local Governments in India have had a long history. In ancient and medieval India there were real, effective and "resplendent local self-governments" even called as "republics". In nature normally, they were essentially gerontocratic than democratic. During the British rule they became statutory, regulated, centrally and bureaucratically controlled. After Independence democratization of local governments in line with the democratic Constitution of India took place. But, they remained subordinate and state government - dependent authorities till the 73rd and 74th Amendments to the Constitution. Since these amendments local governments have legally become constitutional and coordinate authorities, constituting the third layer of the federal governments.

But, in reality neither their status nor capacities have changed much. The old culture of bureaucrats and state level politicians of treating local governments as subordinate authorities has not changed. To some extent their political stability of existence and financial resources also have improved. Yet, leadership in local bodies is deliberately not allowed to grow and their administrative services are kept at meager levels and, as more bureaucratic than managerial in capacities, facilitating domination by higher governments. Capabilities of local governments to face the challenges of fast growing urbanization, development, and needs of climate change have a big deficit.

3.5.1. Their Demands for a Better Future

A. A second tranche of constitutional reforms

The 73rd and the 74th Amendments improved their status and resources to some extent. New Constitutional Amendments to provide capable structures, resources (administrative and financial) and powers to function autonomously from State Governments are needed.

B. Bold democratic, managerial and technocratic design and solutions

The terms 'Panahcyat' and 'Municipality' with their 'small village' or 'small town' local and 'direct democracy' or 'town assembly' type of self-government connotations are fast becoming dated. The challenges of size and problems at local level are now immense. The 'Municipalis' (small town) is now increasingly replaced by the 'Metropolis' (The Chief/ Capital/Big City) and the latter itself is being replaced by the 'Megalopolis' (Urban region). For example, Mumbai with its population of 2 crores, area size of more than 2,200 square kms, and an annual budget of Rs. 37,000 Crores is an awesome local body. The old 'town council' form of local government is a dwarf answer for the present challenges. All local bodies including villages and towns are moving fast towards this situation. Bold democratic, managerial and technocratic designs and solutions are called for. The following minimum suggestions are briefly given below:

1. ***Establishment of keri/street sabhas and councils:*** The local problems begin and are at the *Keri* / Street level where the people really live. The bottom of governance and people's participation 'should begin here. It builds community and protects commons'.
2. ***Directly elected (unreserved) presidents and mayors:*** This promotes popular, strong, accountable and above all a stable (fixed term) local leadership and local governments capable of facing challenge from below and above.
3. ***Cabinet form of municipal government:*** This provides integrated and accountable (Portfolio-wise) local government. It makes parastatal bodies now contributing to chaos irrelevant.
4. ***Establishing specialized local government managerial and technical services:*** This eliminates dependence on generalist bureaucracy and contributes to capacity building for local governance.

Today, the era of subordinated local governments needs a relook as these bodies have become 'constitutional' and 'coordinate' authorities rather than mere 'statutory' bodies. Real and substantial decentralization of powers and resources for effective decentralized planning, development and democracy are the need of the hour. These are very dear to the heart of our beloved scholar Prof. Abdul Aziz. Governance local and national have to move ultimately towards the Gandhian dream of Sarvodaya in concentric and federating circles of coordinate and able governments from Keri/Street to the National Level.

NOTES AND REFERENCES

[1] Altker AS. (1958). State and Government in Ancient India, Motilal Banarasidas Delhi Third Edition, p. 225

[2] Umapathy M. (1985). History of Local Self-government in Rural Karnataka, Prasaranga, University of Mysore, p. 15.

[3] Ibid Ch. 2. p. 22

[4] Loc cit

[5] Ibid P. 21 and Sharma M.P. and Sadana BL. (1956). *Public Administration in Theory and Practice Kitab Mahal 43rd Edition,* Ch. 26 "Local Government", p. 641.

[6] Umapathy, M. (1985) Op. Cit., p. 28

[7] Dikshit, G.S. (1964). Local Self-government in Medieval Karnataka, Karnataka University, p. 181.

[8] Altekar (1958). Op. Cit., pp. 220–224 and 323.

[9] Umapathy, M. (1985). Op. Cit., pp. 24–28.

[10] Ibid, p. 25

[11] Ibid, pp. 27–28

[12] Ibid, pp. 28–29

[13] Ibid, pp. 31–32

[14] Ibid, p. 32

[15] Siddiqui Kamal (*ed.*) (1992). *Local Government in South Asia – A Comparative Study*, University Press Ltd., Dhaka, p. 18.

[16] Sharma, M.P. and Sadana, B.L. (2006) Op. Cit., p. 845.

[17] Umapathy, M. (1985). *Op. Cit.*, 3: 39–43

[18] Ibid See Ch. 4, 5 and 6

[19] Ibid See Ch. 5 4 to 6

[20] Sharma, M.P. and Sadana, B.L. (2006). Op.Cit., pp. 862–3

[21] Ibid, p. 862

[22] Ibid, pp. 863–867

[23] Umapathy, M. (1985). Op. Cit. See. Ch. 7.

[24] Ibid. Ch.8 Also read

a) Umpapthy, M. (1995). *"Panchayati Raj in Karnataka A Status Report" in Souvenir Indian Public Administration Association 15th Annual Conference, Department of Studies in Political Science Manasagangotri, Mysore*, pp. 24–29.

b) Umapathy, M. and Ramanathan, S. (1998). "Panchayati Raj in Karnataka", *In*: Ramanathan, S. (*ed.*), Landmarks in Karnataka Administration, Indian Institute of Public Administration, Karnataka Regional Branch, Bangalore and Uppal Publishing House, New Delhi, pp. 35 to 64.

[25] Umapathy, M. (1995). Op. Cit., pp. 25–26.

[26] Umapathy, M and Ramanathan, S. (1998). Op. Cit., p. 38.

[27] Umapathy M. (1995) Op. Cit., pp. 25–26.

[28] Ibid, pp. 26–28

[29] Ravindra, A. (1998). "Urban Administration", *In*: Ramanathan, S. (*ed.*), Op. Cit., pp. 65–82.

[30] Ibid, pp. 71–75

[31] See Arora Ramesh, K. and Goyal Rajanish (1996). "Municipal Administration in India; Some Problem Areas", pp. 278 to 284 in Ch. 16 "Urban Local Government" in their *Indian Public Administration: Institution and Issues 2nd Edition*. Vishwa Prakashan, New Dehi and Sivaramakrishnan, KC. and Lestica Green (1986). Metropolitan Management: The Asian Experience, New York, Oxford.

4

Democratic Decentralisation, Good Governance and Inclusive Development in India

SATYANARAYANA SANGITA[4]*

ABSTRACT

India is one of the few postcolonial countries, which has sustained not only democracy and remained as a nation for the last seven decades. However, it has failed to promote inclusive development in addressing issues like poverty, malnutrition, unemployment, illiteracy, inequality, human rights and corruption. The failure in promoting inclusive development can be attributed to democratic deficit particularly at the grass root level (district and sub-district levels) and political parties. The paper analyses the role of Decentralized Government (DG) in promoting good governance and inclusive development. The paper argues that the DG promotes good governance and inclusive development by enabling minorities and disadvantaged groups to share power in the governance of the country. It also facilitates people's participation and representation to formulate and implement policies reflecting the needs and aspirations of the people. DG also ensures accountability of elected leaders and administrators to reduce wastages and corruption and improve the provisioning of various services. In spite of these advantages, the DGs are not able to function as an autonomous institution in areas of planning, administration and finances due to interference from the higher-level governments.

[4] Former Professor and Head, Centre for Political Institutions, Governance and Development, Institute for Social and Economic Change, and Visiting Professor, National Law School of India University, Bengaluru-560072, Karnataka.

**Corresponding author:* Email: snsangita@nls.ac.in; satyansangita@gmail.com

SECTION-I

4.1. INTRODUCTION

India is one of the few postcolonial countries, which has opted and sustained democracy for the last seven decades. Elections are conducted regularly and governments have been changed under different political parties. Unlike many other countries, all sections of society (irrespective of religion, region, caste, sex, and education) are given voting rights to select responsive leaders. Unrestricted freedom for political parties, interest groups and press has been enabling them to reflect and articulate diverse views and interests. Institutions like Judiciary, Human Rights, Minority, SC/ST and Women Election Commissions are given autonomy to act independent of governments to safeguard citizens' rights.

This has enabled India to survive as a nation (disproving the hypothesis of western scholars) and resolve conflicts (language, regional, religious, and other ethnic) within the democratic framework, unlike many other developing countries. Parliamentary democracy and federal form of government (sharing power among centre, states and local) have also enabled to articulate the contesting interests of small groups and parties (Muslims, Christians, Bodos, Nagas) through their elected representatives. Democracy has also facilitated persons with humble background and from disadvantaged groups to occupy highest positions (President, Prime Minister, and Chief Minister). Furthermore, it has helped to moderate the extremist persuasions, ideologies, political parties and insurgent groups and separatist movements (like Punjab, North-East, and Kashmir) to fall line with mainstream thinking. Democracy has been partly responsible for making India as world leader in areas of information, nuclear, space and bio-technologies.

In spite of seventy years of democracy, India's significant chunk of population is poor, malnourished, unemployed and illiterate. Human development index is very low when compared to semi-democratic countries like China and South-East Asia countries. Sadly, India is ranked as one of the most corrupt countries, according to the transparency international. Ethnic (religion, caste, language and so on) tensions and conflicts are widespread. Disparities among regions and classes are increasing. Human rights violations are on rise. Radicalism and fundamentalism are spreading to a number of districts. So is also criminalism and corruption. The failure in promoting inclusive development/governance can be attributed to democratic deficit particularly at the grass root level (district and sub-district levels) and political parties. In other words, the improper institutionalization of third tier of democratic local governments at the district and sub-district levels and absence of internal democracy in political parties (not the focus of this paper) is a major constraint for removing economic, social and political inequalities and reducing poverty. Against this background, the paper analyses the role of decentralized rural government (Panchayat Raj) in promoting good governance and inclusive development. Analytical framework has been developed to examine these issues. The study is mainly based on secondary sources.

The second section discusses with the conceptual and analytical framework of Decentralized Government (DG) for promoting good governance and inclusive development. The third section deals with the empowerment and representation of disadvantaged (SCs/STs/ Women/Minorities) in DG to share power along with the dominant sections. The fourth section deals with the participation, representation, responsiveness and accountability of DG in provisioning of services through decentralized government in an efficient and in equitable manner to promote inclusive development and enjoy trust and confidence from the minorities and disadvantaged groups. The fifth section discusses about the constraints (due to lack of political from higher level governments) for efficient and effective functioning of DG with autonomy and accountability to achieve the desired goals/outcomes. The last section concludes with the policy implication

SECTION-II

4.2. DEMOCRATIC DECENTRALISATION AND GOOD GOVERNANCE: CONCEPTUAL AND ANALYTICAL FRAMEWORK

Decentralisation normally refers to transfers of authority, resources and responsibilities from higher level governments (central and state) to the lower level units/organs of government or non-government organizations (community or peoples' or non-profit or voluntary organisation) or private or profit organisation. Such transfers/powers in the form of deconcentration, devolution, delegation and privatization empower the local units to decide the allocation and distribution of public resources, to implement programmes and policies and to raise and spend public revenues for these and other purposes. These three powers referred as political, administrative and financial decentralisation respectively.

However, democratic decentralisation implies more than the transfer of the powers, resources and responsibilities to the local bodies. Crucially, it entails a system of governance in which citizens possess the right to hold local public officials to account through the use of elections, protests (movements by opposition, civil society, interest groups representing SCs, STs women, minorities and poor), media (print and electronic), grievance and other accountability mechanisms (courts, ombudsman, citizen charter, Sakala, public hearing and social audit).

4.2.1. Decentralized Government, Participation and Representation

DG enjoys trust and legitimacy from the people particularly minorities and disadvantaged as it promotes political stability and good governance in four ways. The first two are relating to participation and representation to empower and enable the disadvantaged to share power with the dominant communities and rural rich and to protect social, cultural and economic rights. The second two are relating to responsiveness and accountability of DG (political leaders and administrators) to people in delivering various benefits and services efficiently and equitably.

4.2.2. Democracy, Participation and National Integration

People's participation in governance (voting right) of country to elect leaders and policies without any discrimination (on the basis of caste, class, religion, sex and literacy) is critical for trusting the democracy (government) and owning the nationhood. Similarly, the other political rights like freedom of expression (press), association (political parties and interest groups), and contest (highest positions of the land including President and Prime Minister) further enhances peoples trust in government and loyalty to nation. India can be mentioned in this regard. India is one of the few countries in the world which has been holding regular elections and changing governments. Even it has been able resolve many conflicts and survived as a nation in spite of complexity and diversity in terms of ethnicity, religions, languages castes and classes. However, some sections of society are alienating from the government which is manifested in terms of naxalism, terrorism, and fundamenta-lism, low percentage of voting, poverty, human rights violations, violence, and conflicts and so on. However, this can be addressed by third tier of government, along with central and state governments as follows.

Firstly, DG enjoys legitimacy and trust, since they are elected by the local people. While governments nominated or imposed by the higher level governments do not enjoy the same confidence. Locally elected governments allow the community to identify more with its political institutions and fostering a sense of ownership and belongingness to its governance and resources. Secondly, the DG which makes participation easier for people particularly minorities and vulnerable groups to articulate their interests and rights (Blair, 1997).

4.2.3. Decentralized Governance and Representation

Representation in political and administrative system helps people to respect and identify with the government. People on some occasions want to see leaders from their own race, caste irrespective of their competence and commitment for public service. There are occasions, where caste groups come in support of known criminals and corrupt and prevent the government to prosecute and punish the guilty. In other words, representation is considered good governance rather than the efficiency. People prefer to govern by their own people rather than by the outsiders, even they are competent.

Secondly, the local people own the government, since its elected leaders are representative of the population in terms of ethnicity, caste, region, language and so on. The representative character of DG has been further strengthened with the reservation of seats for the disadvantaged. It thus promotes participation and representation which are critical for legitimacy and trust.

4.2.4. Decentralized Government and Responsiveness

DG also enjoys respect from people, since they reflect the needs and aspirations of the people. By its very nature, DG brings government closer to the people, making the translation of community preferences into responsive policy and programmes more likely. It generates incentives for people to own the decentralized government, since newly assigned responsibilities and resources relevant to them. Locally based decisions are often more practical and sustainable in that they acknowledge and accommodate local diversities and historic complexities that may exist within a particular locality. Only with the full cooperation of the local community, then, can development projects succeed (Steytler Nico, 2008: 20).

Even DG tends strongly to enhance speed, quantity and quality of responses from government institutions. It has both authority and resources to respond quickly to problems and pressures from below without waiting for approval at higher levels. DG has more and better information regarding their constituents and better able to enforce and coordinate policies and programs (Bardhan, 1996). DG also harness creative energy of the local people and can promote innovation. It helps to mobilize both human and financial resources as well. One of the underlying rationales of decentralisation is the possibility for innovation and experimentation that it offers sub national units (Nico Steytler, 2008: 21). Thus, DG promotes expected improvement in allocative efficiency, welfare and equity through increased participation, transparency, empowerment and responsiveness.

4.2.5. Decentralized Government and Accountability

Political decentralisation is said to strengthen the accountability and contain corruption. The proximity of citizens to their elected representatives also makes it easier to call the latter to account (Nico Steytler, 2008: 21). In DG, citizen finds it easier to hold government accountable through voter information, participation, and monitoring.

However, some studies differ with these arguments. DG, according to them, is frequently not inclusive in terms of political representation or decision-making, resulting in policies and actions that often do not address the needs of disadvantaged groups, including women. It is well documented that, in general, women and weaker sections are under-represented in DG.

In many DGs, the gap between the rich and poor is so wide. The poor, often living on employment and wages without assets and skills do not always have access to the basic services. Their voices are not heard on the need for access to housing, water, fuel, transport, and security. Poverty is a main constraint, women who bear the brunt of poverty. Women, more than men, deal with the basic services such as water, fuel, sanitation, primary health care, waste disposal, and transport. Illiteracy or poor education exacerbates the difficulties of access to basic services (Nico Steytler, 2008: 25).

The exclusion of disadvantaged groups from policy attention is a further manifestation of some DGs becoming inwardly focused – benefits for self-serving elites – rather than being community centered and development directed. The ultimate form of a self-serving institution is corruption in its various forms. Corruption and elitism, even if they exist only as perceptions, are a real threat to an effective DG as participation in elections and other processes decreases where the image of politicians and institutions is poor. Becoming inwardly focused is often the product of poor leadership; democratic institutions are not seen or used as vehicles to advance the community (Nico Steytler, 2008: 25).

In this paper, the expected out comes from democratic decentralisation are good governance and inclusive development. Political decentralisation enables the minorities and disadvantaged groups to share power with the dominant communities on the basis of numerical strength and affirmative action. Their representation in DG helps to trust and own the government. They are unlikely to support secessionist and separate movement. They prefer to stay with the main stream population and share power with the dominant communities. People also trust the DG, since it promotes good governance (responsiveness and accountability) and inclusive development. DG facilitates participation of people to formulate policies to reflect their needs and aspiration. Even their participation in policy implementation and monitoring ensures accountability of DG to disadvantage groups and thereby redress their grievances.

The function of DG depends upon the autonomy and accountability of DG from higher level governments. Whether DGs are enjoying autonomy (in terms of functions, finances and functionaries) to promote good governance and inclusive development?

SECTION-III

4.3.1. Is Third Tier of Government at District Level a Solution?

The foundation for the third tier of local self government known as Panchayat Raj (PR) at the district, taluk and village level came into existence in late 1950s on the basis of the recommendations of the Balwantaray Mehta Committee report. This attempt has not been institutionalized due to lack of political and administrative will. Both central and state governments undermined the significance of these institutions for promoting good governance. Most of these institutions are viewed as agents of the state governments to implement various development programmes. State governments are not enthusiastic in devolving powers and resources and holding the elections regularly.

With the Constitutional Amendments (73rd and 74th in 1992), the third tier of government (along with the central and state governments) for rural and urban areas with independent powers and resources has been stabilized in 2000s.

After the constitutional amendment, Panchayat Raj Institutions (PRIs) are emerging as units of local self-governments for promoting good governance and inclusive development. Powers, functions and resources have been devolved to these institutions to involve local people of various ethnic groups (religious, linguistic and caste) in the governance of the country (numerical strength facilitates Christian, Muslim and other ethnic minorities to provide leadership in some decentralized governments which is difficult at higher level governments). Reservation of seats and positions in decentralized government enable the disadvantaged (SCs/STs/OBCs/Women) to share power with the dominant communities and influence the policies and deliver goods and services benefiting them. PRIs thus enjoy political, administrative and financial autonomy in many respects. Firstly, all major responsibilities along with resources (Central and State Plan Schemes, Programmes and Resources) are transferred to PRIs for preparation and implementation of plans. Many centrally sponsored schemes have been transferred to PRIs in many states. All 29 functions as mentioned in Eleven Schedule and resources are transferred to PRIs (assigns 30 specific subjects to Gram Panchayats (GPs), 28 to Taluk Panchayats (TPs) and 28 to Zilla Panchayats (ZPs) in Karnataka). PRIs can prepare plans for subjects like agriculture, animal husbandry, primary and secondary education, public health, rural roads and housing, women and children, social welfare, public distribution, public libraries and so on. GPs can undertake regulatory functions such as issue of licenses, approval of building plans, and maintenance of common properties, assets and buildings. They can provide basic services such as drinking water and sanitation and maintain village roads, buildings and streetlights. The elected heads of PRIs are entrusted with the executive powers and control over officials and women. Seats and offices are reserved for SCs, STs and women (in proportion to their population and women, not less the one third) in PRIs to represent and influence policies benefiting them. The State Election Commission is entrusted with the responsibility of holding free and fair elections. State Finance Commissions are constituted to devolve financial resources to the PRIs.

District planning committees are constituted to enable decentralized government to formulate and implement plans based on local needs and resources. Even plan grants and resources available to DG under flagship programmes of the central government like Mahatma Gandhi National Rural Employment Guarantee Act (MGNREGA), National Rural Health Mission (NRHM), Universalisation of Education (Sarva Shiksha Abhiyan), Bharat Nirman, Swachh Bharat Abhiyan, Public Distribution System (PDS) and Smart Cities Mission to build necessary infrastructure and expanding access to health and education. Many governance institutions like Grama Sabha (village assembly), ward committees, social audit, ombudsman, RTI, and so on are introduced to make DG accountable and minimise the role of higher level governments in monitoring development programmes.

SECTION-IV

4.4.1. Panchayat Raj Institutions and Good Governance in India

This section mainly analyses the contribution of PRIs in promoting good governance. These issues are analysed in terms of participation, representation, responsiveness and accountability.

4.4.2. PRIs, Participation and Good Governance

PRIs facilitated the participation people in local governance in terms of voting, campaigning, contesting, Grama Sabha meetings and other development, welfare and cultural activities. Firstly, the establishment of small PRI structures/units nearer to the people (6,000 and 400 population for GP and ward respectively) and regular elections motivates people to participate in PR elections with highest turnout. The polling percent in GP elections was around 60–90 as against 40–70 in the state and central elections.

Secondly, people's participation during local elections in various forms (campaigning, mobilisation, contributions, and membership, contesting, and voting and so on) reflect their interest and trust in decentralized government. Even women participation in elections is quite significant. For instance, nearly 50 lakh women candidates file nominations for 10 lakh positions in PRIs; three women candidates for each position (Baviskar and Mathew, 2009: 11). Extensive participations in PR elections help to select right leaders and policies. This is evident from people's assertion in defeating, non-performers (sitting members and incumbent regimes) in PR elections.

Thirdly, Grama Sabha (village assembly) enables people to take correct decisions in selecting the beneficiaries and localities. Even they can raise their voice if their needs are not fulfilled and wrongs are committed by the PRIs. People's planning and campaign in Kerala can be mentioned in this regard. Not only large numbers of residents have been mobilised in this process, there have been extensive debates that have led to the writing of local histories and preparation of village plans (Vyasulu, 2008: 69).

4.4.3. District Governments and Minorities and Disadvantaged

DG rather higher tier governments are more ideal for ensuring representation in two ways. Firstly, small ethnic groups located in particular territory are likely to have better representation in DG. For instance, Muslims, Sikhs, Christians who constitute minority in India are in majority in some states. This is more so at the district levels. For instance, Muslims constitute majority in 20 out of 593 districts in India as shown in the Table 4.1. In 9 districts, they constitute more than 75 percent, as against 38 districts with above 25 percent population. Similarly, Christians constitute majority in some districts for which information is not available. STs constitute majority in 75 districts (Table 4.1). However, SC population is not concentrated geographically. There is only one district with majority population as 50 districts with the population above 25 percent. The districts with minority population may go further, if other ethnic groups like Bodos, Goorkhas Kodagus (Coorgs) and so on are taken into considerations.

Table 4.1: Category-wise composition of population in districts (in %).

Sl. no.	*Particulars*	*SCs*	*STs*	*OBCs*	*Muslims*	*Christians*	*Sikhs*	*Others*
1	Above 75%	0	40		9			
2	Above 50%	1	35		11			
3	Above 25%	*50	**31		38			
4	Less than 25%	542	518					
	Total	593	593		593			

Note: *Above 26 percent; **Above 30 percent

***Source*:** (1). GoI, Planning Commission, Compiled from "Report of the Task Group on Development of SCs and STs: On Selected Agenda Items of the National Common Minimum Programme", 2005 (2). Sachar Committee Report.

It is evident from the above analysis that the third tier of government is most suited to accommodate minorities in governance structures. The existence of autonomous Hill Districts Councils (HDC) in the North Eastern States is a testimony to protect the social, cultural, political and economic rights of tribals.

4.4.4. PRIs, Representation and Empowerment of Disadvantaged

Reservation enabled to select disadvantaged to positions in PRIs and municipal governments as shown in the Tables 4.2 and 4.3. For instance, around 36–38 percent of women, 17-20 percent SCs, and 7-11 percent STs got elected to the positions in GP, TP and ZP accounting to the total elected members 27,31,199. In fact, the participation of SCs, STs and women has increased over the years. The SCs membership in Village Panchayat (VP) had been increased to 18.15 percent in 2010 from 12.5 percent in 2000. The corresponding percent for Taluk Panchayat and Zilla Panchayat is 21.09 and 12.81 and 18.13 and 12.47 respectively. Similarly, the representation of STs in GP had gone up to 12.13 in 2010 from 8.74 in 2000. The corresponding figure for TP and ZP are 743 and 5.69 and 10.27 and 7.43 respectively. The women membership in GP had been increased to 38.4 in 2010 from 31.37 in 2000. The corresponding figures for TP and ZP are 37.19 and 20.71 and 35.80 and 31.80 respectively.

Although a majority of states reserved at least 33 percent of seats for women, they accounted for 44.52 percent in PRIs–1.26 million (Alok, 2011 cited in Sudipta Biswas, 2016). Reservation is the main factor for the entry of women in great number. For instance, according to a study in Madhya Pradesh, Rajasthan, and Uttar Pradesh (with a sample of 1200), 97 percent of women got elected for the first time and even women are getting elected from general constituency. For instance, according to the Ministry of Panchayat Raj (MoPR, 2008) 6 percent of women elected from unreserved seats (Sudipta Biswas, 2016).

Women's association with PRIs has brought transformation in their attitude, empowerment, self-confidence and political awareness. The women who reluctantly entered into politics showed great maturity in outlook, enthusiasm, political consciousness and perception of their role and responsibility. Most of the women who got elected for the first time without political experience started asserting control over resources and officials and challenging male authority and supremacy. Initially many

Table 4.2: Elected members in PRIs in India (in percent).

Categories	*Elected members of PRIs in India*									*Total members*		
	Grama panchayats			*Panchayat samitis*			*Zila parishads*					
	2000	*2008*	*2010*	*2000*	*2008*	*2010*	*2000*	*2008*	*2010*	*2000*	*2008*	*2010*
SCs	12.55	18.76	18.5	12.81	20.72	21.09	12.47	17.3	18.13	12.56	18.86	18.66
STs	8.74	11.91	12.13	5.69	7.28	7.43	8.07	10.84	10.27	8.58	11.65	11.83
Women	31.37	36.36	38.4	20.71	36.37	37.19	31.8	36.64	35.8	31.14	36.36	39.11
Others	47.34	32.97	30.97	60.79	35.63	34.29	47.66	35.22	35.8	47.72	33.13	30.4
Total	100	100	100	100	100	100	100	100	100	100	100	100

Note: Meghalaya, Mizoram, Nagaland States have Traditional Councils.***Source:*** Ministry of Panchayat Raj, Government of India.

Table 4.3: Political empowerment and participation of disadvantaged in country's governance.

Sl. no.	*Details*	*No. of units*	*Total elected members*	*SCs*	*STs*	*OBCs*	*Women members*	*Women ministers/ Presidents*
1	Nation		*793					
2	State	28 + 7	4508					
3	Municipal corporation	112						34 (30.36)
4	Municipalities	3551	68554					
5	Town municipalities < 3 lakh population	1430						476 (33.29)
6	Nagar panchayats	2009						670
7	District panchayats	537	15694				5779 (36.82)	198 (1.26)
8	Intermediate panchayats	6094	156609				58094 (37.09)	1970 (1.26)
9	Village panchayats	232913	2656476				975116 (36.71)	77210 (2.91)
8	All panchayats	239544	2828779	853931(30.19)			1038989 (36.73)	79378 (2.81)

Note: *543 Lok Sabha and 250 Rajya Sabha. ***Source:*** Compiled from George Mathew and Rakesh Hooja, Republic of India, in Nico Steytler (*ed.*), *A Global Dialogue on Federalism*, Volume 6, McGrill Queens University Press, London, 2007, p. 178.

of the women who are first timers and illiterate depend upon their men folk (husbands and other male representatives) for conducting the Panchayat activities and to shield them from the PR officials. Gradually, they become independent and exercising control over officials. This has also resulted for a change in the power relations between husband and wife. Besides, the women from the labour and lower caste take much interest in PRIs than the higher cast women. Now women come forward to fight for election, come out of homes to attend panchayat meetings and sit with men of different caste and age groups is a great transformation in regard to women empowerment (Baviskar and Mathew, 2009: 16).

Studies found that the participation of weaker sections (SC/ST, women) in meetings and in decision-making is quite satisfactory (Litvack *et al.,* 1998; Klitgaard, 1988). He found that about 80–90 percent of women particularly from lower income attended the PRIs meeting regularly. They are responsible for changing working culture in PRIs and improvement of female literacy. Chattopadhyay and Duflo (2001) found that the women leaders of village councils concentrate more in infrastructure that is relevant to the needs of rural women (drinking water, fuel and roads). Women member in PRIs were very effective in developmental role (Palanithurai, 2001). Similar observations are offered regarding other disadvantaged groups such as SCs/STs/OBCs.

Studies also pointed out that reservation has improved the perception levels of women and it has created an urge in them to participate in the governance. Twenty five percent of women members found visible change in their status within the family after they have been elected. About 60 percent of women said that they would encourage women to contest election. The same percent is contemplating to contest election (PRIA, 2000).

Their representation has helped the disadvantaged to articulate their views and improve their livelihoods. The weaker sections' power over resources has increased through PRIs. In states like West Bengal, Maharashtra, Gujarat, UP, the SCs started asserting their rights demanding egalitarian treatment. They are critical of any discrimination. They are vocal and freely expressing their views and taking full advantage of the welfare schemes meant for them. The members belonging to dominant community started respecting the SC president which was not the situation in earlier PR (they were ill-treated by making them to sit separately, or on floor, and having separate cups for tea) (Bavisker and Mathew, 2009: 10). Same is the case with the

STs. ST Presidents are protecting the interests of their community, although it is symbolic in some places. It has been found that many SCs, STs and women beneficiaries under different schemes who crossed the poverty line have experienced upward occupational mobility and many of them started repaying their loan (Aziz *et al.*, 2002).

4.4.5. PRIs and Responsiveness (Allocative Efficiency)

PRIs response to local needs and aspirations is very high. This is also known as allocative efficiency in economics terminology. According to them, PRIs improve efficiency, since there is a perfect match between preferences and provision of services. It reduces cost, improves output and more efficiently utilise resources (Smith, 1985: 4).

Allocative efficiency is high in DG rather than the higher level governments. It facilitates perfect match between resources and needs. Local information and needs can be ascertained by DG more accurately and there by identify project/schemes which have maximum utility or welfare gain. Selection/location of projects/members is very effective, whenever they are selected by the people. The involvement of Grama Sabha (GS) has brought down the selection of wrong places and persons. This is more so where needs are more diversified. For instance, some village needs water facility rather than road. In such situation the utilisation of the former is more than the latter provided by the Central Government. Many centrally sponsored rural development programmes in the past have failed due to wrong priorities, design and location. Roads, school building, tanks, field channels built were not effectively used as they were not strategically located to the needs of people. Similarly, many hand pumps were out of order, since people never had the feeling of owning them. Ultimately maintenance and sustenance of such projects and schemes under decentralized government appears to be very high (Sangita, 2002).

4.4.6. PRIs and Accountability (Productive Efficiency)

Productive efficiency is also high in decentralized government due to participation of people in implementation and monitoring of the development programmes. Firstly, people's involvement in formulation and implementation results in reduction in transactional cost (such as administrative costs, salaries, complex procedures, waste, leakages and corruption). Late Rajiv Gandhi, former Prime minister used to say that only 15 paisa out of one rupee spent reaches the poor by various anti-poverty programmes. People's monitoring contributes to minimise wastages and leakages. Their close observation prevents the procurement of substandard inputs like goods and materials. Close monitoring by PRIs helps to improve the attendance of teachers and doctors in schools and hospitals respectively.

Decentralisation also contributes towards better compliance and enforcement with low cost, since decisions regarding selection of schemes and design of projects are taken in consultation with the various stakeholders. This is particularly so in the management of community property resources like forests and water tank where law enforcement and punitive regulations are minimal. Democratic institution's monitoring mechanisms also help to improve the administrative efficiency. Regular monitoring by elected representatives (monthly review and surveys) help to assure that the policies and programmes serve the intended purposes. Further, the increased transparency and accountability that result from the civil society oversight enhances efficiency by decreasing the potential for diversion of resources due to patronage or corruption (Brinkerhoff, 2000: 604).

The productive efficiency also increases due to transparency and accountability in delivery of services (Aziz, 1994). Regular PR election has become a powerful mechanism for ensuring accountability. This is because if the elected leaders do not work devotedly for the upliftment of rural society, they will not be able to win the election next time. The defeat of large percent of sitting members in PR elections reflects this trend. Studies even mentioned that the accountability of officials to the elected representatives has increased. Responsible officials (like PHC medical officer, agricultural and veterinary officer etc.) can be asked for their presence in the PRIs meetings. In the meeting an officer may be asked/questioned for his/her performance. Productive efficiency can also be improved through social auditing and monitoring. Social audit (Jamabandi) through Grama Sabha (GS) and Ward Sabha (400 population) in Karnataka has enabled citizen to monitor the progress of works and ensure administrators accountable for the entrusted tasks and responsibilities (Sivanna and Babu, 2004).

Productive efficiency can be achieved by reduction of corruption under PRIs. Study finds that decentralized government enhances greater transparency and reduces the incidence of grand corruption. Another study found that corruption among PRIs functionaries was minimal where media and civil society were effective. The rent seeking is more in areas where institutions like Grama Sabha, media and civil society organisations are non-functional.

Productive efficiency can also be improved in decentralized government. It helps to mobilise additional resources (voluntary contribution like land, capital and labour) for promoting rural development. Such contributions accounted for 20 to 40 percent of the expenditure of the community development blocks in 1950s. Many villagers donated lands for construction of schools and hospitals. Even instances such as repair of field canals and tanks, and construction of buildings and roads were evident. Even people's involvement has also helped to manage village common property resources. People's involvement is also resulted in improving the collection of levies, betterment and user charges.

4.4.7. PRIs and Service Delivery

PRIs have improved the public provision of the service. Sectors like education and health improved substantially under PRIs. It was observed that there was a significant improvement in the area of medical and public health facilities and the supply of drugs in Karnataka. The attendance of doctors and paramedical staff improved considerably under the constant monitoring of local leaders in many PHCs and hospitals. GP leaders played a positive role by exerting moral pressure on the staff not to avoid their regular duties. Availability of doctors and paramedicals in medical centers are 74 percent and 93 percent respectively. 31 and 26 percent of households were satisfied with the behaviour of doctors and teachers respectively.

The utilisation of resources which has been transferred to the PRIs is much better than it used to be under line departments. Developmental works are being executed more speedily and field staffs are better controlled under PRIs (Meenakshisundaram, 1994). In Madhya Pradesh, Grama Panchayats and Janpad Panchayats played a very important role in improving literacy in 1990s (Vyasulu, 2008: 69).

4.4.8. PRIs and Service Delivery (Equity)

Decentralized governance ensured effective delivery of services like education, health care and poverty elimination programmes. Decentralized governance is more sensitive to poverty and unemployment according to World Bank (2002) and John (2000).

According to these studies, PRIs in India have done remarkably well in respect of devolution of power, implementation of the centrally sponsored employment generating and anti-poverty programmes especially in Karnataka, West Bengal, Andhra Pradesh, Madhya Pradesh, Rajasthan and Kerala and so on.

Westergard's (1986) study suggested that NREP had considerable success in providing employment of the rural poor. Some studies of food for work programme accorded the programme some success. Dreeze (1990) also found that IRDP overwhelmingly benefitted landless labourers. Swaminathan (1990) has also noticed similar success while comparing the state performance in implementing IRDP in West Bengal and Tamil Nadu. Webster (1992) found that the benefits under the employment generation programme and IRDP had gone to the poor and improved their living condition.

Leakages and wastages have come down under PRIs in implementation of poverty alleviation programmes. Bardhan and Mookherjee (2004) in their study on IRDP and agricultural mini-kits during 1978–98 in West Bengal found that the proportion of Grama Panchayat seats secured by landless doubled (10 percent to 20 percent). Distribution of IRDP leakage rate to the medium and large landowners was quite small (less than 4 percent) as against 87 percent of benefits for small and marginal farmers.

In West Bengal, in the late 1970s and early 1980s, the Grama Panchayats played an important role in the implementation of Operation Barga — identifying those who tilled land and registering their rights. Agricultural output has shown a dramatic increase in the state since then (Vyasulu, 2008: 69).

SECTION-V

4.5.1. Constraints for Effective Functioning of Decentralized Government

Decentralized governments in both urban and rural India, although constitutionally mandated, have a very weak existence in their own right. They are controlled by the state governments, which have retained numerous powers. Among them is the power to make rules, to make changes in the content of schedules, to appoint officials, to dismiss the Sarpanch, to cancel resolutions or decisions of panchayats, to dissolve panchayats, and to inspect records and works. Decentralized governments are hence sub-servient to state governments. The DGs have no power to legislate, nor have they the capacity to approach the courts to rule upon disputes over the respective constitutional powers of the second and third orders of the government. In fact, there is no case law on decentralized government in India as there is in the United States (Horst *et al.,* 2008: 9).

The constitution of in-charge ministers for districts further undermines the autonomy of the rural decentralized government. The in-charge minister is responsible for all activities including developmental, welfare and social security. He heads the committee to monitor and review the implementation of development and welfare programmes particularly central and state sponsored schemes. The ZP president is one of the members in the committee. Similarly, in Karnataka, MLAs used to chair the committees at taluk level to identifying beneficiaries for schemes like allotment of houses, sites, as well as selection of water supply schemes (Chandrasekhar, 2011).

The non-constitution and ineffective functioning of district planning committees is also a major constraint for autonomous functioning of DGs. The participative district planning has received prominence with the eleventh five year plan emphasis on inclusive development. District planning is an important instrument to achieve the optimum outcome in terms of balanced development with convergence of resources and enforcement of inter sectoral priorities. Unfortunately, many state governments have failed in supporting the district planning committees with the required capacity, expertise and resources to prepare long and short-term plans matching the resources and needs and aspirations of people (Kumar and Sangita, 2011).

Most of the centrally sponsored schemes dealing with employment, education, health, nutrition, child and women care, infrastructure and so on are outside the purview of PRIs. The implementation of flagship programmes of the central government like Mahatma Gandhi National Rural Employment Guarantee Act (MGNREGA), National Rural Health Mission (NRHM), Universalisation of Education (Sarva Shiksha Abhiyan), Bharat Nirman Programme, Indira Awaas Yojana, Midday Meal, Public Distribution System (PDS), Smart Cities Mission can be mentioned in this regard. These schemes were very significant in terms of number, administrative network and resources. They accounted around 213 in 2003–04, although their number had come down to 147 in 2011–12 (planning to reduce further to 49). Secondly, the resources spent under the flagship programmes in the districts, taluks and villages levels constitute around 70–80 percent of the development expenditure. Thirdly, parallel level bodies (parastatal bodies or registered societies) with administrators, experts and NGOs are constituted outside the PRIs. Such bodies account 10-40 at each of the levels (state, district, taluk and village). For instance, special agencies like District Rural/Tribal/ Watershed Development Agency for implementing CSSs can be mentioned in this regard. For instance, 571 District Rural Development Agencies (DRDAs) cells were working for implementing IRDP in the country in 2004 (Chandrasekhar, 2011: 50). Same is the case at the taluk and village levels. Most of these bodies are headed by the ministers, Deputy Commissioner/Collector at the district level, while administrator, MLA, or taluk president at taluk level (Chandrasekhar, 2011: 50).

The constitution of parallel bodies to implement programmes/schemes (State and Central Governments and International Organisations) appropriates the functions of GP. In ever village, 5–10 committees with separate office bearers and budgets for activities like development, health, water, sanitation, education, forest and so on appropriates the functions of the GP. Most of these committees are constituted with the representatives of stakeholders, NGOs, PRIs and administration. Some times the budgets of these committees are many times higher than the GP budget. Even there were instances, where keen contests were taken place for the positions in these organisations.

Some of these committees are above the GP (vertical), while others are horizontal. The former is known as village development committees with nominated members to supervise and monitor the development activities including Village/Grama Panchayat. The Village Development Committee in West Bengal Gram Vikas Samiti in Haryana, Gram Swaraj System in MP and Vigilance Committee in Himachal Pradesh can be mentioned in this regard (Chandrasekhar, 2011: 62). While the latter include the village committees for water, forest, health, education. The committees are responsible for formulation and implementation of plans as well as their operation and maintenance.

The organisation of many development programmes by the State Chief Ministers also undermines the functioning of PRIs. For instance, Andhra Pradesh Chief Minister, Chandrababu Naidu, started a massive programme known as Janmabhoomi claimed to be a government at the door steps (Prajalu Vaddaku Palana) to address the problems of villagers. This is the biggest event of the state government held twice in a year for 2–4 weeks. The cluster meetings are held in the villages in which ministers, MPs MLAs/MLCs, elected representatives of local bodies and officials with big budgets and support of entire district administration outside the purview of PRIs. The structure of Janmabhoomi Programme was dominated by bureaucrats, NGOs and political leaders and there was practically no role for elected leaders of PR except in a customary way. The activities reserved for PRIs including major development programmes are performed by the Janmabhoomi. They include: enrollment, immunisation, organisation of free medical camps, desiltation of tanks, laying down of roads, construction and white washing of school buildings, chlorination of water and so on. (Chandrasekhar, 2011: 83). Even identification of beneficiaries for pensions, houses, sites available under various programmes of central and state governments are undertaken in these meetings. The succeeding CMs have followed similar programmes with different names. For instance, the programme is titled as Rancha Banda by Dr. Rajsekhar Reddy who succeeded Chandrababu Naidu, Pallebata by Kiran Kumar Reddy and now Chandrababu Naidu again with Janmabhoomi. The Racha Banda and Pallebata programmes resemble Janmabhoomi in many respects.

The allotment local area development fund/grants to federal and state legislators (MP/MLA/MLC grants) also undermines the effective functioning of these institutions. Members of Parliament Local Area Development (MPLAD) was introduced in 1993 and each MP was given Rs. One Crore (now Rs. 5 Crore) for each year to undertake development works for creating durable assets in his/her constituency with the support of DC. This scheme is not only implemented out side PRIs and but also result in duplication and wastage of resources. They are isolated without integration with the local planning and also without accounting and accountability. Similar schemes are introduced by the state governments. For instance, Karnataka Legislator's Local Area Development Scheme (KLLADS) was introduced in 2003 (Chandrasekhar, 2011: 58).

Decentralized governments are yet to achieve the financial autonomy. They still depend upon 70–80 percent of their expenditure on higher level governments, in spite of transferring 42 percent of central tax revenues to states on the recommendations of Fourteenth Finance Commission. The total expenditure of decentralized government as a proportion of the combined expenditure of union, states, and decentralized governments amounted to 6.4 percent in 1998–99 and 5.1 percent in 2002–03. The decline in the expenditure of Panchayats (which covers nearly 73 percent of the population) from 3.9 percent in 1998–99 to 3.3 percent in 2002–03 is quite disturbing. While it is 20–35 percent for some countries and 45 percent for Denmark (Oommen, 2006: 897). Even the revenues raised by Panchayats from the sources assigned to them are very low. For instance, the revenues of panchayats constitute around 0.07 percent of GDP and 0.35 of total public revenues (central, state and local revenues taken together) in 2002–03 (Rao and Rao, 2008: 56). The own resources of revenue of decentralized government is only 0.39 percent of GDP in 2003–02 (of more than 82 percent is from urban local bodies), (Oommen, 2006: 897).

Decentralized governments in many states are yet to develop their own cadre of administrators. Most of the senior level staff is drawn from higher level governments, against whom the decentralized government has no control. Although decentralized government has a constitutional status, they are unable to function as units of self-government. They are dependent on state governments, which have conceded only political decentralisation and not the fiscal or the administrative decentralisation of powers and functions (Horst *et al.*, 2008: 9).

4.5.2. Enabling Environment for Success of PRIs

The effective functioning of decentralized government depends upon the commitment of the central and state governments and the support of civil society organizations and movements as well. Political regimes (parties and leaders) with strong commitment towards decentralisation and development are responsible devolving adequate powers and resources to decentralized government. For instance, the PRIs have come into existence with the initiative of congress party under the leadership of Nehru and SK Dey in late 1950s. Similar attention was received by Rajiv Gandhi in 1990s which ultimately resulted for constitutional status to PRIs. Janata Party Chief Minister, Ramkrishna Hegde along with dedicated brand of bureaucrats was responsible for devolving major powers along with resources to PRIs in 1980s in Karnataka. Democratic decentralisation has not been received sufficient attention in some states. Powers given to them were withdrawn and elections were not held regularly.

Leftist governments in Kerala and West Bengal have provided supporting legislations along with the resources to strengthen PRIs for reducing poverty and promoting social development. At the same time, the civil society organizations and movements are instrumental in mobilizing the people for devolving powers and resources to PRIs. Reform minded political parties in Kerala and West Bengal created opportunities for collective action from below by mobilising the small and marginal farmers and landless to take advantage of the benefits from PRIs and anti-poverty programmes (Robinson, 2007). Even civil society organizations and movements have mobilized the people to devolve powers and resources to PRIs. Even some of them have empowered PRIs by protests, advocacy, and capacity building and so on. In recent years, NGOs in Karnataka have fought for the rights of the PRIs, when State government was trying to dilute the powers given to PRIs. Similarly, Kerala Sastra Sahitya Parishad has played a significant role in shaping and implementing the people's campaign for decentralized planning in the late 1990s (Robinson, 2007; Crocker, 2008).

SECTION-VI

4.3. CONCLUSIONS

It is evident from the above review that democratic decentralisation promotes good governance and inclusive development by enabling minorities and disadvantaged groups to share power in the governance of the country. People's participation promotes trust in the decentralized government, since they got an opportunity to select their own governments and policies. The representation also enables the people to trust their government. Thirdly decentralized government enables to formulate policies reflecting the needs and aspirations of the people. Fourthly, DG promotes accountability and there by reduces wastages and corruption. Inspite of these advantages, the decentralized governments are not able to function as an autonomous institution due to political, administrative and financial interference from the higher-level governments.

REFERENCES

Aziz Abdul, Sivanna, N., Babu M. Devendra, Shekar Madushree and Charles Nelson (2002).

Decentralised Governance and Planning: A Comparative Study in three South Indian States. New Delhi: Macmillan.

Bardhan Pranab (1996). The Nature of Institutional Impediments to Economic Development. Working Paper, No. 1041. UC Berkely: Institute for Business and Economic Research.

Bardhan Pranab and Mookherjee Dilip (2004). Capature and governance at local and national levels. *American Economic Review*, 90(2): 135–39.

Blair Harry (1997). 'Participation and Accountability at the Periphery: Democratic Local Governance in Six Countries'. *World Development,* 28(1): 21–39.

Brinkerhoff (2000). Democratic governance and sectoral policy reform: Tracing linkages and exploring synergies. *World Development,* 28(4): 601–615.

Chandrashekar Lalita (2011). Undermining Local Democracy: Parallel Governance in Contemporary South India, Routledge, New Delhi.

Chattopadhyaya, R. and Duflo, E. (2001). *Women as Policy Makers: Evidence from a India Wide Randomized Policy Experiment.* Unpublished, Cambridge Mass.

Crocker David, A. (2008). *Ethics of Global Development: Agency, Capability and Deliberative Democracy*, Cambridge, New York.

Litvack Jennie, Ahmad Junaid and Bird Richard (1998). *Rethinking Decentralization in Developing Countries.* Washington DC: World Bank.

Mathew George (2009). The Functioning of Local Governments and their Relationship with Upper Levels of Government (Sub-theme paper). *In*: Kincaid John and Chattopadhyay Rupak (*eds.*), *Unity in Diversity: Learning from Each Other, Volume 4 – Local Government in Federal Systems*, Viva, New Delhi, pp. 36–54.

Meenakshisundaram (1994). *Decentralisation in Developing Countries.* New Delhi: Concept.

Palanithurai, G. (2001). *The Genre of Women Leaders in Local Bodies: Experience from Tamil Nadu.*

PRIA (2000). Programme for Strengthening Panchayati Raj Institutions: Narrative Report. New Delhi: PRIA.

Rao, M. Govinda and Vasanth Rao, U.A. (2008). Expanding the resource base of panchayats: Augmenting own revenues. *Economic and Political Weekly*, 43(4): 54–61.

Rao, M. Govinda, Bird Richard, M. and Litvack Jennie, I. (1998). 'Fiscal Decentralisation and Poverty Alleviation in a Transitional Economy: The Case of Viet Nam'. *Asian Economic Journal*, 12(4): 351–378.

Risse Horst, Caroline Andrew, Singh Dalbir and Keswani Suresh (2008). *Local Government in Federal Systems* (Sub-theme paper), *In*: Kincaid John and Chattopadhyay Rupak (*eds.*), *Unity in Diversity: Learning from Each Other, Volume 4 – Local Government in Federal Systems,* Viva, New Delhi, pp. 3–18.

Robinson Mark (2007). Does Decentralisation Improve Equity and Efficiency in Public Service Delivery Provision. *IDS Bulletin,* (38): 1.

Ronald Wats, L. and Kincaid John (2008). Introduction, *In*: Kincaid John and Chattopadhyay Rupak (*eds.*), *Unity in Diversity: Learning from Each Other, Volume 4 – Local Government in Federal Systems*, Viva, New Delhi, pp. XI–XVII.

Sangita S.N. (2002). Administrative reforms for good governance. *The Indian Journal of Political Science*, 63(4).

Sangita S.N. (2007). Decentralisation for Good Governance and Service Delivery in India: Theory and Practice. *The Indian Journal of Political Science*, LXVIII(3): 447–484.

Singh Mahendra Prasad (2008). Reorganisation of States in India. *Economic and Political Weekly,* 43(11): 70–75.

Sivanna, N. and Badu Devendra (2004). *Panchayat Jamabandhi in Karnataka: A Case of Transparency and Accountability in Good Governance,* Working Paper No. 142, ISEC, Bangalore.

Smith, B.C. (1985). *Decentralisation: The Territorial Dimension of the State,* George Allen and Unwin, Boston.

Steytler Nico (2008). Enhancement of Democracy through Empowerment of Disadvantaged Groups (Sub-theme paper), *In*: Kincaid John and Chattopadhyay Rupak (*eds.*), *Unity in Diversity: Learning from Each Other, Volume 4 – Local Government in Federal Systems*, Viva, New Delhi, pp. 19–35.

Vyasulu Vinod (2008). The Functioning of Local Government in Federal Systems: Perspectives from India (Sub-theme paper), *In*: Kincaid John and Chattopadhyay Rupak (*eds.*), *Unity in Diversity: Learning from Each Other, Volume 4 – Local Government in Federal Systems*, Viva, New Delhi, pp. 55–70.

Webster Neil (1992). Panchayati Raj and the Decentralisation of Development Planning in West Bengal. Calcutta: K.P. Bagachi and Company.

Westergard Kirsten (1986). *"People's participation, Local government and Rural Development: The case of West Bengal"*. CDR Research Report.

World Bank (2002). *Decentralizing Indonesia: A Regional Public Expenditure Review, Overview Report* "East Asia". Washington DC: World Bank.

5

Centrality of Panchayats in Rural Development Programmes: Rhetoric or a Reality?

H.S. SHYLENDRA[5]* AND S.S. RAJPUT[5]

ABSTRACT

Forging a strong link between the Centrally Sponsored Schemes(CSSs) and panchayati Raj Institutions (PRIs) is seen as a solution which can both help CSSs to shed their top-down character for better outcomes, and enable PRIs to emerge as institutions of real self-governance. This paper presents the emerging experiences and challenges focusing on six major CSSs from eight major states representing four broad geographical regions of India. The analysis reveals that the thrust for actual linkage comes mainly from attaining programme specific goals than the aim of deepening the devolution process. As a result neither the goal of improving grassroots delivery of CSSs nor the cause of empowering panchayats is addressed fully. The findings reveal wide variations across schemes and states in the involvement of PRIs. Overall, the PRIs are found involved largely in some aspect of programme implementation and monitoring. Prominent among the factors hindering progress are inadequate and slow progress towards devolution, continued top-down nature of CSSs that act as programmatic constraints affecting the potential role of PRIs. A meaningful linkage is possible by resorting to restructuring of CSSs to come out of their top-down mould and enable the states to deepen the decentralisation process.

[5] Professor of Economics, Institute of Rural Management, Anand, Gujarat
[5] Research Associate, Institute of Rural Management, Anand, Gujarat.
**Corresponding author:* E-mail: hss@irma.ac.in; shriprakashsingh.rajput@gmail.com

5.1. INTRODUCTION

The Centrally Sponsored Schemes (CSSs), a type of special purpose grants made available by the central government to states, have raised two major issues. The first is about the relevance of the method of their working in a federal system like ours (Garg, 2006; IRMA, 2008). The second relates to the question about the efficacy of their delivery at the grassroot level and the resultant outcomes on the development goals (GoI, 2008a). CSSs are conceived under the provision of Article 282 of the Indian Constitution with the avowed objective of tackling developmental problems of national importance. But their ever increasing number and funds allocated have been seen as potent threats to some of the basic principles of federalism in India. The funds which flow more in the nature of conditional grants, are perceived to undermine the role the state governments are expected to play for development on their own volition. CSSs which emerged initially to look at the issues of inter-state nature sub-sequently have been extended to cover a wide range of issues across sectors. The state governments in general have been compelled to accept them as partnership programmes by providing matching contributions of varying degree. The method of direct release of funds under many of these CSSs to district and local agencies by passing the state governments also has raised further consternation about the role of CSSs. CSSs have been largely criticized for their poor performance on equity and efficiency counts (GoI, 2002; 2008a). Some consider them to be a major drain on public resources as they tend to focus mainly on achieving financial and physical targets through a supply-driven approach to the neglect of more sustainable outcomes. On the equity front, a major criticism is that their benefits get largely garnered by better-off regions or sections of society owing to poor targeting. Another major issue is the suggestion and attempt for strengthening their linkage with the Panchayati Raj Institutions (PRIs) as they exist under the framework created in the aftermath of 73rd Amendment. While the issue of forging linkage between rural development and decentralisation has been advocated since the launch of the Community Development Programme (CDP), a centrally supported programme launched in the 1950s, the interface being newly sought to be established between CSSs and PRIs is the result of several challenges and compulsions that have emerged more recently. One of these challenges relates to bringing compatibility of CSSs in their present form with the framework of decentralisation created under the 73rd Amendment. A list of twenty-nine subjects has been delineated under the Eleventh Schedule of the Constitution creating a clear domain for the Panchayats. The state governments are called upon under Article 243G to endow Panchayats with powers and authority to emerge as institutions of self-government especially to prepare and implement plans for economic development and social justice. Simultaneously, District Planning Committees (DPCs) have to be constituted which would help in the emergence of true decentralized planning involving PRIs.

Given such a framework, it is argued that CSSs which are generally formulated and implemented in a top-down manner contravene the constitutional provisions pertaining to the role of PRIs. The Eleventh Five Year Plan (GoI, 2008a) lamented that CSSs exist more as standalone silos lacking in integration and convergence with local governance. In a similar tone, the Expert Group on grassroots planning argued that CSSs are even coming in the way of real emergence of decentralized planning (GoI, 2006). In the process, the Panchayats have been compelled to act merely as agents for channelizing CSSs funds rather than emerge as empowered institutions for development planning. Further, with the economic reforms gaining grounds, the developmental programmes including CSSs have come under severe scrutiny. The Eleventh Five Year Plan (GoI, 2008a) highlighted that several of these developmental schemes have not generated the results commensurate with the allocations. The Plan attributes the poor results to factors such as their inadequate convergence, rigid and inconsistent design and approach, and weak professional support. The Plan calls for radically altering the structure of CSSs by giving a pivotal role to local governments in their planning and implementation.

Simultaneously, PRIs are found languishing owing to inadequate responses of the state governments to devolve powers and authorities. Some of the recent assessments have highlighted the fact that PRIs have been neither able to emerge as credible institutions of local self-government nor able to deliver on the expected political and economic outcomes very significantly (Jayal, 2006; Singh, 2007).

The issue of according centrality to PRIs in CSSs has mainly emerged in the above context. It is seen by the advocates as a possible solution to the problems being faced both by PRIs and CSSs as highlighted above (GoI, 2006; GoI, 2008b; GoI, 2008c). Several mechanisms have been identified to ensure centrality of Panchayats under CSSs. A more instrumental way suggested is to modify the guidelines of various CSSs in consultation with the concerned ministries and departments to give a central role to PRIs in the planning and implementation of CSSs. However, an exercise carried out to this effect was found to be ineffective as the ministries and departments could not make the required progress to ensure centrality to PRIs. Another suggestion is to make the release of central government funds conditional so that states are able to fulfil their obligations towards decentralisation (GoI, 2008b). It is argued that CSSs can be leveraged to enforce states and their departments to devolve the needed functions and functionaries to Panchayats so that they can play an active role. However, there are views that CSSs alone cannot be used as instruments for empowering Panchayats which would need adoption of a broader process of decentralisation (IRMA, 2008).

The Expert Group (GoI, 2006) which looked at the ways of fostering decentralized planning came up with a framework under which PRIs could attain centrality. The group argued for integrating CSSs under the district planning process to be carried out by DPC in a more holistic way involving Panchayats up to the village level. The district plan would look beyond schemes and programmes and focus on addressing broader developmental goals like human development, poverty alleviation, and sectoral development. CSSs would get subsumed into district planning. Ultimately, there would be only one plan for a district and not a set of standalone plans as prepared currently for CSSs. To help PRIs prepare such a holistic plan, the Expert Group recommended some specific steps including carrying out activity mapping by each ministry to clearly delineate the role of Panchayats based on the principle of subsidiarity. The guidelines of CSSs are to be then fully realigned with activity mapping. Local governments at different levels are to be vested with powers to fully implement and manage the schemes. All standalone sub-committees of various CSSs would be integrated as the sub-committees of Panchayats to ensure convergence. The line departments as well as parallel bodies promoted by the government or donor support programmes would be brought under Panchayats so that *panchayats* will have primacy for grassroots planning and development.

From a conceptual perspective, the linkage between CSSs and PRIs can be related to the perceived role of decentralisation for rural development as advocated either by the liberal interventionist approach or the radical populist approach (Gurukkal, 2006). Under the liberal interventionist approach, the linkage could be seen as one of tapping decentralized institutions like PRIs more in an instrumental way for attaining efficient programme results. Local government's *vis-à-vis* centralized systems are considered more efficient for delivery of public interventions because of their ability to target and monitor resource use in a much better way. Decentralisation hence is considered to be an obvious choice for improving the efficiency of resource allocation of public programmes. From the perspective of radical populist approach, strengthening the linkage between CSSs and PRIs is seen as an attempt to transform structurally hierarchical system of planning which is politically and economically disempowering for the poor. Decentralisation done more in the form of devolution here becomes as an end in itself for empowering local communities. However, under both approaches outcomes of decentralisation are considered uncertain and predicated upon the existence of several desirable conditions. The interventionist approach may fail if there is inadequate delegation of powers, lack of capacity among local governments for planning, and local elites end up capturing the delegated power and resources. Similarly, the radical approach for empowerment may fail if enabling socio-economic conditions of participation fail to materialize for the poor.

Given such a tenuous conceptual linkage and a weaker available empirical evidence about the role decentralisation can play in rural development (Shylendra, 2008), the attempt to give centrality to PRIs under CSSs raises several challenges and questions. Can according centrality to PRIs help address the problems afflicting CSSs with regard to their outcomes on efficiency and equity? What has been the progress in tuning CSSs to make PRIs become active participants? What are the right approaches to ensure centrality of PRIs under CSSs? Can merely altering the guidelines in an instrumental way would help or does it need a more holistic approach whereby CSSs get integrated with decentralized planning? Can CSSs be leveraged for ensuring states to carry forward the devolution process? Can the grants of CSSs be made conditional to make such a progress? Moreover, what are the constraints of the state governments in giving due role for PRIs? What are some of the social and economic challenges for strengthening the relationship between developmental programmes like CSSs and Panchayats?

The present study is an attempt to look at critically some of these issues pertaining to the linkage between CSSs and Panchayats. More specifically, the following objectives have been examined in this study:

(i) What is the nature and extent of the involvement of PRIs under the CSSs, and what has been the progress towards assigning centrality to PRIs?

(ii) What is the emerging experience, and what are some of the outcomes of the involvement of PRIs for decentralised planning and development?

(iii) What are the constraints in enhancing the role of PRIs, and what is the possible ways forward in strengthening the linkage between the PRIs and the CSSs?

The study is focused on analysing the case of six major CSSs: National Rural Employment Guarantee Scheme (NREGS), Indira Awaas Yojana (IAY), Sarva Shiksha Abhiyan (SSA), National Rural Health Mission (NRHM), Integrated Child Development Services (ICDS), and Accelerated Rural Water Supply Programme (ARWSP)/Swajaldhara. The six schemes were selected not only because they have comparatively a higher financial outlay but are also aimed at addressing some of the crucial development issues like rural employment, housing, education, health, drinking water, and nutrition.

Eight major states representing four broad geographical regions of India (North, South, East and West) were selected for the study. The states are Assam, Bihar, Gujarat, Himachal Pradesh (HP), Karnataka, Madhya Pradesh (MP), Rajasthan, and Tamil Nadu (TN) (Table 5.1). Data were collected at four levels for each scheme: State, Zilla Panchayat (ZP), Intermediate Panchayat (IP), and Village Panchayat (VP). A relatively backward district was selected for a case study in each state to examine the role being played by PRIs at three levels. Respondents included elected leaders of Panchayats, officials in charge of selected schemes (from state to block level), field level functionaries, and members of village community. On the basis of the review of guidelines of the selected schemes a schedule was prepared for discussions and data gathering.

Table 5.1: Selected sample states, districts, blocks and villages.

States	***Districts***	***Blocks***	***Villages***
Assam	Morigaon	Bhurbandha	Mikirbheta, Azarbari
Bihar	Gaya	Bodh Gaya	Padariya
Gujarat	Sabarkantha (Anand)	Bhiloda (Anklav, Sojitra)	Jaisinghpura, Bhusawal (Koshindra, Maghrol)
HP	Mandi	Sunder Nagar	Mahadev
Karnataka	Davangere	Jagalur	Kechchanhalli
MP	Mandala	Mandla (Narayanganj) (Sikoshi)	Hirdenagar, Koregaon
Rajasthan	Ajmer	Pisangan	Ganahera
TN	Villupuram	Kallakurichi	Ariyaperumanoor, Mathur

Units given in the brackets were covered for pilot study/additional information.

The attempt is to capture for each programme some of the underlying processes of involving of PRIs in planning, implementation and monitoring. There is no attempt made to evaluate the impact of an involvement of PRIs as such. For each programme, an overview is given in terms of its basic goals, broad structure of implementation, and major provisions made for involving PRIs according to the programme guideline or framework. This is followed by a descriptive analysis of the primary data gathered for each scheme. Finally, an attempt has been made to compare and synthesize the findings across the schemes.

The study, given its objectives and the methodology adopted suffer from few limitations. Given the time constraint, only eight states have been studied to capture the national level scenario. In each of the states, primary data were collected using a case study methodology by selecting one particular ZP/district, one IP/block, and one or two Village Panchayats. Again time was a constraint to explore in detail all the relevant issues adequately. Uniform data could not be collected for each scheme across all states. Moreover, relevant circulars and official documents could not be accessed for some of the states/schemes. Though the attempt is to present both *de facto* and *de jure* scenarios about the status of involvement of PRIs, in many cases only one of the scenarios has been shown depending upon data availability.

5.2. ANALYSIS OF SELECTED CENTRALLY SPONSORED SCHEMES

5.2.1. Indira Awaas Yojana

The Indira Awaas Yojana (IAY) was launched during 1985–86 as a sub-scheme of the Rural Landless Employment Guarantee Programme (RLEGP). IAY continued thereafter as a sub-scheme of the Jawahar Rozgar Yojana (JRY) which was launched in 1989 and focused on Scheduled Castes (SCs) and Scheduled Tribes (STs) families in rural areas. From 1993–94, the scope of IAY was extended to cover all Below Poverty Line (BPL) households. IAY was de-linked from JRY and made an independent scheme from January 1st 1996.

IAY is a CSS of the Ministry of Rural Development to provide houses to the poor in rural areas, funded on cost-sharing basis between the Government of India and State Governments in the ratio of 75:25. According to 2004 guidelines (GoI, 2004), the major target groups for houses under IAY are below poverty line households living in rural areas belonging to SCs/STs, freed bonded labourers and non-SCs/STs BPL rural households, and widows. The objective is primarily to help construction/upgradation of dwelling units of members of the target groups by providing them financial assistance.

The Department of Rural Development under the Ministry of Rural Development is the apex body for overall implementation of IAY in the country. At the state level, generally the department/s of rural development and Panchayati Raj look after IAY. A state level vigilance and monitoring committee for rural development programmes which has a representative or nominee of the Ministry of Rural Development, GoI monitors the programme.

The District Rural Development Agency (DRDA) and/or Zilla Panchayat (ZP) looks after the implementation of IAY at the district level. As per the GoI guidelines, ZP/DRDA on the basis of allocations made and targets fixed will decide the number of houses to be constructed/ upgraded Panchayat-wise during a particular financial year. This will be intimated to the Village Panchayat (VP) concerned. Thereafter, the Grama Sabha (GS) will select the beneficiaries from the list of eligible BPL households restricting this number to the target allotted. The selection by the GS is final and no approval by a higher body is required. ZP/DRDAs and the Intermediate Panchayat (IP) should however be sent a list of selected beneficiaries (GoI, 2004).

The ZP/DRDA concerned may certify that a particular category is exhausted or not available in a district so that these allocations may be utilized for other categories. The funds of IAY are operated by ZP/DRDA at the district level. The Central Government funds are released in two installments subject to the progress of the scheme. The State Government has to release its share to ZP/DRDA within a month.

The beneficiary has to be involved in the construction of his/her house and can seek the help of ZP/DRDA in acquiring raw material at controlled rates. ZP/DRDA will not employ contractors but can seek expertise or material help to make the houses cost-effective and durable. ZP/DRDA has to ensure through monitoring completion of the previously sanctioned housing units before seeking fresh allocations.

5.2.2. Field Observations

IAY has been in existence for a long period. It has been standardized to ensure targeted and speedy release and utilization of funds from the

State Government to the VP level. The state governments implement the programme largely according to the guidelines issued by the central government with only minor deviations to suit local realities. Under IAY, the central government gives annual targets up to the district level. Attempts are being made to monitor the release of funds and implementation of the programme up to the household level using web-based technology. Officials at state government level in many of the states (Bihar, TN, HP and Gujarat) are of the view that IAY has been streamlined well and the present system helps in the better implementation of IAY. They felt that the current role given for PRIs under IAY is adequate and there is no need for any further devolution. A few states not only have their own housing schemes (Gujarat, Karnataka, MP and TN) but also make some additional allocation (Gujarat, Rajasthan and TN) to IAY households to meet the cost of housing.

ZP level

Some of the major issues observed at the district level pertain to the allocation of targets, release of funds, and monitoring progress. As to whether it is DRDA or ZP which plays the key role depends upon the role assigned to ZP by the state government and also the status of DRDA in relation to ZP. In states like Karnataka, MP, and Rajasthan (where DRDA is merged with ZP), district level issues are handled by ZP. However, in Karnataka the final allocation across talukas/blocks and villages is done by a state level rural housing corporation which is the nodal agency for implementation of the scheme. In states like Assam, Bihar, TN and Gujarat, DRDAs have been assigned the role to handle district level issues. ZPs play no active role. In states like MP and HP where DRDA functions under ZP, ZP handles district level issues in co-ordination with DRDA. In states like MP and Rajasthan, ZPs have been given additional roles. In MP, ZP can exercise discretion up to 3 percent in allotting houses to certain needy sections like widows and handicapped households. In HP, ZP ensures that at least two houses are allotted to each VP. In Rajasthan and MP, the chief executive officer (CEO) of ZP even releases funds directly to Village Panchayats/selected households at the village level. About the request or appeal for changing the status of BPL, no role has been assigned to ZPs. In Bihar and Rajasthan the second appeal can be made to the District Collector for changing the status. In TN and Gujarat, DRDA authorities have been given the role in this regard. In TN, the consent of DRDA project officer (PO) is needed for the Block Development Officer (BDO) to change the

BPL status of a household on appeal. In all the states, ZPs overall monitor the progress of IAY. This is done mostly as a part of the review of all development programmes implemented in the district.

IP level

The Intermediate Panchayats (IP) play a very limited role directly. IPs receives the list of selected BPL households from VPs. IPs may do only a general verification of the list before they pass it on to ZP/DRDA. In MP, IPs verifies the list to ensure that the roster has been followed in the allocation. The fund release is handled by BDO/TDO. In states like TN and HP, BDOs release funds to VPs. In Assam, Bihar, Gujarat, and Karnataka (till recently), BDOs released funds to beneficiaries directly. In some states, block level officials have been given additional powers or roles. In TN, though VPs release funds to beneficiaries, the bank would release funds only on receiving advice from BDO. In Assam, the junior engineer at the block level is a joint signatory with the beneficiary for withdrawing money from the bank. IPs take up general monitoring of IAY mostly on a voluntary basis. Junior Engineers (JE) and other technical people under IP provide technical supervision and advice (TN, Gujarat, Assam) to households to ensure quality and also provide utilization certificates (Rajasthan). In Gujarat, the IP president is a member of the land management committee which recommends land to landless IAY beneficiaries.

VP level

In the given structure of IAY, VPs play relatively a more active role than ZP/IPs. They are the implementers of the programme at the village level. The BPL waitlist which is the basis for allotting houses under IAY is supposed to have been approved by the Grama Sabha. Given the fact that the BPL list as prepared in 2002 has been faulty, VPs in some of the states are found proactively prioritizing the households based on actual need. VPs in many states (Gujarat, HP, Karnataka, TN, and MP) reported that they resort to such a change with approval from the Grama Sabha. Given the rigid norm of adhering to the BPL list, this proactive role of VPs seems to be helping in mitigating the problems of the faulty BPL list.

In most states, houses are allotted only to households with a house site. In TN and Gujarat, VPs can recommend allotment of land to landless by higher level agencies. In terms of fund release, only a few states (TN, HP and Karnataka) have allowed VPs to release funds to beneficiary households directly. Many states (Assam, Bihar, and Gujarat) release funds from district or block level directly to beneficiary households (Table 5.2).

Table 5.2: Release of IAY funds to households.

State	*PRI*	*Actors involved*
Assam	–	BDO
Bihar	–	BDO
Gujarat	IP	BDO
HP	VP	VP President and Secretary
Karnataka	VP	VP President and Secretary
MP	VP	VP Secretary with consent from construction committee having VP members and engineer
Rajasthan	ZP	CEO-ZP
TN	VP	VP President and Vice-President/BDO/Advise Bank.

In Karnataka, the state level Rajiv Gandhi Rural Housing Corporation Ltd. (RGRHCL) releases funds to VPs directly for release to beneficiary households.

Some of the states (Assam, Rajasthan) have reversed the system wherein the VP or VP president released funds to selected households. This has been done apparently with the intention of eliminating corruption at the VP level. In Karnataka, instead of IP, VP has now been entrusted with the role of disbursing funds to beneficiaries in order to ensure better monitoring at the ground level. The same instrument of fund release is being perceived and utilized differently by different states as per their local reality or experience for ensuring transparency and monitoring. Corruption or leakage was reported by the households or elected leaders in the release of assistance in many places (Assam, Bihar, and TN).

Coming to the monitoring at the VP level, different systems and mechanisms have been put in place. The most common method is the system of construction of the house by the beneficiary household. As per the guideline, IAY houses are to be built by beneficiary households ontheir own. It is believed that this would help beneficiaries take interest in their own house and complete it within time by adding own resources wherever possible. This is also expected to reduce unnecessary leakage in funds to contractors. While this seems to have helped in proper utilization of assistance, there are also situations where this does not seem to have worked effectively. In Assam, now to ensure proper utilization of assistance at the household level, JE at block level has been made a joint signatory of the beneficiary's account. While the officials have generally welcomed the idea, PRI representatives have opposed it as it leads to excessive bureaucratic intervention at the local level to the neglect of VP's role in monitoring.

In all states the funds are being released to households in two to four installments. Except in Bihar and to some extent in Assam, the fund release is dependent upon the progress achieved by the household. VPs monitor the progress with the help of their own staff. In a few cases, staff from block level also helps VPs (Rajasthan and MP) in monitoring. In Bihar it is now mandatory to release the second installment of assistance within 60 days of the first release irrespective of the progress in construction. The state government has introduced the system in order to reduce the hassles faced by households in getting the second installment. In Assam, it was reported that the second installment is to be released before March end so that funds do not lapse. The district officials said that, as a result of such an automatic release of funds, progress in construction of houses is found to be either low or slow.

Overall, by design IAY is a highly structured and standardised programme. The scope for PRIs to play a more proactive role is very limited. How far within the given scope PRIs at three levels have been able to play due role depends upon the nature of devolution. Largely, IAY is being implemented by bureaucratic agencies. At the district level the role of ZP is also dependent upon the status of DRDA. In states where DRDAs exist as parallel institution, the role of ZP has been curtailed. In other states, ZPs are able to participate in the programme in allocation of targets and disbursement of funds besides generally overseeing the progress. About IPs, again because of the nature of the programme the role is largely perfunctory. The elected body was found having hardly any role in planning. However, the administrative and technical staffs like BDO/TDO and engineers in most states are found playing key role in activities like releasing funds, providing technical support, and certifying the progress of house construction. It is here that they tend to dominate over elected representatives which also give a scope for rent-seeking by them.

It is the VPs which have had relatively a more prominent role in actual planning, implementation, and monitoring of the scheme. Despite the rigidity that exists in the BPL list, VPs, given their closeness to households, are found playing a proactive role to ensure that to the extent possible the needy get the assistance given limited allotment. Wherever such prioritisation has happened it has been done mostly with the involvement of Grama Sabha. However, we also observed that VPs in some cases have shown favour or bias. Regarding involving VPs in releasing funds, the scenario is mixed. In some states VPs are bypassed in releasing funds to the beneficiaries. But wherever the VPs release funds, they are found actively involved in monitoring the progress of house construction. To conclude, the involvement of PRIs in IAY is conditioned by the guidelines, the extent of devolution attempted by the states, and the emerging local experience with various aspects of programme implementation.

5.3. INTEGRATED CHILD DEVELOPMENT SERVICES

The Integrated Child Development Services (ICDS) programme was launched in 1975 to provide an integrated package of services for the holistic development of the child through convergence of services under various schemes/programmes. It mainly aimed at providing pre-school education on one hand and breaking the vicious cycle of malnutrition, morbidity, reduced learning capacity, and mortality on the other (GoI, nd.a). ICDS is a universal programme meant for the entire population irrespective of socio-economic status. ICDS specifically reaches out to children below six years of age and their mothers, especially from vulnerable and remote areas.

The Ministry of Women and Child Development looks after the ICDS programme at the national level with a central project management unit. ICDS is implemented through the state governments and the status is reviewed through regular meetings with state secretaries. A comprehensive Management Information System (MIS) for ICDS is used for regular flow of information and feedback between and across units. ICDS is implemented at the block level by a team comprising Anganwadi Helpers, Anganwadi Workers, Supervisors, and Child Development Project Officers (CDPOs). At the district level District Programme Officers (DPOs) coordinate and oversee programme implementation. The Anganwadi Worker (AWW) is a woman selected from the local community and works as the frontline ICDS worker in the Anganwadi Centre (AWC).

Subsequent to the 73rd Amendment to the Constitution, the Central Government has issued instructions to involve PRIs in the implementation, monitoring, and supervision of the scheme. It is also envisaged to ensure synergy between women's self-help groups and the ICDS programme. Although there are no specific areas of intervention for PRIs mentioned in the ICDS guidelines, the proposed ICDS-IV Project (2008–13) has made some proposals for the involvement of PRIs and the community in ICDS. The guiding principle would be to strengthen partnerships with PRIs, NGOs/CBOs, and public and private sectors to foster decentralisation, and to bring in flexibility and community-based locally responsive childcare approaches into practice (GoI, 2008d).

5.3.1. Field Observations

ICDS has been in operation for over three decades. Being also a donor supported programme, there have been several systems which have been put in place for a more structured delivery of the services. The administrative staff and reporting structures of the programme have been largely given. However, in order to ensure effective coverage and delivery of services, state governments have tried out several mechanisms according to the local situations.

It could be seen that ICDS is placed under either the Social Welfare or Women and Child Development Department. In some cases, a separate directorate has been created for overseeing ICDS. The states were found confronted with many challenges like universalizing the services, ensuring adequate staff, creating good infrastructure like buildings with water and toilet facilities for AWCs, reducing leakage or diversion of food and supplies provided, and monitoring the implementation. Involvement of PRIs and community is being seen as a solution to address many of these challenges. Some of the states have attempted to devolve a few functions and functionaries of ICDS to PRIs (Karnataka, Bihar, MP, and Gujarat) and some have proposed to devolve in future (HP and Rajasthan). Some states have reversed or modified the involvement of PRIs especially that of VPs based on experience (Karnataka and MP). Some states have adopted a decentralized system to procure supplies at the local level in coordination and consultation with the community and VP members. In other cases, supplies are procured at the state or district level by the project authorities in coordination with civil supplies agencies or private sources and delivered to AWCs.

ZP level

Whatever role the ZPs can possibly play under the current programme structure is found dependent upon whether ICDS or the department under which it comes is placed with ZP or not. Four of eight states have placed ICDS or its department under ZP (Karnataka, MP, Rajasthan, and Gujarat). In states like Karnataka and Gujarat even funds are channelized through ZP. In other states (Assam, Bihar, HP, and TN), ICDS is placed under or overseen by the District Collector (DC)/District Magistrate (DM). In terms of planning, given the nature of the programme ZPs had found very limited scope for their involvement. Planning in terms of mapping of AWCs and providing buildings for them is largely being done by DPOs in coordination with CDPOs. ZPs are found identifying and recommending AWCs more on a Voluntary Basis (HP). The states where ICDS is under ZPs, ZPs approve the budget and action plan. In other states the plan is found before ZP only for information (HP). In cases where ICDS is under DC/DM like in TN, all the issues and needs are taken up with DC/DM who in turn tries to arrange by coordinating with other line agencies. ZPs which have been given the overseeing role are using some formal mechanism for the purpose. In Karnataka, the standing committee of ZP on social welfare reviews ICDS progress. In Rajasthan, a ZP representative is on a review committee of ICDS. In states where ZPs are not entrusted the ICDS responsibility, monitoring takes place more in a voluntary and discretionary way. For example, in TN a ZP president reported that she visits AWCs out of personal interest to monitor the working and provide support.

IP level

At the IP level, largely a situation is similar to the district level could be seen. However, the involvement of IPs is relatively much higher than ZP as the project is actually implemented at the block level. Like at the district level, some of the states (Karnataka, Gujarat, and Rajasthan) have placed ICDS under IP. Even the funds are also channelized through IPs. In Gujarat, CDPO felt that such a system is helpful for the project as urgent fund needs can be met from IP's resources whenever there is a delay. CDPO coordinates with BDO/TDO who appraises IP members about such needs. IPs in this case also takes up monitoring work either directly or through committees. However, in all the states the involvement of IPs in planning is found to be limited. IPs, not in many states, could come with their proposal for AWCs. Only in HP it was reported that IP could recommend an AWC. IPs were found approving new AWCs in Karnataka and Bihar. CDPO of the block we visited in Bihar argued that IPs could no longer play such a role which was contested by the IP president. Day to day monitoring of programme delivery is carried out in all states by CDPOs through field supervisors. In Karnataka, CDPO works with the executive officer of IP to procure supplies through tender.

VP level

At the VP level while some states have tried to increase the role for VPs (Bihar and TN), others have tried to reduce it (Assam, MP, HP, and Karnataka). At the same time, most states have tried to involve the community in ICDS management and monitoring. States like MP and HP had made attempts to entrust major responsibilities of overseeing the working of AWCs and their staff to VPs. However, these states have now tried to reduce the role given to VPs.

In most states, VPs provide land or building, help construct building, and arrange water or electricity to AWCs. In states like TN, Gujarat, HP, and Karnataka, VPs were found providing the above facilities as and when there is a need or approached by the ICDS staff. However, we could observe during field visits in TN and Karnataka, that AWCs had broken doors or a non-working toilet. VPs in these villages were either not sure as to how to arrange for these facilities or not keen to take the initiative. In states like MP, Rajasthan, and Bihar VPs are expected to play a much more prominent role. They along with the Grama Sabha can help map needs for new AWCs, allot land, and arrange for building. In Rajasthan, VP could select AWW and helper through the Grama Sabha. In Bihar, the VP president has to certify the attendance of AWC staff for release of their salary.

A most common way in which VPs are being involved is through having the president and/or ward members on the committees created to help in the working of AWCs (Table 5.3). In all the states visited except Gujarat, village level or AWC level committees have been constituted for helping in enrolment, supervision, procurement, and monitoring the working of AWCs. These committees mostly are broad based in nature involving VP head or ward members, representatives of SHGs, and community members, especially the mothers of the children enrolled in AWC. In MP and Rajasthan there are exclusive mothers' committees constituted for the purpose. In these committees, generally AWW acts as the convener or member-secretary, and is the joint signatory with the committee head for handling the bank account.

Table 5.3: Role of VP/VP members in ICDS programme.

State	*VP/Grama Sabha*	*VP President or Member*
Assam	_	On AWC Monitoring Committee (AWCMC)
Bihar	Map AWC need and arrange building	Certify attendance of staff; Member of *Poshahar Karyanvayan Samiti* (PKS)
Gujarat	Help arrange buildings	_
HP	Help as per needs	On village level coordination committee
Karnataka	_	On Bal Vikas Samiti (BVS)
MP	Building construction; monitoring	Not on Mothers' Committee
Rajasthan	Select AWW/ helper; arrange building/land	On *Poshahar* Committee
TN	Help as per needs Committee (VLMC)	On Village Level Monitoring

Insights from the field visits revealed that the performance of VPs or their representatives has been of a mixed nature. As discussed earlier, some states (MP and HP) have tried to curtail the role of VPs because of several limitations faced. Currently, the VP members are found taking a more of discretionary interest (despite some training and orientation) and hence unable to make any significant impact on the working of the committee. In Karnataka, a women ward member refused to become the member/head of the committee (Bal Vikas Samiti); in Gujarat VP members are found contributing ration whenever there has been delay in supplies to AWC. In Assam, when the VP member's attention was drawn to the problem of non-availability of food in the local AWCs, they expressed the view that it was the department's responsibility.

Overall, the involvement of PRIs across states and levels in ICDS is of varying degree and type. Not in all states is ICDS integrated with ZP/IP. In many states ICDS continues to work under the overall supervision or control of the district collector at the district level. In both cases the involvement of ZP/IP in planning and implementation is of a limited nature. Even monitoring is done perfunctorily more on a personal or voluntary basis. The involvement of IP is found to be limited despite ICDS being implemented at the block level as a project. Only in those states where ICDS comes under IP, there is some involvement in planning, implementation, and monitoring. Otherwise, it is largely managed by CDPOs with their supervisory staff. With regard to VPs, the role is relatively more significant than PRIs at other two levels. While some states have tried to curtail the role of VPs based on their ineffective performance, others have tried to increase it with the hope that VPs would help improve the performance of ICDS. In all the states there is a trend towards involving community members along with VPs and their representatives. This could be seen both as a step to broadbase participation as well as to curtail the dominant role of VP or its president. A glaring aspect that could be observed at the VP level in many states is the lack of feeling of ownership towards the programme.

5.4. SARVA SHIKSHA ABHIYAN

The National Policy of Education 1986 provided for setting up of a national mission for the achievement of the goal of Universal Elementary Education (UEE). The Government of India came with a resolution in 2001 to lay foundation for the setting up of a national mission called the Sarva Shiksha Abhiyan (SSA). SSA is a holistic and convergent approach to UEE aimed at the following major objectives: (i) All children of 6–14 years age in school/EGS centre/bridge course by 2003; (ii) All children of 6–14 years age complete five year primary education by 2007; (iii) All children of 6–14 years age complete eight years of schooling by 2010; and (iv) Universal retention by 2010 (GoI, 2008e).

The SSA a National Mission is an independent and autonomous wing of the Department of Elementary Education and Literacy under the Ministry of Human Resource Development (MoHRD). The Mission has a governing council chaired by the Prime Minister. An executive committee chaired by the minister of HRD is empowered to execute the decisions of the governing council. Six sub-missions at national level have been constituted to develop, implement, and review certain specific aspects of SSA. One of these sub-missions is on social mobilization, community involvement and role of PRIs. The SSA framework allows states to have their own management structures but there is an illustrative structure for this purpose so that decentralisation can be monitored.

The programme framework (GoI, 2008e) calls for community ownership of the interventions through effective decentralisation. It is envisaged that involvement of community and PRI representatives for UEE would ensure full transparency. There will be a district level committee comprising members of ZP, CEO of ZP, and district officials. The education sub-committee of ZP is assigned the mandate to monitor SSA at the district level. A block level education committee with PRI representatives will supervise block level interventions. At the VP level a standing committee or a sub-committee of VP is recommended to act as nodal body for all matters relating to elementary education. This is to be operationalised through constitution of a Village Education Committee (VEC) and a School Management Committee (SMC) having PRI representatives. For planning, a community based approach is recommended with each habitation serving as a unit of planning. These local plans will form the basis for formulating the district plan for elementary education.

5.4.1. Field Observations

In most states, SSA is being implemented largely based on the framework. No clear information could be obtained about the induction of PRI leaders on the state level missions. In Karnataka, a state for which information could be obtained; there are no PRI leaders on the governing council or on the executive committee of SSA society. About the role visualized for PRIs under SSA, the discussions with the state level officials revealed contrasting responses. In one of the states (Gujarat) a view was expressed that involving PRIs in a mission-based programme like SSA is not desirable. In Assam it was felt that PRI leaders, given the context, lack social orientation which would be a handicap for them to play any meaningful role. Some of the state officials expressed the view that they have attempted considerable degree of decentralisation under SSA including spending a significant amount of funds at the local level (Karnataka). VECs are found playing a major role in this regard especially for civil works (TN). In many states, the current level of role assigned for PRIs is found to be adequate (MP, Gujarat, TN and HP), and any further role could be given only in areas like monitoring (Rajasthan).

ZP level

The visualized role for ZPs under the SSA framework is largely for planning and monitoring. The district level governance structure is mostly in the form of a district implementation committee which works as an independent or autonomous unit. In many of the states these committees are under the district collector/magistrate with the District Primary Education Officer (DPEO) acting as its member-secretary and district programme coordinator. Not in many states these committees are found headed by ZP presidents. In Karnataka, the District in-charge Minister is the Honorary President of the Committee (Table 5.4).

Table 5.4: Head of district level committee of SSA.

State	***Head***
Assam	District Collector
Bihar	District Magistrate
Gujarat	Committee not constituted
HP	District Collector
Karnataka	ZP President (but under district in-charge Minister)
MP	District Collector
Rajasthan	District Collector
TN	District Collector

In Gujarat no separate Committee has been constituted for SSA. The District Education Committee of ZP generally oversees even SSA, and has DPEO as its member-secretary. A separate account has been created for SSA with DPEO having withdrawal powers.

Coming to planning under SSA which is visualized to be a bottom-up exercise, not in many states such an integrated planning process has been adopted. The annual plan is being prepared mainly by the district committee with inputs from Block Resource Centres (BRCs). Only in two states (MP and Rajasthan) ZPs were found involved in SSA planning to some extent. Even for monitoring ZPs are not found playing any major role in most of the states. ZPs in some states (MP, Bihar, Rajasthan and Gujarat) are entrusted with the responsibility of recruiting and supervising regular or para-teachers.

Overall, the role being played by ZPs is found to be of a limited nature. The members of ZPs with whom we discussed in many districts said vehemently that ZP is hardly playing any role in SSA.

IP level

The extent of involvement of IPs is found relatively better than ZPs. In five states IP presidents are found heading the SSA block level committee (TN, Karnataka, Bihar, Assam, and MP). However, in Karnataka the local MLA is designated as the honorary president of the committee which is headed by the IP president. Again one or two IP members are also found on the block level committee in these states. In Bihar, IP members are even nominated to the village level committee. In Rajasthan they are nominated to the BRCs. With regard to planning, IPs are found taking part either directly (MP) or through the block level committee (Karnataka, Assam and TN). In states like Assam and Gujarat, IP have proposed either school or rooms. Through the block committees, IPs and their leaders monitor the implementation of SSA interventions. IPs are found monitoring more voluntarily in the case of Gujarat and HP.

VP level

Coming to the role of Village Panchayats, there are again variations across states. VPs and their members are being involved mostly through the creation of VECs or other committees as visualized under the SSA framework (Table 5.5). Only in MP a direct and full-fledged involvement of VP could be seen. In MP, VECs have been abolished and their responsibilities have been transferred to VPs or the standing committees. In Karnataka there are no VECs.

Table 5.5: SSA committees at village panchayat level.

State	*Committees*	*Head*
Assam	VEC/SMC	Ward member/Respectable person
Bihar	VSS	Ward member
Gujarat	VEC	VP President
HP	VEC	VP President/Ward member
Karnataka	SDMC	No VP member
MP	No VEC	——
Rajasthan	VEC/SDMC	VP President/Ward member
TN	VEC	VP President/Ward member

There are School Development and Management Committees (SDMC) in Karnataka, consisting of community members, students and ex-officio representatives including the school headmaster. SDMCs are constituted for each school and are supposed to work as part of the VP's civil amenities committee. In states where VECs exist, they are either headed by the VP president or by the ward member. VECs are mostly constituted for each school, and in case where there is more than one VEC, ward members generally head these committees (TN). In Bihar and Karnataka the previous committees were headed by the VP presidents. Now, while in Bihar a ward member heads VEC called the Vidyalaya Shiksha Samiti (VSS), in Karnataka there are no representatives of VP on SDMCs.

In addition to VECs, in some of the states school level development and monitoring committees also have been created (Assam and Rajasthan). The leadership and composition of these committees varies across the states. In Rajasthan they are headed by a ward member; in

Assam as well as in Karnataka they are headed by a community member elected by the committee. VECs and SDMCs have been constituted in a broad based way to have representation from community, students, and local institutions like school, AWC and Primary Health Centre (PHC). In most cases, there are specifications to have representatives from various weaker sections on these committees.

VECs and SDMCs are primarily expected to provide support to ensure community ownership of school based interventions aimed at UEE. However, field observations in these states found highly varied in participation and contribution of these committees especially involving VP leaders. The direct role of Panchayat in planning and monitoring could be observed only in Madhya Pradesh. The plans are being prepared mostly by VECs or SDMCs as per the suggested formats. These plans are to be discussed and consolidated at the VP level before they are passed on to the cluster/block level. But that does seem to be happening. For example, in Karnataka, SDMCs are found not sharing these plans with VPs.

A major activity under SSA at the village level is the construction and maintenance of school buildings and rooms. Here again there are variations across states in the involvement of VPs or SSA committees. In Gujarat and Madhya Pradesh construction works are being carried out by the civil works/amenities committee of VPs. In HP and TN, it is the VEC which is carrying out construction work. In Karnataka, Assam and Rajasthan it is the SDMCs which are involved in civil works.

The involvement of VPs or their leaders has been mixed as per the insights gained from field observations. In TN, at the state level it is felt that involvement of VECs especially in construction work has resulted in the creation of good quality school buildings at a lower cost. This is attributed to additional local resource mobilization as well effective monitoring. In many instances, on the other hand, there are delays in completing civil work. In Bihar where VSSs have been reconstituted to involve the broader community, we observed that in many places they were dominated by the local elites. This has come in the way of effective participation of weaker sections in the activities. Though there are limited instances of corruption by VECs, VP presidents are found harassing teachers in the joint management of funds. In Gujarat and HP not all VP members show equal interest in the affairs of the committees. A need was expressed for VPs and their leaders to play a more voluntary and proactive role in educational activities. In states where both SDMC and VEC exist together (Assam and Rajasthan), the former is found to be more active than the latter. This was attributed to the fact that SDMCs in these states have been allotted more funds than VECs. A concern was also expressed that the head masters/teachers who act as member-secretary on these committees are found spending more time on civil works than teaching.

5.5. NATIONAL RURAL EMPLOYMENT GUARANTEE SCHEME (NREGS)

The National Rural Employment Guarantee Act (NREGA) was notified on September 7, 2005. The first phase of NREGS commenced on February 2, 2006; and it has now been extended to cover the rural areas in the entire country.

The Act is an outcome of a discourse on right-based law for providing a strong social safety net programme for the vulnerable groups of society. The major objective of NERGA is "to enhance livelihood security in rural areas by providing at least 100 days of guaranteed wage employment in a financial year to every household whose adult members volunteer to do unskilled manual work" (GoI, 2008f). Simultaneously, the Act aims atcreation of durable assets and strengthening the livelihood resource base of the rural poor. The Act provides for an incentivized structure for the states to implement NREGA earnestly as 90 percent of the costs are borne by the Central Government. There is also a provision for paying unemployment allowance by the state government in case the employment demanded is not provided. At the national level the Ministry of Rural Development oversees the implementation of the Act. A central employment guarantee council has been constituted which advises the Central Government on NREGS besides helping in monitoring its implementation.

The states are supposed to first formulate the state specific employment guarantee scheme conforming to the provisions of the Act and the operational parameters delineated in the guidelines of the central ministry. For each state there will be a State Employment Guarantee Council (SEGC) which acts as an advisory body on the matters of implementation, evaluation, and monitoring of NREGS.

The thrust of NREGS is to build a model of governance, based on the principles of transparency and grassroots democracy. The scheme advocates a pivotal role for PRIs at all levels in achieving the goals. As per the Act, the village, intermediate, and district panchayats will be the principal authorities for planning and implementation of the scheme.

It also provides that all three levels of PRIs can be the implementing agencies with a condition that at least 50 percent of the works in terms of cost will be allotted to VPs for implementation. The district and intermediate Panchayats can identify and implement respectively schemes which have inter-block or inter-village linkages. The district programme coordinator (the District Collector/CEO of ZP/any other Equivalent Official) at district level and the programme officer at the block level (BDO or Equivalent Officer) coordinate the implementation of NREGS.

As per the operational guidelincs, the Grama Sabha is supposed to assist in identification of households, identify and recommend developmental works, and conduct social audit of the programme. Based on the Grama Sabha's recommendation, the VP will identify a shelf of projects to be taken up in its area, will forward to the programme officer for scrutiny. IP has a limited role of consolidating the plans of VPs into a block plan after including its own proposals and forwarding it to ZP for further approval. ZP is supposed to finalize and approve block-wise shelf of projects to be taken up for implementation. Based on the approved plan, implementation responsibilities are assigned to PRIs and line agencies. Works are to be implemented in such a way as to maintain a ratio of 60:40 between wage and material components without the involvement of contractors and machinery.

5.5.1. Field Observations

Being a right-based programme, NREGS envisages a decentralized approach involving PRIs to deliver on the goals of employment guarantee. With an inbuilt disincentive of paying compensation to wage seekers for failure to provide employment, there is a major on us on the states to put in place an effective delivery mechanism.

Of the eight states visited, seven have constituted SEGC to guide and deliberate on matters concerning NREGS implementation. In Gujarat, SEGC is not yet been constituted, though there is a notification of the rules. In all states where SEGC has been constituted, leaders of PRIs from various levels have been nominated as members to bring local level issues to the attention of state level authorities. However, we could not look into the actual involvement of these leaders in the deliberations of the council.

Largely, states are found implementing NREGS as per the guidelines though there are some deviations arising out of the local situations.

About involving PRIs, varying approaches are seen. While the guidelines specify that at least 50 percent of the funds may be spent by VPs, we saw that some of the states (TN, Rajasthan and Karnataka) are veering towards a VP-centric implementation and are aiming to make VPs spend 100 percent of the eligible funds. Such a strategy, as could be discerned from the discussions, is based on the perception that VPs are the best agency to plan and execute a scheme like NREGS.

In most states, efforts have been made to meet the additional personnel needs, both technical and non-technical, through deputation and new recruitment. However, the progress has been of a varying nature. Some of the states (Karnataka and MP) are yet to recruit fully key local staff like Panchayat Rozgar Sevaks (PRS) to support PRIs. In TN, an attempt has been made to involve representatives of Community Based Organizations (CBOs) and para-development workers to provide support.

ZP level

As can be seen from Table 5.6, six states have designated the District Collector/Magistrate as the DPC, while two have designated CEO of ZP and the District Development Officer (DDO) of DRDA as DPC. A general preference towards the District Collector as DPC can be apparently seen.

Table 5.6: NREGS at ZP/District level.

States	*District Programme Coordinator (DPC)*	*Plan approval agency*	*Fund Management*	*ZP can have own projects*
Assam	DC	ZP	DRDA	Yes
Bihar	DC	ZP	DRDA	Yes
Gujarat	DDO-DRDA	ZP	DRDA	Yes
HP	DC	ZP	DRDA	Yes
Karnataka	CEO-ZP	ZP	ZP	Yes*
MP	DC	ZP	ZP	Yes
Rajasthan	DC	ZP	ZP	No
TN	DC	DC	DRDA	No

*Now not allowed

The guidelines assign only a perfunctory role for ZP in plan approval. ZPs compile all block level plans into a district level plan and pass them within 15 days after verifying whether IPs and VPs have broadly followed the norms prescribed for the schemes. ZPs may add their own schemes into the district plan. Except in TN, ZPs are found involved in approving the district plan for NREGS. In TN, the District Collector approves the district plan. These plans are found to be merely a compilation of the shelf of projects as identified by different levels of Panchayats. In most states, ZPs are found identifying and adding their own schemes into the district shelf of projects. In TN and more recently in Karnataka, ZPs are not being allowed to formulate their own schemes and this has led to dissatisfaction. Even in states where ZPs have been allowed to have their works, ZPs are feeling constrained owing to the difficulty in identifying schemes which are inter-block in nature and lack of cooperation from VPs.

Monitoring is largely found to be a bureaucratic exercise. ZPs have not been able to get involved in the monitoring process of NREGS. DPCs are found monitoring on a regular basis because of pressure from state governments.

IP level

IPs are largely in the same position as ZPs when it comes to NREGS. The BDOs or their equivalents have been designated as the Programme Officer (PO) in most of the states. In Karnataka and MP, Executive Officers (EO) of IP are designated as POs. In Bihar and Rajasthan contractual appointees have been assigned these responsibilities in order to relieve the regular BDOs from NREGS work. In all states, IPs consolidates through PO the VP level shelf of projects and approves them after verification. IPs then passes them on to ZP or district level authorities for approval. IPs adds their own projects in all the states except TN and Karnataka. Technical personnel either with IP or line agencies give technical sanction for the schemes selected by VPs/IPs. Funds and muster rolls are released by PO to VPs based on the demand and as per the norms specified. In Gujarat, wages to workers are being released by IPs through TDO (Taluk Development Officer) directly. The responsibility for releasing wages has been withdrawn from VPs and is placed with IPs.

Like at the district level, monitoring is carried out by POs with the help of technical and other staff. Only to a limited extent the elected leadership is found involved in monitoring NREGS. In Rajasthan, Gujarat and MP, IPs reported that they monitor the programme more on their own volition.

The elected leader of IPs in many of the states strongly expressed dissatisfaction at the fact that IPs are not able to get involved in NREGS in an active manner like VPs. In TN, IP leaders disapproved the VP-centric approach of the state government. In Assam, IP leaders said that VPs do not cooperate with them. Moreover, IPs are unable to easily identify projects of inter-village nature.

VP level

The involvement of VPs could be seen in all three types of activities, *viz.*, planning, implementation and monitoring. VPs have tried to identify a shelf of projects through Ward Sabha/Grama Sabha. Given the multiple schemes identified, VPs are also seen (in Gujarat and Madhya Pradesh) prioritizing the works in consultation with the Grama Sabha and the technical staff of IP or line agencies. In some of the states, fund limits have been specified for VPs. In Assam, VPs are given a limit of Rs. 5 lakh for a project. In Karnataka this is Rs. 10 lakh and anything above this limit can be sanctioned only by EO of IP. In TN, VPs have to take up a work upwards of Rs. 3 lakh.

Implementation is taken up by VPs after obtaining administrative and technical sanction. At least in four states (TN, MP, HP and Gujarat), VP Presidents are found involved in the execution of the works along with other staff. In states like Assam and Bihar, VP Presidents are not directly involved in execution and are assisted by a variety of technical and administrative staff of IP or VP or line agencies. In many states, specialized staffs like PRS have been appointed to assist them in issuing job cards, preparing muster rolls, supervising the work, and making wage payments. Technical works like site selection and measurements are being carried out by technical assistants or junior engineers.

Wage payments are being made to workers through cheques signed by the VP President along with the Secretary or PRS in all states except Gujarat and TN. In Gujarat, payment is made by PO on the basis of the muster roll prepared by VP. The responsibility for wage payment has been withdrawn by the state government from VPs. In TN where a decision has been taken to make cash payment, a committee headed by the VP President oversees direct payment to workers.

VPs are found involved in monitoring the performance in a variety of ways. The Grama Sabha is involved in monitoring directly and indirectly in several states like TN, Bihar and Assam. Vigilance and monitoring committees or beneficiary committees have been constituted in most states for the purpose of monitoring. Community members, workers, and Panchayat staff are part of these committees. Social audit initiatives have also been taken up in a few states either directly through the Grama Sabha (TN) or through the beneficiary committees.

Overall, VPs are found involved more prominently than PRIs at other levels. The efforts of VPs appear to have contributed significantly in the take-off and speedy progress of a scheme like NREGS. Apparently, states like TN, Rajasthan and Karnataka are also the states where VPs have a prominent role in implementation. The role assigned to the Grama Sabha in planning seems to be helping in identification of many need-based schemes like water harvesting structures and roads as could be observed from field visits. VP leaders in TN supported the primacy given to the VPs. They argued that VPs are much closer to the people than other PRIs (IP/ZP) which helps them in mobilizing people easily for work.

Many negative outcomes could also be identified despite the involvement of PRIs. At least in three states (Assam, Karnataka and TN) there were complaints of leakage or corruption. These complaints were made by officials, PRI leaders and members of the community based on their observations of the prevailing situation. Another major issue is the poor quality of assets created under NREGS. This is attributed to the political nature of the scheme aimed at providing proactive employment and to the inability of VPs to monitor and ensure work quality. Other concerns are favour being shown by VP president in work allotments (Bihar), lack of adequate response from VP leaders to take up NREGS work (Gujarat), technical staff imposing projects not favoured by local community (Rajasthan), and excessive focus of VPs on NREGS to the neglect of other schemes.

5.6. ACCELERATED RURAL WATER SUPPLY PROGRAMME/ SWAJALDHARA

The Government of India launched the Accelerated Rural Water Supply Programme (ARWSP) in 1972–73 to assist the states with 100 percent grants-in-aid to implement drinking water schemes in problem villages. The states were given powers to give technical and administrative approval for the schemes under ARWSP beginning from 1995. They could decide on the implementing agencies for the programme. A nodal department was to be entrusted the responsibility to avoid duplication of efforts and dovetail the activities with other schemes. The responsibility for planning, implementation, supervision and monitoring of the approved schemes under ARWSP rested with the nodal department. The Public Health and Engineering Department (PHED) or Rural Development/Panchayati Raj department or a board or corporation generally implemented the programme. At district level, either DRDA or the nodal department was the implementing agency. PRIs were to be involved particularly in selecting the location, operation, and maintenance and fixing of water cess or tariff (GoI, nd.b).

Simultaneously, the government approved major policy reforms under the rural water supply programme during the Ninth Five Plan period. Sector reform projects initiated on a pilot basis in 1999 culminated in the launch of the Swajaldhara programme in 2002 (GoI 2003). The aim was to give freedom to communities to have schemes of their choice and to participate actively in project planning, implementation and operation and maintenance. The thrust was to move from a supply-driven to a demand-driven decentralized approach wherein the role of government would be one of facilitator. Apart from giving prominence to PRIs and community participation, the schemes under sector reforms aimed at partial capital cost sharing and total responsibility for Operation and Maintenance (O & M) by the users.

A State Level Water and Sanitation Mission (SWSM), registered as a society, and was suggested for the effective implementation of Swajaldhara. SWSM was to provide the policy guidance, conduct review of implementation, and ensure the convergence of schemes in the sector. The Swajaldhara guidelines suggested an institutional set-up which gave prominent role to PRIs at all three levels. PRIs were to be the implementing agencies.

ZP is supposed to perform all the functions of the District Water and Sanitation Mission (DWSM). In the absence of an elected body, DWSM can be constituted under the chairmanship of the District Collector and perform similar tasks. DWSM is supposed to consider and review the implementation of Swajaldhara projects. At the village level, VP or the Village Water and Sanitation Committee (VWSC) is supposed to be the implementing agency. The states are expected to provide support to PRIs by vesting them with functions, finances and functionaries to carry out the responsibilities. The VWSCs will work as committee of VPs.

ARWSP and Swajaldhara have now been subsumed under the new National Rural Drinking Water Programme (NRDWP) introduced in April 2009 (GoI, 2009).

5.6.1. Field Observations

The drinking water scenario has been characterized by the presence of multiple schemes of centre, state and donor agencies having varied strategies for execution and O & M. The involvement of PRIs also has varied. Because of the diverse strategies, mixed policy signals have been given to the communities about the need and nature of their participation. This was highlighted as one of the major reasons for the general failure of the Swajaldhara scheme. Given both unmet and emerging needs of drinking water, and the dismal performance of sector reforms programmes, the states are currently faced with a challenge of identifying suitable strategies including involving PRIs. The states could be seen transitioning from ARWSP to the new NRDWP. NRDWP's basis of giving some weightage, among other things, to the criterion of extent of rural population managing rural water schemes has apparently made many states to take note of the need for decentralisation.

A supply driven programme, ARWSP is implemented largely through technical line agencies like the Public Health and Engineering Department (Assam, Bihar, MP, and Rajasthan), and Drinking Water Boards (Gujarat and TN). Even O & M is handled by these agencies in many of the states. Since long, some of the states like TN and Karnataka have tried to involve panchayats under ARWSP for local O & M and collection of tariff. A more specific strategy to involve panchayats and user groups has been initiated since the launch of sector reform programmes. Most states have constituted state water and sanitation missions to give thrust to the reforms process. In states like TN and Assam, the existing nodal agencies themselves have tried to address the sector reform programmes.

ZP level

Wide variations are seen in the involvement of ZPs across states. In three states (HP, Karnataka and MP) the district water and sanitation mission has been constituted as a part of ZP. ZP presidents are found heading the mission (separately or as part of ZP) in all states except Gujarat. In Rajasthan and Assam, the DWSM handles mainly the Total Sanitation Campaign (TSC). ZP presidents in MP, HP and Assam head

DWSC. The District Collector or Magistrate heads DWSC in three states (Gujarat, Rajasthan and TN); while in Bihar, DWSC is headed by the Deputy Development Commissioner (DDC). In Karnataka DWSC has not been constituted and ZP is entrusted fully with the responsibilities of drinking water.

The actual role played by ZPs varies across states depending mainly on the extent of transfer of responsibilities. In states like TN, Gujarat and Bihar; ZPs do not play any role in planning and implementation. In Karnataka, MP and HP, the ZPs are found involved in planning and scrutinizing drinking water schemes of both the central (ARWSP and Swajaldhara) and state governments. However, implementation in almost all the states is the responsibility of line agencies like the public health engineering department or water supply boards. These agencies play a more prominent role in the state supported schemes. Only in Karnataka, ZP handles both planning and implementation as the panchayat rural engineering department has been brought under ZP by the state government. ZP here also releases O & M funds to VPs. ZP leaders in this state were even found taking initiatives to handle any emergency O & M or execution work.

IP level

The role of IPs is found to be different from that of ZPs. In some of the states (Assam, Gujarat and MP), IPs are not involved in ARWSP or under Swajaldhara. In Gujarat IPs can propose schemes for consideration by DWSC. Providing technical help for O & M of the water schemes is found to be major activity of IPs in four states (Bihar, TN, Rajasthan and Karnataka). In Karnataka, IPs till recently looked after the O & M of hand pumps through a technical mobile unit placed at their disposal. Some of the other roles found being played by IPs across states include releasing funds to VPs for O & M (TN), monitoring and capacity building (HP), and sanctioning hand pumps to individual households using funds made available under the 12th Finance Commission (Assam). In three states (Bihar, MP and Rajasthan), block-level water and sanitation committees have been formed. However, in two states (Bihar and Rajasthan) there is no representation of IP leaders. In MP, in the block we studied, the committee existed only on paper. In Assam, members of the IP visited had allocated the funds released under the 12th Finance Commission equally among them to provide hand pumps to BPL households of their choice. The IP head, however, agreed that it was not a good step on their part, and would try and rectify it in future.

VP level

As mentioned above, many states have involved VPs in O & M of water schemes even before the launch of the sector reform programmes. However, programmes like Swajaldhara have brought newer focus on the role of VPs. The VWSCs are found constituted only in those areas or districts where Swajaldhara has been implemented. In some states (HP) VWSCs have become even dysfunctional (Table 5.7). In Assam, efforts are being made to create VWSCs more for the purpose of implementing TSC. Only in Gujarat, VWSCs have come up in a more widespread way as the state government has proactively extended the sector reform programmes in several districts. WASMO, a specialized agency designated as SWSM in Gujarat, has played a key role in promoting VWSCs through grassroots mobilization and awareness creation.

Table 5.7: Involvement of VPs in Drinking Water.

States	*VWSCs*			*Role of VP for other schemes*	
	Constituted	*Status*	*Role*	*Role*	*Problems*
Assam	Yes	Separate for water and TSC	O&M	No role	Reluctant to take up O&M
Bihar	Yes	Only in SJ area	Planning, Implementation and O&M	Construct and look after HPs	Role withdrawn
Gujarat	Yes	More widespread	Planning, Implementation and O&M	O&M of HP and other sources	Collection depends on performance
HP	Yes	Only in SJ area but not functional	Scheme selection, O&M	O&M	Reluctant to take over
Karnataka	Yes	Only in SJ area	Planning and O&M	O&M tariff collection	Neglet of HPs
MP	Yes	Only in SJ area	—	Planning and O&M	Depends on VP leaders
Rajasthan	Yes	Only in SJ area	O&M of HPs	Planning, O&M of HPs	Lack of funds
TN	Yes	Only in SJ area	Planning, implementation and O&M	O&M and tariff collection	Poor collection of tariff

Source: Field survey. HPs: Hand Pumps; SJ: Swajaldhara.

The formation of VWSCs has been confined largely to the Swajaldhara areas. Even here a major problem faced is the failure to mobilize the capital cost contribution from water users. The differentiated norm adopted between Swajaldhara and other schemes for users' contribution is the major cause for poor response. Involvement of VPs and their leaders also did not help in addressing the problem. Even in Gujarat, the response has been varying across districts and is found to be relatively better in better-off areas than in backward areas despite the lower contribution norm fixed.

Coming to other schemes especially like spot sources or hand pumps implemented by state governments, VPs are found involved in O & M including collection of tariffs. In some of the states VPs are even involved in planning and execution of these schemes (Bihar, MP and Rajasthan). In Bihar, till recently VPs were given responsibilities to construct hand pumps. However, this role has been withdrawn because of the poor technical capacity and failure of VPs to submit the utilization certificates.

Field observations brought out quite a few issues about the role and capacity of VPs. A local VP is considered better suited for O & M than a distance line agency (TN) as VP can address the problem quickly. In Karnataka, ward members who are also members of the VWSC made personal fund contribution, pending reimbursement by VP. This was done to take up immediate replacement of the defunct pump as the formal approval process would take a long time. Again, VP and other PRI leaders are found actively and voluntarily visiting worksites to keep track of the progress and quality of work.

We observed that VP leaders are found biased when it comes to allotting hand pumps. Better-off sections or members of own groups are shown favour in such allotments (Bihar and Assam). In general, O & M is found to be poor. VPs are found to be poorly equipped to take care of the technical aspects, especially of bigger projects (Gujarat and Karnataka). Fund constraint is found to be a common complaint in maintenance of hand pumps (Karnataka). Collection of water tariff by VPs is found to be generally poor. This was attributed to factors like poor performance of the schemes, illegal water connections, preference shown by users for public sources, and local politics. VPs in some states expressed reluctance to takeover hand pumps or other schemes for O & M (Assam and HP).

5.7. NATIONAL RURAL HEALTH MISSION

The National Rural Health Mission (NRHM) was launched on April 12, 2005; as an effort to integrate the ongoing programmes of health and family welfare through a sector wide approach to enable efficiency in health service delivery. NRHM specifically seeks "to provide effective health care to the rural population, especially the disadvantaged groups including women and children, by improving access, enabling community ownership and demand for services, strengthening public health systems for efficient service delivery, enhancing equity and accountability and promoting decentralisation" (NIHFW, nd).

In order to ensure smooth implementation of NRHM, a broad operational framework (2005–2012) for the health sector has been suggested by the government (GoI, nd.c). The structure of NRHM at the national level has a Mission Steering Group (MSG) to be headed by the union minister for health and family welfare to provide policy support and guidance to the mission. An Empowered Programme Committee (EPC), headed by the union secretary for health and family welfare, is responsible for the implementation of NRHM. There is also a provision for a NRHM mission at the state level with the Chief Minister as the chairperson and the minister of health and family welfare as co-chairperson. Among other members, there is a category of nominated representatives from PRIs and local bodies on the state mission. A state health and family welfare society is constituted to be headed by the chief secretary/development commissioner and the convener is the officer designated as the mission director. A programme management support unit functions as the secretariat to provide technical assistance to the state mission.

The NRHM framework envisages "to empower the PRIs at each level *i.e.*, Grama Panchayat, Panchayat Samiti (Block) and Zilla Parishad (District) to take leadership to control and manage the public health infrastructure at district and sub district levels" (GoI, nd.c). The district level structure has a District Health Mission (DHM) as the apex body, to be chaired by the ZP chairperson. The District Collector is the co-chair and the chief medical officer is the mission director. Other members are the chairperson of the standing committee of the ZP and chairpersons of IPs.

The mission is supported by the District Health Society (DHS) which has a governing body chaired by either the District Collector/Magistrate or CEO of ZP. The CEO could be either the chief medical officer or the civil surgeon of the district. DHS is responsible for planning and management of all rural and urban health and family welfare programmes in the district. The mission would work towards inter-sectoral convergence and preparation of an integrated district health plan (GoI, nd.d).

The states are supposed to indicate their commitments to PRIs in their MoUs for greater devolution of funds, functionaries, and programmes for health. The DHM will guide and manage all public health institutions in the district including Primary Health Centres (PHCs) and Community Health Centres (CHCs). An attempt would be made to bring CHCs under community ownership. IPs are supposed to help in coordinating the work of VP in their jurisdiction and thereby act as a link between VP and DHM. There will be Village Health and Sanitation Committees (VHSCs) to oversee all NRHM activities and develop the village health plan. There is an annual provision of untied fund of Rs.10,000 to each sub-centre to be utilized by ANM in consultation with VHSC to meet local needs. VPs are entrusted with the task of recruiting ASHA workers who will be accountable to VPs.

5.7.1. Filed Observations

Though the programme was introduced in 2005, some states (Bihar, MP and HP) are yet to fully put in place the decentralized structures as visualized under the framework. The states we studied have constituted respective state health missions for guiding programme implementation. Information could not be obtained about the nomination of PRI representatives on the general body of the state health missions for all states. Karnataka and Assam have nominated PRI leaders on the mission general body. In the discussions, many NRHM officials felt that the role assigned for the PRIs is adequate. Some expressed the view that the involvement of PRIs is not appropriate for a sector like health, and the situation has deteriorated further with the induction of panchayat leaders.

ZP level

ZP's involvement is visualized through DHM and DHS. There were variations across states with regard to adoption of the framework provisions or suggestions. TN and MP have not constituted DHM though there are DHSs headed by the District Collector. As a result, the visualized role at least for the ZP president had not materialized in these states. In Karnataka till recently, the district in-charge minister was the chairperson of DHM and the District Collector and the ZP President were the co-chairpersons. The reconstituted district health committee now has the ZP President as the chairperson. DC is now the chairperson of the executive committee. It is clear that, while the District Collector/Magistrate is involved in the district level structure of NRHM (DHM or DHS) in all states, this was not the case with the ZP President (Table 5.8). This possibly shows the preference being given to involving District Collectors over political leaders in the district level governance structures of developmental programmes like NRHM. In HP, the chief medical officer of the district we visited was not sure of the constitution of either DHM or DHS. He said possibly they existed on paper only.

Table 5.8: ZP president and district collector in district level structures of NRHM.

States	*ZP President*	*District Collector/Magistrate*
Assam	Yes	Yes
Bihar	Yes	Yes
Gujarat	Yes	Yes
HP	NA	NA
Karnataka	Yes	Yes
MP	No	Yes
Rajasthan	Yes	Yes
TN	No	Yes

NA: Not available

Another aspect we examined at the district level was the preparation of district health plans. In the districts we visited, though the district health plan has been prepared the involvement of either ZP or DPC was found missing. Also, ZP's approval as such has not been sought or obtained for the district health plan. In HP and Rajasthan there was consultation with ZP about the district plan. This was, however, found to be a mere perfunctory exercise.

In almost all the cases the district health plan has been prepared without looking at the plans of the lower level committees. Moreover, not in all states there were attempts made to prepare block plans or village level plans which can feed into the district plan. Thus, the planning exercise being carried out under NRHM at district level was found to be top-down in nature. In Assam there was a view among the health officials that ZP members hesitated to participate in health related meetings or camps owing to absence of incentives. In Bihar and

MP, ZP members expressed the view that they did not get full information about schemes like NRHM.

IP Level

There was a highly mixed kind involvement of IPs across states. Not in many states we could observe the constitution of block level mission or committees involving IPs. In three states, there was attempt made to involve IPs. Karnataka has created a taluka level committee for planning and monitoring involving, among others, IP president, EO of IP, and head of the general standing committee of IP. Previously, this committee was headed by the local MLA. The committee is also constituted as a sub-committee of IP to bring it within the fold of IP. In Rajasthan, there is a Block Health and Sanitation Committee (BHSC) involving the IP President and is entrusted with task of preparing the block health plan.

In MP, a standing committee of IP looks after planning and monitoring. In states like TN, Assam, and Bihar, the IP president or members are found involved in committees like the patient welfare society or peripheral management committees meant for managing CHCs and PHCs. Not in many states we could observe systematic efforts in block level planning to involve IPs which can feed into the district plan. Only in few states (Rajasthan, HP and Assam) an attempt has been made to arrive at block plan with some involvement of IPs and VHSCs.

The following issues emerged also with regard to the role of IPs in health. In Bihar, the IP President certifies the attendance of contractual staff for salary payment. In Rajasthan IPs can propose new sub-centres (SC) for consideration by the agencies concerned. In TN the standing committee of the IP was not working regularly.

VP level

The involvement of VPs could be seen at two levels: village and PHC/SC. At the village level, VHSCs have been constituted involving VP leaders, community members, and staff of health and other interventions (Table 5.9). VHSCs have been formed mostly for each revenue village and are headed by the VP president or a ward member. They also have community representatives and staff of other agencies like PHC, ICDS and school. Some of the states have specified that a minimum number of women and representatives of weaker sections should be part of these committees. However, VHSCs were not found in the study district of Bihar. In Bihar, in the study district the district programme manager mentioned that frequent turnover of district programme managers has come in the way of constituting VHSCs. In MP, it was reported that VHSCs have been formed only in certain districts.

Table 5.9: Role and involvement of VPs in NRHM in study districts/states.

States	*VHSC Constituted in study district*	*Head of VHSC*	*Joint signature for untied fund*	*ASHA Identification*	*Constitution PWS/RKS involving members*
Assam	Yes	Ward	Ward member	VHSC/GS Member/ASHA	Yes
Bihar	No	—	President/ANM	VP President	Yes
Gujarat	Yes	VP President	FHW/ Teacher	VP	Yes
HP	Yes	VP President	—	—	Yes
Karnataka	Yes	Ward member,	President		
VHSC/GS	Yes	VP President	and AWW		
MP	Yes	VP President	President and ANM	VP/GS	Yes
Rajasthan	Yes	VP President/ Ward member	President and ANM	VP/GS	Yes
TN	Yes	VP President	President and VHN	VHSC	Yes

VP leaders are also found involved in the committees of PHC or SC. These are mostly Patient Welfare Societies (PWSs) constituted for the management of PHC. The third level of participation of VP representatives could be seen in Karnataka where a certain number of heads of PHC committees could be nominated on the taluka level NRHM committee.

The role of VHSCs in planning is yet to emerge. As district level plan preparation itself is in a nascent stage, the involvement of VHSC has not been attempted in any significant manner. Other activities in which the involvement of VHSCs could seen across states are sanitation and hygiene, creation of facilities at PHC or SC level, creation of awareness, and defraying the medical expenses of poor households utilizing the untied funds. Some of the VHSCs are found involved in chlorination and village cleaning activities. VHSC in the study village of Karnataka went on a cleaning campaign after a diarrhea breakout. In states like

Assam and Bihar, VHSCs are found utilizing funds to meet medical expenses of poor households. In Assam, VHSCs are found disbursing Rs. 300 each to selected IAY households for construction of toilets under TSC using their untied funds. Health officials in many states said that VHSCs or VP members now quickly bring to their attention breakout of any disease so that they can take immediate action. Even ASHA workers expressed the view that they are able to approach women easily for health awareness through the help of VP members.

In Assam, Karnataka, and TN, VHSCs are also found involved in selecting and recommending ASHA workers for appointment by block level officials. In other states, the ASHAs are being selected either by the VP President or by VP in consultation with the Grama Sabha. For utilizing the untied funds in all states except Gujarat, the VP President or ward members are found to be the joint signatories. In Gujarat the signing power has been entrusted to the government staff (FHW and a teacher) to avoid any misappropriation.

The role of VPs in monitoring is very limited. VPs reported they monitor the work of PHC staff. VPs found it difficult to monitor the working or attendance of doctors. In Bihar, the VP president has been entrusted with the role of certifying the presence of PHC staff like ANM for release of salary. In Karnataka, the government took a decision asking ANMs to sign every day at the VP office. ANMs protested against the decision and forced the government to reverse the order. AWWs of ICDS expressed dissatisfaction at their role as joint signatories with the VP president or ward member for untied funds of VHSC. They felt that they could be pressurized by the VP leaders in utilizing the funds.

5.8. CONCLUSIONS

The issue of forging links between CSSs and PRIs has been seen as a possible solution to help CSSs to shed their top-down character and enable PRIs to emerge as institutions of self-government. The study has looked at the experiences and challenges focusing on six major CSSs in eight states. All the programmes in their guidelines/frameworks have fairly elaborate provisions to involve PRIs at various levels. However the actual linkage is being approached more in an instrumental than in an integrated manner. This could be discerned both with regard to the purpose and the method adopted for such linkages. Therefore, neither the goal of improving the grassroots delivery of CSSs nor the cause of empowering panchayats is being fully addressed.

About the purpose of involving PRIs under CSSs, the apparent thrust has come mainly from the compulsion of attaining the programme specific goals than help deepen the devolution process as such. Like in the case of drinking water (Swajaldhara), the focus on PRIs has emerged in the context of implementing the demand-driven sector reform programmes. Similarly, under NREGS the prominent role being assigned to PRIs comes from the major concern of scaling-up speedily the programme in more a transparent way all across the country. Under ICDS and IAY which already have well established bureaucratic structures for planning and implementation, the involvement of PRIs comes from the concern of ensuring effective monitoring. Given such overriding programmatic aims, PRIs have largely ended up as mere agents of delivery rather than as local self-governments that can contribute towards integrated decentralized planning.

Coming to the actual scenario of involvement of PRIs and the role they are able to play, wide variations could be seen across schemes. Even within a scheme there were variations across states and across three layers of PRIs. The variations could be attributed to factors like difference in the degree of devolution achieved by the states, the nature of the programme, and the guideline provisions for involving the PRIs.

States where there is relatively a greater degree of devolution, the involvement of PRIs is much higher. In states like Karnataka and MP where the transfer of functions and functionaries to PRIs has been attempted in a more significant way, the involvement of PRIs at least under some of the CSSs could be seen happening more naturally. Even the merger of DRDA with ZP in these states, is helping ZPs to oversee CSSs like IAY automatically.

Similarly, with a line agency like the panchayat rural engineering department coming under ZPs in Karnataka, ZPs are able to execute their own drinking water schemes. However, the general scenario in most states is that PRIs are yet to be fully given their due role and powers.

The bureaucracy and parallel agencies continue to dominate over PRIs. At the district level across schemes and states, the District Collector or Magistrate remains a key person for governing and administering CSSs. Largely, the involvement of PRIs is being attempted merely out of the compulsion of following programme guidelines. Given a choice, many states may prefer other arrangements which are convenient to them. This could be seen in the case of own schemes of some states for housing or water. While under IAY the states are trying to involve PRIs as per the guidelines, for their own rural housing schemes they have put in place a different mechanism where PRIs get only a limited role in identifying the needy and programme implementation. At the same time, it could be seen that bureaucracy at various levels is found not well disposed towards devolution. The response from top officials is that the current role given for PRIs is more than adequate under CSSs, and there is no need for devolving any further powers to them. Some even hold the view that involvement of PRIs is not desirable in schemes like SSA and NRHM. Moreover, there has been resistance from the bureaucracy for transferring functionaries to PRIs. The states have shown reluctance for any large scale transfers of regular functionaries. Some states have even reversed such transfers.

When a CSS gets recast and comes up with a newer mandate for decentralisation like SSA and NRHM, there is inadequate response to shed powers by the well entrenched bureaucracy. This is also one of the reasons why the committees of these CSSs get constituted mostly as parallel bodies to PRIs. Many of the programme guidelines insist that such committees be constituted as sub-committees of PRIs. However, not in many schemes/states such integrated committees could be seen. The officials do not even fully share the information about these schemes with PRIs. The women PRIs leaders, especially from weaker sections, face even greater hurdles in dealing with the officials.

Given the nature of CSSs we studied, PRIs are found involved largely in some aspects of implementation. Monitoring is taken up to a certain extent. The role of PRIs in planning is highly insignificant. Even in schemes like SSA and NRHM which visualize decentralized district and local plans, line agencies carry out planning with only perfunctorily involving PRIs. In NREGS, PRIs are able to participate in the planning process to some extent. However, planning is confined merely to identification of shelf of projects. In none of the schemes, attempt has been made to bring district planning committees into the picture.

Major fallout of such a planning process is the absence or lack of local ownership among PRIs, especially VPs, who do not identify themselves fully with these schemes. For example, in the case of ICDS, neither the absence of ration nor the poor infrastructure has evoked any proactive response from PRIs. At the same time, PRIs have been constrained to come up with their own initiative for local development. Invariably, much of their time and effort is focused on implementing schemes from the centre or state government.

In programme implementation which is the main area of their involvement under CSSs, PRIs have displayed much strength wherever possible. In IAY, VPs have to strictly go by the BPL list for allocation. As the BPL list has been generally found to be faulty, PRIs have difficulty in targeting the real needy. However, we could be observe that VPs to an extent have been able to prioritize the list and identify the needy based on their understanding. In SSA, the involvement of VECs has helped achieve cost effectiveness in civil works owing to better monitoring. PRI leaders in many places are found taking immediate action to address problems faced in O & M of water schemes. There were also individual level voluntary actions or contributions by PRI leaders for addressing local problems.

PRIs also face several limitations or constraints in effective programme implementation. Lack of technical expertise and capacity is found to be a major problem. Lack of adequate information on schemes is another major constraint. The standing committees of PRIs at all three levels are found to be inactive or dormant leading to ineffective role in monitoring. A common feature reported across different states is equal sharing of funds by PRI leaders under several schemes. Funds are being utilized more according to individual preferences than based on real needs of the community. Many PRI leaders demand that they should be provided with adequate remuneration or honorarium so that they can fully participate in local governance. In a few cases, the compulsions of making own livelihood needs has limited the role of PRI representatives.

To conclude, the attempt to bring PRIs and CSSs together has not produced the desired results. Neither the purpose of improving programme delivery nor the objective of empowering PRIs has been realized significantly because of the linkages that exist now. There are systemic and programmatic hurdles coming in the way of forging an effective linkage between the two. Systemically, the inadequate and slow progress towards devolution by the states is the major constraint for the PRIs to make a significant contribution. The continued top-down approach of the CSSs is the programmatic constraint which nullifies the potential role of PRIs for bottom up planning and development. Hence mere strengthening the provisions in the programme guidelines to include PRIs becomes perfunctory and can produce only limited outcomes for decentralisation. The way forward for a meaningful linkage lies not only in restructuring CSSs to shed their top-down character but also in simultaneously enabling the states to appreciate and deepen the decentralisation process further as envisaged in the constitution.

ACKNOWLEDGEMENTS

The paper is based on a study carried out for 'The State of the Panchayats: An Independent Assessment, 2008-09' Commissioned by the Ministry of Panchayati Raj (MoPR), Government of India. Support received from the MoPR for the study is gratefully acknowledged. We would like to place on record our sincere thanks to all the villagers, elected panchayat representatives, government officials/programme functionaries in the eight states for sharing their precious time, experiences and views. The usual disclaimers apply.

REFERENCES

Garg, SC. (2006). "Transformation of central grants to states: Growing conditionality and bypassing state budgets". *Economic and Political Weekly*, 41(48): 4977–84.

Government of India (GoI) (2002). *Ninth Five Year Plan: 1997–2002, Vol. I.* New Delhi: Planning Commission.

Government of India (GoI) (2003). *Swajaldhara Guidelines*. New Delhi: Ministry of Rural Development, Department of Drinking Water Supply. Retrieved May 8, 2009. from: *http://ddws.gov.in/popups/swajal_pop.htm*

Government of India (GoI) (2004). *Guidelines for Indira Awaas Yojana (IAY).* New Delhi: Ministry of Rural Development.

Government of India (GoI) (2006). *Planning at the Grassroots Level: An Action Programme for the Eleventh Five Year Plan, Report of the Expert Group*. New Delhi: Ministry of Panchayati Raj.

Government of India (GoI) (2008a). *Eleventh Five Year Plan, 2007–12, Volume 1, Inclusive Growth.* New Delhi: Planning Commission.

Government of India (GoI) (2008b). 'Centrally Sponsored Schemes: Identifying a Domain for the Panchayati Raj Institutions'. *In*: *The State of Panchayats: 2007–08, Vol. 3: Supplementary.* New Delhi: Ministry of Panchayati Raj, pp. 337–45.

Government of India (GoI) (2008c). Report of the Empowered Sub-Committee of the National Development Council on Financial and Administrative Empowerment of the Panchayati Raj Institutions. New Delhi: Ministry of Panchayat Raj.

Government of India (GoI) (2008d). ICDS-IV Project: State PIP Guidelines. New Delhi: Ministry of Women and Child Development. Retrieved May 26, 2009. from: *http://wcd.nic.in/*

Government of India (GoI) (2008e). *Sarva Shiksha Abhiyan: Framework for Implementation*. New Delhi: Ministry of Human Resource Development, Department of School Education and Literacy. Retrieved May 25, 2009. from: *http://ssa.nic.in/page_portletlinks?foldername=ssa-framework*

Government of India (GoI) (2008f). The National Rural Employment Guarantee Act 2005 (NREGA): *Operational Guidelines*. New Delhi: Ministry of Rural Development, Department of Rural Development.

Government of India (GoI) (2009). National Rural Drinking Water Programme: Framework for Implementation. New Delhi: Ministry of Rural Development,

Department of Drinking Water Supply. Retrieved February 2, 2010. from: *http://ddws.gov.in/popups/RuralDrinking Water_2nd April.pdf*

Government of India (GoI) (nd.a) (2009). *Integrated Child Development Services (ICDS) Scheme*. New Delhi: Ministry of Women and Child Development. from: *http://wcd.nic.in/icds.htm*

Government of India (GoI) (nd.b) (2009). ARWSP Guidelines. New Delhi: Ministry of Rural Development, Department of Drinking Water Supply. Retrieved May 8, 2009. from: *http://ddws.gov.in/popups/swajal_pop.htm*

Government of India (GoI) (nd.c) (2009). National Rural Health Mission: Framework for Implementation 2005–12. New Delhi: Ministry of Health and Family Welfare. from: *http://ddws.gov.in/popups/RuralDrinkingWater_2ndApril.pdf*

Government of India (GoI) (nd.d) (2009). National Rural Health Mission: Institutional Setup at State Level. New Delhi: Ministry of Health and Family Welfare. from: *http://www.mohfw.nic.in/NRHM%20state%20and%20district%20health%20mission-institutional%20setup.htm*

Gurukkal Rajan (2006). *"Democratisation at the Grassroots: Problems of Theory and the Politics of Praxis". Gandhi Marg*, 28(2): 149–65.

Institute of Rural Management Anand (IRMA) (2008). *The* State of Panchayats: 2007–08, Vol. 1: Thematic Report. Anand: IRMA, pp. 135–163.

Jayal, Niraja Gopal (2006). "Introduction", *In*: Jayal Niraja Gopal, Prakash Amit and Sharma Pradeep, K. (*eds.*), *Local Governance in India: Decentralisation and Beyond*, New Delhi: Oxford University Press, pp. 1–26.

National Institute of Health and Family Welfare (NIHFW) (nd) (2010). *National Rural Health Mission: Frequently Asked Questions*. from *http://nihfw.nic.in/ndc-nihfw/html/NationalRuralHealthMission.htm*

Shylendra, H.S. (2008). "Delivering Rural Development Programmes: Can Panchayats Make a Difference?" Working Paper No. 206. Anand: Institute of Rural Management.

Singh Satyajit (2007). "Introduction", *In*: Singh Satyajit and Sharma Pradeep, K. (*eds.*). *Decentralisation: Institutions and Politics in Rural India*. New Delhi: Oxford University Press, pp. 1–34.

6

Decentralised Planning in India: A Historical Perspective

M. DEVENDRA BABU[6]*

ABSTRACT

The paper outlines the large number of factors that have hindered decentralised planning and implementation in India in a historical perspective. The discussion includes non- devolution of functions, functionaries and finance to panchayats and urban bodies, non-constitution of District Planning Committees, planning and implementation of central flagship programmes through District Rural Development Agencies by states rather than merging this agency with panchayats, involvement of large number of parastatal agencies at the local level, poor knowledge and capacities of elected and non-elected members of local governments in the plan preparation and implementation. The paper argues that success of decentralised planning in India depends on strengthening the local bodies with powers, functions and finances, capacity building of functionaries, giving autonomy in evolving their own schemes and programmes.

6.1. INTRODUCTION

Soon after independence, India adopted FiveYear Plans to accelerate economic growth and at the same time to reduce poverty, unemployment, inequalities and regional disparities. Centralised planning (top-down approach) was practiced at the national and state levels. Macro planning undertaken in the country from 1951 had succeeded in promoting growth of Gross Domestic Product (GDP) and changing the structure of

[6] Honorary Professor, Karnataka State Rural Development and Panchayat Raj University, Gadag, Karnataka.

**Corresponding author*: E-mail: devendrababu@yahoo.com

the economy in favour of secondary and tertiary sectors from a primary sector orientation. However, the country could not overcome the problems of poverty, social and economic inequalities between individuals and regions even after decades of planning. A view was developed during the late 1960s that planning should be taken down from the national and state capitals to district level also.

Meanwhile an upsurge of interest is witnessed towards decentralised planning and administration in the last two decades in the third world countries. Why this shift in the planning approach? According to Cheema and Rondinelli (1983: 14) the shift in favour of decentralised planning is not only to the disillusionment with the results of central planning and the shift of emphasis to growth-with-equity policies, but also to the realisation that development is a complex and long term process that cannot be easily planned and controlled from the Centre. Similarly, Harris (1983) came out with the opinion that the national governments are likely to be ineffective and inefficient in the matters of provision of local services. Stiefel and Pearse (1982: 146) furthering the cause of decentralisation, argued that it would help redress the existing regional disparities and the popular participation would lead to increased control over resources and regulative institutions in a given social situation; and also groups and movements of those hitherto excluded from such control. Not only this, the grassroots governance is essential to build genuine self-reliance and sustainability (Parajalu and Kothari, 1998: 25).

From the fiscal angle many economists argue for decentralisation. Their argument revolves around the allocative efficiency of fiscal decentralisation (Oates, 1972). Sundaram aptly sums up that the decentralised planning seeks to look in greater detail into the aspirations and requirements of specific local areas and communities and to take suitable measures for meeting these, so as to take maximum advantages of the local initiative, potentials, capacities and resources (1997: 181).

Thus the above views strongly come up in favour of local (decentralised) planning in place of centralised planning. The advantages of decentralised planning may be summarised as follows:

- It is more responsive to the needs and aspirations of the people;
- It understands local problems better and avoids mismatch problem;
- It assesses local natural and human resources, and the growth potential of the area;

- It is possible to rope in the services of local people and non-governmental organisations in the formulation and implementation of plans;
- It is possible to mobilise local contribution to support own resources;
- It delivers services at lower costs.

6.2. OBJECTIVES AND METHODOLOGY

In the above background, this paper critically evaluates the problems and prospects of decentralised planning in India. The analysis is made on the quantitative and qualitative information. The former is based on secondary data and the latter on the observations and discussion had with the elected members, officials and citizens during field visits under various studies in Karnataka.

6.3. REFORMS AND REALITIES IN DECENTRALISED PLANNING

In India, the importance of decentralised planning was highlighted in the First Five Year Plan (1951–56) itself. However, the process of decentralised planning in the country was initiated from 1970s where many states introduced planning at the district level. The district plans took the shape of disaggregation of the state plans. The role of the district planners was mainly consultation and supervision, and the district plans continued to be formulated at the state level and implemented by the official machinery responsible to the heads of departments at the state level (Aziz, 1993; Babu, 2010).

Further, the Central Government constituted many expert committees to suggest ways and means of adopting planning from below. The history of initiatives in decentralised planning in India is given in Table 6.1.

It is to be noted that our Five Year Plans beginning with the first one emphasised the importance and adoption of decentralised planning. The various committees/commissions such as Balwantrai Mehta and Dantwala Committees and Administrative Reforms Commission had strongly advocated for local governments and their meaningful involvement in planning and development. In the midst of adoption of numerous rural development schemes in the 1980s the GVK Rao and Hanumantha Rao committees suggested the potential for rural local governments in the effective planning and rural development. The 73rd Constitution Amendment Act (CAA), of course provided the much needed

Table 6.1: Initiatives in decentralised planning in India.

Year/Period	*Committee/Programme*	*Ideas/Concepts*
First Five Plan Year (1951–56)	Community Development Programme	To break up planning exercise into national, state, district and local community levels.
Second Five Year Plan (1956–61)	District Development Councils	Drawing up of village plans and popular participation in planning through the process of democratic decentralization.
1957	Balwantrai Mehta Committee Report	Establishment of village, block, district panchayat institutions.
1967	Administrative Reforms Commission, GoI	Provision of resources/ accommodation of local variations, purposeful plan for area.
1969	Planning Commission	Formulated guidelines; detailing the concept of the district plan and methodology of drawing up such a plan on the framework of annual plans, medium term plans and perspective plans.
1978	M.L. Dantwala Committee Report	Block level planning to form a link between village and district level planning.
1983–84	Centrally Sponsored Schemes/RBI	Strengthening district plan and district credit plan.
1984	C.H. Hanumantha Rao Committee Report	Decentralisation of functions, powers and finances; setting up of district planning bodies and district planning cells.
1985	G.V.K. Rao Committee Report	Administrative arrangements for rural development; district panchayat to manage all development programmes.
1992	Constitution of India	Legal status to local bodies and assignment of function of local development.
2006	Ministry of Panchayati Raj (Government of India)/V. Ramachandran Committee Report	An action programme for the Eleventh Five Year Plan.
2008	Planning Commission	Manual for Integrated District Planning

Source: Various documents/Reports of Government of India.

Constitutional power for rural local governments and their important role in rural development. For capacity and knowledge building of functionaries of local democratic governments in planning and implementation, the Ramachandran Committee (MoPR, 2006) and the Planning Commission (2008) prepared manuals and made available to them.

6.4. 73RD AMENDMENT AND PLANNING

At the Central level, Article 243(G) of the Constitution 73rd Amendment Act, 1992 had provided that, the state Legislature by law, may, endow the Panchayats with such powers and authority as may be necessary to enable them to function as institutions of self-government (Government of India, n.d). The Article further provided that such law may devolve to panchayats powers and responsibilities of:

1. a. Preparing plans for economic development and social justice; and

   b. Implementing schemes for economic development and social justice as may be entrusted to them.

   Further, it identified 29 subjects/functions to be devolved to Panchayats by the state governments - the details of which were appended to the Act as the Eleventh Schedule.

2. Again, Article 243(ZD) of 74th CAA provides for constitution of a District Planning Committee (DPC) at the district level in every state. The main objective of DPC is to consolidate the plans prepared by the Panchayats and the municipalities in the district and to prepare a draft development plan for the district as a whole.

3. With respect to DPC, the Legislature of a state, by law, make provision to:

   a. The composition of the DPCs;

   b. The manner in which the seats in such committees shall be filled;

   c. The functions relating to district planning which may be assigned to DPCs; and

   d. The manner in which the Chairpersons of DPCs to be chosen.

Every DPC shall, in preparing the draft development plan have regard to:

a. Matters of common interest between the Panchayats and the municipalities including spatial planning, sharing of water and other physical and natural resources, the integrated development of infrastructure and environmental conservation; and

b. The extent and type of available resources whether financial or otherwise.

The Chairperson of DPC to forward the development plan prepared by the Committee to the state government.

6.5. GRAMA SABHA

After 73rd Amendment, a three-tier PRIs namely, Grama/Village Panchayat (GP) at the village level, intermediate Panchayat at the Taluk/Block (TP) level and Zilla/District Panchayat (ZP) at the district level were established in almost all the states in the middle of 1990s. Grama Sabha (GS) below the Grama Panchayat was incorporated in the State Panchayat Raj Acts. Planning divisions have been created at the zilla/district panchayat by many states to carry out the planning activities. The tasks of this division include preparation of draft and action plans for the district, consolidation and integration of taluk and grama panchayats' plans in the district plans, distribution of plan grants across the TPs and GPs and monitoring of the plan programmes.

6.6. DECENTRALISED PLANNING: THE REALITIES

As stated earlier almost all the states in India keeping the mandate of the 73rd CAA, established Panchayats during 1993 and 1994 and repeated periodically thereafter. However, with regard to devolution of functions, functionaries and finance to Panchayats a large number of states have not shown genuine interest. Many states transferred on paper a large number of programmes and schemes (subjects) to Panchayats but without commensurate transfer of functionaries and finances (Table 6.2). As a result, the role of PRIs (except in a very few states) is confined only to some basic services and agency functions. The bureaucracy/line departments at the district level carry out the plan (allocation of outlays) under the supervision and guidance of state and state level officials.

Along with functions fiscal devolution is utmost important for the success of decentralised planning. The fiscal independence of the government is the share of own source revenue in the combined revenues of all level governments. The Table 6.3 reveals the share of own source revenue and expenditure of PRIs in India. The information in the Table reveals that the share of own revenue (less than half percent) and expenditures (2 to 4%) of PRIs among the three level governments is very negligible.

Again, the information given in Table 6.4 unfolds the pathetic position of local governments in the fiscal matters in India as compared to other countries. In India the ratio of revenue and expenditure of local governments in the GDP is very low. Overall the fiscal autonomy of

Table 6.2: Devolution status in major states of India.

State	*Number of functions, funds and functionaries transferred to panchayats*		
	Functions	*Funds*	*Functionaries*
Andhra Pradesh (including Telangana)	10	10	Very few
Assam	29	7	Very few
Bihar	5	8	Very few
Jharkhand	3	–	^
Gujarat	13	14	14
Haryana	10	0	0
Karnataka	29	29	29
Kerala	29	29	29
Madhya Pradesh	19	22	13
Chhattisgarh	12	^	9
Maharashtra	18	11	18
Orissa	21	9	11
Punjab	7	0	0
Rajasthan	10	10	10
Tamil Nadu	29	0	0
Uttar Pradesh	16	4	6
Uttarakhand	11	14	14
West Bengal	29	12	12

Note: ^- No information
Source: Website of "Ministry of Panchayati Raj", Government of India, Accessed on 6–5–2016.

Table 6.3: PRIs share of own revenue and expenditure in the combined revenues and expenditures in India (in percent).

Particulars	*2002–03*	*2003–04*	*2004–05*	*2005–06*	*2006–07*	*2007–08*
Share of own source revenue	0.4	0.4	0.4	0.4	0.3	0.3
Share of expenditure	2.5	2.9	3.1	3.7	3.9	3.7

Source: Oommen, 2013

local governments is weak. Again, own revenue share (self financing) is very low at the local government level in India as compared to Canada and China.

6.7. DISTRICT PLANNING COMMITTEE

Another important facilitator for planning at the grassroot level is DPC. As stated earlier Article 243ZD of 74th CAA places a big role for DPC in

Table 6.4: State-local fiscal transfers – a comparative perspective.

Indicator	*Canada*	*China*	*India*
Local Government (LG) Role: Percent of GDP	7%	11%	<2%
LG role: Percent of total government expenditure	19%	66%	6%
LG Autonomy: Political/ Fiscal/Administrative	Strong/Strong/ Strong	Moderate/ Moderate/Weak	Strong/Weak/ Weak
Self-financing: Urban/Rural	90%/75%	60%/47%	52%/7%
Vertical fiscal gap at the local level	15%	47%	75%

Source: Shah, 2016

the district planning. With regard to DPC, in a large number of states they have not been constituted and wherever they existed they remained toothless (Babu, 2009). In some states where DPCs were constituted, the bureaucrats/ ministers were made chairpersons, which is against the spirit of decentralisation. The position of DPCs in the country can be seen from Table 6.5.

Table 6.5: Status of district planning committees in major states of India.

State	*Status*	*Chairperson of DPC*
Andhra Pradesh	Not yet constituted	—
Assam	Not yet constituted	—
Bihar	Constituted	Chairperson of ZP
Chhattisgarh	Constituted	District in-charge Minister
Gujarat	Not yet constituted	—
Haryana	Constituted	*
Jharkhand	*	*
Karnataka	Constituted	Chairperson of ZP
Kerala	Constituted	Chairperson of DP
Madhya Pradesh	Constituted	District in-charge Minister
Maharashtra	Not yet constituted	—
Orissa	Constituted	District in-charge Minister
Punjab	Not yet constituted	—
Rajasthan	Constituted	Chairperson of DP
Tamil Nadu	Constituted	Chairperson of DP
Uttar Pradesh	Not yet constituted	—
Uttaranchal	Constituted	District in-charge Minister
West Bengal	Constituted	Chairperson of ZP

Note: *No information
Source: Website: Ministry of Panchayati Raj, Government of India.

6.8. ROUND TABLE MEETINGS

Having observed the pathetic situation in not only district planning but also on other important aspects of PRIs in various states in the post 73rd Amendment period the then Central Minister for Panchayat Raj Mr. Mani Shankar Iyer had drawn up certain measures to strengthen these institutions. He had organised seven Round Table Conferences of Panchayat Ministers of States on different issues in different places of India. The Fourth Round Table Meeting of Ministers, in particular, resolved to initiate decentralised planning in their respective states. As a precursor to this the states started the process of constituting DPCs and making provision for Elected Members/Chairperson of the District/ Zilla Panchayat as its Chairperson.

6.9. DISTRICT RURAL DEVELOPMENT AGENCY

Similarly, the District Rural Development Agency (DRDA) at the district level, which is the nodal agency for implementing rural development and poverty alleviation programmes of Central Government, remained independent of Panchayats in several states. As a result planning for these programmes remained outside the purview of Panchayats. The

Table 6.6: State-wise status of district rural development agency in India.

	Major states	*Status of DRDA*
1.	Andhra Pradesh	Not merged with ZP
2.	Assam	Not merged with ZP
3.	Bihar	Not merged with ZP
4.	Jharkhand	No information
5.	Gujarat	Not merged with ZP
6.	Haryana	Not merged with ZP
7.	Karnataka	Merged with ZP
8.	Kerala	Merged with ZP
9.	Madhya Pradesh	Merged with ZP
10.	Chhattisgarh	Merged with ZP
11.	Maharashtra	Not merged with ZP
12.	Orissa	Merged with ZP
13.	Punjab	Not merged with ZP
14.	Rajasthan	Merged with ZP
15.	Tamil Nadu	Not merged with DP
16.	Uttar Pradesh	Merged with ZP
17.	Uttarakhand	No information
18.	West Bengal	Merged with ZP

Source: Planning Commission, 'Five Year Plan 2002–07', Vol. III, Appendix 5.1, GoI

status of DRDA indifferent states is given in Table 6.6. It can be seen from the Table that eight states out 18 have not amalgamated the DRDA with ZP/DP and in another two states there is no information on the status of DRDA.

6.10. RECENT DEVELOPMENTS IN DISTRICT PLANNING

The Central Government after observing the lackadaisical approach of states in strengthening PRIs and that of grassroot planning initiated many policies and programmes as shown in Box 6.1. The crucial requirements for planning and development by PRIs are funds, capacities and guidelines/information. To provide more financial resources at the disposal of PRIs and to take up rural development activities introduced the development programmes like Backward Region Grant Fund (BRGF) programme, Rashtriya Krishi Vikas Yojana (RKVY) with huge budgetary support. Further, as stated earlier knowledge/ capacities of elected representatives of local governments is very important particularly in preparing integrated and long term vision district plan. For building capapcities of PRI functionaries in the

Box 6.1: Recent initiatives by central government towards decentralised planning.

1. Backward Region Grant Fund (BRGF) Programme (2006–07)
2. Rashtriya Krishi Vikas Yojana (RKVY) Fund (2007–08)
3. Rajiv Gandhi Panchayat Sashaktikaran Abhiyan (RGPSA) (2012) RGPSA seeks to:
   a. Enhance capabilities and effectiveness of Panchayats and the Grama Sabha;
   b. Enable democratic decision-making and accountability in Panchayats and promote people's participation;
   c. Strengthen the institutional structure for knowledge creation and capacity building of Panchayats;
   d. Promote devolution of powers and responsibilities to Panchayats according to the spirit of the Constitution and PESA Act;
   e. Strengthen Grama Sabhas to function effectively as the basic forum of people's participation, transparency and accountability within the Panchayat system;
   f. Create and strengthen democratic local self-government in areas where Panchayat do not exists; and
   g. Strengthen the constitutionally mandated framework on which panchayats are founded.
4. V. Ramachandran Committee - Manual for Decentralised Planning (2006)
5. Planning Commission – Manual for Integrated District Planning (2008).

planning aspect a programme namely, Rajiv Gandhi Panchayat Sashaktikaran Abhiyan (RGPSA) was introduced in 2012 by the Central Government. The various components of this programme is shown in Box 6.1. Again, the Central Government focused its objective on inclusive growth during Eleventh Five Year Plan. To achieve this objective the Government felt the need for active participation of decentralized governments. It felt that the experience of local governments till Tenth Five Year Plan was one of preparing and implementing disjointed annual plans instead of five year period plan as practiced by Central and States since beginning. To syncronise with the plans of Centre and States the Planning Commission instructed the states to initiate preparing a five year plan for the Eleventh Five Year Plan period at the district level too with active participation of local governments and DPC. For this, the MoPR (2006) brought out a manual (Ramachandran Committee) for the benefit of functionaries of local governments. A Similar kind of manual was brought out by Planning Commission in 2008 and made it available to the stakeholders in the same year.

As a result of above initiatives by the Central Government the local governments (rural and urban) for the first time prepared five year plan coinciding with the Centre's Eleventh Five Year Plan – 2007–12. The local governments prepared two sets of plans – One for agriculture sector namely, 'Comprehensive District Agriculture Plan – 2007–12' (CDAP) and the other a plan for all the sectors at the district level namely, 'Comprehensive District Development Plan – 2007–12 (CDDP). The DPCs were activated (at least in some states) in these plan preparations. The enthusiasm shown by the local governments in the preparation of the above plans, however, fade away by the time the Twelfth Five Year Plan preparation was under way.

6.11. CONCLUSIONS AND SUGGESTIONS

The foregoing information on the status of rural local governments in India in general and grassroot level planning in particular are self-revealing. They are far from becoming self-governing institutions. With very few functions and resources at their command, the expectation of a move towards a true decentralised planning in India has yet remained an unfulfilled dream. In a majority of states the PRIs depend largely on Central Government programmes and funds. Almost all rural development and poverty alleviation schemes of Central government are being implemented through PRIs. The Central grants are tied to schemes. Even most of the grants provided by states to PRIs are tied to the schemes. As a result there is no leverage for PRIs to allocate resources according to local needs and priorities. The share of own revenue and total expenditure of PRIs among the three level governments in India, is abysmally low with 0.3% and 3.7% respectively during 2007–08 (Oommen, 2013). The functionaries available at the local government level is grossly inadequate and lack technical expertise. Besides, the local governments have very little supervision and control over the majority of officials as they are deputed from state bureaucracy. Notwithstanding the introduction of Panchayat strengthening measures by some states and also the Central Government, the grassroot level planning, by and large, has not moved forward in an intended manner and speed. In these states the preparation of perspective plans and vision document is sporadic in nature. As and when push comes from the above *i.e.,* the Central Government (as in the case of preparation of Comprehensive District Development Plan for Eleventh Plan Period) there will be some activity at the grassroot level in plan preparation without perpetuating the same on their own thereafter.

In these circumstances the question that arises is what needs to be done to take forward the much eulogised planning from below? The discussion and understanding of decentralisation both from governance and outcome point of view is varied and it depends on how one grasp it. Decentralisation per se is not bad. The failure of the system is largely due to empowerment problems. Hence there is need for empowerment of PRIs both by the states and Central Government.

As brought out earlier, the success of decentralisation depends on the extent of provision of requisites/conditions such as political power, devolution of responsibilities according to the subsidiarity principle, own revenue raising powers and devolution of grants-in-aid to meet the needs, creation of exclusive local bureaucracy and above all capacity building of functionaries of PRIs on a continuing basis and awareness creation among the citizens in the art of governance and planning.

Though certain provisions are there in the 73rd CAA towards empowering the PRIs particularly in the matters of responsibilities and finances. But they are not mandatory in nature and left to the respective states to make legislations in devolving them. It is the states which are reluctant to share power below the state. The studies pointed out that in those countries where meaningful devolution were effected they experienced higher economic growth (World Bank, 1988). In India the on us of empowering PRIs rests largely with the states.

Along with this, the local democratic institutions need to learn and function effectively. The effectiveness in the governance occurs when the sub-institutions within the PRIs such as standing committees, social audit, grama sabha etc. function according to the laid out framework. The active participation of citizens in the local governance is very important. It is the responsibility of local government to ensure peoples' participation in the processes of its governance and planning which in turn lead to transparency, efficiency and accountability.

REFERENCES

Aziz Abdul (1993). *'Decentralised Planning: The Karnataka Experience'*, Sage, New Delhi.

Babu M. Devendra (2009). District Planning Committee and Grassroot level Planning: Some Issues with Reference to Karnataka. *The Grassroots Governance Journal,* II(1 & 2).

Babu M. Devendra (2010). 'Decentralised Planning in Karnataka: Realities and Prospects'. *Social and Economic Change Monographs 19*, Institute for Social and Economic Change, Bangalore.

Cheema, G., Shabbir and Rondinelli Denis, A. (*eds.*) (1983). *'Decentralization and Development: Policy Implementation in Developing Countries'*, Sage, Beverly Hills, CA.

Government of India (n.d) (1992). 'Seventy-Third Constitution Amendment Act, - The Panchayats', New Delhi

Harris, R. (1983). Centralisation and Decentralisation in Latin America. *In*: Cheema, G.S. and Rondinelli, D.A. (*eds.*) (1983). *Decentralisation and Development: Policy Implementation in Developing Countries*, Beverly Hills, CA: Sage.

MoPR (Ministry of Panchayati Raj) (2006). *Planning at the Grassroots Level: An Action Programme for the Eleventh Five Year Plan, Report of the Expert Group*. New Delhi: Government of India.

Oates, E. Wallace, 1972, *'Fiscal Federalism', Harcourt, Brace and Jovanovich*, New York.

Oommen, M.A. (2013). *Fiscal Decentralization*, *In*: George Mathew (*ed.*), *Status of Panchayati Raj in the States and Union Territories of India -2013*, Institute of Social Sciences and Concept, New Delhi.

Parajalu Pramod and Kothari Smitu (1998). *Struggling for Autonomy: Lessons from Local Governance, Development,* 41(3).

Planning Commission (2008). *Manual for Integrated District Planning*, Government of India.

Shah , Anwar , (2016). State Fiscal Transfers to Local Governments: Principles and Lessons from the International Practice, *Iin*: Workshop on 'Fiscal Decentralisation and the Role of State Finance Commissions, ; 18–19th January 2016, New Delhi, India.

Stiefel, M,. and d A Pearse, A. (, 1982). *UNRISD's Popular Participation Programme: An Inquiry into Power, Confilict, and Social Change, Assignment Children*, Vol. (59/60).

Sundaram, K. V., (1997)., *Decentralised Multilevel Planning: Principles and Practice (Asian and African Experiences)*, Concept, New Delhi.

Wallace Oates, E. (1972). *'Fiscal Federalism', Harcourt, Brace and Jovanovich*, New York.

World Bank (1988). '*World Development Report*, New York, Oxford University Press.

7

Some Landmark Developments in the Evolution of India's Federal Finance

B.S. SREEKANTARADHYA[7]*

ABSTRACT

This paper discusses some landmark developments in the evolution of India's Federal Finance. The recent years have witnessed a few landmark developments in India's federal financial relations. First, there has been a fundamental shift in the structure of financial transfers from the centre to the sub-national governments. The Constitution (Eightieth Amendment) Act 2000 facilitated augmentation of the centre's resources available for transfers by including the proceeds of all central taxes in the divisible pool. Further, the Successive Finance Commissions of India increased the percentage share of the states from the divisible pool. The recommendation of the Fourteenth Finance Commission, in particular, is very significant in this regard. Its recommendation to increase the share of the states to 42 percent of the divisible pool was a landmark decision as it contributed to higher empowerment and enhancement of the autonomy of the states with the availability of more untied transfers.

7.1. INTRODUCTION

A systematic approach to the federal financial relations in independent India started with the First Finance Commission's award (1952–57). Since then, over a period of more than six decades, the centre-state financial relations have evolved. Successive Finance Commissions have tried to bring about significant improvements in the system of statutory transfer of financial resources to the sub-national governments. In

[7] Former Professor, Department of Economics and Cooperation, University of Mysore, Karnataka.

**Corresponding author*: E-mail: bss_aradhya@yahoo.com

addition, non-statutory transfers recommended by the erstwhile Planning Commission and the different ministries of the central government also became an important component of the federal finance. Thus, India's federal finance includes both statutory and non-statutory transfers.

Equity or fairness in the distribution of financial resources between the centre and the sub-national governments is the biggest issue in inter-governmental financial relations. Under India's federal set-up, there is both centralization and decentralization, as it is necessary that certain functions have to be centralized and certain others have to be decentralized. The real problem in this regard is one of asymmetry between the spending responsibilities and the financial resources. While the centre has more financial resources at its command, the states and the local bodies taken together have more spending responsibilities. Thus there is the problem of vertical fiscal imbalance *i.e.*, imbalance between the centre and the states. This phenomenon of centralization of taxing powers and decentralization of spending has been repeatedly highlighted in the literature on the subject (Chellaiah, 2005; Rangarajan and Srivastava, 2011). There is also the problem of horizontal fiscal imbalance *i.e.*, imbalance among the states in respect of levels of development and capacity to raise financial resources.

To tackle the problems mentioned above, it is necessary to transfer financial resources from the centre to the states which have to find resources not only to meet their own requirements, but also to transfer resources to the local bodies which have assumed great importance in the federal set-up after the 73rd and 74th Amendments to the Constitution.

Federal fiscal devices such as sharing of the tax proceeds of the Centre and grants-in-aid from the Centre have been employed to tackle the problems of vertical and horizontal fiscal imbalances. Both statutory and non-statutory transfers should ensure equity and efficiency. The federal financial relationships have to be developed in such a way that they ensure higher degree of empowering and autonomy to the states and also provide impetus to the decentralization process in the country. It is interesting to analyse some of the landmark developments in India's federal finance which have contributed to the enhancement of the autonomy of the states and also to the strengthening of the decentralization process. An attempt is made here to highlight those significant steps in respect of both statutory and non-statutory fiscal transfers which have gradually paved the way for a cooperative federalism. Section I analyses the changes in vertical devolution and Section II highlights the developments with regard to the transfer of resources for the benefit of the local bodies. Section III looks into the changes in non-statutory transfers with special reference to the recent restructuring of the Centrally Sponsored Schemes (CSSs) and Section IV presents the concluding remarks.

I

STATUTORY TRANSFERS: DEVELOPMENTS IN TAX SHARING

7.2. VERTICAL DEVOLUTION

Though both vertical devolution and horizontal devolution are equally important, only the former has received good attention while no major change has been made in respect of the latter. No doubt, the criteria selected and the weights assigned to them have been modified over time. Up to the Seventh Finance Commission, population and collection in respect of income tax and indicators of backwardness in respect Union excise duties were the criteria employed for the *inter se* distribution among the states. Later on, other criteria like area, income distance, index of infrastructure, tax effort, fiscal discipline and forest cover were considered and the weights assigned to them were modified by the successive Finance Commissions. But all this has been no more than mere tinkering with the criteria and the weights. Critics have pointed out that these changes were subjective and needed to be replaced by a more rational system (Sarma, 1997). But nothing of that kind has taken place.

Vertical devolution is extremely important from the point of view of higher empowerment and autonomy of the states. The transfers which the states get in the form of a share from the central taxes are untied which can be used by the states for whatever purpose they want according to their own needs. For transfers to be effected in this form, the divisible pool should be widened and a higher percentage of this should be shared with the states. States have always argued for widening the divisible pool and for increasing their share from this pool. Successive Finance Commissions have tried to meet this demand and with the result, the divisible pool has grown considerably over time.

We shall first see what constitutes the divisible pool and how it has expanded over time. From the First Finance Commission to the Tenth Finance Commission, the only central taxes shareable with the states were the non-corporate income tax and the Union excise duties. In addition, there was grant-in-lieu of railway passenger fare tax and share of additional duties of excise in lieu of sales tax.

The share from the income tax and Union excise duties given to the states from the First Finance Commission to the Tenth Finance Commission is shown in Table 7.1.

Table 7.1: Share of the states in income tax and union excise duties (in percent).

Finance commission	*Share of income tax*	*Share of union excise duties*
Finance Commission-I	55	40
Finance Commission-II	60	25
Finance Commission-III	66 2/3	20
Finance Commission-IV	75	20
Finance Commission-V	75	20
Finance Commission-VI	80	20
Finance Commission-VII	85	40
Finance Commission-VIII	85	45
Finance Commission-IX	85	45
Finance Commission-X	77.5	47.5

Source: Reports of the Finance Commissions - I to X.

The share of income tax proceeds in the central transfers to states increased from 55 percent recommended by the First Finance Commission to 85 percent recommended by the Seventh Finance Commission. The Eighth and Ninth Finance Commissions retained it at the same level before the Tenth Finance Commission reduced it to 77.5 percent on the ground that "the authority that levies and administers a tax should have a significant and tangible interest in its yield..". Since the corporation tax was not included in the divisible pool, the share of the income tax itself had to be increased by the successive Finance Commissions. The share of the Union excise duties was reduced from 40 percent recommended by the First Finance Commission to 25 percent recommended by the Second Finance Commission and from the Third Finance Commission to the Sixth Finance Commission it remained at 20 percent. One reason for the reduction in the percentage share was the increase in the revenue from the Union excise duties as a result of the increase in the revenue due to the increase in the commodity coverage.

The Seventh Finance Commission raised the share of the Union excise duties to 40 percent and the Eighth and the Ninth Finance Commissions recommended a share of 45 percent and the Tenth Finance Commission raised it to 47.5 percent. Thus, the share of both income tax and the Union excise duties was raised over time. But still this system had serious deficiencies which needed to be addressed.

The deficiencies of the tax sharing system that prevailed up to the Tenth Finance Commission were the following:

a. The divisible pool was very narrow despite the increase in the percentage share of the income tax and the Union excise duties.
b. To increase devolution, the share of the income tax was raised to such an extent that what remained with the centre after sharing with the states got reduced to such an extent that it proved to be a disincentive for the centre to make serious effort to raise additional revenue from the income tax. Nearly half of the revenue collected from the Union excise duties was also shared with the states. With the result, a high percentage share from limited number of taxes went to the states.
c. With the rapid growth of the corporate sector over time, the revenue from the corporation tax increased far exceeding the revenue from the income tax. States were unhappy that a more elastic source of revenue was not shareable.
d. Another factor which contributed to the narrow divisible pool was the exclusion of cesses and surcharges from sharing with states.

7.3. ALTERNATIVE SCHEME OF VERTICAL DEVOLUTION

As a result of the deficiencies of the tax devolution procedure described above, states were highly dissatisfied with the then existing system of tax sharing and the demand for an alternative scheme of devolution was intensified and the expert opinion also favoured a change. The Eighth Finance Commission and the Sarkaria Commission favoured the inclusion of the corporation tax in the divisible pool and the Chelliah Committee on Tax Reforms favoured sharing 25 percent of the aggregate tax revenue of the Centre with the states and even the Government of India favoured inclusion of all the central taxes in the divisible pool (Report of the Tenth Finance Commission, 1995).

The Tenth Finance Commission made out a strong case for a new tax sharing mechanism under which all central taxes would be pooled and a proportion of this would be devolved to the states. It pointed out that the following benefits would accrue from the new arrangement:

a. With a given share being allotted to the states in the aggregate revenue from central taxes, states will be able to share the aggregate buoyancy of central taxes.
b. The Central Government can pursue tax reforms without the need to consider whether a tax is shareable with the states or not.
c. The impact of fluctuations in central tax revenues would be felt alike by the central and state Governments.
d. Should the taxes mentioned in articles 268 and/or 269 form part of the arrangement, there will be a greater likelihood of that being tapped.

A Constitutional Amendment was necessary to introduce the alternative vertical devolution outlined above. The Constitution (Eightieth Amendment) Act 2000 permitted the new pattern of vertical devolution and according to the new article 270 in the Constitution, the net proceeds of all central taxes except the duties and taxes referred to in Articles 268 and 269 and surcharges and cesses could be shared with the states. The new approach hailed as a landmark in the evolution of India's federal finance conferred on the states the benefit of a share from the widened divisible pool. With this radical departure from the past, the states were expected to benefit from the buoyancy of the central taxes. The long standing demand of the states was met with this new arrangement.

7.4. INCREASES IN THE SHARE FROM THE DIVISIBLE POOL

Apart from widening the divisible pool, attempts have been made to increase the percentage share of the states from this divisible pool. The Tenth Finance Commission which made the proposal to pool the proceeds of all central taxes also proposed that the states' share from the divisible pool could be fixed at 29 percent (26% + additional 3% of gross tax revenue as share of additional excise duties in lieu of sales tax). The Eleventh Finance Commission actually recommended a share of 29.5 percent of the net tax revenue (not gross tax revenue) of the centre. (28% + 1.5% as share of additional excise duties in lieu of sales tax) The Twelfth and the Thirteenth Finance Commissions raised the share to 30.5 percent and 32 percent respectively. The Fourteenth Finance Commission recommended a big jump from 32 percent to 42 percent. States have immensely benefited by the widening of the divisible pool and the increased share they get from this divisible pool. As pointed out by the Fourteenth Finance Commission "....increasing the share of tax devolution to 42 percent of the divisible pool would serve the twin objective of increasing the flow of unconditional transfers to the states and yet leave appropriate fiscal space for the Union to carry out specific-purpose transfers to the states." It is rightly said that "The FC XIV recommendations have resulted in a fundamental shift in the structure of transfers. For all states put together, unconditional tax devolution would now account for more than 70 percent of total central transfers" (Chakraborty, 2016). Though there is further scope for widening the divisible pool by including the proceeds of cesses and surcharges and non-tax sources of revenue like sale proceeds of spectrum and off-shore royalties, the improvement brought about till now marks a big departure from the past and it has contributed to higher empowerment and enhancing of the autonomy of the states, since transfers in the form of tax share constitutes untied transfers. With higher tax devolution, states' fiscal space has been enhanced and they are now in a position to determine their priorities.

II

7.5. IMPETUS TO THE DECENTRALIZATION PROCESS

The impetus given to the decentralization process by adopting a system of central transfers to supplement the Consolidated Fund of the state to augment the financial resources of the Panchayats and Municipalities is a truly landmark development in the evolution of India's Federal Finance.

It is very well recognized that decentralization of the development process is an essential requirement for effectively meeting the local needs of the people such as drinking water, sanitation, primary education, primary health care, roads etc., in rural areas and adequate civic amenities in urban areas. Though the local bodies have been functioning since a long time, their role received a new emphasis with the passing of the 73rd and 74th Amendments to the Constitution. Before this amendment, the mandatory duty of the Finance Commission under Article 280 of the constitution was to recommend sharing of centre's tax proceeds with the states and grants-in-aid to the states. After the amendment, two sub-clauses (bb) and (c) were added to Article 280. As pointed out by the Tenth Finance Commission, "These sub-clauses make it obligatory upon the Commission to recommend the measures needed to augment the Consolidated Fund of a state to supplement the resources of the Panchayats/Municipalities in the state on the basis of the recommendations made by the Finance Commission of the State". The finances of the local bodies being very poor because of lack of opportunities for raising sufficient resources on their own, their resource crunch is a serious problem. Even after the transfer of financial resources from the states, the local bodies generally face the problem of lack of resources to carry out the responsibilities entrusted to them. Therefore, after enlarging the scope of Article 280 of the constitution, the Tenth Finance Commission was urged to look into the question of central transfers for the benefit of the local bodies. Even though this issue was not included in the terms of reference, the Tenth Finance Commission examined this question and recommended *ad hoc* grants to supplement the Consolidated Fund of the State for the purpose of augmenting the resources of the local bodies.

The question of grants-in-aid to local bodies was included in the terms of reference of the Eleventh Finance Commission for the first time and thereafter it became a permanent feature. The quantum of grants recommended by the successive Finance Commissions has greatly increased over time as shown in Table 7.2.

Table 7.2: Quantum of grants recommended for the local bodies (Rs. crores).

Finance commission	*PRIs*	*ULBs*	*Total*
Finance Commission-X	4,380	1,000	5,380
Finance Commission-XI	8,000	2,000	10,000
Finance Commission-XII	20,000	5,000	25,000
Finance Commission-XIII	63,051	23,111	86,162
Finance Commission-XIV	2,00,292	87,143	2,87,436

Note: PRIs – Panchayat Raj Institutions; ULBs – Urban Local Bodies.
Source: Reports of the Finance Commissions - X to XIV.

Grants to PRIs increased from Rs. 4,380 Crore recommended by the Tenth Finance Commission to Rs. 2,00,292 Crore recommended by the Fourteenth Finance Commission and the grants to urban local bodies increased from Rs. 1,000 Crore recommended by the Tenth Finance Commission to Rs. 87,143 Crore recommended by the Fourteenth Finance Commission. The total grants to local bodies increased from Rs. 5,380 Crore recommended by the Tenth Finance Commission to Rs. 2,87,436 Crore recommended by the Fourteenth Finance Commission. Thus, between the Tenth and the Fourteenth Commissions there has been a quantum jump in the transfer of financial resources to the local bodies.

Successive Finance Commissions have recognized the need for substantially larger outlays by the local bodies to discharge their responsibilities with regard to the local needs of the people. The Thirteenth Finance Commission said, "There is an undisputed need to bolster the finances of the rural as well as the urban local bodies. All local bodies need to be supported through a predictable and buoyant source of revenue, substantially higher than the present levels, in addition to their own tax revenue and other flows from state and Central Government". *Ad hoc* approach followed by the previous commissions was given up and a decision was taken by the Thirteenth Finance Commission to recommend a certain percentage of the divisible pool as the share of the local bodies. After deciding the percentage share, this was converted into grants-in-aid under article 275 as there is no provision for sharing the tax proceeds of the Centre with the local bodies. The Thirteenth Finance Commission recommended 2.28 percent of the Centre's divisible pool of the previous year as the share of the local bodies. This is a very significant development since it ensures that the local bodies also benefit from the buoyancy of the central taxes. The Fourteenth Finance Commission pointed out that the states demanded that the share of the local bodies from the divisible pool should be increased to 5 percent. But in its recommendation the Commission makes no mention of the share of the divisible pool, but only says that it has worked out the size of the grants for the local bodies and recommended that amount to be transferred.

7.6. CRITERIA AND WEIGHTS FOR *INTER SE* DISTRIBUTION

The Tenth Finance Commission based its recommendations for *inter se* distribution on the state-wise rural population in the case of Panchayats and inter-state ratio of slum population in the case of urban local bodies. The subsequent Finance Commissions have adopted different criteria and weights. Eleventh and Twelfth Finance Commissions adopted more or less similar criteria and weights: population (20%), distance from the highest per capita income (10%), geographic area (10%). While the Eleventh Finance Commission adopted index of decentralization as one of the criteria and assigned 20% weight, the Twelfth Finance Commission gave up this and adopted index of deprivation and assigned 10 percent weight.

The Thirteenth Finance Commission increased the number of criteria and assigned separate weights to panchayat raj institutions and urban local bodies as shown in Table 7.3.

The Fourteenth Finance Commission changed over to a much simpler formula and adopted only population (2011) and area and adopted weight of 90 percent and 10 percent respectively for both PRIs and ULBs.

Table 7.3: Criteria and weights assigned by the FC XIII to PRIs and ULBs (Percent).

Criteria	*PRIs*	*ULBs*
Population	50	50
Area	10	10
Distance from the highest per capita sectoral income	10	20
Index of devolution	15	15
SC/ST proportion in the population	10	
FC local body grants utilization index	5	5
	100	100

Source: Report of the Thirteenth Finance Commission.

Successive Finance Commissions have done well in increasing the quantum of grants to the local bodies and also in adopting suitable criteria and weights for inter se distribution. They have also made several recommendations for augmenting the own resources of the local bodies. But there seems to be no serious effort to give effect to those recommendations. Several improvements are needed to streamline the whole process of Finance Commissions' work in respect of the central transfers to the local bodies. The Finance Commission is supposed to give its recommendation on the basis of the work of the State Finance Commissions. But in practice, the Central Finance Commission is handicapped because of the poor quality of work of the State Finance Commissions and also because of lack of synchronization between the period covered by the Central Finance Commission and the State Finance Commissions. Different states appoint State Finance Commissions at different points of time and their recommendations are not available to the Central Finance Commission before it finalises its report. State Finance Commissions should be appointed in such a way that their recommendations are available to the Central Finance Commission before it finalises its recommendations. There are also problems with regard to the data base of the local bodies, utilization of the central transfers by the local bodies etc., which need to be addressed to fully benefit from the central resources transferred to the states for augmenting the resources of the local bodies. In spite of some of these problems, increased central transfers for the benefit of the local bodies have gone a long way in providing an impetus to the decentralization process.

III

7.7. NON-STATUTORY TRANSFERS

Central transfers to states other than those made by the Finance Commissions constitute a significant part of federal finance. They are plan funds from the centre transferred to the states in the form of central plan assistance and centrally sponsored schemes.

Central assistance for the states' plan which occupied a premier place until recently has now lost its importance. With the increased devolution from the centre recommended by the Fourteenth Finance Commission, states get more untied funds and therefore, block grants have been discontinued since 2015–16 (NITI Aayog, 2015). The erstwhile Planning Commission was the authority vested with the powers to recommend plan assistance to states. Even before the dismantling of the Planning Commission, there was a gradual reduction in the untied block grants. However, while identifying the landmark developments in the evolution of India's federal finance, the procedure adopted for allocating plan funds cannot be ignored as it represents a particular phase in India's federal finance and therefore a brief description of the way in which the erstwhile Planning Commission allocated plan grants to states is given below taking it as a matter of historical significance.

Plan grants to states in the first three Five Year Plans were discretionary and not based on any criteria. Criteria and weights for allocation of central plan grants were adopted for the first time in the Fourth Five Year Plan. This marked a departure from the past as it made way for a rational approach for allocation of grants to states for plan purposes. The formula known as Gadgil formula formed the basis for allocation of plan grants among the states in the Fourth Plan. A modified Gadgil formula was introduced in 1980 and subsequently in 1991 Gadgil-Mukherjee formula was introduced.

Out of the central funds available for distribution as plan grants among the states 30 percent was first set apart for the special category states and the remaining 70 percent was allocated among the states on the basis of the formula adopted by the Planning Commission. Plan assistance to states was in the form of loans and grants in the ratio of

70:30 for many years and later on the loan component was given up as states were asked to borrow directly in the market instead of borrowing from the Centre.

Population which was given 60 percent weight in the original Gadgil formula was reduced to 55 percent weight in the modified Gadgil formula, but it was again raised to 60 percent in the Gadgil-Mukherjee formula. Per capita income which was given 10 percent weight in the original Gadgil formula was raised to 25 percent weight in both the revised Gadgil formula and the Gadgil-Mukherjee formula. Ongoing irrigation and power projects and social problems were given 10 percent weight each in the modified Gadgil formula and in the Gadgil-Mukherjee formula. Tax effort which was given 10 percent weight in the original Gadgil formula was given up in the modified Gadgil formula and again it was included in the Gadgil-Mukherjee formula and given 7.5 percent weight. Fiscal management was assigned 5 percent weight in the modified Gadgil formula only and special development problems were given 15 percent and 7.5 percent weight respectively in the modified Gadgil formula and Gadgil-Mukherjee formula. This approach was criticized on the ground that it only amounted to tinkering with criteria and weights and that it favoured large states and ignored the interests of small states. There was a proposal to replace this formula by a composite development index suggested by the Raghuram Rajan Committee (Government of India, 2013). Allocation of central funds to states on the basis of this index would have assured more transfers in favour of relatively backward states. But before any decision was taken on the implementation of this recommendation, the Planning Commission itself was dissolved and the central plan assistance was discontinued after the Fourteenth Finance Commission recommended higher vertical devolution. However, the significance of the formula based approach to allocation of plan funds to states followed from the Fourth Plan to Twelfth Plan cannot be underestimated as it marked a departure from the discretionary approach to a formula based approach. As normal central assistance has been discontinued from 2015-16, the focus has to be on the mechanism of transfer from the centre for the remaining schemes like Centrally Sponsored Schemes (CSSs).

7.8. RESTRUCTURING OF CENTRALLY SPONSORED SCHEMES

The centre has been transferring huge amounts to states under the CSSs. Since several aspects of these schemes were unacceptable to states, under the NITI Aayog regime, restructuring of CSSs is being attempted and the changes proposed are extremely important and they constitute a major departure from the past and thus this may be treated as another landmark development in respect of non-statutory transfers under India's federal finance.

Centrally sponsored schemes are those which are designed by the Centre and implemented by the states. They are schemes in the areas of rural development, agriculture, irrigation, education, health etc., which are extremely important, but states are unable to take up on their own because of resource crunch. The Centre finances these schemes and the states also have to bear a part of the cost.

Several problems were identified with regard to CSSs. First, there was a proliferation of such schemes, some of which involved small investment. Schemes with small outlays were found to be not useful (Chaturvedi, 2011). Second, schemes were of one-size-fits-all nature and they were not tailored to the specific local needs and the states had to simply go by the guidelines issued by the Centre or in other words, the schemes lacked flexibility. Third, because of the requirement of partial contribution by the states, sometimes states were unable to fully utilize the funds available under the CSSs (NITI Aayog, 2016). In view of these difficulties, the states in general wanted pruning of the CSSs and favoured more of untied central transfers. NITI Aayog considered the views of the states and appointed a Sub-Group of Chief Ministers on Rationalisation of CSSs (2015) and on the basis of the recommendations of this group, CSSs have been restructured.

The new approach marks a great departure from the past. First, the number of CSSs has been greatly reduced. There were 360 schemes in the Ninth Plan Period, 155 in the Tenth Plan Period and 147 in the Eleventh Plan Period. The number was further reduced during the Twelfth Plan Period and there were 66 schemes in 2014–15 (NITI Aayog, 2015). Under the new restructured scheme, the number is reduced from 66 to 28 umbrella schemes, out of which 6 schemes have been categorised as core of the core schemes and 20 have been categorised as core schemes, and 2 as optional schemes. Core schemes are compulsory for all states. In the case of optional schemes, the participation is by choice. This has been modified in the 2017 budget, according to which there are no optional schemes and the number of core schemes has been increased to 22.

Existing pattern of assistance is applicable to core of the core schemes. For core schemes, the share between the Centre and the states is in the ratio of 90:10 in the case of North East and Himalayan states and for other states it is in the ratio of 60:40. For optional schemes, it is 80:20 for North East and Himalayan states and 50:50 for others.

The most important departure from the past is the end of the one-size-fits-all approach and the flexibility allowed to states to meet state-specific requirements. Another significant departure from the past is the end of the discretionary powers enjoyed by the Central Ministries in allocating transfers to states under CSSs. The new decision is that "Inter-state distribution shall be on the basis of criteria evolved by a committee comprising Secretary of Nodal Administrative Ministry as Chairman, Financial Advisor of the Ministry and Advisor concerned of NITI Aayog" (NITI Aayog, 2015).

Under the new dispensation, there is also good institutional arrangement to ensure effective implementation of the schemes. There will be a standing committee consisting of the CEO of NITI Aayog as Chairman, representatives from every state/ UT and from the Concerned Ministries and the Finance Ministry for this purpose. There will also be independent evaluation and monitoring of the schemes by the NITI Aayog.

Restructuring of the CSSs on the above lines, removes the major deficiencies experienced earlier and allows flexibility so that the states may take greater interest in the implementation of the CSSs.

IV

7.9. CONCLUDING OBSERVATIONS

In a federal set-up, it is necessary to ensure stable, predictable and adequate financial resources to the sub-national governments. It is even more important to promote their autonomy and strengthen the decentralization process. Some of the landmark developments in India's federal finance that have taken place over time have served these requirements well. The Eightieth Amendment to the Constitution facilitated the widening of the divisible pool from which the centre transfers funds to the sub-national governments and their share from the divisible pool has also increased considerably meeting the demand that the major transfer should be in the form of tax sharing which provides untied funds. The widening of the divisible pool and the enhancement of the share from this have increased the autonomy of the states. After the 73rd and 74th Amendments to the Constitution, the flow of central funds to the local bodies has increased greatly contributing to the strengthening of the decentralization process. With the restructuring of the CSSs under the NITI Aayog regime, the states' demands such as reducing the number of schemes, proper classification of the schemes, allowing greater freedom to states in the designing and implementation of the schemes and subjecting the transfers to some formula have been met. These significant developments, on the whole, have paved the way for strengthening cooperative federalism.

REFERENCES

Chakraborty Pinaki (2015). "Finance Commissions' Recommendations and Restructured Fiscal Space". *Economic and Political Weekly,* 50(12).

Chakraborty Pinaki (2016). Evolving Centre-State Financial Relations. *Economic and Political Weekly,* 51(16).

Chaturvedi, R.K. (2011). Report of the Committee on Restructuring of Centrally Sponsored Schemes.

Chellaiah Raja, J. (2005). *"Malady of Continuing Fiscal Imbalance". Economic and Political Weekly,* 40(31).

Government of India (1995). Report of the Tenth Finance Commission.

Government of India (2000). Report of the Eleventh Finance Commission.

Government of India (2004). Report of the Twelfth Finance Commission.

Government of India (2009). Report of the Thirteenth Finance Commission.

Government of India (2015). Report of the Fourteenth Finance Commission.

Government of India (2013). Report of the Committee for Evolving a Composite Development Index of States.

NITI Aayog (2015). Report of the Sub-group of Chief Ministers on Rationalisation of Centrally Sponsored Schemes, Government of India.

NITI Aayog (2016). Office Memorandum, August, 17.

Rangarajan, C. and Srivastava, D.K. (2011). *Federalism and Fiscal Transfers in India,* Oxford University Press, New Delhi.

Sarma, J.V.M. (1997). *"Federal Fiscal Relatios in India – Issues of Horizontal Transfers". Economic and Political Weekly,* 32(28).

8

Fiscal Dependence of Local Bodies: Insights from Karnataka

K. GAYITHRI[8*@]

ABSTRACT

This paper on Fiscal Dependence of Local Bodies, analyses the sources of finances of the local bodies. The paper observes that local governments in India in general and Karnataka in particular have depicted a large-scale dependence on state government financial support in discharging their functions and provision of services. It is argued that the excessive dependence of the local bodies on transfers leads to a situation where in the decentralization process tends to get vitiated and the performance of local bodies becomes vulnerable to any adverse changes in the resource transfer. Further the extent and nature of transfers is largely dependent on the fiscal capacity of the state government supporting the local bodies even while providing adequate resources for the state's own commitments. The paper observes that devolution to local bodies is observed to be highly vulnerable to State's overall fiscal position creating uncertainty in the flow of funds. This phenomenon is reported to be more predominant for the PRIs as the share of ULBs is observed to be by and large on the increase albeit it's smaller share in total. This is more with reference to plan / development funding than the non-plan funding which largely is towards salary. Uncertainty / unpredictability of fund support and hamper the developmental activities of the local bodies.

[8] Professor, Institute for Social and Economic Change, Nagarbhavi, Bangalore, Karnataka.

@ An earlier version of this paper was published in the Aarthika Charche: FPI Journal of Economics and Governance,vol. 3, No. 2, July-December 2018, Permission obtained to reproduce Copy Right material

**Corresponding author:* E-mail: gayithri@isec.ac.in

8.1. INTRODUCTION

Decentralisation efforts have a long history in the state of Karnataka. Abdul Nazir Sab was the visionary who redesigned Panchayat Raj System in the early 80's. This system was taken as the model system for the Panchayat Raj and subsequently the 73rd Amendment has given Constitutional status to Panchayati Raj Institutions (PRI) at village, block and district levels. Karnataka Panchayat Raj Act came into force in 1993 as a comprehensive act replacing the act of 1987 to establish a three tier PRI system at the village, taluk and district level in the state.

Local governments in India in general and Karnataka in particular have depicted a large-scale dependence on state government financial support in discharging their functions and provision of services. The excessive dependence of the local bodies on transfers leads to a situation where in the decentralization process tends to get vitiated and the performance of local bodies becomes vulnerable to any adverse changes in the resource transfer. Further the extent and nature of transfers is largely dependent on the fiscal capacity of the state government supporting the local bodies even while providing adequate resources for the state's own commitments. Hence, the resource transfers to the local bodies are largely determined by the fiscal space available with the state government that gets created by augmenting the revenue resources and attaining allocative efficiency in expenditure.

Fiscal performance of Karnataka state has been observed to be sound as evident from the trends in broad fiscal indicators such as fiscal and revenue deficits, development and non-development expenditure and own tax resource generation. This has been especially the case since the enactment of Fiscal Responsibility Act by the State Government in 2002. The state's performance on account of non-tax revenue however has been very weak. The state's committed expenditure which includes state commitments with reference to expenditure items such as salaries, pensions, interest payments, subsidies, administrative expenditure and devolution to PRIs and ULBs has increased from 89 percent of uncommitted revenue receipts to 95 percent in 2012–13 which has further decreased to 82 percent. (GoK, Economic survey, 2015–16) In understanding the state's fiscal capacity to enhance the quantum of devolution to the local bodies a more detailed analysis of the Non Loan Gross Own Revenue (NLGORR) and Non Loan Net Own Revenue Receipts (NLNORR), that have been used as the base for devolving resources in the past along with a disaggregate analysis of state expenditure and their likely trends in future is required. In doing this it is important to factor in the likely fiscal impact of the policy changes like Goods and Services Tax (GST), the enhanced share in tax devolution due to the Fourteenth Finance Commission and reduction in the support extended by the central government to the state governments for various centrally sponsored schemes.

Despite the long history and acclaimed decentralisation efforts, the local bodies have been heavily dependent on transfers from the state and central governments, the former being much more predominant. The inherent advantages that the decentralisation processes provide in attempting grassroots development to reflect the local needs get nullified if not backed by own resources and more so when the external resource support is available but with conditions attached. The large-scale dependence nullifies the very fundamental principles of decentralisation.

The present paper makes an effort to understand the fiscal dependence of the local bodies on the transfers meted out by the higher levels of government and their implications, taking the case of Karnataka.

8.2. TRANSFERS TO LOCAL BODIES: LONG TERM TRENDS AND ISSUES[9]

The resource base of the local bodies comprises of State Finance Commission (SFC) Grants, Central Finance Commission (CFC) Grants, State Government and Central Government Grants for maintenance and development purpose. This paper presents an analysis of the trends in local bodies from the state government over time. Transfers to local bodies in Karnataka from the state government has increased from Rs. 3320.81 Crore in 1997–98 to Rs. 35538.62 Crore in 2016–17 amounting to 9.7 times increase over the initial year (Table 8.1). The distribution of the resources transferred between the urban and local bodies reveals that while the share of urban local bodies has doubled from 8.28 percent to 16.83 percent that of rural local bodies has declined from 91.72 percent to 83.17 percent. However, on an average rural local bodies account for a much larger share in the total with almost 85 percent share with the urban local bodies accounting for 15 percent share in the state government total. It can also be observed that while transfers to urban local bodies has increased by 21 times that of rural local bodies has increased by 8.7 times.

[9] For more details see the author's report submitted to the Fourth State Finance Commission, Government of Karnataka, 2017.

The rates of growth too reveal that transfers to the urban local bodies have been by and large much larger than that of rural local bodies, however, the former has revealed considerable fluctuation over time and at times has even been negative (Fig. 8.1).

Table 8.1: Trends in transfers to local bodies (Rs. crore).

	Transfers to local bodies			*% Share to total*		
Year	***ULBs***	***PRIs***	***Total***	***ULBs***	***PRIs***	***Total***
1997–98	274.81	3046.00	3320.81	8.28	91.72	100.00
2000–01	531.43	4432.20	4963.63	10.71	89.29	100.00
2004–05	798.00	4893.41	5691.41	14.02	85.98	100.00
2007–08	1926.00	9024.13	10950.13	17.59	82.41	100.00
2010–11	2978.00	13464.97	16442.97	18.11	81.89	100.00
2013–14	5020.44	20510.18	25530.62	19.66	80.34	100.00
2016–17	5980.31	29558.31	35538.62	16.83	83.17	100.00

Note: Data on allocation to ULBs from 2002–03 to 2004–05 and 2010–11 is taken from MTFP rest of the years is from GoK, Finance Department. Data on allocation to PRIs from 2002–03 to 2004–05 and 2010–11 is taken from GoK, Link Documents; rest of the years is from GoK, Finance Department.

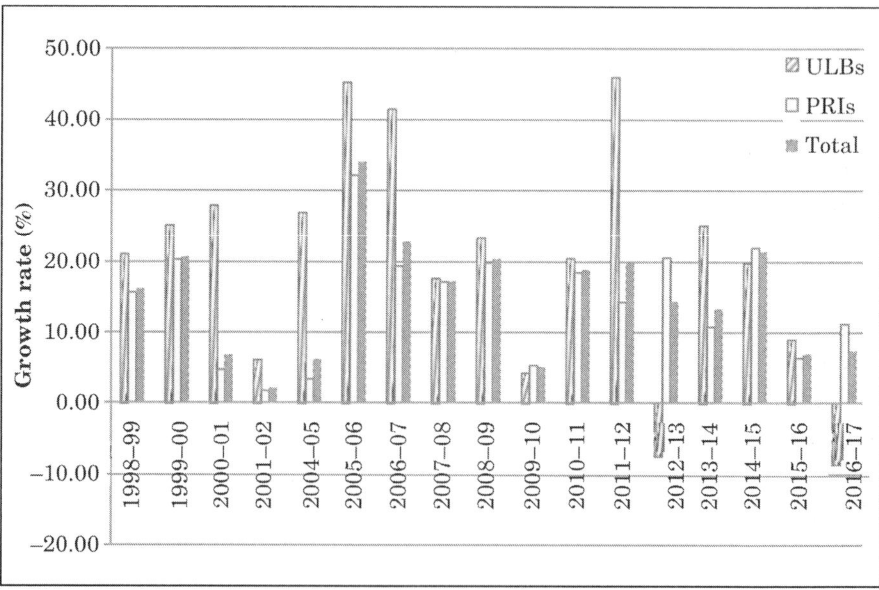

Fig. 8.1: Growth of allocation to local bodies

8.3. TRANSFERS *VIS-À-VIS* STATE'S FISCAL POSITION

Analysis of the share of allocation to the local bodies in the state's aggregate expenditure (Revenue and Capital account) over time reveals that there has been an overall decline from 1997–98. The variations in the share clearly reveal that the allocations are largely reflecting the overall state's fiscal situation. The share declined during 1997–98 till 2004–05, subsequent to which there has been some increase until 2008–09, the decline that has occurred in 2009–10 has more or less continued at the reduced level for the rest of the reference period. Karnataka's fiscal situation was precarious until 2003–04, substantially improved with the framing of Fiscal Responsibility Act in 2002–03 resulting in a substantial improvement in the resource position. The global recession that occurred in 2008–09 adversely affected the state's resource position once again due to the tax concessions that were provided and stimulus measures in the form of enhanced spending.

An important policy concern in this context is with reference to the fact that despite an absolute overall increase in the transfers provided over time, they are very often adversely affected by the state's overall fiscal position. The state's fiscal adversities get clearly reflected in the shared resources with the local bodies that have suffered a decline during 1997–98 until 2004–05 and once again from 2009–10. The World Bank (2004) observes that, "Local plan allocation is also vulnerable to another feature of the inter-governmental arrangement in Karnataka; the devolution to sub-state bodies is vulnerable to expenditure compression. When budgets are tight, state transfers to local governments can be under-funded, or postponed".

The allocation to local bodies as a percent share in Gross State Domestic Product (GSDP) is small and has revealed similar pattern with the overall share declining from 4.89 percent in 1998–99 to 4.5 percent in 2015–16 dropping further to 3.18 percent in 2016–17 (Fig. 8.2).

8.4. TRANSFERS IN RELATION TO NLNORR

It is important to examine the trends in share of transfers in the Non-Loan Net Own Revenue Resources (NLNORR) which basically comprises of state's own revenue inclusive of both tax and non-tax sources after netting out the cost of collection charges. The third State Finance Commission appointed by the Government of Karnataka had recommended that NLNORR be used as the divisible pool as opposed to

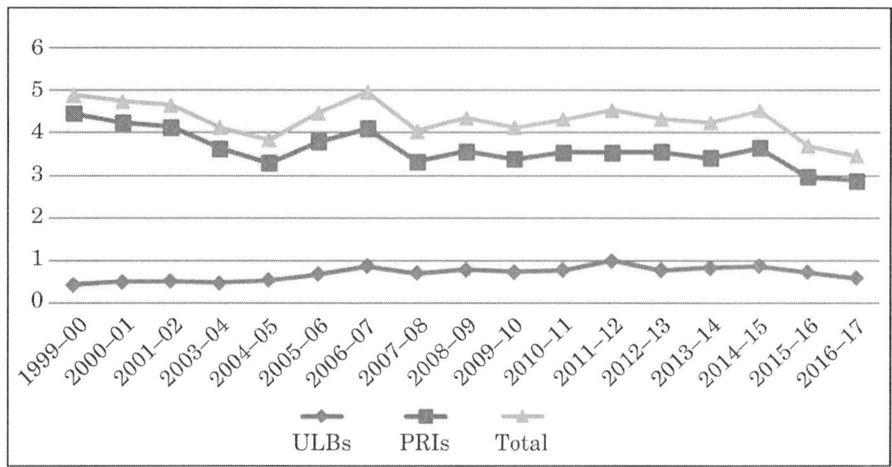

Fig. 8.2: Allocation to local bodies: Share of GSDP.

the first and second State finance commission that had recommended Non-Loan Gross Own Revenue Receipts (NLGORR). The divisible pool should consist of net proceeds of taxes, tolls, duties, fees levied and collected by the state government.

In order to make the long-run comparison meaningful, the overall trends in the transfers to the local bodies have been traced as a percent to NLNORR.

These trends have revealed that the share of total transfers to the NLNORR has declined from 44.62 percent in 1997–98 to 40.28 percent in 2016–17. In addition, there is no uniform trend *i.e.,* either a gradual increase/decrease revealed during the reference period, on the contrary considerable fluctuations have been observed. The share was at the highest in 1999–00 at 51.71 percent and at the lowest in 2004–05 with 28.25 percent share (Table 8.2). On an average, the total transfers account for 40.93 percent share in NLNORR; while the average share of urban local bodies share is 6.16, rural local bodies account for 34.71 percent. The paths of increase/ decrease are clearly discernible in Fig. 8.3. The fiscal stress experienced by the government of Karnataka in late nineties and early years of the last decade had resulted in a declining share to the local bodies in the NLNORR, the improved state's fiscal health had resulted in a considerable increase in its share from 2005–6 till 2008–09. There has been a decline after that owing to the set back to the state's resource position caused by the global melt down. PRIs seem to be more vulnerable to the fiscal stress of the state as the

Table 8.2: Transfers to local bodies (Rs. in crore).

	Transfers to local bodies			***NLNORR (Rs. in crore)***	***Ratio of transfers to NLNORR***		
Year	***ULBs***	***PRIs***	***Total***		***ULBs***	***PRIs***	***Total***
1997–98	274.81	3046.00	3320.81	7441.63	3.69	40.93	44.62
2000–01	531.43	4432.20	4963.63	10386.94	5.12	42.67	47.79
2004–05	798.00	4893.41	5691.41	20143.69	3.96	24.29	28.25
2007–08	1926.00	9024.13	10950.13	28895.33	6.67	31.23	37.90
2010–11	2978.00	13464.97	16442.97	41286.49	7.21	32.61	39.83
2013–14	5020.44	20510.18	25530.62	64775.78	7.75	31.66	39.41
2015–16	6548.92	26575.81	33124.73	80690.68	8.12	32.94	41.05

Source: State's own tax and Non-tax revenue GoK, Accounts at a Glance 1960–2015, Data on Total Fiscal Services from both Annual Financial Statments (Gok) and Finace Accounts (CAG, GoI).

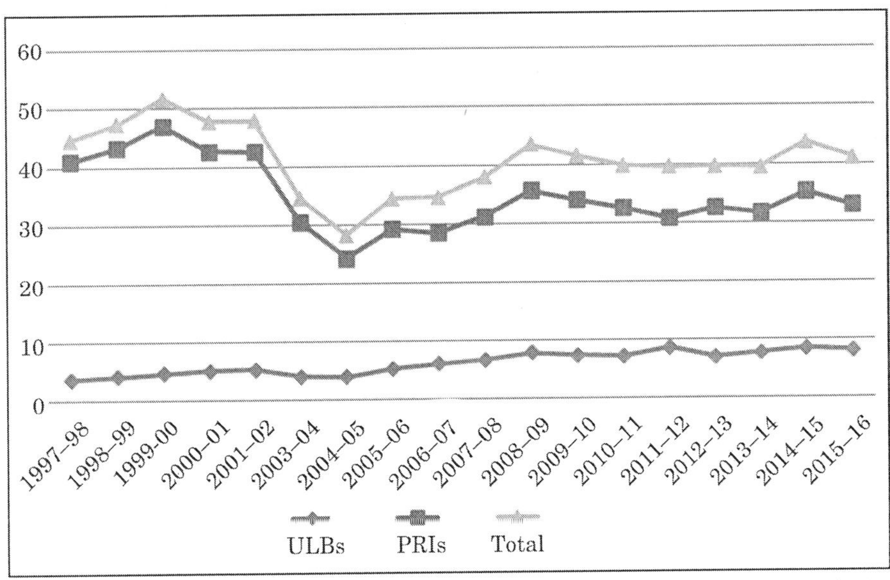

Fig. 8.3: Allocation to local bodies: Share in NLNORR.

fluctuations are more in the case of PRIs and the ULBs continue to have a steady increase albeit a much smaller share as compared to the PRIs. Yet another important observation from the trends is that the transfers effected to the local bodies do not seem to be in total compliance with the recommendations of State Finance Commissions constituted from time to time. For instance, transfers observed during 2011–12 to

20115–16, the period applicable for Third State Finance Commission, have exceeded the recommended level of 33 percent. Similar trends prevailed for the earlier periods too. These trends by and large account for adhocism in the transfers affected to the local bodies albeit enhanced allocations over time and is an important matter of policy concern from the point of view of assured and predictable support received by the local bodies in the discharge of their development function.

It is also important to examine the trends in the share of allocation to the local bodies in the state's total expenditure. The long-run trends reveal a clear decline as depicted in Fig. 8.4 from 1998–99 till 2004–05 after which it increased until 2008–09 followed by a decline that continued till the end of the reference period. This decline is more for PRIs than ULBs as the share of ULBs continued to increase. The share of the budget allocation to the local bodies in state's total expenditure well above 25 percent in late nineties had dropped to 20 percent in 2004-05, the increase in the subsequent period however never reached the level prevailing in late nineties.

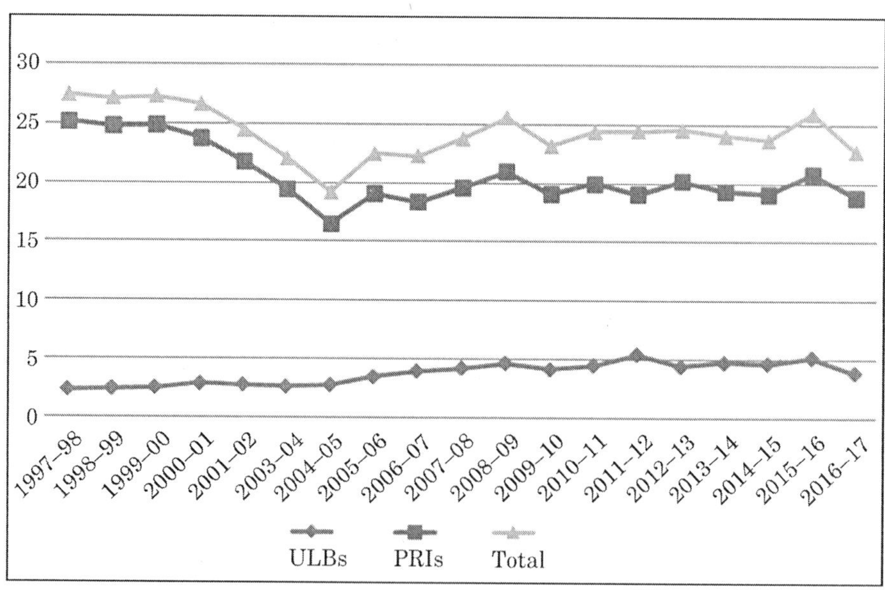

Fig. 8.4: Allocation to local bodies: Share in total expenditure.

8.5. ALLOCATION TO PRIS BY LEVELS

Distribution of the resources allocated to the three tiers of local bodies *i.e.,* Zilla Panchayat (ZP), Taluk Panchayat (TP) and Grama Panchayat (GP) are presented in Table 8.3 and Fig. 8.5. The largest share accrues to the TPs followed by the ZPs and lastly the GPs. While the share of the former two tiers has declined during the reference period that of the third tier *i.e.,* GPs has increased significantly from 4.84 percent in 2003–04 to 16.06 percent in 2016–17. However, ZPs and TPs together constituted over 80 percent share throughout the reference period.

Table 8.3: Transfers to local bodies by each level.

Year	***Total allocation in Rs. in crore***				***Share of total allocation (in %)***		
	ZP	***TP***	***GP***	***Total***	***ZP***	***TP***	***GP***
2004–05	1784	2701	409	4893	36.45	55.19	8.36
2007–08	3422	4848	1355	9625	35.55	50.37	14.08
2010–11	5227	7023	1215	13465	38.82	52.16	9.02
2013–14	9141	11476	1930	22547	40.54	50.90	8.56
2015–16	9568	14002	3006	26576	36.00	52.69	11.31
2016–17	9633	15178	4748	29558	32.59	51.35	16.06

Source: Government of Karnataka, Link documents: Various years.

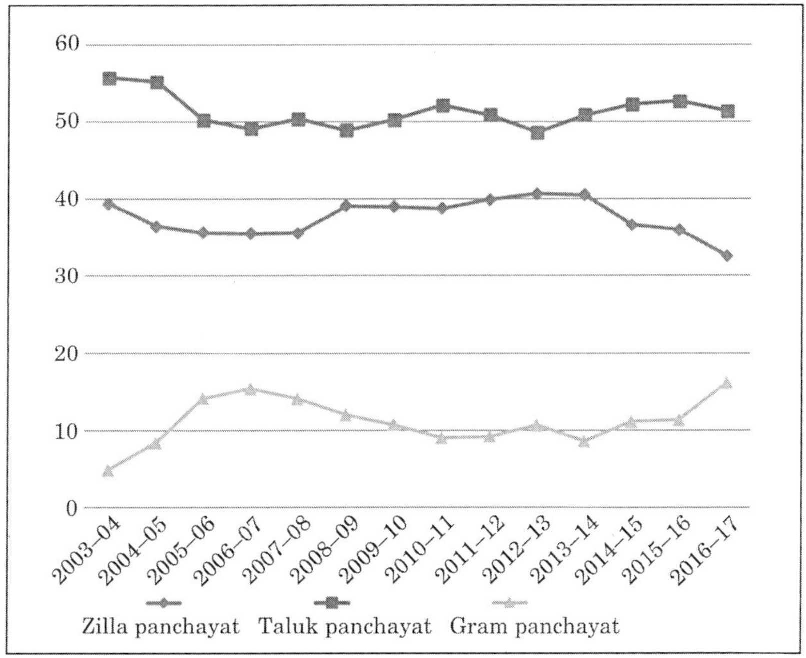

Fig. 8.5: Percentage share of ZPs, TPs, and GPs in total allocation to PRIs.

8.6. DISTRICT SECTOR PLAN OUTLAY IN THE STATE'S PLAN OUTLAY

Devolution of plan funds to the rural local bodies as a percentage of the state's total plan outlay has reduced by more than half from 34.85 percent in 1991–92 to 15.43 percent in 2015–16. This decline has occurred both in the state plan outlay and also the allocations under central schemes. While that of state's plan outlay has declined from 18.43 to 14.68 percent that of centrally sponsored schemes has declined in a much more significantly from 16.42 percent to 1.2 percent. The decline has been very sharp for both state plan and central plan between 2002–03 to 2004–05 and 2008–09 onwards. The state plan has more or less supplemented the significant central plan support that has occurred after 2014–15. Two key issues that concern the rural local bodies development relates to, first a significant decline in the support to the development spending, which is a serious of concern as the dependence of the local bodies on higher levels of government is high due to very small size of their own resources. Secondly, the plan funding support is not steady and is subjected to considerable variations depending on the state's fiscal position. This leads to unpredictability of funding support and thus hamper developmental activities in a significant manner (Fig. 8.6).

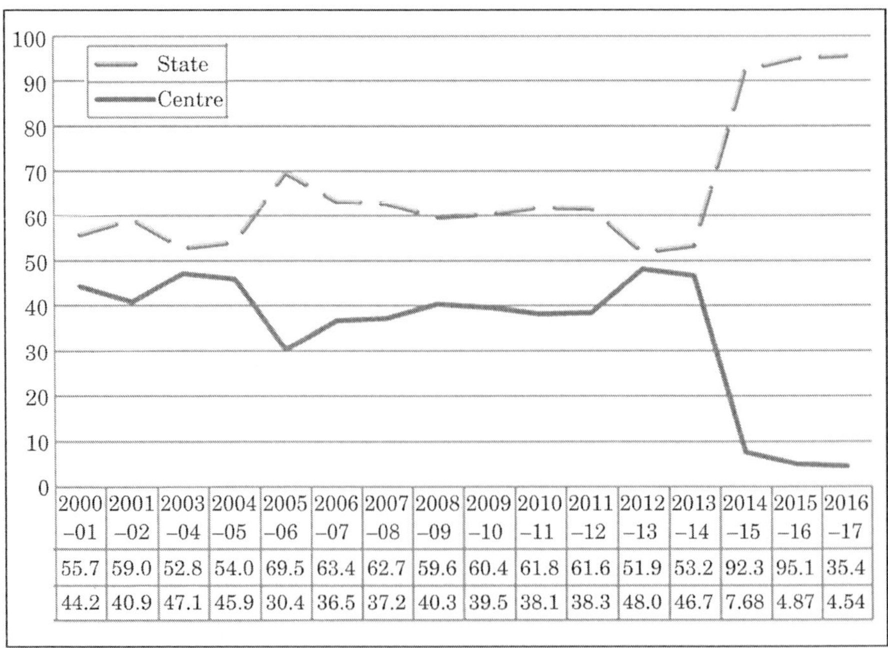

2000–01	2001–02	2003–04	2004–05	2005–06	2006–07	2007–08	2008–09	2009–10	2010–11	2011–12	2012–13	2013–14	2014–15	2015–16	2016–17
55.7	59.0	52.8	54.0	69.5	63.4	62.7	59.6	60.4	61.8	61.6	51.9	53.2	92.3	95.1	35.4
44.2	40.9	47.1	45.9	30.4	36.5	37.2	40.3	39.5	38.1	38.3	48.0	46.7	7.68	4.87	4.54

Fig. 8.6: Percentage share if state and centre in the total allocation to PRIs.

8.7. PLAN AND NON-PLAN ALLOCATION

The plan and non-plan breakup of the resources allocated to the PRIs (Table 8.4) reveals that plan has had a larger increase and thus has an increased share in the total.

Table 8.4: Plan and non-plan allocation to PRIs.

Year	*Allocation in Rs. crore*			*% Share of allocation*	
	Plan	*Non-plan*	*Total*	*Plan*	*Non-plan*
2004–05	1425	3468	4893	29.13	70.87
2007–08	3571	6054	9625	37.10	62.90
2010–11	4870	8595	13465	36.17	63.83
2013–14	8730	13817	22547	38.72	61.28
2015–16	11328	15248	26576	42.62	57.38
2016–17	12513	17046	29558	42.33	57.67

Source: GoK, Link documents: Various years.

However, when one analyses the PRI plan outlay share in the state's plan outlay it can be observed that (Table 8.5 and Fig. 8.7) it has declined from a little over 25 percent in 1993–94 to a little less than 15 percent. The recent decrease is largely on account of the central plan schemes.

Per capita transfers to local bodies are depicted in Fig. 8.8 which reveals that there is a fivefold increase in the transfers affected to the local bodies in Karnataka.

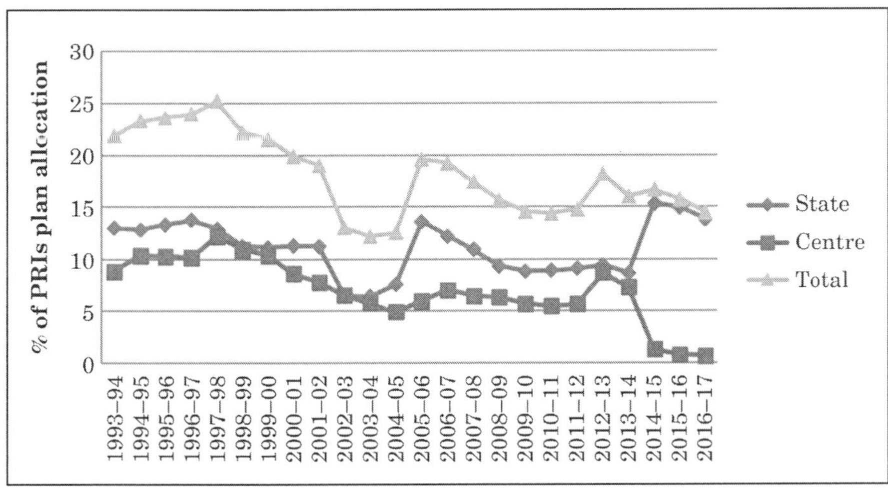

Fig. 8.7: Percentage share of PRIs plan outlay to the total state plan outlay.

Table 8.5: Percentage share of state and centre in the total plan outlay to PRIs.

Year	*State*	*Centre*
1994–95	55.29	44.71
1997–98	51.55	48.45
2000–01	56.69	43.31
2004–05	60.73	39.27
2007–08	62.76	37.24
2010–11	61.81	38.19
2013–14	54.27	45.73
2015–16	95.13	4.87

Source: Economic survey of Karnataka (2016–17).

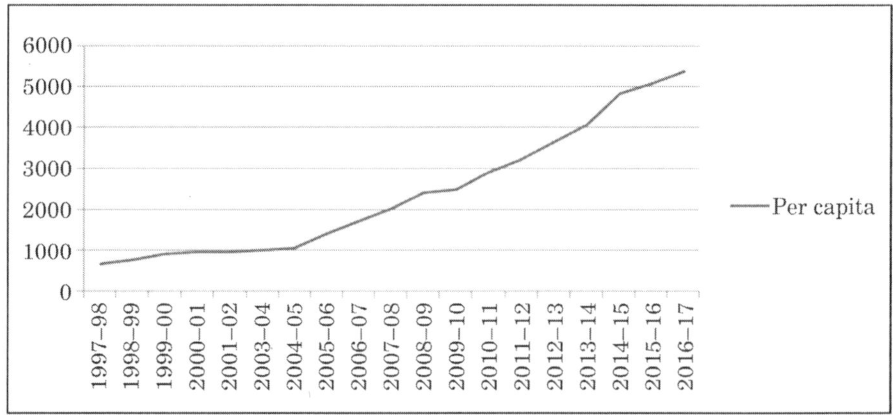

Fig. 8.8: Per capita transfers to the local bodies.

8.8. STATE FINANCE COMMISSIONS' RECOMMENDATIONS *VIS-À-VIS* ACTUAL ALLOCATION OF FUNDS

As per the Karnataka Panchayat Act state government has to constitute a State Finance Commission once in five years to make recommendations on the sharing of proceeds of taxes between the state and the local bodies, grants to be given from the State's Consolidated Fund and the share of Urban and Rural local bodies. Karnataka has appointed four SFC s till date with the first SFC award covering the period 1997–98 to 2001–02; second SFC award covering 2006–07 to 2010–11 and third SFC award covering 2010–11 to 2015–16. While the first two commissions have used NLGORR the third one has used NLNORR. Details of the SFC recommendations *vis-à-vis* the actual devolution by each of the SFC periods are presented in Table 8.6 and Figs. 8.9 to 8.10. It can be

Table 8.6: SFC recommendations *vis-a vis* actual transfers (Rs. crore).

Year	*Actual transfers to local bodies*			*Allocation recommended by SFC*			*Difference b/w actual and SFC allocation*		
	ULBs	*PRIs*	*Total*	*ULBs*	*PRIs*	*Total*	*ULBs*	*PRIs*	*Total*
First State Finance Commission									
1997–98	275	3046	3321	415	2349	2763	–140	697	558
1998–99	332	3520	3853	454	2574	3029	–122	946	824
1999–00	416	4232	4648	505	2863	3368	–89	1369	1280
2000–01	531	4432	4964	578	3275	3853	–47	1157	1111
2001–02	564	4507	5071	591	3350	3941	–27	1157	1130
Second State Finance Commission									
2006–07	1639	7712	9351	2192	8768	10960	–553	–1056	–1609
2007–08	1926	9024	10950	2348	9390	11738	–422	–366	–788
2008–09	2374	10802	13176	2464	9857	12322	–90	945	854
2009–10	2474	11374	13848	2713	10852	13565	–239	522	283
2010–11	2978	13465	16443	3347	13386	16733	–369	79	–290
Third State Finance Commission									
2011–12	4344	15375	19719	4992	11483	16475	–648	3892	3244
2012–13	4018	18531	22550	5690	13087	18777	–1672	5444	3773
2013–14	5020	20510	25531	6478	14898	21376	–1458	5612	4155
2014–15	6011	24988	30999	7089	16305	23395	–1078	8683	7604
2015–16	6549	26576	33125	8069	18559	26628	–1520	8017	6497

Source: GoK, Finance Department.

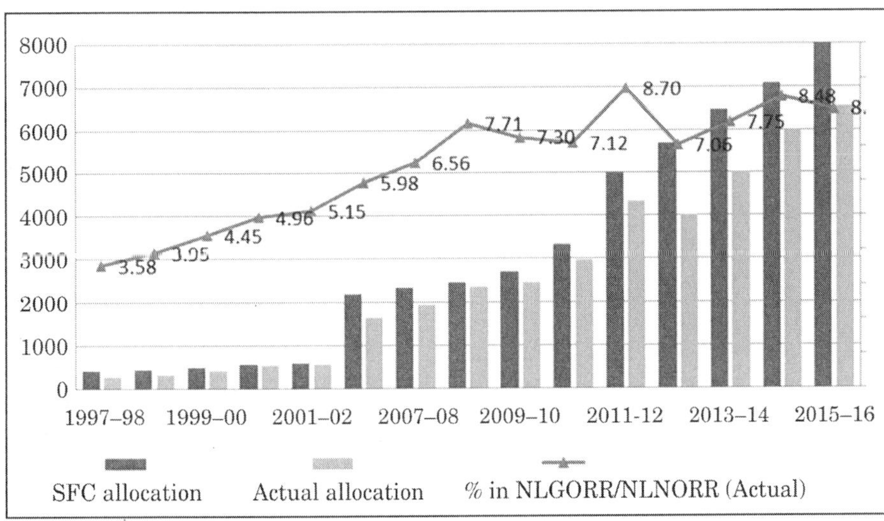

Fig. 8.9: State Finance Commissions' recommendations and actual allocation to ULBs (Rs. in Crores).

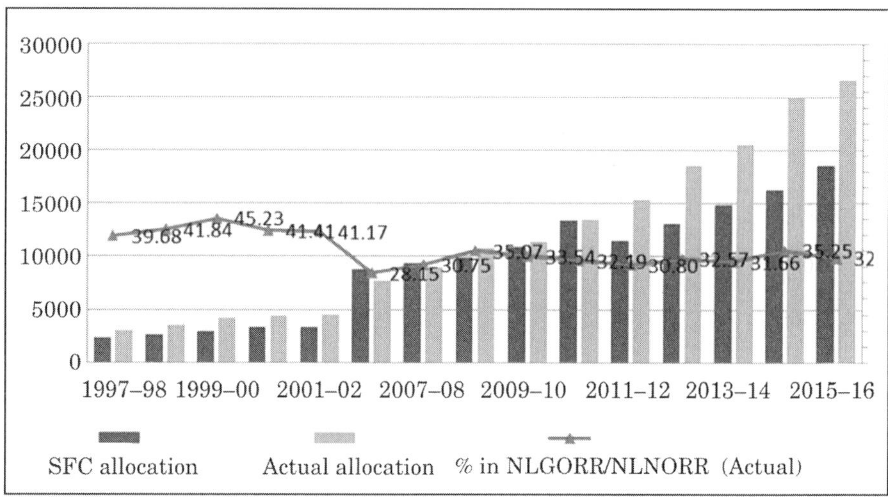

Fig. 8.10: State Finance Commissions' recommendations and actual allocation for PRIs (Rs. in Crores).

observed that by and large there has been considerable deviation between the SFC recommendations and the actual assignment to the local bodies, there has been however larger flow of resources as compared to the recommended level.

While the urban local bodies have largely had an under funding thus having lesser resource availability as opposed to the recommended level, PRIs have had larger absolute allocations during most of the years with the exception of two years during the second SFC period. An important aspect to be remembered is that as discussed earlier urban development is supported by the state government by way of funds provided to various parastatals. PRIs' support is on the contrary largely limited to the SFC funds. Figs. 8.9 to 8.11 also depict the percent share of allocations to ULBs, PRIs and total to the respective base used by the various SFCs *i.e.*, NLNGORR in the case of first two SFCs and NLNORR in the case of third SFC. While the recommended share to the urban local bodies has increased over each SFC the recommended share has not been assigned. Rural local bodies share on the contrary has declined from 30.6 percent in first SFC to 32 in second and 23 percent in the third SFC.

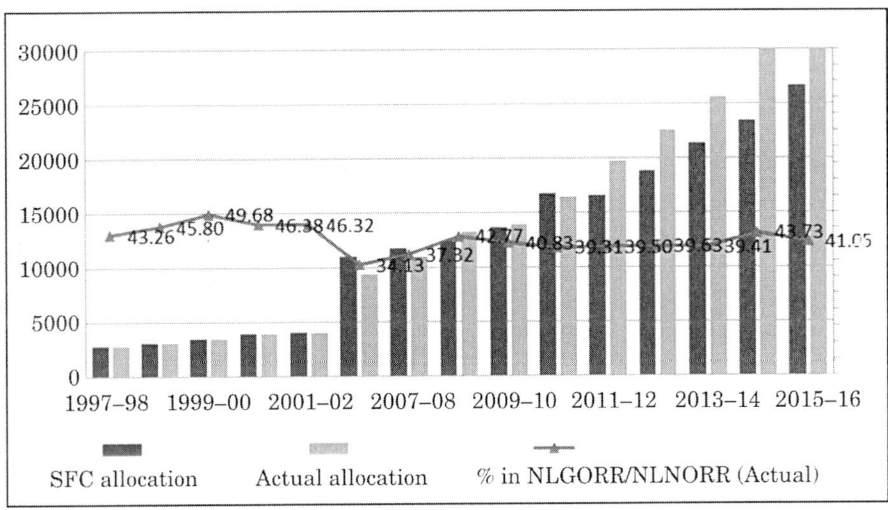

Fig. 8.11: State Finance Commissions' recommendations and actual allocation for LBs (Rs. in Crores).

8.9. CONCLUDING OBSERVATIONS

Devolution to local bodies is observed to be highly vulnerable to State's overall fiscal position creating uncertainty in the flow of funds. This phenomenon is more predominant for the PRIs as the share of ULBs is observed to be by and large on the increase albeit it's smaller share in total. This is more with reference to plan/development funding than the non-plan funding which largely is towards salary. Uncertainty/ unpredictability of fund support and hamper the developmental activities of the local bodies.

There has been a sharp decline in plan funding from the state's plan outlay from both the state and center sources reiterating the fact that while development funding is receiving a setback, the salary component continues to be on the rise. It remains a debatable issue if salary expenditure has to be relegated to secondary importance, especially with reference to services such as health and education wherein the services of doctors and teachers are the most important inputs in the service delivery. The support provided by the Centre and states are not complementing each other rather they are substituting for one another, which once again raises the issue of predictability of assured funding.

By and large there has been considerable deviation between the SFC recommendations and the actual assignment to the local bodies, there has been however larger flow of resources as compared to the recommended level. While the urban local bodies have largely had an underfunding thus having lesser resource availability as opposed to the recommended level, PRIs have had larger absolute allocations during most of the years with the exception of two years during the second SFC period. An important aspect to be remembered is that urban development is supported by the state government by way of funds provided to various parastatals. PRIs' support is on the contrary largely limited to the SFC funds.

There is however, need to considerably improve the quality of support rendered to the local bodies. The study's results have shown that while there has been an increase occurring overtime, there are uncertainties prevailing. This is in view of the fact that whenever the state has revenue shortfall or fiscal adversity, there has been a reduction in the transfers. In addition, the share of plan funding to the local bodies in the total state plan outlay has declined in a significant manner implying that the development funding to the local bodies has suffered a decline. The salary component has a huge share although on a marginal decline. The support extended by the state also is considerably influenced by the central support, any increase in the central support is marked by a reduction in state support and *vice versa*. This can amount to considerable amount of unpredictability and hamper developmental activities of the local bodies. Studies have also highlighted considerable regional differences in per capita support to the local bodies which unfortunately is adversely affecting the backward districts. Irrespective of the factors leading to such developments, be it poor absorptive capacity or utilization, the overall development of the state in general and backward regions in particular would pose serious concerns.

Most importantly, it is necessary that the local bodies tone up their own revenue generation in a significant manner.

REFERENCES

Gayithri, K. 2017, Karnataka State fiscal transfers to local bodies: The current status and the state's fiscal capacity, an unpublished report submitted to the Fourth State Finance Commission, Government of Karnataka.

Government of Karnataka, 2016, Economic Survey of Karnataka (2015-16) Planning, Programme monitoring and Statistics Department, Bengaluru.

Government of Karnataka, 2016, Accounts at a glance, 1960-2015, Finance Department, Bengaluru.

Government of Karnataka, 2016, Accounts Reckoner, 2007-2015, Finance Department, Bengaluru.

Government of India (Various Years), State Finance Accounts, Comptroller and Auditor General of India, New Delhi.

Rao, Govinda, M, T.R.Raghunandan, Manish Gupta, Polly Datta, Pratap Ranjan, Jena and H.K.Amarnath, 2011, Fiscal Decentralization to Rural Local Governments in India: Selected Issues and Reform Options, National Institute of Public Finance and Policy (Report of the Study Sponsored by Ministry of Panchayath Raj, GoI), New Delhi.

The World Bank, 2004, India: Fiscal decentralisation to rural local governments, Washington, D.C

9

Decentralized Governance Process and Its Implications for Development: The Case of Karnataka

PROF. N. SIVANNA[10]*

ABSTRACT

Decentralized governance in India has effectively begun with the 73rd Amendment to the Constitution, which opened a new era in the history of Panchayati Raj. Set in this context, this paper attempts to look at the journey of decentralization in the state of Karnataka over the last two decades. The analysis has been carried out keeping in view of the processes involved in decentralizing the power and authority and their implications on the development outcomes. It reveals that the Karnataka state has been progressive in empowering the three-tier panchayats and has been steadily evolving by constant efforts to enable Panchayats to function as 'institutions of self-government' and the instruments of rural development. More and more government programmes and schemes are implemented through Panchayats with a clear budgetary allocation for district sector to expedite the development process. In spite of the well institutionalised processes of decentralized governance, there are certain structural and social constraints that prevent Panchayats from delivering the development outcomes at the local level.

9.1. INTRODUCTION

Decentralisation is a process of governing away from the centre. Globally the turn towards decentralising power and authority has evolved

[10] Chief Executive Officer, Karnataka Panchayat Parishad, Bengaluru and Hon. Professor, Karnataka State Rural Development and Panchayat Raj University, Gadag, Karnataka

*Corresponding author: E-mail: sivanna55.n@gmail.com

strongly since early 1990s. Even before this period, there were experiments of decentralised reforms in many countries. However, the push for decentralisation reforms has gained prominence with the emergence of globalization and liberalisation of the economy. In the context of developed nations, the decentralisation reforms aimed at institutional, organisational restructuring of the central governments. Whereas in developing countries of Africa, Latin America and Asia region, the objectives of decentralisation have been to improve the quality of governance through accountability and transparency and to enhance the efficacy of delivery of public services.

The effective participation of people in local decision-making process and development is critical in improving the delivery of public goods and services. A decade ago, estimates of number of decentralization experiments ranged from 80 percent of the World's countries to effectively all of them (Manor, 1999). The goals of decentralisation can be broadly categorised into administrative (deconcentration/delegation), fiscal (economic/market/privatisation) and political (devolution) dimensions. Among these, devolution is considered as the most appropriate form as it transfers legislative, executive and judicial responsibilities to the local governments on the basis of the *principle of subsidiarity*.

Decentralized governance can be understood as "the restructuring of authority so that there is a system of co-responsibility between institutions of governance at the central, regional and local levels according to the principle of subsidiarity (UNDP, 1997: 4)". It is more of a sharing responsibilities between different tiers of government rather than regulating lower level of governments by its higher counterparts. The inherent potentials of decentralization have attracted the national governments to opt for the decentralized reforms apart from its popularity.

The expected benefits of decentralized measures are accountability of the government, efficiency in the delivery of public services and goods, involving people in the decision-making process. Engaging people is critical as "participation and decentralisation are considered to have a complementary relationship in that a good decentralisation scheme requires participation of some kind to ensure that the local government is responsive to local needs (John and Chathukulam, 2015: 20)".

9.2. DECENTRALIZATION IN INDIA

Panchayats in India have been institutionalised through 73rd Constitutional Amendment Act (hereafter CAA) of 1992 after the recommendations of various committees. The objectives of democratic decentralization are:

- To deepen the local democracy
- To engage people in decision-making, especially disadvantaged sections (Women, Scheduled Castes and Scheduled Tribes)
- To improve the delivery of local public goods.

The twin objectives of 73rd CAA is to ensure local 'economic development' and 'social justice' through Panchayati Raj Institutions (hereafter PRIs). The institutional journey of PRIs from 1992–2017 in India represents one of the most fascinating and challenging aspects of decentralized governance and its implications on delivering the developmental outcomes. Karnataka is one of the few states apart from Rajasthan (1959), Andhra Pradesh (The Andhra Pradesh Grama Panchayats Act, 1964) and Maharashtra (Bombay Village Panchayats Act, 1958) where the decentralization reform has started even much before the 73rd CAA. In particular, 'The Karnataka Zilla Parishads, Taluk Panchayat Samithis, Mandal Panchayats and Nyaya Panchayats Act, 1983' had ushered a radical beginning of decentralized governance in the country. The Act was passed on the basis of Ashok Mehta Committee recommendations. One of the unique features of this Act is reservation of seats for Women, SC and STs which is seen as one of the steps to involve people in the decision-making process, who are traditionally excluded in power relationships. With this backdrop, the paper attempts to explore Karnataka State's decentralization experience with reference to post-73rd CAA phase. It specifically deals with the functioning of PRIs, their role in enabling political inclusion and rural development.

9.3. KARNATAKA GRAMA SWARAJ AND PANCHAYAT RAJ ACT 1993

In Karnataka there were efforts to redesign PRIs, by the then new government, and this was done keeping in view the broad framework of the 73rd Amendment. It is significant to note that Karnataka was the first State to pass a new legislation in 1993, namely, The Karnataka Panchayat Raj Act, 1993, which is now rechristened as 'The Karnataka Gram Swaraj and Panchayat Raj Act, 1993'. The new Act provides for a three-tier structure of Panchayat Raj with Zilla Panchayats (at the district level) Taluk Panchayats (at the Taluk level or Intermediate level) and Grama Panchayats (at the village level). The Bill for constituting

Panchayats, which was introduced on 1st April 1993, came into force from May 18, 1993.

All the three Panchayats are directly elected bodies. To facilitate and motivate people's participation in governance and planning, the recently amended Act provides for the constitution of 'Habitation Sabha', Ward Sabha' and 'Grama Sabha', termed them as "Units of Grama Swaraj", convened twice in a year, with the functions of mobilising voluntary labour and contributions, identifying beneficiaries for the development schemes and rendering assistance in the implementation of programmes/ schemes pertaining to the village. In its preamble the 1993 Act resolves for promoting greater participation of the people and ensuring more effective implementation of rural development programmes. It also recognises Panchayats as 'Units of Local-Self Government'. Further, as stated in the Annual Report of the Department of Rural Development and Panchayat Raj, the vision of the department lies in promoting sustainable and inclusive growth of overall rural development along with empowerment of PRIs.

One of the salient features of 1993 Act, compared to previous Acts, is that it has provided reservation not only to membership seats but also to executive positions - adhyaksha and upadhyakshas. It has provided reservation to women (fifty percent in each category of seats), backward classes (one-third) and to Scheduled Castes and Scheduled Tribes (with a minimum of 18 percent) in proportion to their population. One fifth of the Grama Panchayat adhyakshas are represented in the Taluk Panchayats by annual rotation and the adhyakshas of the Taluk Panchayats in the Zilla Panchayats. In conformity with the Eleventh schedule of the Constitution, the 1993 Act has entrusted a wide range of functions (Schedules I, II and III) to Panchayats. To carry out these functions, the Grama Panchayat receives at present Rs. Ten lakh as annual grant (Grama Panchayats with more than 8000 population receive Rs. Ten lakhs, and those with less than 8000 population Rs. Eight lakhs) and has powers to levy tax on buildings and lands, levy water rate, tax on entertainment, vehicles, advertisement and hoarding, market fee, fee on bus stands and on grazing cattle. Both Taluk Panchayats and Zilla Panchayats are allowed to charge fee on their property used by others and they do not have powers to levy taxes. In addition, both Grama Panchayats and Taluk Panchayats get proceeds from cess on land revenue and surcharge on stamp duty levied by the State Government respectively. Except for these, the Panchayats have to depend solely on the resources transferred from the Government.

9.4. BRIEF PROFILE OF PRIS IN KARNATAKA

Karnataka comprises 60242 Grama Panchayats, 176 Taluk Panchayats and 30 Zilla Panchayats. It has to its credit for entrusting major responsibilities and devolving all the 29 functions (a first State to do so in the country as a whole) as enlisted under the Eleventh Schedule of the Constitution 73rd Amendment. In recent years, the Karnataka Government has taken a number of steps to strengthen the Panchayats to improve rural decentralisation governance. Entrusting the responsibility of plan formulation and implementation to the panchayats by transferring the functions, functionaries and finances is one of the administrative innovations. The Rural Development and Panchayat Raj Department (RDPRD) has issued guidelines to prepare district perspective plans; introduction of social auditing in the form of *Jamabandi* to ensure transparency in the system. The Government of Karnataka has evolved a detailed range of 'Activity Mapping' for all the three Panchayats. Broadly, the activity mapping visualises both Zilla Panchayats and Taluk Panchayats as planners, facilitators and owners of common executive machinery, Grama Panchayats as the cutting edge of local service provision, and Grama Sabha and Ward Sabhas as instruments of downward accountability. The new activity mapping framework devolving functions has to be accompanied by adequate devolution of finances and functionaries.

It is significant to note that the Panchayat Raj Act of 1993 has undergone several changes since its inception. The Government of Karnataka has made significant Amendments to 1993 Act on the basis of recommendations made by various committees starting from 1995. Till now, the Act has been amended twenty times during the period from 1993 to 2015. In particularly, the Amendments made in 2010 are critical from the viewpoint of building the institutional capacities of the Panchayats. Some of the important Amendments are instituting a development officer [Panchayat Development Officer (PDO) Amending Act 24 of 2010] exclusively for the Grama Panchayats, creating Panchayat Ombudsman (Amending Act 34 of 2011) and fifty percent reservation of seats for Women (Amending Act 17 of 2015). The reservation of half of the seats to Women in Panchayats is a strong precursor of gendered governance to enable *political equality*. Creation of Ombudsman for Panchayats is one of the ways to make the local governments accountable and transparent to the needs of citizens.

The recent Amending Act 44 of 2015 is one of the most comprehensive Amendments. It consists of a broad template for the decentralised governance through Panchayats to enable *Gram Swaraj*. It is very ambitious in nature yet it is the need of hour. Some of the important provisions in this Amendment are as (i) Constitution of Habitation and Habitation Sabha, (ii) Providing Staff to the Panchayats, (iii) Responsibility Map, (iv) Directive Principles of Panchayat Policy (DPPP), (v) Preparation of vision plan by GP based on the "priority ranking" method, (vi) Consolidation of GP plans by the Taluk Planning and Development Committee (TPDC), (vii) Conduct, duties and responsibilities of Panchayats Elected Members, (viii) Establishing Commissioner rate of Panchayati Raj, (ix) Karnataka Panchayat Administrative Service (KPAS), (x) Karnataka State Decentralized Planning and Development Committeem (xi) Grievance redressal authority and (xii) Revenue generation and mobilising capacity of GPs.

By enacting these Amendments to the Panchayat Raj Act, Karnataka has become the first State in the country to delineate Directive Principles of Panchayat Policy (hereafter DPPP) in line with that Directive Principles of State Policy (hereafter DPSP) of the Indian Constitution. It also widened the Constitutional horizon of the Panchayats to make integral part and parcel of the federal structure of governance. It can be understood as DPSP are fundamental to the *governance* of the country DPPP are fundamental to the *local governance*. It is significant to note here that the amended Act while making provision for constituting 'Habitation Sabhas', in addition to Ward Sabhas and Gram Sabhas and regarding these sabhas as "*Units of Gram Swaraj*", is almost realising the Mahatma Gandhi's dream of 'Gram Swaraj'. In moving these Amendments, the then Chief Minister of Karnataka, Sri. Siddaramaiah, observed in his Budget Speech 2014–15 (Para, 277) that *"It is our prime duty to make the "Gram Swarajya" dream of Mahatma Gandhi into a reality".*

9.5. GENDER AND SOCIAL COMPOSITION OF ELECTED REPRESENTATIVES OF PANCHAYATS IN KARNATAKA

More than one lakh members are representing their constituencies in the Panchayats of Karnataka- 1083 Members in Zilla Panchayats; 3903 in Taluk Panchayats and 96,968 members in Grama Panchayats. Of the total, 50.05 percent of the members are women, slightly more than the assigned quota of fifty percent, Scheduled Castes 19.98 percent, followed by Scheduled Tribes with 10.94 percent, other backward classes 18.07 percent and members from general category 51.01 percent. In terms of membership the women members almost equal representation along with men members. Tables 9.1 and 9.2 illustrate the social composition of Panchayats in Karnataka,

Table 9.1: Details of membership in PRIs in Karnataka.

Sl. no	*Panchayat tiers*	*Total members*	*Women*	*SCs*	*STs*	*OBCs*	*General*
1.	Zilla Panchayats	1083	548	212	95	223	553
2.	Taluk Panchayats	3903	1998	771	387	744	2001
3.	Grama panchayats	96,968	48484	19393	10666	17454	49455
4.	Total	101954	51030	20376	11148	18421	52009
5.	Percentage to the total	100	50.05	19.98	10.94	18.07	51.01

Source: RDPRD, Government of Karnataka.

Table 9.2: Panchayat Elected Women Representatives (PWERs) in India and Karnataka.

	Total no. of Panchayat Elected Representatives	*Total no. of Women Elected Representatives*	*% of Women Elected Representatives*
India	2916961	1345990	46.14
Karnataka	95307	50892	53.4

***Source*:** Lok Sabha starred question no. 122, Ministry of Panchayati Raj, GoI, 2016.

The data in Table 9.2 and Fig. 9.1 indicate the gradual increase of women's entry in PRIs. Karnataka has been witnessing continuous growth in the number of women entrants into the Panchayats and ahead

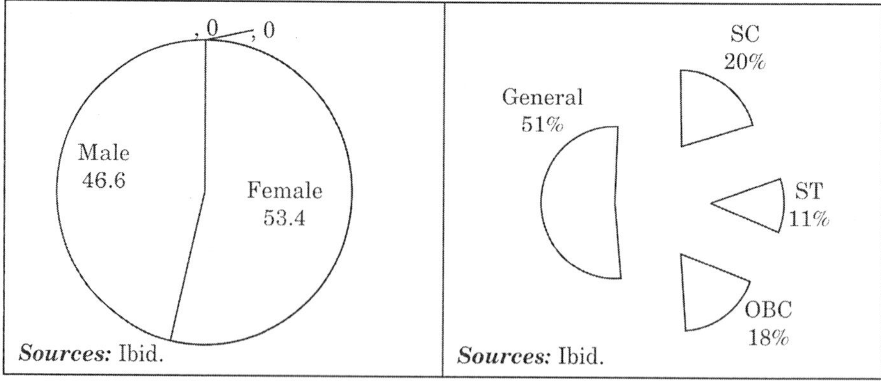

Fig. 9.1: Gender and social composition of Panchayat elected members in Karnataka.

of many other states in empowering women at the grassroots. It also reveals a fact that the proportion of Panchayat elected members, especially SCs/STs is more than the population percent of the Karnataka State. As per the Census 2011, Karnataka State has 17.5 percent of SCs and 6.95 percent of STs.

9.6. DECENTRALIZED GOVERNANCE AND DEVELOPMENT: AN ANALYTICAL FRAMEWORK

Among the important dimensions of political/administrative decentralization is the devolution. Devolution is considered as a genuine form of decentralization as it devolves the authority and decision-making powers to the local government institutions. It also aims to empower the local government institutions by granting autonomy in policy making and its implementation. Devolution is a political act. It facilitates the participation of politically excluded communities in the decision-making process by creating necessary institutional structures. It aims to empower citizens through participation in democratic deliberation and discussion to have informed choices on the matters pertaining to their daily lives. In the forthcoming analysis, we undertake devolution as an indicator of political/administrative decentralization in explaining its implications for the development and public services delivery.

Decentralized governance is one of the potential ways to ensure development by enabling the people's participation in the conduct of individual and community affairs. The development is an outcome of the processes such as citizen's participation in the governance. Citizens especially the disadvantaged sections will be able to actively participate in the local governance only when there are enabling institutional arrangements and social environment. The following analytical framework (Fig. 9.2) has been used to understand the extent of decentralized governance processes in Karnataka State and their implications on the local development outcomes.

Decentralised governance and planning is crucial for the process of development. In the following discussion an attempt has been made to explore the working of decentralized governance system in the State of Karnataka and its implications on the developmental outcomes. Karnataka is one of the few States that allotted more than the stipulated percentage of budget funds to its PRIs of the plan grants for the year 2016–17, Zilla Panchayats have been allocated Rs. 5,412.79 Crore, followed by Rs. 4,316.67 Crore for Taluk Panchayats and Rs. 2,783.07

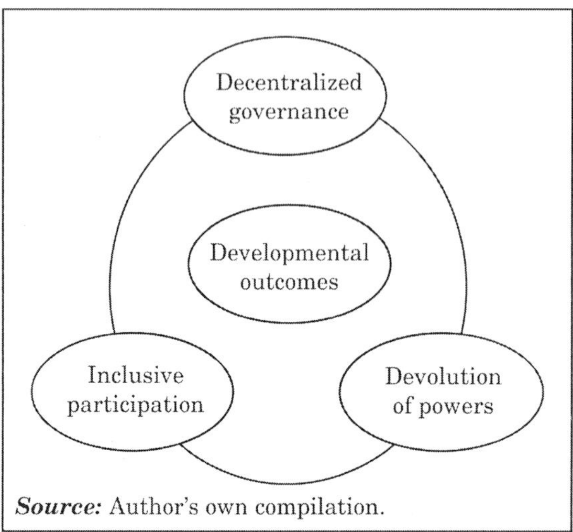

Fig. 9.2: Decentralized governance and development: Analytical framework.

Crore for Grama Panchayats in the State. Under the non-plan sector, Taluk Panchayats have been allocated Rs. 10,860.93 Crore, followed by Rs. 4,220.33 Crore allocated to Zilla Panchayats and Rs. 1,964.52 Crore for Grama Panchayats. However, Taluk Panchayats got a lion's share in the non-plan (mostly salary component) allocation followed by Zilla and Grama Panchayats. The recent Amendment Act (44 of 2015) provides for the Constitution of Karnataka State Decentralised Planning and Development Board to enable the State Government to formulate development plans and the Annual Economic Review to be presented along with the Budget Document to the State Planning Board. Section 309B of the Act delineates the provisions for Decentralised Planning for Panchayats:

1. Panchayats as institutions of self-government shall achieve all-round development coupled with social justice, empowered by total and simultaneous devolution of functions functionaries and funds to them Panchayats.
2. Development shall be planned from the grassroots level to assess determine and prioritize the needs of all sections of the people with emphasis on the interests of the vulnerable sections

The decentralised planning process as described in the plan documents begins with the determination of annual plan size at the state level, and allocation of funds to the district sector. The district sector allocation for various programmes is done in consultation with the Chief Executive Officer of each Zilla Panchayat, District Level Sectoral Officers and State level Department officers. After this, the data will be supplied to Finance Department to integrate the district sector data with the State and also to print budget link documents.

Based on the allocation, the action plans will be prepared by the Zilla Panchayat, Taluk Panchayat and Grama Panchayat and after its discussion and approval by the respective Standing Committees and General Body. With the consolidation and approval by the District Planning Committee, the draft district plan will be sent to Planning Department for the final approval. In the preparation of plans, the Ward Sabhas and Grama Sabhas play a crucial role and their recommendations and suggestions do figure in such action plans emphasising the fact that the plans so prepared are the by-product of people's wishes and demands. Thus, the entire planning process can be termed as 'participatory planning process'.

A close look at the sector-wise expenditure, incurred by the Zilla Panchayats in the initial years, shows that out of the total expenditure incurred on different sectors, expenditure on social infrastructure took the major share. On an average, 45.64 percent of the expenditure was incurred for promoting social sectors like education (within it the largest was on salary), nutrition, water supply and sanitation. This was true even at the state-level. Next in the priority in spending was on the rural development sector, which included expenditure on rural employment (JRY grant) and other special rural development programmes. On an average 21.24 percent of the total expenditure was incurred on this sector whereas, the expenditure on agriculture and allied activities accounted for 17.90 percent only. The last priority was the welfare of SCs and STs; only 7.31 percent of the total was spent towards this. Even at the state-level the expenditure incurred was nowhere near the desired expenditure of 20 percent (Sivanna, 1999: 41–42). The expenditure pattern of Grama Panchayats revealed that the major share of expenditure was on public development works (21.54 percent), public security works (24.45 percent) like purchase of street lights, civic amenities etc, (Ibid).

Significantly and interestingly similar scenario continues even now that sectors like social infrastructure, which includes allocation to education, and rural development, much of its share is taken by rural employment schemes such as MGNREGA, continue to be priority sectors in terms receiving allocations compared to other sectors (See Table 9.3).

Table 9.3: Sector-wise allocation of the district sector state plan funds during 2014–15 to 2016-17.

Sl. no.	*Sector*	*Annual plan (Rs. In lakh)*				
		2014–15	*2015–16*	*2016–17*	*Average for three years*	*In %*
1.	Rural development	278930	270229	290750	279969	24.42
2.	Social infrastructure	302598	342886	370548	338677	29.61
3.	Agriculture and allied activities	26381	26651	29464	27498	02.42
4.	Welfare of women and children, nutrition and disabled	154689	165171	172276	164045	14.33
5.	Rural housing	101999	102000	114700	106233	09.27
6.	Public health and Family welfare	65838	71701	72305	69948	06.13
7.	Welfare of SCs, STs, OBCs and minorities	76023	86455	120962	94480	08.25
8.	Rural water supply	23652	51488	62586	45908	04.03
9.	Roads and bridges	15920	13935	15205	15020	01.33
10.	Village and small scale industries, labour, cooperation and handlooms and textiles	1885	2079	2255	2073	00.19
11.	Science and technology	157	176	202	178	00.02
	Total	1048072	1132771	1251253	1144032	100.00

Source: Economic survey 2016–17, Department of Planning, Programme Monitoring and Statistics, Government of Karnataka.

Social infrastructure and rural development received 29.61 percent and 24.42 percent respectively compared to other sectors and there has been an increasing trend over the years both in terms of overall allocation and percentage terms. As referred to, rural employment, aiming at providing employment opportunities to rural people, has a major share in the total allocation made to rural development in particular and to other sectors in general. It can also be seen that there is a perceptible increase in the allocation made to these sectors across the years. As per the budgetary allocations (for the period 2017–18) to different development sectors- Zilla Panchayats, Taluk Panchayats and Grama Panchayats-wise-allocation to general education is to the tune of 42.82 percent, shared by both Zilla and Taluk Panchayats followed by allocation to other rural development programmes (13.98 percent), welfare of SCs/ STs/OBCs (8.85 percent) and rural employment (MGNREGA grant) 5.43 percent, a substantial cut compared to previous years allocation and these have an edge over other sectors like water supply and sanitation

(4.95 percent) and housing (4.59 percent). This clearly indicates the importance that is being given to social and rural development sectors. Seen in terms of Panchayat–wise allocation, Zilla Panchayats receives 31.56 percent (including NREGA 5.43 percent), Taluk Panchayats 49.49. In Karnataka all these programmes are being implemented by the Rural Development and Panchayat Raj Department (RDPRD).

9.7. EFFICACY OF GRAMA SABHA- PEOPLE'S PARTICIPATION IN DEVELOPMENT

Grama Sabha and Ward Sabha are considered as soul of the Panchayati Raj system. They are the only available platforms to exercise direct democracy in our representative system of democracy. The broader vision is to transform representative to participatory democracy. It is the place to deliberate, discuss the local development issues. In the context of decentralised planning, it is the place where prioritisation takes place based on local people's concerns, demands and needs. Grama Sabha is a decision-making body and the Panchayat has to ensure that the decisions taken in the Grama Sabha should reflect in the local plan preparation and the same is being implemented. However, it has been observed that

"Most of the Panchayats have failed to execute the decisions taken of the Grama Sabha. However the recent experience reveals that there is a growing awareness among the rural people about the significance of Grama Sabha functions. For example the states like Karnataka, Kerala, Tamil Nadu, Rajasthan and Sikkim have successfully implementing the decisions of Grama Sabha (Dwarakanath, 2013: 6)".

There is a general critique about the poor participation of people in the discussion and decision-making process *via* Grama Sabha is prevalent not only in Karnataka but also throughout the country. Grama Sabhas have been increasingly reduced to an identification/selection of beneficiaries for the State and Union Government schemes. Voices of Women, SCs/STs have not been given much importance in the meetings of Grama Sabha. The Table 9.4 illustrates the rate of people's participation in Grama Sabha in Karnataka State.

The Table 9.4 provides glimpses of the extent of people's participation in the Grama Sabha meetings. As per the Panchayat Act, 2015, 1/10 percent of the total electorates or 100 is the minimum quorum required to conduct Grama Sabha meetings. On an average only 39 (minimum)

Table 9.4: People's participation in Grama Sabha.

Taluk	*Total number in electoral rolls*	*Total number on rolls attended the "Grama Sabha" in the project period*						
		2006–07	*2007–08*	*2008–09*	*2009–10*	*2010–11*	*Project average*	*Per-cent*
Basavakalyan	58675	1301	1123	1131	894	1599	1210	2.06
Deodurga	46639	810	1897	1073	1152	1080	1202	2.57
Gubbi	57537	882	1205	1275	1063	1606	1206	2.09
Kudligi	47926	773	1129	1019	1079	1643	1129	2.35
Total	210777	3766	5354	4498	4188	5928	4747	2.25
Average per year	5269	126	162	145	135	180	149	
Each Grama Sabha		39	55	43	47	58	48	

Source: Adopted from Government of Karnataka, 2012:22.

and 58 (maximum) person's have participated in Grama Sabha. In terms of percentage only three percent of the electorates have participated in the deliberations of the Grama Sabha. These statistics show that the levels of people's participation are very poor in all the four Taluks which is much lower than a quorum requirement.

Apart from low people's participation, various studies (Sivanna, 2016; Naik, 2010; Reddy *et al.*, 2010) have found that the Grama Sabha meetings were dominated by influential caste groups of the village. They also revealed untouchability and other social discriminatory practices in the Grama Sabha meetings. To illustrate, Untouchability is still being practiced in almost all the villages of the GPs in Gulbarga, Bellary, Bagalkot and Mandya districts of Karnataka. The Fig. 9.3 represents the number of respondents in the GP who admitted to having faced discrimination due to the practices of untouchability.

It is clear that the Grama Sabha as an institutional set up has not yet persuaded into the minds of people to come forward and to participate in the decision-making process. The potentialities of Grama Sabha as an instrument of political inclusion and direct democracy is yet to be achieved. Strengthening of Grama Sabha is critical for the success of Panchayats to function as 'institutions of self-government' as envisioned in the 73rd CAA. There are arguments in favour of amending Grama Sabha provisions in the State Panchayat Acts in line with the Grama Sabha provisions of PESA, 1996.

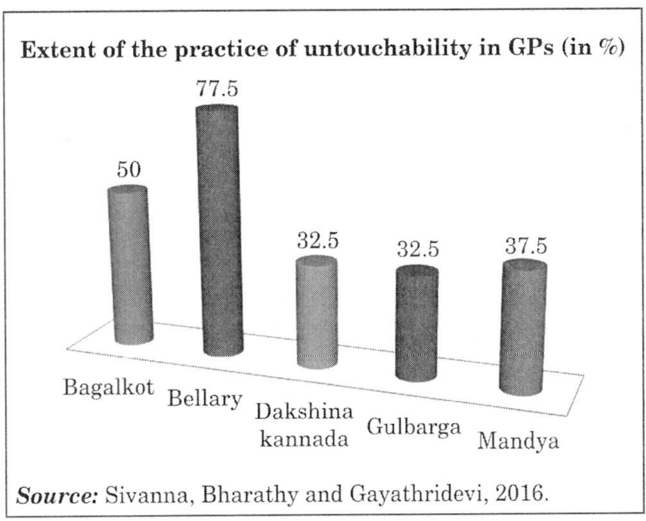

Fig. 9.3: Practice of untouchability in Panchayats

9.8. DEVELOPMENTAL ACTIVITIES

The relationship between the level of decentralisation and the extent of development is not a very exact one, but is expected to be positive and mutual. A better involvement of people in local governance is expected to stimulate better quality of development, and in turn, with better levels of literacy, health and general wellbeing, people are more inclined to participate in local bodies. This is not only because they are more politically aware, but also because they feel that their participation results in concrete outcomes. An Index of Participation[1] and Human Development Index (HDI) are prepared by the Department of Planning, Government of Karnataka (2015). We find that the districts of Kodagu, Uttara Kannada, Udupi, Dakshina Kannada and Chikkamagaluru rank high on the HDI Index, and they perform equally well on the participation index. On the other hand Yadgir, Bijapur, Gulbarga performs poorly on both the HDI and Index of Participation. The co-efficient of correlation between the Index of Participation and HDI across 30 districts of Karnataka turned out to be positive at 0.348 and statistically significant at 6 percent. There are deviations from the overall positive correlation. The most obvious one is Bangalore Urban District which ranks first on the HDI, but very low on participation. On the other hand, the district of Gadag has high levels of participation, but ranks very low on the HDI. In spite of this contrasting picture, by and large, in the districts of Karnataka we observe that decentralisation does have a positive impact on development outcomes.

At a micro level, it can be observed that Grama Panchayat perform three to four important development activities such as supplying drinking water, providing houses to the houseless, providing sanitation and working towards improving health and education condition of the villagers. As a norm the GP should provide drinking water to all the residents to the extent at least 40 to 55 litres of drinking water per day per person (LPCD). The water programs that are implemented at the GP level include '*Jala Nirmala Yojane*', '*Swajaladhare*' and '*Rajiv Gandhi Water Scheme*'. As regards housing the GP implements four main schemes *viz.,* Indira Awaas Yojana, Ambedkar Housing Scheme, Ashraya and Basava Schemes; the funds for the first two schemes are shared both by the Central Government and State Government where as the remaining two exclusively by the Karnataka Government. The Ashraya scheme, sponsored by the Karnataka Government, is meant for the rural houseless poor covering SCs/STs households as well as general category in the ratio of 50:50. Currently, Rs. 40,000 has been provided as financial assistance and for SCs/STs the full grant and for others half the grant and the remaining half as a loan. The Ambedkar housing scheme, is a fully subsidized scheme to help SCs/STs households to construct a house on their own sites and is being implemented only in rural areas. Under the scheme each beneficiary gets Rs. 40,000 as a grant and it is released in four installments of Rs. 10,000. The Indira Awaas Yojana (IAY) is also a centrally sponsored programme meant for upgrading of unserviceable kutcha houses to pucca/semi-pucca houses. This scheme targets BPL households. Of them, 60 percent should belong to SCs/STs categories, while other 40 percent can be other categories. The total amount of assistance is Rs. 40,000. As per Section 51 of the Act, the GP should provide every year at least ten percent of the families with toilet facilities, construct community toilets to meet the demands of those who do not have individual toilets and construct and maintain drainage system. However, the GPs have a limited role to play in implementing programmes related to health and education. In addition, the GP has the responsibility of constructing and maintaining public roads, providing and maintaining street lights, and more importantly, collection of taxes.

However, in terms of spending towards these schemes, the data collected from the selected five Grama Panchayats is not so impressive. For example, during the period 2011–12, the Panchayats have hardly spent on these civic amenities. On average, each Grama Panchayat had spent just 2 percent for providing houses under Ashraya schemes and about 4.27 percent under IAY scheme and spending was very meager towards providing drinking water and construction of toilets. Seen in contrast, the expenditure on the executing MGNREGA programme was to the extent of 41 percent by each panchayat thereby indicating the fact that the Grama Panchayats have been giving prime importance to the flagship programmes sponsored by the Central Government.

A recent study (Poojary, 2010: 224–5), conducted with a comparative perspective, in the selected coastal and interior regions of Karnataka reveal that the Grama Panchayats of coastal Karnataka have done better compared to Panchayats of interior Karnataka in organizing members and village council meetings, better distribution of houses to houseless and BPL families, following norms for the selection of beneficiaries and rare altering of the lists that were finalised by the Grama Sabhas. The study further reveals that 'higher the stock of social capital the better is the institutional performance' of institutions like Panchayats. As per the findings of the study the Panchayats of interior Karnataka (having low stock of social capital) were low in their performance compared to Panchayats of coastal Karnataka (having higher stock of social capital). Panchayats of coastal Karnataka showed better performance in practicing procedural democracy like organising public meetings and managing development activities like providing housing, drinking water and sanitation (Ibid: 174).

9.9. CONCLUDING OBSERVATIONS

It has been a long journey for the Panchayats to transform from traditional role of maintaining community affairs at the local level in attaining the constitutional status as "institutions of self-government". The failure of centralized planning in post second world war most of the developing countries have initiated decentralized reforms with an intent of involving people in decision-making thereby improving the effectiveness of delivery of public services at the local level. In India, Panchayati Raj System has started in 1959 with an understanding that Panchayats can deliver better services compared to State or Union Governments. Karnataka State is one of the progressive states as far as implementing the decentralized governance reform is concerned; successive amendments in the Panchayat Raj Act indicates the will of the State Government to devolve the 'power to the people'.

The foregoing narration informs us the various processes involved in decentralizing the power and authority to the local government institutions and more so to rural areas. Initiatives such as decentralized planning through people's participation at the local level is relatively successful in institutionalizing the bottom-up planning. And thereby, we can witness a considerable change in the priorities of local development shifting from infrastructure to rural employment and social sectors. However, the development outcomes are not satisfactory and this can be attributed to the factors such as low people's participation especially by the Women, SCs/STs and youth in the Grama Sabha meetings. It has serious implications on the efficacy of Grama Sabha and its role in enabling decentralised planning process for the development.

An important observation is that even now the basic amenities such as education and health are delivered through respective departments. Although these subjects are enumerated in Eleventh Schedule (Article 243) and has to be devolved to PRIs, sadly Grama Panchayats have a least role in the implementation of education and health related programs/schemes. Structural barriers such as influence of dominant castes and their role in dictating the agenda of Grama Sabha, in the selection of beneficiaries especially for the housing schemes, practices of untouchability, not heeding the voices of disadvantaged sections of the society all these impede the deepening of democracy thereby altering the development priorities.

The gradual increase in the budgetary allocations to rural development, social infrastructure and welfare of women, SCs/STs indicates the financial commitment to attain the better outcomes of social well being. However, providing functional and financial allocations are not sufficient for the successful decentralized governance. It also requires adequate human and institutional capacities. The recent Amendment in PR Act of 2015, the Karnataka State government has promulgated a separate cadre for the Panchayats *i.e.,* Karnataka Panchayat Administrative Services (KPAS). This may bring the required human personnel to enable Panchayats for better function to cater the needs of rural people and development. Heavy reliance of Panchayats for the funds is still a serious concern. Revenue generation by Panchayats is very weak.

Addressing the above mentioned human and institutional concerns may pay the way for better prospects for the decentralised governance. Once the system in place with necessary provisions such as staff, capacity building of the elected representatives, local bureaucracy and most importantly the citizens, then one can expect the desired changes in the societal development. Achieving rural development through Panchayats remains as a slogan if people do not perceive the system as their own and is there for their well being.

REFERENCES

Dwarakanath, H.D. (2013). *'Grama Sabha - A Milestone for Sustainable Development in Rural India'*. *Kurukshetra*, 61(7): 5–8.

Government of Karnataka (2012). *'A Study on the outcome indicators of Gram Swaraj Project in selected Taluks of Karnataka – A Review'*. Prepared by Decentralization Analysis Cell Gram Swaraj Project, Bangalore: Rural Development and Panchayati Raj Department.

Government of Karnataka (2016). *Economic Survey of Karnataka 2016–17*, Department of Planning, Programme Monitoring and Statistics, Bengaluru: Directorate of Economics and Statistics.

John, M.S. and Chathukulam, J. (2015). *Theoretical Perspective of Decentralisation, Citizenship, Participatory Democracy*. *Mainstream Weekly*, LIII(26): 19–30.

Manor, J. (1999). *'The Political Economy of Democratic Decentralization'*, Washington: World Bank.

Naik, S.K. (2010). Grama Sabha experience in four districts of Karnataka, *In:* Ahsraful Hasan, S.A. and Ganesh Prasad, G.S. (*eds*). *Proceedings of the National Seminar on Grama Sabha, Abdul Nazir Sab State Institute of Rural Development, Government of Karnataka, Mysore: Kamal Impressions*, pp. 182–90.

Poojari M. Chandra (2010). *Institutions, Decentralization and Development*, Prasaranga Kannada University, Hampi.

Reddy, G., Bandi, M. and Reddy, R. (2010). Changing role of Grama Sabha in decentralised governance – An overview of Andhra Pradesh experience. *In*: Ahsraful Hasan, S.A. and Ganesh Prasad, G.S. (*eds.*), *Proceedings of the National Seminar on Grama Sabha, Abdul Nazir Sab State Institute of Rural Development, Government of Karnataka, Mysore: Kamal Impressions*, pp. 135–50.

Sivanna, N. (1999). Decentralisation and Rural Development: The Case of Karnataka. *Indian Social Science Review*, I (1): 29 49.

Sivanna, N., Bharathy, M. and Gayathridevi, K. (2016). 'Engendering Rural Local Governance: A Case from Rural Karnataka'. *Monograph No. 49*, Institute for Social and Economic Change, Bengaluru.

UNDP (1997). Decentralized Governance Programme: Strengthening Capacity for People -Centered Development, Management Development and Governance Division, Bureau for Development Policy.

10

Decentralized Governance Process in Telangana State and Its Implications for Development

M. GOPINATH REDDY[11]*

ABSTRACT

Decentralization of power to the local units of government and management is one of the best ways of empowering people, promoting public participation and increasing efficiency. Decentralization with its potential benefits coupled with the declining legitimacy of centralized systems has attracted support from a diverse range of ideological schools. This paper probes into decentralized governance process in the new State Telangana and its implications for local development. It is striking to note in the ranking of Devolution Index, the State of Telangana's aggregate position stands at 17 among the 25 states in India. Interms of some recent initiatives launched by the new Government of Telangana such as 'Mana Ooru Mana Pranalika' (our village our planning) and 'Gram Jyothi' Programme did not create much impact in the countryside. Recently the Government has brought out New Panchayati Raj Act for the State Telangana where far reaching changes are contemplated. It needs to be watched keenly to what extent these reforms will usher in genuine decentralization regime thus paving way to overcome 'decentralisation deficit' status that the present state is in.

10.1. INTRODUCTION

In recent times there is an increasing realization that genuine decentralization leads to development. It is also felt that decentralization

[11] Professor and Head, Division for Sustainable Development Studies (DSDS), Centre for Economic and Social Studies (CESS), Begumpet, Hyderabad-500016.
*Corresponding author: E-mail: mgopinathreddy@gmail.com

of power to the local units of government and management is one of the best ways of empowering people, promoting public participation and increasing efficiency. Decentralization can help mobilize resources, introduce locally and regionally diverse solutions and promote equitable growth by bringing the poor into mainstream development.

It is also often argued that decentralization is a more effective and efficient framework for delivering pro-poor programmes. The perceived benefits of decentralization range from stimulation of economic growth and alleviation of rural poverty to strengthening civil society and reducing the responsibilities of the center (Manor, 1999). It was observed that project costs are four times higher in centralized systems when compared to decentralized systems. Besides, asset maintenance is much better in the decentralized systems (Bardhan, 1996).

Decentralization with its potential benefits coupled with the declining legitimacy of centralized systems has attracted support from a diverse range of ideological schools. While decentralized systems are found to be superior in terms of intra-regional targeting efficiency, their delivery systems target better in low poverty regions and not as well in high poverty regions (Bardhan and Mukharjee, 2000). As stated above, there are many virtues of decentralization to act as an efficient service delivery mechanism.

The PRIs since the beginning of 1960's saw the phases of 'ascendency' (1959–1966), 'stagnation' (1967–1976) and 'decline' (1977–1991) due to a number of reasons that include, poor political will on the part of the state government; insufficient powers and finances to the local bodies; and fear on the part of state level leaders that parallel leadership was emerging from the grassroots level etc. One main reason of the decline of the local bodies is that they are not backed by the constitutional mandate as PRIs are placed in the Directive Principles of State Policy (Article 40 of the Constitution) which are non-justifiable.

This situation paved the way for pushing constitutional status to PRIs. After lot of trails and tribulations, in the year 1993, 73rd Constitutional Amendment Act became a reality that embedded in the Constitution as part IX. Now, it is more than two and half decades that PRIs/ institutions of local self-government came into operation in all the states which passed State Conformity Acts as soon as the Central Act came into being. Thus, local governments crept into the statute book in 1993. Part IX was inserted by the Constitution (73rd Amendment) Act, 1993 with effect from 24th April 1993 for Panchayats and Part IXA was inserted by the constitution (74th Amendment) Act 1992 with effect from 1st June 1993 for Municipalities making state legislatures responsible for devolving power and authority to local governments in order to enable them to carry out devolved functions. Institutions of Local self-governments have the following mandatory provisions:

- Establishment of State Election Commission (Article 243K),
- Holding regular Panchayat Election (Article 243E),
- Reservation of seats for SCs/STs (Scheduled Castes/Scheduled Tribes) and women (Article 243D),
- Constitution of State Finance Commission at regular intervals (Article 243I), and
- Setting up of District Planning Committees (Article 243ZD).

And, yet another milestone in this process was that in the year 2005–06, Ministry of Panchayati Raj (MoPR), Government of India had introduced Panchayat Empowerment and Accountability Incentive Scheme (PEASIS) to (a) Motivate states to empower the panchayats, and (b) Motivate Panchayats to put in place accountability systems to make their functioning transparent and efficient (Alok, 2014).

10.2. DECENTRALISATION AND DEVELOPMENT - A CONCEPTUAL FRAME

It is realized that, decentralization to rural local governments is meaningful only when the Panchayats have adequate untied funds to provide public services assigned to them. Assignment of adequate and appropriate revenue sources to rural local governments is extremely important in the Indian context. The inability to assign potent revenue sources has led to local governments carrying on unfunded mandates and this has resulted in poor service delivery. Inadequate assignments combined with low levels of effort by the rural local governments have led to high levels of transfer dependence and low fiscal autonomy (Rao and Rao, 2008).

Article 243G of the Constitution empowers Panchayats to function as institutions of self-government for the purposes of preparing plans and implementing schemes for economic development and social justice in their respective areas for various matters, including those listed in the 11th Schedule which is merely illustrative and indicative. Unlike the division of powers and functions enumerated in the Union List and State List, no clear demarcation exists between the state and

Panchayats. It is for the state legislature to make laws regarding the devolution of powers and functions to the Panchayats. Almost all states and UTs (union territories) claim that they have transferred responsibilities in varying degrees to the Panchayats, by enacting laws in conformity with the Constitutional Amendment Act (CAA), 1992 passed by the Parliament of India. However, the functional domain of Panchayats pertains only to traditional civic functions in several states.

Another challenge before the state government has been the allocation of activities to the appropriate tier of the Panchayat system. Traditionally, the lowest-level Panchayat— the Village Panchayat— has been the most active in almost all states. Generally, the Village Panchayats carry out major functions, including core functions, whereas Intermediate (Block) and District Panchayats in most states are allotted supervisory functions or act mainly as executing agents for the state government (Jha, 2004).

When the authority and power in respect of certain activity is transferred from the state to the Panchayats, the latter should have the prerogative of making 'decisions,' in respect of planning and implementation of such activity. In the sphere of devolution of responsibilities to lower levels of governance, some important principles should be kept in view. In the first place, the principle of 'subsidiarity' needs to be given adequate attention. The principle of subsidiarity postulates that any function which can be performed by a lower tier, should be handled by that tier alone and not by any higher tier of PRI. Second, the state government should not unilaterally withdraw responsibilities and power already granted to the Panchayat without adequate justification and prior consultation with the latter. Third, responsibilities, authorities and powers granted to the Panchayats should be extremely specific, clear and simple in order to be comprehended by the Panchayats. Lastly, whenever, functions and responsibilities are transferred to the Panchayats, it should be ensured that the necessary funds, functionaries and freedom in decision-making also accompany such transfer (Government of India, 2014).

There is a trend for governments throughout the world to become increasingly decentralized fiscally, administratively and politically. Some of the reasons for this include a growing critique of central state planning, whereby centrally-administered bureaucracies can represent an inefficient and uninformed means of allocating resources. It is argued that central state agencies lack the local knowledge to implement policies and programmes that reflect people's real needs. Decentralization is therefore intended to create institutional arrangements to strengthen the relationship between citizens and the state, giving citizens the capacity to impose sanctions on local authorities – such as voting, recourse to higher-level authorities (Johnson, 2003). Additionally, basic services that ought to be the responsibility of the state are not reaching their target populations, particularly the poor (World Bank, 2003; Ahmad *et al.*, 2005). Some studies suggest that one of the reasons why government spending does not translate into better outcomes is that centralized control means that money often does not reach frontline providers at the local level (Ahmad *et al.,* 2005). Thus, the rationale behind decentralization is that service delivery will improve if more decision-making functions are given to local authorities. For these reasons, which relate to the potential for increased economic efficiency and democratization, there have been significant international and national political pressures in favor of decentralization.

However, the experience of decentralization to date has been mixed. The problems most frequently encountered include: the risk of funds failing to arrive from the center; the lack of capacity at sub-national levels of government to take responsibility for public service provision; the disjuncture between political decentralization and administrative decentralization, with central governments still having almost total control of policy formulation and programme funding, and local governments having very limited scope for decision-making; and the potential for local elites to take charge of initiatives or to capture a large share of public resources, which limits the potential for pro-poor outcomes (World Bank, 2003; Ahmad *et al.*, 2005; Johnson *et al.*, 2005).

More than an outcome in itself, decentralization is a process, aimed at improving the delivery of programmes and services at the grassroots level. However, views on the outcomes of decentralization to date have been mixed. Support for decentralization is often based on criticism of centralized planning on account of the inefficiencies of large bureaucracies, which lack the 'time and place knowledge' to implement policies and programmes that reflect people's real' needs and preferences (Johnson *et al.*, 2005). Other proponents argue that decentralizing power from the center to districts or villages enables people to participate in decision-making more directly and, potentially, can lead to relations between governments and citizens that allow a greater degree of accountability (Crook and Mannor, 1998). On the other hand, those who are more critical of decentralization suggest that unless it is truly democratic, with structures in place that allow for real accountability, the process may simply transfer power from one set of elites to another (UNDP, 2002; Cagatay *et al.*, 2000).

It could be argued that the reason why decentralization does not always lead to desired outcomes is the insufficient political commitment to reform on the part of national governments (or state governments in the case of India). This means that reforms are merely superficial, and control over decision-making and use of funds remains centralized (Jones *et al.*, 2007). Thus, decentralization must be accompanied by citizenship-building, information-sharing, transparency over decision-making and use of funds, and capacity-building for local functionaries, so as to increase the level of accountability and improve local governance (Bardhan, 2002).

10.3. STATUS OF DEVOLUTION OF FUNCTIONS, FUNDS AND FUNCTIONARIES: ALL INDIA SCENARIO

The index of devolution in practice for the year 2014–15 allows us to analyze the devolution happening in the field and validate the data obtained from the state governments across the country. The indicators chosen also reflected on actual control of Panchayats over transferred institutions, functions and functionaries, financial autonomy and utilization of development funds and the status of infrastructure and administrative system in place.

Table 10.1 provides the ranking of the states by the index of development in practice. Kerala stands out as the top performing state on this index followed by Sikkim, Karnataka, and Maharashtra in that order. The important states like Uttar Pradesh, Bihar, Andhra Pradesh, Punjab are found not doing well with poor rankings.

10.4. NEW STATE OF TELANGANA - REFORMS INITIATED

The Panchayat Raj Conformity Act of 1993 relevant to United Andhra Pradesh continued to be in operation after the new state Telangana came into being. It is well documented (Reddy, 2003; Haragopal and Reddy, 2013) that in United Andhra Pradesh PRIs were not treated well by the respective governments – both Telugu Desam Party (TDP) and later by Congress party. In fact, during TDP rule (from 1996–2004) Panchayats were clearly undermined by starting number of parallel bodies – in particular mention may be made to 'Janma Bhoomi' programme where 'Nodal Officer Raj' reigned supreme at the cost of

Table 10.1: Ranking of states in the component and aggregate indices of devolution in practice.

State	*Functions*	*Functionaries*	*Finances*	*IGT*	*Aggregate DPr*
Kerala	1	1	1	1	1
Sikkim	3	2	13	3	2
Karnataka	2	6	11	6	3
Maharashtra	11	4	2	8	4
Himachal Pradesh	14	9	3	4	5
Assam	10	3	10	13	6
Tripura	9	5	4	12	7
West Bengal	5	22	21	2	8
Madhya Pradesh	6	18	6	7	9
Uttarakhand	4	8	17	16	10
Gujarat	8	14	15	15	11
Odisha	19	12	12	9	12
Chhattisgarh	7	21	18	10	13
Rajasthan	21	7	23	11	14
Tamil Nadu	20	17	5	14	15
Haryana	18	25	9	5	16
Telangana	13	16	16	18	17
Uttar Pradesh	17	23	8	17	18
Punjab	16	13	20	19	19
Andhra Pradesh	12	19	14	20	20
Jharkhand	23	15	22	22	21
Bihar	22	24	19	21	22
Manipur	15	11	25	23	23
Arunachal Pradesh	24	10	7	24	24
Jammu and Kashmir	24	20	24	25	25

Source: Devolution Report, 2014–15, TISS and MoPR, 2015.

democratically elected Panchayati Raj representatives. A number of other parastatal agencies were created — Water Users Association, Watershed Association, Vidya Committees and Parents Committees etc., which were not integrated with the democratically elected PRIs at the grassroots level. The functional and financial devolution as per the constitutional amendment act was not done — only few insignificant functions were devolved without necessary funds and functionaries. Most of the functions were still being discharged by the line departments. Congress Party which came to power in 2004 had promised a lot to strengthen PRIs. However, in practice Nodal Officer Raj was replaced by 'MLA Raj'. Once again undermining locally elected people's representatives.

Once separate state agitation started from early 2000, after TRS party was formed in 2002, the whole issue of local governance took a backseat and entire governance was centred around how to tackle Telangana movement. Once Telangana State became reality under the leadership of K. Chandra Sekhar Rao of TRS that came to power, initially nothing much has happened on the decentralization front. The new government's focus is more on rebuilding new Telangana (Bangaru Telangana) and the main issues handled were increasing more water resources, getting more revenues and correcting the imbalances in the employment situation of the educated unemployed in Telangana.

i) 'Mana Vooru-Mana Pranalika (MVMP)' (Our Village Our Planning)

On the rural front some important initiates were started by TRS Government which had some implications for local development. MVMP was directed to bring in people's participation in terms of identification of needs and priorities and planning decision making at grassroot level. MVMP focused on six themes (i) health and nutrition; (ii) education; (iii) agriculture and land use; (iv) *haritha haram* (increasing green cover); (v) employment and livelihood; and (vi) infrastructure.

An evaluation study conducted by Council for Social Development (CSD, 2014) brought forth serious lapses in the implementation of MVMP and its various components. One of the important findings of the study is the awareness and participation of the people in MVMP is relatively low as only 30 percent of the people were aware of the programme and only 10 to 20 percent of people have participated in the Grama Sabhas that were conducted for preparing the village plans under MVMP.

ii) Gram Jyothi Programme

The Government of Telangana launched Gram Jyothi Programme (Gram Panchayat Development Plan-GPDP) as a logical continuation of Mana Ooru-Mana Pranalika. The objective of Grama Jyothi is to improve the service delivery to the people in core sectors through the strengthening of the Grama Panchayats by bringing together the efforts of various departments working at the Grama Panchayat level which are hitherto working independent of one another. Grama Jyothi aims synergise the developmental activities of the departments by achieving functional and financial convergence through preparation of Grama Panchayat Developmental Plans. Grama Jyothi seeks to exploit the enormous collective energy of the people by making those active partners in the development process, decision-making and take good advantage of the social capital at the village level. The goal of Grama Jyothi is to bring in much desired accountability, transparency in the functioning of public institutions working at Grama Panchayat level and make them responsive to the needs of the people.

The progress of the Gram Jyothi Programme is not satisfactory. The critics have seen it as a parallel institution to Grama Panchayats. The core functions and responsibilities that are supposed to the discharged through this institution are actually the domain of the Grama Panchayats as per the 11th schedule. Instead of strengthening the local bodies with sufficient funds and functionaries the institution of Gram Jyothi programme to improve the service delivery to the people is seen as a brazen violation of the spirit of the 73rd Amendment Act.

10.5. NEW STATE PANCHAYAT RAJ ACT – 2017

The Telangana Government has recently brought in New State (Telangana) Panchayat Raj Act, (The Hindu, 18 November, 2017). In the proposed Act it is intended to bring in the best practices of decentralisation of England and South Africa. The new Act fix as responsibilities and make the sarpanches accountable to the delivery of services. An Ombudsman covering two to three districts with some decision- making powers will oversee the functioning of Grama Panchayat/Sarpanches, who now treat their position as a political power centre, will be accountable for efficiently discharging their duties in delivery of basic amenities or else may lose their position. Increasing the accountability is key in the new State Panchayati Raj Act.

The Government, under the new Act, wants to release sufficient funds directly to the sarpanches coming from various sources, including the Centre and in fact, according to Government, the Panchayats should be more functional with responsibilities attached. The New Act will be all the more important since Government intends to create new Panchayats reducing the habitations in the present Panchayats for effective delivery.

10.6. PROGRESS OF DISTRICT PLANNING COMMITTEES IN ANDHRA PRADESH AND TELANGANA STATES

District Planning Committees (DPCs) shall be constituted at the district level in every State to consolidate the plans prepared by the Panchayats and the Municipalities in the district and to prepare a draft development plan for the district. The Constitution therefore enjoins upon the DPCs two specific responsibilities. In preparing the draft development plan, the DPC shall have regard to matters of common interest between the Panchayats and the Municipalities including spatial planning, sharing of water and other physical and natural resources, the integrated development of infrastructure and environmental conservation and the extent and type of available resources, both financial and otherwise.

Earstwhile Andhra Pradesh was a late starter as compared to many states, in constituting the DPCs. Andhra Pradesh Government despite its proposed commitment to strengthen planning process could not bring the Act of District Planning Committee 2005 until 2006 (Act No. 40 of 2005). However, the necessary guidelines for the working of DPCs have yet to be formulated to make these institutions functional. Of late, DPCs have become non-performing institutions in both AP & Telangana States.

10.6.1. Few Comments on the Working of the DPCs

After the notification of DPCs the process of elections to DPC has been completed.

1. In all the districts DPC have been constituted in the month of the September by completing the formalities of nominations of the members to the DPC (G.O. Ms. No. 418 dated: 06–09–2007) besides elected members.
2. However, in the thirteen BRGF districts DPCs have conducted their meetings quite hurriedly in view of the deadlines for submission of proposals to get BRGF funds. In the process the comprehensive plans required to be prepared at the level of village, intermediate and districts, as required by the Act have not been under taken thus negating the spirit of bottom-up planning.
3. Since the rest of the districts are not BRGF districts, no meetings have been conducted yet.

10.7. THE STATUS OF PANCHAYATS EXTENSION TO SCHEDULED AREAS (PESA) ACT

There are four PESA districts in Telangana - Adilabad, Khammam, Warangal (Partly) and Mahaboobnagar (Parts of the district). There are few important PVTGs in Telangana such as Gonds, Chenchus, Pradhans etc. PESA implementation started in United Andhra after passing the PESA Act in 1998. However, rules for the implementation of PESA Act were prepared after a gap of 13 long years *i.e.,* in the year 2011. The new state of Telangana is expected to give desired push to the PESA implementation as the share ST population in the new state has gone up to more than nine percent (in United AP the share of the ST population was about 6.5%). Activating the Grama Sabha is crucial in the implementation of PESA as it is important institution to address the developmental concerns of the tribals.

A full-term (2014–19) rule of the present government shows that not much of pace is infused in strengthening PESA. The present government has passed Tribal Sub-Plan (TSP) Scheduled Caste Sub-Plan by amending the United AP Legislation which is praise worthy. However, PESA strengthening is equally important for the tribal governance and management of their resources.

10.8. CONCLUSIONS

It emerges from the above narrative that United AP always remained a 'decentralisation deficit' state. Unfortunately, the new state Telangana is in the same order at the moment. Thus, decentralization deficit status has serious implications for local development. The inadequate devolution of 3 Fs has serious implications in developing overall basic infrastructure by the PRIs. Secondly, strengthening PESA is of utmost importance in the 5th Scheduled areas of Telangana. The planning apparatus of the District Planning Committees is yet to emerge as serious planning units for decentralized planning of rural and urban areas.

The new state of Telangana has a task cut out with regard to strengthening decentralization ecosystem and come out of a decentralization deficit status. It is hoped that the recent reforms ushered by the TS Government will bring in desirable changes in the ecosystem of democratic decentralization status of Telangana State.

REFERENCES

Alok, VN. (2014). *'Measuring Devolution to Panchayats in India: A Comparison across States Empirical Assessment – 2013–14,'* Indian Institute of Public Administration, Sponsored by Ministry of Panchayat Raj, Government of India, pp. 1–6.

Ahmad Junaid, Shantayanan Devarajan, Khemani Stuti and Shah Shekhar (2005). 'Decentralization and Service Delivery: World Bank Policy Research,' Working Paper 3603, pp. 1–27.

Bardhan Pranab (2002). *'Decentralization of Governance and Development'. The Journal of Economic Perspectives,* 16(4): 185–205.

Bardhan Pranab and Mookherjee Dilip (2000). *"Capture and Governance at Local and National Levels". American Economic Review*, 90(2): 135–39.

Bardhan Pranab (1996). *"Decentralized Development". Indian Economic Review,* XXXI(2): 139–56.

Crook Richard, C. and Manor James (1998). *'Democracy and Decentralization in South Asia and West Africa: Participation, Accountability and Performance',* Cambridge University Press, Cambridge, pp. 1–335.

Cagatay Nilufer, Keklik Mumtaz, Lal Radhika and Lang James (2000). *'Budgets as if People Mattered: Democratizing Macroeconomic Policies,' UNDP SEPED Conference Paper Series No. 4.*

Government of India (2014). *'Report of the Fourteenth Finance Commission 2015–2020,' New Delhi,* pp. 1–481.

Haragopal, G., Reddy M. Gopinath and Rao, C.V. (2013). 'Andhra Pradesh', in Status of Panchayati Raj in the States and Union Territories in India', George Mathew (*ed.*), Institute of Social Sciences, Concept Publishing Company, New Delhi.

Jha Shikha (2004). *'Panchayats: Functions, Responsibilities, and Resources'. Paper Commissioned by the National Institute of Rural Development (NIRD), Hyderabad on behalf of the 12th Finance Commission of India.*

Johnson Craig (2003). *'Decentralization in India: Poverty, Politics and Panchayati Raj'.* ODI Working Paper 199, London, UK, pp. 1–60.

Johnson Craig, Deshingkar Priya and Start Daniel (2005). *'Grounding the State: Devolution and Development in India's Panchayats'. The Journal of Development Studies,* 41(6): 937–970.

Manor James (1999). *"The Political Economy of Democratic Decentralization," Directions in Development Series.* Washington DC: World Bank, pp. 1–133.

Rao Govinda, M. and Rao U.A. Vasanth (2008). *"Expanding the Resource Base of Panchayats: Augmenting Own Revenues". Economic and Political Weekly,* 43(4): 54–61.

Reddy M. Gopinath (2003). *"Status of Decentralised Local Bodies: Post–73rd Amendment Scenario". Economic and Political Weekly*, XXXVIII(12 and 13).

Reddeppa, L. *et al.* (2014). 'Mana Vooru Mana Pranalika: Telangana A Rapid Concurrent Survey', CSD, Hyderabad.

The Hindu, 18th November (2017).

UNDP (2002). *Human Development Report: Deepening Democracy in a Fragmented World, United Nations Development Program,* New York, pp. 1–277.

World Bank (2003). *Making Services Work for Poor People, World Development Report 2004,* The World Bank, Washington, DC.

11

Redressal of Regional Imbalances in Karnataka

B. SESHADRI[13] AND K. GAYITHRI*

ABSTRACT

The paper is a contribution to a theoretical understanding of regional imbalances and an empirical verification of regional imbalances in Karnataka. The paper tracks the historical circumstances in which regional imbalances have emerged in the state of Karnataka and their threat to the overall state's development. The paper argues that regional imbalances are congenital to the state of Karnataka since 1956, the formation of state of Karnataka with the merger of lagging districts of Bombay- Karnataka, Hyderabad-Karnataka, Madras Presidency and the 'C' state of Coorg with the relatively developed old Mysore state. The paper proves that, what is achieved is significant, but what remains to be achieved is more significant. The paper makes out a case for putting in place, a well defined and flexible regional policy by the government. It is further argued that the current practice of thinly spreading resources should be stopped and adequate funds released fully and on time which further get completely utilised in time can help in redressing the regional disparities.

11.1. INTRODUCTION

An inquiry into the development history of the world — particularly of the post- Industrial Revolution — inter alia, leaves one with the inescapable impression that regional imbalances in development have been an integral and inseparable part of the development process. The roots of areal dualism, which are to be found in the two bold voyages –

[13] Professor and Head (Retd), Department of Development Studies, Kannada University, Hampi, Karnataka.

**Corresponding author*: E-mail: gayithri@isec.ac.in

the Western Voyage of Columbus (1492) and the Eastern Voyage of Vasco-da-Gama (1498) — resulted in a chain of events that made the world one, but not yet ceased to widen the disparities between the areal groupings of mankind. The areal disparities, so initiated by these geographical discoveries, got good grounding in the disparity-engendering Industrial Revolution of the 18th Century. The ongoing mega process of globalization has been exacerbating the historically inherited hardened antecedent regional imbalances; the line of demarcation between the developed and the lagging regions is getting thickened. The problem has come to acquire global dimension: It is found in the developed as well as in the less developed and developing countries; the former have some backward regions, and the latter, besides backward pockets, have some developed pockets. Another dimension of the problem is that, globalization has given rise to a paradoxical situation in which higher growth rates and increasing regional imbalances have become simultaneous processes.

In development literature, the problem of regional imbalances goes by the name "North-South" problem. Strictly speaking, it is a post-war (World War II) phenomenon. Here, "North" refers to relatively developed industrialized regions, whereas, "South" refers to relatively less developed lagging regions (Seshadri: 1991). Since the problem is found in every part of the world, it is not something peculiar to India, as a nation, and Karnataka, as a state. We do find inter-state disparities at the national level and intra-state disparities at the state level.

But what is peculiar about them is that in spite of seven decades of independent existence, over six decades of planned development and a host of redressal measures, they present a sad spectacle of development-deprivation disparities. As far as Karnataka is concerned, it presents another peculiarity. Strangely enough, North Karnataka Region (NKR), comprising two divisions – Belgaum and Gulbarga – exhibits most of the characteristics of the lagging "South", and the South Karnataka Region (SKR), comprising two divisions – Bangalore and Mysore – exhibits most of the characteristics of the relatively developed "North". Of course, backwardness is found in both the halves; but it is more pronounced in NKR than in SKR.

With these prefatory observations, the present paper is structured as follows:

Part One: Carries two sections. The first section gives a brief note on the historical circumstances in which regional imbalances emerged and the threat they have been posing to the enlarged state of Karnataka.

The second section, as a necessary background for the empirical analysis of regional imbalances, presents a succinct summary of some of the important theories of regional imbalances.

Part Two: Is split into two sections, and it is devoted for the discussion of the measurement of regional imbalances between the two regions – SKR and NKR – and among the four divisions. Aggregative metrics are used in the first section to measure development-deprivation disparities. And disaggregative indicators are used in the second section to capture regional disparities.

Part Three: Is devoted for the discussion of some of the important measures taken by the government to redress regional imbalances in the state.

Part Four: Concludes the paper by giving a brief summary of the aforesaid discussion. It also makes some suggestions for making redressal measures more effective in reducing interregional and intra-regional imbalances in the state.

PART ONE

I

11.2. A NOTE ON THE EMERGENCE OF REGIONAL IMBALANCES IN KARNATAKA

Regional Imbalances are congenital to the enlarged state of Karnataka which came into existence on November 1, 1956. They emerged with the merger of the lagging districts of Bombay-Karnataka, Hyderabad-Karnataka, Madras Presidency and the 'C' State of Coorg with the relatively developed Old Mysore State. That is not the real problem: the real problem is the persistence and widening of disparities even in 2015, inspite of the development experienced by the lagging parts of the state. As such, even today, the state presents a sad spectacle of united existence and divided development. The linguistic integration, per se, has not been able to bring about economic integration between NKR and SKR. This should not lead us to the hasty conclusion that nothing significant has been achieved so far. However, it does mean that what is achieved is significant, but that which remains to be achieved is more significant. Since the 1990s, the persisting disparities have been posing a threat to united Karnataka. The very inhabitants of NKR, who led the long drawn-out struggles for their merger with SKR, have been posing a threat to break away from the united Karnataka and form an independent state for themselves.

The simmering discontent of the separatists of NKR, which used to manifest itself in relatively peaceful debates and discussion turned into a large scale mass movement for separation in September 1997 as a reaction to the statement made by the then Chief Minister J.H. Patel in the first ever cabinet meeting held outside Bangalore (*i.e.,* at Hubli) on September 22, 1997. He said that there were no regional imbalances in the state. But slowly the movement fisteled out only to stage a comeback with higher force at Hubli as a violent reaction to the Report of the Committee of Judges of the Karnataka High Court which did not favour the setting up of a High Court Bench in NKR. A similar movement started in Gulbarga for cessation and formation of an independent state for Hyderabad-Karnataka Region (HKR). But, the separatist movement came to acquire disastrous dimensions at Hubli. The Action Committee Constituted by the Hubli-Dharwad Bar Association went to the extent of designing and unfurling a tri-colour flag (green, white and blue), and also unveiling a separate map of North Karnataka State comprising 12 districts. The Committee also made a public declaration: "From today (June 21, 2000) we are the citizens of the new state of Uttara Karnataka".

This development came as a rude shock, not only to the unity-loving Kannadigas of both the halves (NKR and SKR), but also to the Congress Government headed by S.M. Krishna. With a view, among other things, to holding the two halves together, S.M. Krishna Constituted a High Power Committee for Redressal of Regional Imbalances under the Chairmanship of Dr. D.M. Nanjundappa in December 2000, to address the problem of regional imbalances in the state. The Committee submitted its Final Report, with a number of recommendations, including the well-known 8-year Special Development Plan (SDP), in June 2002. But it was kept in cold storage till 2007–08 — The year in which it was implemented by the BJP-led government, of course, with some deviations. The 8-year SDP period ended in 2014–15. Yet the imbalances continue to persist. Realising the seriousness of the problem, the then Congress Government headed by Siddaramaiah has extended the period for the implementation of the SDP by another 4 years from 2015–16, and has provided an annual grant of Rs. 3000 Crore for 4 years (a detailed discussion on this is taken up in Part Three). This, in brief, are the struggles of the, lagging NKR for securing spatial equity and regional justice in terms of overall development.

II

11.2.1. Theoretical Framework

With a view to facilitating a proper understating of the North-South problem in Karnataka, a succinct summary of some of the important theories of regional imbalances is given in this section. Though the rudimentary roots of areal dualism are to be found in the two bold Voyages – of Columbus (1492) and Vasco-da-Gama (1498) – the awareness about the emergence and persistence of regional imbalances is mostly a post-war (World War II) phenomenon. And in course of time, areal disparities came to induce economists to develop theories and hypotheses about the temporal behavior of divergence and convergence in the growth path of nations. The French Regional Economists, F. Perroux and Bondeville, who developed the concept of "Growth Pole" in 1955 were the pioneers in arguing that growth does not appear everywhere and all at once; it appears in growth poles with variable intensities and it spreads along diverse channels and has varying terminal effects for the whole economy. But operationally useful theorizing on regional disparities got a major breakthrough in the writings of Gunnar Myrdal (1957), A.O. Hirschman (1958), J.R. Hicks (1958), J.G.Williamson (1959) and William Alonso (1968). (For a detailed discussion of their theories, see Seshadri, 1991).

Most of them believe and agree that growth or economic progress does not appear everywhere at the same time, and that once it appears, powerful forces make for a spatial concentration of economic growth around the initial points. John Friedman and William Alonso opine that such centres grow so rapidly as to create problems of an entirely new order, but also act as suction pumps, pulling in the more dynamic elements from the more static regions. Such regions get relegated to a second class peripheral position, and as a result income differences between the centre and the periphery tend to widen.

For Myrdal also growth in a free market economy, does not appear everywhere at once. In his opinion, that once growth starts in a region, the ever increasing internal and external economies would fortify and sustain the continuous growth of the growing region at the expense of other regions, where relative stagnation becomes the pattern. He explains the process of cumulative causation which perpetuates interregional income differentials with two consecutive forces – "Backwash Effects" and "Spread Effects." The former ones refer to unfavourable forces which cause divergence whereas, the latter ones refer to favorable forces which cause convergence. In his view, spread effects are weaker than backwash effects, and as such, in the absence of external influence, regional disparities persist. And on the basis of the results published in the Economic Survey of Europe in 1954, he has drawn two conclusions: (i) the regional inequalities are more wider in poor countries than in the richer countries; and (ii) while regional inequalities are diminishing in the richer countries, and the tendency is the opposite in the poorer countries.

Another important theorist is A.O. Hirschman. He like Myrdal, argues that progress does not appear everywhere at the same time, and once it appears, powerful forces make it for a spatial concentration of growth around the initial points (1958). For him also, growth is necessarily unbalanced. As such, he considers interregional/international inequality in growth an inevitable concomitant and condition of growth itself. Like Myrdal, he also uses two forces, namely "trickling down effects," favouring convergence, and "polarization effects" which cause divergence. In his analysis, the latter ones become powerful and cause divergence, but, in the long run, the former ones become powerful and bring about north-south rapprochement. But he considers deliberate economic policy to be an important influence in correcting regional imbalances.

Almost as a sequel to the theories of Myrdal and Hirschman J.R. Hicks (1958), argues that once unequal rates of growth develop and tend to perpetuate themselves, the growth rates may even increase. He uses two terms, centrifugal force and centripetal force, to explain the alternating phases of divergence and convergence. The growth in the dynamic area is capable of acting as centrifugal force by trickling down the growth to lagging regions. It is also equally capable of acting as a centripetal force by draining the growth potential of the lagging peripheral regions. He also believes in the ability of government intervention in reducing spatial inequalities. In his view, it is not difficult to induce the economic forces to move a little further or a little faster than they would have done without government intervention.

J.G. Williamson, in the preface to his pioneering empirical study (1965) on regional inequalities gives a crystal-clear theoretical analysis of the emergence of divergence and its final convergence. For him, if significant economic growth appears in one region, it should occasion no surprise if absolute differentials between rich and poor regions should persist even if they grow at the same percentage rate after the "fortuitous" random shock in the North. The centripetal forces which come to dominate the early stages of national development are bound to give way to centrifugal forces at a later stage. In short, he holds the view that regional disparities diverge initially only to converge later on.

From the foregoing discussion, we may draw the following inferences on the nature of regional imbalances:

i. Growth, per se, does not appear everywhere at one and the same time, and as such, it is necessarily unbalanced;
ii. The divergence-causing centripetal forces which dominate the growth-path initially are bound to give way to convergence-causing centrifugal forces at a later stage;
iii. Regional imbalances are more pronounced in poorer countries/ regions than in richer countries/regions;
iv. Regional imbalances persist for long, even if the lagging regions grow at the same rates as the advanced regions; and
v. Government intervention can make a positive difference – it can narrow down regional disparities by consciously creating an enabling environment in which the lagging regions are enabled to grow at a faster rate than those which are ahead of them.

PART TWO

I

11.3. MEASUREMENT OF REGIONAL IMBALANCES

11.3.1. Introduction

Most leaders believe in the dictum that, that which can be measured alone can be managed. And those who are charged with the responsibility of redressing regional imbalances must first get the disparities measured by using reliable metrics. We know that disparity is a multidimensional phenomenon and a multivariate function. As such, it becomes necessary to use such indicators and indices which are helpful in quantifying the interregional imbalances and their temporal behavior — a crucial input in the redressal exercise. Here, we have used both aggregative and disaggregative metrics to measure areal disparities among divisions and regions of the state. While doing so, the districts as well as taluks are also brought into the disparity discussion. This part is split into two sections. The first section analyses and interprets disparities by using aggregative measurers such as Comprehensive Composite Development Index (CCDI), Cumulative Deprivation Index (CDI),

Human Development Index (HDI) and District Composite Develoment Index (DCDI) etc.

These indices give an average picture of development and deprivation: they measure the overall performance of the regions and divisions; and they become helpful in measuring their overall relative performance. The second section measures regional disparities with reference to individual indicators (or variables) which have direct bearing on the development-deprivation levels of the regions concerned. They include literacy, school drop-out rates, SCs and STs population, cultivators and landless agricultural labourers etc. The outcomes of these measures would the useful in recommending redressal measures.

11.3.2. Measurement of Regional Imbalances by Aggregative Metrics

Comprehensive composite development index

CCDI is the most comprehensive composite index available for measuring regional imbalances. The High Power Committee (HPC) presented its findings in its Final Report submitted to the government in June 2002. The disparity analysis is done for 27 districts and 175 taluks (now there are 30 districts and 176 taluks). The committee has used 35 indicators in constructing CCDI. The 35 indicators are grouped under 5 dimensions: of them, 9 indicators represent "Agriculture and Allied Activities", 5 indicators represent "Industry, Trade and Finance", 9 indicators represent "Economic Infrastructure", 7 indicators represent "Social Infrastructure" and 5 indicators represent "Demographic Aspects." (For details, see the Final Report 2002). The CCDI value of the taluks is the basis for measuring the relative development and backwardness of the taluks, districts, divisions, and regions. The CCDI value of 1 (one) – the state average level of development – is used as the benchmark for determining the relative positions of the 175 taluks.

Based on CCDI value, the taluks whose CCDI value is 1 (one) and > 1 are considered Relatively Developed Taluks (61 taluks), the taluks whose CCDI value lies between 0.53 and 0.79 are regarded as Most Backward Taluks (39 taluks), the taluks whose CCDI value ranges from 0.80 to 0.88 are regarded as more Backward Taluks (40 taluks), and the taluks whose CCDI value lies between 0.89 and 0.99 are classified as Backward Taluks (35 taluks). Of the 175 taluks, broadly there are 61 Relatively Developed Taluks and 114 Backward Taluks. The relative shares of the four divisions and two regions in these four categories tell us about their relative development and backwardness. The details are presented in Table 11.1.

Table 11.1: Division-wise, Region-wise and Taluk-wise CCDI values.

Sl. no.	*Divisions/ Regions*	*Relatively developed taluks (nos.)*	*Most backward taluks (nos.)*	*More backward taluks (nos.)*	*Back-ward taluks (nos.)*	*Total number of taluks (nos.)*
1	*2*	*3*	*4*	*5*	*6*	*7*
1.	Bangalore division	18 (35.29)	11 (21.57)	13 (25.49)	09 (17.65)	51 (100.00)
2.	Mysore division	22 (50.00)	02 (4.54)	10 (22.75)	10 (22.73)	44 (100.00)
3.	South Karnataka Region (SKR)	40 (42.11)	13 (13.38)	23 (24.21)	19 (20.00)	95 (100.00)
4.	Belgaum division	18 (36.74)	05 (10.20)	12 (24.49)	14 (28.57)	49 (100.00)
5.	Gulbarga division	03 (9.68)	21 (67.74)	05 (16.13)	02 (6.45)	31 (100.00)
6.	North Karnataka Region (NKR)	21.(26.25)	26 (32.50)	17 (21.25)	16 (20.00)	80 (100.00)
7.	Karnataka state	61 (34.86)	39 (22.28)	40.(22.86)	35 (20.00)	175 (100.00)

Source: Derived from the data available in the Final Report of HPCFRRI (2002). pp. 166–168/223–226.

Note: The figures in brackets indicate the percentage of taluks of the total taluks of the divisions and regions concerned.

From the data presented in Table 11.1, we may draw the following inferences on the incidence of development and backwardness in the four divisions and two regions:

i. The data in columns 4, 5 and 6, pertaining to backward taluks, we get the impression that there is no glaring disparity between SKR and NKR; of the 114 backward taluks, 55 are in the former and 59 in the latter. The real picture emerges when we consider column 4 which reflects the intensity of backwardness; of the 39 most Backward Taluks in the State, 26 are in NKR and only 13 in SKR. In other words, 32.50% of NKR's 80 taluks, and only 13.38% of SKR's 95 taluks are in this category. This shows that backwardness is more pronounced in NKR than in SKR; the number of such taluks in NKR is twice their number in SKR.

ii. Among the four divisions, Gulbarga division, with 21 Most Backward Taluks (67.74% of its taluks) emerges as the most backward division in the state. Whereas, with only 2 of its taluks (4.54% of its taluks) Mysore emerges as the least backward division in the state. The second and third positions, in terms of the incidence of backwardness, go respectively to Bangalore (11 taluks:

21.56%) and Belgaum (5 taluks: 10.20%). Thus, intra-regionally, in SKR, Bangalore division is far more backward than Mysore division, whereas in NKR, Gulbarga division attracts the tag of the most backward division and Belgaum division the tag of the least backward division.

iii. At the state level, 22.28% of its taluks (175) are in the most backward category. But it is disheartening to note that the corresponding figure of Gulbarga division (67.74%) is more than three times the state average of 22.28%. Whereas, the corresponding figures of the remaining three divisions are less than the state average.

iv. Regionally speaking, SKR's figure is far below the state's by 8.90 percentage points, and on the contrary, NKR's figure lies far above the state's by 10.22 percentage points. We get altogether a dramatically opposite picture, when we view the disparity situation from the point of relatively developed taluks. Of the 61 such taluks in the state, 40 are in SKR (42.11% of its taluks), and 21 in NKR (26.25% of its taluks). The former's figure is far above and the latter's figure far below the state average of 34.86%. These data provide concrete evidence to say that SKR is far above NKR in terms of development.

v. Among the divisions, Gulbaraga, which carries the first position in terms of backwardness, with only three of its taluks (9.68% of its taluks) in the relatively developed category, occupies the last position. Whereas, Mysore which carries the last position in terms of backwardness, with 22 taluks (50% of its taluks) in terms of development, occupies the first position. The second and third positions go respectively to Belguam and Bangalore divisions.

In sum, in terms of backwardness, NKR occupies the first position and SKR the second position. And in terms of development, SKR occupies of first position and NKR, the second position.

11.3.3. Deprivation Distances as per CDI

The High Power Committee, besides developing CCDI for measuring development disparities, developed Cumulative Deprivation Index (CDI) for measuring regional imbalances in terms of deprivation levels of the two regions and four divisions. According to HPC, additional development funds required for narrowing down the imbalances should be distributed among the 114 backward taluks in proportion to the degree of their deprivation measured in terms CDI values. The HPC has worked out the CDI values for all the backward taluks. The CDI value is derived from the formula: CCDI value of 1(one) – the state average minus the CCDI value of a given taluk is its CDI, which indicates its deprivation level. The CDI values worked out by the HPC for the four divisions and two regions and their deprivation levels are presented in Table 11.2.

Table 11.2: Particulars of division-wise and region-wise CDI values and their deprivation levels.

Sl. no.	*Divisions/Regions*	*CDI values*	*Deprivation levels for resource allocation*	
1.	Gulbarga division	8.06	40 percent	8.06./20.26
2.	Belgaum division	4.12	20 percent	4.12/2026
3.	North Karnataka region	12.18	60 percent	12.18/20.26
4.	Bangalore division	5.32	25 percent	5.32/20.26
5.	Mysore division	2.76	15 percent	2.76/20.26
6.	South Karnataka region	8.08	40 percent	8.08/20.26
7.	Karnataka state	20.26	100 percent	—

Source: Final Report of the High Power Committee for Redressal of Regional Imbalances, 2002, pp. 818–819.

The data in Table 11.2 show the relative positions of the four divisions in terms of deprivation distances. From the data we come to know that:

i. Gulbarga division, which occupied the first position in terms of backwardness as per CCDI values, occupies in same first position in terms of deprivation; of the state'stotal deprivation (100%), it claims 40% in it. Its deprivation is equal to the total deprivation of Bangalore and Mysore (25 + 15% = 40%). One good thing about this is that as recommended by the HPC, 40% of the additional resources of Rs. 16,000 Crore provided for the 8-year SDP should go to Gulbarga division (Rs. 6,400 Crore).

ii. As far as the regions are concerned, NKR, with 60% of the deprivation (Gulbarga: 40 + 20% of Belgaum) became eligible for Rs. 9,600 Crore, (Rs. 6,400 Crore of Gulbarga and 3,200 Crore of Belgaum division, which carried a deprivation of 20%) Whereas, SKR, with 40% of the state's deprivation, became eligible for Rs. 6,400 Crore. Of it, Rs. 4000 Crore (25%) went to Bangalore division and Rs. 2,400 Crore (15%) to Mysore division.

iii. Among the divisions, in terms of deprivation-intensity Gulbarga occupies the first position and Mysore the last position. And the second and third positions go respectively to Bangalore and Belgaum.

In sum, the data show that Gulbarga is the most deprived division, and Mysore the least deprived division, and regarding regions, NKR is the most deprived region and SKR the least deprived region in the state.

11.3.4. Net State Domestic Product and Regional Imbalances

The relative shares of the divisions and the regions in Net State Domestic Product (NSDP) are also used as a metric to gauge regional disparities and their inter-temporal trends. Keeping in view the availability of reliable data, we have made an attempt to identify regional imbalances in 2007–08 and 2012–13 and then to capture the intertemporal trends based on the changes in the shares of divisions and regions. The related data are presented in Table 11.3.

Table 11.3: Particulars of the shares of divisions and regions in NSDP: 2007–08 and 2012–13.

Sl. no.	*Divisions/Regions*	*Share in NSDP (at current prices) (Rs. in crore)*	
		2007–08	*2012–13*
1	*2*	*3*	*4*
1.	Bangalore division	1,23,176 (50.69%)	2,31,652 (49.71%)
2.	Mysore division	46,981 (19.33%)	93,156 (19.99%)
3.	South Karnataka Region	1,70,157 (70.02%)	3,24,808 (69.71%)
4.	Belgaum division	42,883 (17.46%)	79,496 (17.06%)
5.	Gulbarga division	30,424 (12.52%)	61,657 (13.23%)
6.	North Karnataka Region	72,862 (29.98%)	1,41,153 (30.29%)
7.	Karnataka State	2,43,019 (100.00%)	4,65,961 (100.00%)

Source: (1) Government of Karnataka, 2008, Economic Survey of Karnataka: 2007– 2008. DES, Bangalore.
(2) Government of Karnataka, 2014–15, DES, Bangalore.

From the data of NSDP presented in Table 11.3 we may draw the following inferences on regional imbalances:

i. The data in column 3 (2007–08) show that there are glaring imbalances not only between the two regions, but also among the four divisions. SKR's share is 70.02% as against NKR's share of 29.98%. Its share is close to two times the share of NKR. In SKR, Mysore division with 19.33% share in the region's NSDP lags behind Bangalore.

ii. Among the four divisions, Bangalore with its share of 50.69% emerges as the most developed division in the state (2007–08).

Not only that, its share is far above the shares of the remaining three divisions, but also the share of NKR.

iii. And Gulbarga, with a share of 12.52% gets the dubious distinction of the least developed or the most backward division in the state. Next to Bangalore, we have Mysore (19.33%), and it is followed by Belgaum (17.46%).

iv. The data pertaining to 2012–13 (column 4), despite improvement in absolute terms, the relative positions of all the four divisions and two regions almost remain the same in terms of their relative shares in percentages. Despite increase in their shares in NSDP between 2007–08 and 2012–13, regional imbalances persist.

v. SKR, with more than two times the share of NKR, embers as the most advanced region in the state. Bangalore continues to be the most advanced division in its, region as well as in the state. As against this, Gulbarga continues to attract the tag of least developed division in its region as well as in the state. The second and third positions go respectively to Mysore and Belgaum divisions.

In sum, the income metric used here to measure regional disparities, tells us that regionally, NKR lags behind SKR, and among the divisions, the first position goes to Bangalore and the last position to Gulbarga. And regional imbalances persists inspite of improvement in the level of income of all the four divisions between 2007–08 and 2012–13.

11.3.5. District Composite Development Index (DCDI) and Regional Disparities

The District Human Development Report (DHDR) 2014, besides carrying data for the construction of composite indices such as Human Development Index (HDI), Gender Inequality Index (GII), Child Development Index (CDI), Food Security Index (FSI), also carries data for constructing DCDI for all the 30 districts of the state. The DCDI is constructed by using 8 indices – Demographic Index, Livelihood Index, Housing and Assets Index, Participation Index, Health Index, Sanitation Index, Water Index and Education Index. The related data available in the DHDRs of 30 districts are used in preparing a chart for the entire state. From that chart, we have identified the top 5 and bottom 5 districts, with a view to capturing the regional disparities between the two regions – SKR and NKR – and among the four divisions – Bangalore, Mysore, Belgaum and Gulbarga. The related particulars are given in Table 11.4.

Table 11.4: Particulars of top 5 and bottom 5 districts as per DCDI values.

Sl. no.	*District*	*Demographic index*		*Livelihood index*		*Housing and assets index*		*Participation index*		*Health index*		*Sanitation index*		*Water index*		*Education index*		*DCDI*	
		Value	*Rank*	*Value*	*Rank*	*Value*	*Rank*	*Value*	*Rank*	*Value*	*Rank*	*Value*	*Rank*	*Value*	*Rank*	*Value*	*Rank*	*Value*	*Rank*
1	*2*	*3*	*4*	*5*	*6*	*7*	*8*	*9*	*10*	*11*	*12*	*13*	*14*	*15*	*16*	*17*	*18*	*19*	*20*
	Top 5 DCDI Districts																		
1.	Bengaluru Urban	0.395	29	0.470	4	1.000	1	0.422	26	0.913	2	0.581	4	1.000	1	0.881	6	0.708	1
2.	Shivamogga	0.611	7	0.299	24	0.350	11	0.784	2	0.459	15	0.753	1	0.660	18	0.889	4	0.601	2
3.	Bengaluru Rural	0.534	13	0.352	13	0.547	2	0.625	9	0.422	18	0.624	3	0.818	8	0.855	7	0.597	3
4.	Dakshina Kannada	0.665	3	0.568	1	0.494	4	0.666	7	0.305	23	0.660	2	0.388	28	1.000	1	0.593	4
5.	Mandya	0.600	8	0.375	9	0.298	17	0.569	13	0.913	1	0.344	12	0.897	4	0.682	22	0.555	5
	Bottom 5 DCDI Districts																		
1.	Bagalkot	0.500	20	0.326	20	0.049	28	0.497	23	0.260	24	0.109	26	0.678	16	0.624	26	0.585	26
2.	Raichur	0.388	30	0.346	15	0.089	25	0.500	21	0.549	1026	0.071	28	0.493	25	0.534	27	0.371	27
3.	Kalaburagi	0.490	23	0.231	30	0.191	22	0.271	29	0.207	26	0.118	25	0.573	22	0.677	23	0.345	28
4.	Vijayapura	0.495	21	0.333	18	0.040	29	0.430	25	0.026	30	0.047	30	0.501	24	0.708	20	0.323	29
5.	Yadgiri	0.478	24	0.346	16	0.025	30	0.421	27	0.059	29	0.063	29	0.426	27	0.393	30	0.276	30

From the data presented in Table 11.4, we may draw the following inferences regarding the relative positions of SKR and NKR in matters pertaining to the incidence of development and deprivation:

i) All the Top 5 districts belong to SKR and all the Bottom 5 Districts belong to NKR; this finding lends support to the generally held view that NKR lags behind SKR.

ii) Among the Divisions of NKR, Kalaburagi (Gulbarga) with three of its districts (out of 5) in the Bottom 5 districts lags behind Belgaum division.

iii) And among the divisions of SKR, Bengaluru division, with three of its districts in the Top 5 districts (out of 5) is better than Mysore division.

In sum, it is to say that development it more pronounced in SKR and deprivation is more pronounced in NKR. And among the four divisions, development is more pronounced in Bangalore division of SKR, and deprivation in Gulbarga division of NKR.

11.3.6. Regional Disparities from Human Development Perspective (HDI)

There has been a slow, but steady shift in development thinking from income-centred approach to people-centered human development approach since the publication of the first Human Development Report in 1990 (HDR 1990) by UNDP. The notion of human development has also been evolving from year to year. India has also been publishing HDRs for India. And Karnataka, as a state, has already brought out two state level HDRs — HDR 1993 and HDR 2005 — and the third one, HDR 2016, is in its final stage. Besides these reports, the state has brought out District Human Development Reports (DHDRs) 2014. In principle, our governments — central and state — do recognize the superiority of the human development paradigm over the income/growth-centred development. But in practice, our government still continues to measure the state's annual development performance by using growth-based metrics. It is more so, with growth-obsessed neo-liberal policies gaining primacy. In this context, it is necessary to point out that income (GSDP) is not only a poor measure of economic progress, but also a bad measure of progress. The Stiglitz Commission goes to the extent of saying that it mis-measures our lives. It measures what is produced but not what is reduced, and it measures what is created but not what is destroyed.

In this background, with a view to capturing a relatively real picture of the quality of life of the people inhabiting 4 divisions, 30 districts and 176 taluks – coming under the 2 regions, SKR and NKR, an attempt is made here to view regional disparities, by using the data available in the 30 DHDRs. It is necessary to point out that low HDI and high HDI districts and taluks are found in SKR as well as in NKR. Two approaches are used here to identify regional disparities: first, by listing the top 5 and bottom 5 districts based on HDI values; and second by listing the top 10 and bottom 10 taluks as well as NKR. The HDI values of the top 5 and bottom 5 districts are given in Table 11.5.

Table 11.5: Particulars of top 5 and bottom 5 districts according to HDI values.

Sl. no.	*District*	*Standard of living index*		*Health index*		*Education index*		*HDI*	
		Value	*Rank*	*Value*	*Rank*	*Value*	*Rank*	*Value*	*Rank*
1	**2**	**3**	**4**	**5**	**6**	**7**	**8**	**9**	**10**
				Top 5 Districts					
1.	Bangalore Urban	1.000	1	0.919	2	0.868	1	0.928	1
2.	Dakshina Kannada	0.647	2	0.848	3	0.600	16	0.691	2
3.	Udupi	0.405	10	1.000	1	0.760	2‘	0.675	3
4.	Kodagu	0.527	6	0.743	8	0.727	4	0.658	4
5.	Chikkamagaluru	0.446	8	0.815	‘5	0.677	5	0.627	5
				Bottom 5 Districts					
1.	Gadag	0.208	23	0.307	27	0.670	7	0.350	26
2.	Vijayapura	0.143	29	0.624	14	0.400	28	0.329	27
3.	Koppal	0.183	27	0.197	29	0.613	13	0.280	28
4.	Yadgir	0.084	30	0.389	26	0.230	30	0.196	29
5.	Raichur	0.179	28	0.110	30	0.231	29	0.165	30

Note: The districts are arranged in the descending order of their HDI values and ranks in the state.

Source: Government of Karnataka; Derived from the district-wise data on HDI values available in the DHDRs (2014) of 30 districts.

From the data presented in Table 11.5 we may draw the following inferences on the relative levels of development and backwardness on the basis of HDI values:

i) It is shocking to note that none of the districts of NKR is found in the list of top 5 districts. All the five districts which occupy the first five ranks in the state belong to SKR. This indicates that NKR lags behind SKR.

ii) If we view the same situation with reference to the divisions of SKR, four out of five districts belong to Mysore division and one *i.e.*, Bangalore Urban belongs to Bangalore division. The second, third, fourth and fifth ranks in the state go to the four districts of Mysore division and the first rank district belongs to Bangalore division. These figures make it crystal-clear that development is concentrated in SKR.

iii) When we see the list of bottom five districts, we cannot but get rudely shocked to know that all the five districts having ranks from 26th to 30th belong to NKR and none to SKR. And in NKR, two districts occupying the 26th and 27th ranks belong to Belgaum division and the remaining three districts occupying the 28th, 29th and 30th ranks belong to Gulbarga division.

This exercise with reference to HDI values also depicts the same situation in respect of development and backwardness, which the earlier two exercises showed about the relative positions of regions and divisions.

11.3.7. Top 10 and Bottom 10 Taluks as per HDI Values

This section is a sequel to section 2.1.5. An attempt is made here to identify the inter-regional and intra-regional development by considering the top 10 and bottom 10 taluks in terms of their HDI values. The related details are presented in Table 11.6.

The data presented in Table 11.6 clearly show that:

i) Development is concentrated in SKR. Of the top 10 taluks, 9 belong to SKR and 1 to NKR and of the 9 taluks of SKR, 5 belongs to Bangalore division and 4 to Mysore division. The one taluk of NKR belongs to Belgaum division and none to Gulbarga division. It means that Gulbarga does not have any place among the ten top 10 taluks in the state. All the first 10 ranks in the state, except rank 7, go to SKR. This shows that development is more pronounced in SKR.

ii) As far as the bottom 10 taluks are concerned, diametrically opposite to the top 10 taluks, 9 out of 10 taluks belong to NKR and one to SKR. Of the 10 ranks, (from 167 to 176, except the 167th rank which goes to SKR, the remaining 9 ranks go to the taluks of NKR. This shows that backwardness is more pronounced in NKR.

iii) Among the 4 divisions, as far as the top 10 taluks are concerned, Bangalore division claims the first position with 5 of its taluks,

Table 11.6: Particulars of top 10 and bottom 10 taluks as per HDI values.

Sl. no.	*District*	*Taluks*	*Standard of giving index*		*Health index*		*Education index*		*HDI*	
			Value	*Rank*	*Value*	*Rank*	*Value*	*Rank*	*Value*	*Rank*
1	2	3	4	5	6	7	8	9	10	11
			Top 10 Taluks							
1.	Bangalore Urban	Anekal	0.870	01	0.794	48	0.674	05	0.775	01
2.	Bangalore Uran	Bangalore North	0.787	02	0.920	09	0.631	14	0.770	02
3.	Tumkur	Tumkur	0.557	13	0.807	40	0.901	01	0.740	03
4.	Dakshina Kannada	Mangalore	0.756	03	0.867	20	0.591	26	0.729	04
5.	Bangalore Urban	Bangalore South	0.599	09	0.935	08	0.662	09	0.718	05
6.	Bangalore Urban	Bangalore East	0.529	20	0.948	05	0.715	03	0.711	06
7.	Uttara Kannada	Karwar	0.516	22	0.948	06	0.693	04	0.697	07
8.	Udupi	Udupi	0.529	21	0.950	03	0.672	06	0.696	08
9.	Hassan	Hassan	0.492	26	0.989	01	0.630	18	0.675	09
10.	Mysore	Mysore	0.716	04	0.814	31	0.502	85	0.664	10
			Bottom 10 Taluks							
1.	Tumkur	Madhugiri	0.245	116	0.473	153	0.200	175	0.285	167
2.	Koppal	Yalburga	0.108	172	0.402	168	0.500	86	0.279	168
3.	Vijayapura	Sindagi	0.098	173	0.643	102	0.363	160	0.279	169
4.	Gulbarga	Jewargi	0.083	176	0.623	111	0.411	143	0.277	170
5.	Gadag	Mundargi	0.160	159	0.206	176	0.583	31	0.268	171
6.	Raichur	Manvi	0.181	150	0.415	165	0.255	171	0.267	172
7.	Gulbarga	Chincholi	0.088	174	0.516	146	0.400	148	0.263	173
8.	Raichur	Sindhanur	0.208	136	0.261	174	0.323	166	0.260	174
9.	Yadgiri	Shorapur	0.132	169	0.433	160	0.270	170	0.249	175
10.	Raichur	Devadurga	0.084	175	0.412	166	0.177	176	0.183	176

Note: The taluks are arranged in the descending order of their HDI ranks in the state.
Source: Government of Karnataka: Derived from the DHDRs (2014) of the 30 districts of Karnataka.

Mysore claims the second position with 4 of its taluks, and Belgaum the last position by having only one taluk in that category. In other words it is to say, that development is concentrated in the two divisions of SKR.

iv) As far as the bottom 10 taluks are concerned, Gulbarga division claims the first position with 7 of its taluks in this list, and Belgaum division occupies the second position with 2 of its taluks in this category. And the last position goes to Bangalore division, which has only one taluk in this category. All this, is to say that backwardness is concentrated in the two divisions of NKR.

In sum, it is to say that the findings of this exercise are in sync with those of the preceding section.

II

11.3.8. Measurement of Regional Imbalances by Disaggregative Metrics

The nature and extent of regional disparities captured in section 2.1 are by using aggregative metrics. As a sequel to it, an attempt is made in this section to gauge regional imbalances by using some disaggregative measures. This exercise helps us to capture micro dimensions of disparities which get concealed in aggregates and averages. Here we have used individual indicators such as literary rate — total, male and female — besides gender gaps in literacy to measure female advantage/ disadvantage, concentration of SC/ST population, workers — with reference to cultivators and landless agricultural labourers — and school drop outs.

11.3.9. Literacy Rates and Regional Disparities

Literacy is one of the important indicators of development and deprivation. It is an integral part of human development. And female literacy has a decisive influence on overall development, besides its implications for matters pertaining to life and death such as, age of marriage, total fertility rate, Infant Mortality Rate (IMR), Child Mortality Rate (CMR), Maternal Mortality Rate (MMR) and reproductive health care. And gender gaps in literacy indicate the extent of female advantage/ disadvantage. Above all, literacy rates – male and female – also have profound bearing on participatory democracy. With this brief preface, the division-wise and region-wise data in respect of literacy rates and gender gaps in literacy for two points of time — 2001 and 2011 — are presented in Table 11.7.

From the data presented in Table 11.7, we may draw the following inferences:

i) One heartening fact is that there has been perceptible improvement in literacy rates – total, male and female – in all the four divisions and two regions. It is also the case with the state. But the improvement is not uniform in all the divisions.

Table 11.7: Particulars of literacy rates by divisions and regions: 2001 and 2011.

Sl. no.	*Divisions/ Regions*	*Literacy rates (in percentage)*							
		Total		*Male*		*Female*		*Gender gap (in percentage points)*	
		2001	*2011*	*2001*	*2011*	*2001*	*2011*	*2001*	*2011*
1	2	3	4	5	6	7	8	9	10
1.	Bangalore division	72.37	80.32	80.28	85.94	63.98	74.42	16.30	11.52
2.	Mysore division	69.11	76.86	76.93	82.91	61.36	70.97	15.57	11.94
3.	South Karnataka Region	71.09	79.07	78.89	84.87	62.98	73.15	16.01	11.72
4.	Belgaum division	65.10	74..38	76.28	82.75	53.48	65.88	22.80	16.87
5.	Gulbarga division	53.60	64.44	65.82	74.20	41.06	54.51	24.76	19.69
6.	North Karnataka Region	60.32	70.13	71.94	79.11	48.29	61.01	23.65	18.10
7.	Karnataka State	66.64	75.34	76.10	82.47	56.87	68.08	19.23	14.39

Source: 1) Census of India 2001, Primary Census Abstract Series 30- Karnataka.
2) Census of India 2011, Primary Census Abstract Series - Karnataka.

ii) The literacy rates of SKR and its divisions are higher than those of NKR and its divisions in 2001 and 2011. Their literacy rates are also higher than those of Karnataka State in 2001 and 2011.

iii) Among the divisions, Gulbarga division merits attention. Notwithstanding the improvement it has registered between 2001 and 2011, its rates in 2011 are far lower than the state average rates of 2011. Further all its rates are far below the averages of SKR and NKR and also of all other divisions in the state. If we consider literacy, a constitutive component of development, Gulbarga division emerges as the most backward division in the state.

iv) The last two columns (9 and 10) clearly show the gender disadvantage that Gulbarga division suffers. Though there is perceptible reduction in gender gap in literacy between 2001 and 2011, it is larger than the gender gaps of all the divisions, regions, and the state average. If gender gap in literacy is an indicator of backwardness in general and that of women in particular, then Gulbarga division cannot but attract the tag of the most backward division in the state.

v) As far as interregional disparities are concerned, NKR lags behind SKR in all the three rates of literacy in 2001 as well as in 2011. It also lags behind the state's performance in both points of time. Its gender gaps in literacy in 2001 as well as in 2011, are larger than those of SKR and the state's figures. This shows that NKR is relatively backward when compared to SKR.

In sum, the literacy data and the data pertaining to gender gaps in literacy, NKR's performance is far below the performance of SKR as well as of the state's. It is also the case with the performance of Gulbarga division. The improvement that has been registered by NKR and Gulbarga between 2001 and 2011 has not been adequate enough to narrow down interregional and intraregional disparities.

11.3.10. School Dropout Rates and Regional Disparities in Karnataka

School dropout rates have direct bearing on the capability-generating variables, and as such, their implication for the capability-centred approach to development. Other things remaining constant, a given region's development varies directly with the quantity and quality of capabilities. So, school dropout rates are used to identify the relative backwardness of regions: lower the dropout rates, lesser the backwardness and higher the dropout rates, higher the degree of backwardness. With this brief note on the importance of school dropout rates, an attempt is made in this section to identify the deprivation distances between SKR and NKR and among the four divisions of the state. The related data are given in Table 11.8.

The data presented in Table 11.8, *inter alia*, reveal the interregional and inter-divisional disparities in school dropout rates, in absolute numbers as well as in percentages. The table reveals the following facts:

i) The school dropout rate between 2004–05 and 2009–10 for the state, as a whole, is 34.24 percent. The corresponding figures for the two regions — SKR and NKR — are 24.07 and 44.70 percent respectively. From these figures, we may infer that NKR is more backward than SKR in terms of school dropouts.

ii) Further, if we compare the regions', dropout rates with that of the state's, it becomes further clear that NKR whose dropout rate is

Table 11.8: Particulars of school dropouts in Karnataka by divisions and regions: 2005–06 and 2009–10 (in numbers).

Sl. no.	*Divisions/ Regions*	*Enrolment in V standard in 2004–05*	*Enrolment in X standard in 2009–10*	*Dropped out students between 2004–05 and 2009–10*
1	2	3	4	5
1.	Bangalore division	3,82,840	2,87,069	95,771 (25.01)
2.	Mysore division	1,98,210	1,54,109	44,101 (22.24)
3.	South Karnataka Region	5,81,050	4,41,178	1,39,872 (24.07)
4.	Belgaum division	3,14,873	1,93,168	1,21,705 (39.92)
5.	Gulbarga division	2,41,364	1,14,416	1,26,948 (52.59)
6.	North Karnataka Region	5,56,237	3,07,584	2,48,653 (44.70)
7	Karnataka	11,37,287	7,48,762	3,88,525 (34.24)

***Source*:** (1) Government of Karnataka 2006, Department of Public Instruction, Samagra Anki-Amsha 2006, Sarva Shiksha Abhiyan Bangalore, pp. 123–130 and (2) Government of Karnataka 2006, Department of Public Instruction, Bangalore, Education in Karnataka State, District Report 2009-10, Sarva Shiksha Abhiyan, p. 190.

Note: The figures in brackets indicate the percentage of students dropped out.

higher than the state's by 10.46 percentage points (44.70 – 34.24), lags far behind SKR whose corresponding figure is less than the state's by 10.17 percentage points (34.24 – 24.07).

iii) Intra-regionally, in SKR, the dropout rate of Bangalore division is higher than that of Mysore – both in absolute numbers and in percentages. However, their figures are far below the state's. Whereas, in the case of NKR, Gulbarga division carries a higher burden of dropouts (52.59 percent) than Belgaum's (39.92 percent) as well as of the state's (34.24 percent).

All this is to say that inter-regionally NKR, by carrying a higher burden of school dropouts, attracts the tag of the more backward region, and Gulbarga division, which carries the highest burden of school dropouts, emerges as the most backward division.

11.3.11. Concentration of SC and ST Population and Regional Disparities in Karnataka

The SCs and STs come under the category of historically excluded and deprived sections of the society. Notwithstanding several measures taken by the government – central and state – under constitutionally provided policy of affirmative discrimination, they have yet to make their meaningful entry into the mainstream development process. The capabilities they have to avail the emerging livelihood opportunities, fall short of the capabilities required in the present globalised world. For diverse reasons, the areas where their concentration is high, are said to be more backward than areas a where their concentration is low. This is what we find in Karnataka. The related data are presented in Table 11.9.

Table 11.9: Particulars of SC and ST population in Karnataka by divisions and regions.

Sl. no.	*Divisions / Regions*	*Unit*	*SCs*	*STs*	*Total of columns 4 and 5*	*Percentage share of SC/ST population in the population of the respective divisions/regions*
1	2	3	4	5	6	7
1.	Bangalore division	Lakhs	39.92	13.12	53.04	23.55 percent
2.	Mysore division	Lakhs	19.57	7.47	27.04	21.52 percent
3.	South Karnataka Region (SKR)	Lakhs	59.49	20.59	80.08	22.82 percent
4.	Belgaum division	Lakhs	20.26	7.58	27.84	18.81 percent
5.	Gulbarga division	Lakhs	24.99	14.30	39.29	35.03 percent
6.	North Karnataka Region (NKR)	Lakhs	45.25	21.88	67.13	25.81 percent
7.	Karnataka	Lakhs	104.25	42.47	147.21	24.01 percent

Source: Compiled from Census of India 2001, Primary Census Abstract, Data Highlights, Karnataka Series 30, Directorate of Census Operations, Bangalore.

The data presented in Table 11.9 reveal the following facts about the relative concentration of SC and ST population between the two regions and among the four divisions:

i) In terms of absolute numbers, the SCs and STs, together, are far higher in SKR than in NKR (column 6). SCs taken separately are far higher in SKR than in NKR (column 4). In the case of STs

NKR excels SKR by a slender margin (column 5). These absolute figures do not help us to draw any useful inference on the concentration of SCs and STs than that and of the relative backwardness of the regions.

ii) The data in column 7 are reliable for drawing some useful inferences on the issue under consideration. The column 7 which provides data on the percentage share of SC and ST population in the total population of the regions concerned shows us the real picture; NKR with 25.81 percent of its total population carries higher concentration of SCs and STs than that of SKR (22.82 percent).

iii) Intra-regionally, in SKR, Bangalore division carries a higher burden of SCs and STs than Mysore division – both in absolute numbers as well as in percentage, share. This means, in SKR, Bangalore division is relatively backward. In the case of NKR, both in absolute numbers and percentage share, Gulbarga emerges as the relatively backward division.

iv) And among the four divisions, Gulbarga, by claiming the highest percentage share (35.03) attracts the tag of the most backward division in the state and Belgaum with the least percentage share gets the tag of the least backward division in the state. The second and third positions in backwardness go respectively to Bangalore and Mysore.

In sum, based on the percentage share of SC and ST population in the total population of a given region/division, NKR emerges as the more backward region than SKR in the state, and among the divisions, Gulbarga emerges as the most backward division in the state.

11.3.12. Cultivators and Landless Agricultural Labourers and Regional Disparities in Karnataka

Regional disparity is a multidimensional phenomenon and a multivariate function. The workers engaged in agricultural operations are also considered in disparity studies. Cultivators, who own land, and landless agricultural labourers, who own nothing but their labour, constitute total agricultural workers. Generally, areas in which landless agricultural labourers are larger in number than cultivators are said to be relatively backward than those in which cultivators excel agricultural labours. In this section, an attempt is made to capture the interregional and interdivisional disparities and also to examine the inter-temporal trends in such disparities. The related data for two points of time – 2001 and 2011 – are presented Table 11.10.

Table 11.10: Particulars of cultivators and landless agricultural labourers by divisions and regions: 2001 and 2011 (in lakhs).

Sl. no.	*Divisions/ Regions*	*Total workers*		*Cultivators*		*Landless agricultural labourers workers*		*Total agricultural*	
		2001	*2011*	*2001*	*2011*	*2001*	*2011*	*2001*	*2011*
1	2	3	4	5	6	7	8	9	10
1.	Bangalore division	82.23 (34.96)	10.23 (39.55)	22.58 (32.55)	22.06 (33.54)	19.82 (26.25)	20.04 (28.03)	38.88 (29.58)	42.10 (30.56)
2.	Mysore division	54.76 (23.28)	53.57 (19.22)	17.34 (25.00)	14.05 (21.36)	10.24 (16.49)	10.14 (14.18)	27.58 (20.98)	24.19 (17.62)
3.	South Karnataka Region	136.99 (58.24)	163.80 (58.76)	39.92 (57.56)	36.11 (54.90)	26.54 (42.74)	30.18 (42.22)	66.46 (50.56)	66.29 (48.29)
4.	Belgaum division	57.09 (24.27)	64.67 (23.24)	18.00 (25.95)	17.76 (27.00)	18.85 (30.36)	21.38 (29.91)	36.85 (28.03)	39.14 (28.52)
5.	Gulbarga division	41.14 (17.49)	50.09 (18.00)	11.43 (16.48)	11.90 (18.09)	16.20 (26.09)	19.92 (13.76)	28.13 (21.40)	31.82 (23.19)
6.	North Karnataka Region	98.23 (41.76)	114.76 (41.24)	29.43 (42.43)	29.66 (45.09)	35.55 (57.25)	41.30 (57.78)	64.98 (49.44)	70.96 (51.71)
7.	Karnataka	235.22 (100.00)	278.72 (100.00)	69.35 (100.00)	65.77 (100.00)	62.09 (100.00)	71.48 (100.00)	131.44 (100.00)	137.25 (100.00)

Sources: (1) Census of India 2001, Primary Census Abstract, data Highlights Karnataka Series 30, Directorate of Census Operations, Bangalore.
(2) Census of India 2011 Primary Census Abstract, Data Highlights, Karnataka Series 30, Directorate of Census Operations, Bangalore.

Note: (1) The figures in brackets indicate the relative shares of divisions and regions in the state's total agricultural workers.
(2) The data in columns 3 and 4 pertain to the total workforce in the state, including agricultural workers.

The Table 11.10 reveals the interregional and intraregional disparities and their inter-temporal trends between the two regions and among the four divisions:

i) The data of 2001 (columns 5 and 7) pertaining to the size of cultivators and landless agricultural labourers show that SKR is in a better position than NKR by claiming 57.56 percent of the state's cultivators and 42.74 percent of the state's landless agricultural labourers as against NKR's figures of 42.43 and 57.25

percent respectively. By this criterion NKR lags behind SKR by carrying higher burden of landless agricultural Labourers.

ii) In 2011, though we find some increase in the percentage share of NKR in the state's figure of cultivators (42.43 in 2001 to 45.09 percent in 2011), it continues to lag behind SKR. Further, the NKR's share in the state's landless agricultural labourers is not only higher than the share of SKR; it has also recorded a marginal increase from 57.25 in 2001 to 57.78 percent in 2011. In both the points of time, NKR, by claiming a lower share of cultivators and higher share landless agricultural labouers in the state when compared to SKR, NKR remains more backward than SKR.

iii) Among the four divisions, Gulbarga has the lowest percentage of cultivators in 2001 and 2011 when compared to the shares of cultivators in the remaining three divisions. Thus, it remains backward in terms of the number of agricultural workers who are cultivators.

iv) The census of India 2011, provides data about another important indicator of backwardness, *i.e.*, female agricultural labourers; higher proportion of female agricultural labourers in total workers is indicative of the relative backwardness. For instance, in Bangalore and Mysore divisions, females in total agricultural labourers account for 51.85 percent, while their share in the total workers of the region is only 33.15 percent. As against this, in Belgaum and Gulbarga divisions, females in the total workers account for 37.97 percent, whereas, their share in agricultural labourers is 56.78 percent. From this we may infer that NKR lags behind SKR.

PART THREE

11.4. REDRESSAL OF REGIONAL IMBALANCES

The regional imbalances that came to the surface with the merger of the relatively more backward districts with those of the relatively developed districts in 1956 to form the enlarged state of Mysore, despite several redressal measures and in spite of some progress achieved in the former group of districts, imbalances persist. The persistence of disparities, among other things, is because of two reasons: first, as already stated, development is essentially imbalanced since it does not appear everywhere at a time, and the areas where it appears, grow at a faster rate than the relatively lagging regions/areas; and second, in the case of Karnataka, the lagging regions were very backward at the time of merger.

In the aforesaid background, it is heartening to note that the government of Karnataka has not only been expressing its verbal concern about the problem of disparities, but has also been converting such concern into action by instituting redressal measures from time to time. Redressal of regional imbalances has the support of our egalitarian constitution. Articles 38(2) and 39(a) (b) (c), among other things, explicitly express the concern about regional imbalances. This concern for balanced development found its expression in our national level Five Year Plans. On the same lines, the Government of Karnataka has been sincerely striving to reduce the development-deprivation distances between the regions, among the divisions and districts. To begin with Fifth Five Year Plan of Karnataka (1974–1979), inter alia, stated: "The plans of the state so far have laid emphasis on overall development through an aggregate and sectoral strategy than on regional planning with a bias towards a redressal of the particular problems and deficiencies of the various regions".

But the problem of devising criteria for identifying backward areas took a lot of time. But here we are not going into the details of that problem. Our focus is on the measures instituted by the Government of Karnataka to reduce regional imbalances. Some such measures are:

11.4.1. Decentralised Planning

The government of Karnataka introduced bottom-up planning; the government started district level decentralized planning in 1978. It devised operationally useful criteria for allocating financial resources giving a weightage of 50 percent for backwardness as measured by agricultural output, irrigation, industrial output, roads and railway facilities, financial infrastructure, medical and health facilities, employment, power supply, problems of weaker sections and special areas like malnad and drought-prone areas. But even to this day in 2016, decentralized bottom-up planning from Grama Panchayats, Taluk Panchayats and Zilla Panchayats continues to be some sort of top-down planning. The District Planning Committees (DPCs) were entrusted with the responsibility of supplanting top-down planning with bottom-up decentralized planning. But most of the DPCs have not become fully functional. So, decentralized planning, in the strict sense of the term, has not yet become a functional reality.

11.4.2. Area Development Boards

With a view to reducing regional imbalances, the government set-up area development boards. The first one to be set up was the Hyderabad Karnataka Area Development Board (HKADB) in 1991. This board's jurisdiction was limited to Gulbarga division. The jurisdiction of other boards which followed HKADB, transcended the boundaries of their divisions in which they were set-up. They include Malnad Area Development Board (MADB) in 1993, Bayaluseeme Development Board (BDB) in 1995, Border Area Development Board (BADB) and Karavali Development Authority and so on. They were given special funds to supplement the planned efforts to accelerate the process of convergence.

The High Power Committee For Redressal of Regional Imbalance (HPCFRRI), popularly known as Dr. D.M. Nanajundappa Committee (DMNC), instituted a study to find out the impact of these Boards in reducing regional imbalances in the state. The task of evaluation was entrusted to the Centre for Multi-disciplinary Research (CMDR), Dharwad. Writing about the performance of HKADB, it said: "Correction of regional imbalances does not seem to the explicit focus of the Board's activities". (Government of Karnataka, 2002, HPCFRRI Final Report, Accompaniment 2, p. 14). The evaluation study has also made a general remark on the performance all the Boards. It has observed: "A close scrutiny of the information gathered from different sources reveals that none of the boards has strictly adhered either the guidelines laid down or the charters provided in respect of holding meetings, allocation of funds, implementation, supervision and monitoring of the progress of the schemes": (Government of Karnataka, HFCFRRI, Final Report, Accompaniment 2: p. 6). From this we may infer that the impact of the boards in reducing regional imbalances has been negligible.

And based on the evaluation report, the HPCFRRI recommended for the abolition of all the area development boards. However, the government could not and did not abolish the boards; they continue to exist.

11.4.3. Eight-Year Special Development Plan: 2007–08 to 2014–15

This is one of the most important redressal measures recommended by the HPCFRRI in June 2002. But, it was kept in cold storage till 2007-08 – the year in which it was implemented. It is of interest to note that unlike other measures, it covers all the regions, divisions, districts and taluks, but its focus is on 114 backward taluks, among the 175 taluks in the state. The study has covered all the 175 taluks – then existing in 2000–2002 – of which, as already stated 61 were Relatively Developed Taluks and 114 Backward Taluks, (39 were most Backward Taluks, 40 more Backward Taluks and 35 Backward Taluks.) Of the 61 Relatively Developed Taluks, 40 were in SKR and 21 were in NKR. And of the 39 most Backward Taluks, 13 were in SKR and 26 in NKR. These figures do indicate the disparities between SKR and NKR. The 8–Year Special Development Plan (SDP) is one of the major recommendations to redress regional imbalances in the state. As already pointed out Rs. 31,000 Crore (of which Rs. 16,000 Crore was the additional fund to be added to Rs. 15,000 Crore – the expected normal development funds that flow into 114 taluks through annual budget allocations.

In this background, an attempt is made in this section to critically examine the implementation of the plan. First, the government implemented, not in 2002, but in 2007–08 and that too without revising the quantum of allocations considering the cost escalation. And during the 8 years of implementation also, government did not bother to carryout revision of indices every year as recommended by the HPCFRRI. Second, even the additional resources (Rs. 16,000 Crore) constituted a part of the budgetary allocations and not as additional resources. Third, while making allocations among the four divisions, the government, using its own formula, instead of the one recommended by the HPC, allocated Rs. 128 Crore less in the first year to Gulbarga division, the most backward division which carried 40 percent of the total deprivation in the state. And when it was brought to the notice of the government by B. Seshadri (a member of the HPC) and T.R. Chandasekhar (Former Consultant for Karnataka State Fourth Finance Commission), the government adopted the Committee's formula from 2008–09 onwards. Fifth, as the following Table 11.11 reveals, the allocations made were not fully released, and the funds released were not fully expended. From these facts, one can imagine to what extent the SDP would have redressed regional imbalances. The details in respect of the annual allocations, releases, and expenditure for 8 years from 2007–08 to 2014–15, are presented in Table 11.11.

We may draw the following inferences from the data presented in Table 11.11.

Of the total allocation made for 8 years (Rs. 20,138.59 Crore), a sum of Rs. 14,246.82 Crore was released, and Rs.13,171.34 Crore was expended in 8 years. In terms of percentage, only 65.40 percent of the

Table 11.11: Year-wise allocation, release and expenditure under 8-Year SDP (Rs. crore).

Sl. no.	*Year*	*Allocation*	*Release*	*Expenditure*	*Expenditure as a percentage of allocation*	*Expenditure as a percentage of release*
1	2	3	4	5	6	7
1.	2007–08	1571.50	827.93	804.48	51.19	97.17
2.	2008–09	2547.34	1344.29	1134.00	44.52	84.36
3.	2009–10	2578.83	1731.12	1543.11	59.84	89.14
4.	2010–11	2584.00	1924.47	1762.54	68.21	91.59
5.	2011–12	2984.14	2529.99	2200.16	73.73	86.96
6.	2012–13	2680.00	2464.83	2402.92	89.66	97.49
7.	2013–14	2925.60	2053.65	2067.56	70.67	100.68
8.	2014–15	2267.18	1370.54	1256.57	55.42	91.68
9.	Total	20,138.59	14,246.82	13,171.34	65.40	92.45

Source: Government of Karnataka 2016, Planning, Programme Monitoring and Statistics Department, Bangalore.

total allocation was expended, and the expenditure, as a percentage of the total releases was 92.45 percent. It is necessary to note that the release of Rs. 14,246.82 Crore fell short of the total allocation of Rs. 20,138.59 Crore by Rs. 5,891.77 Crore. These figures indicate, among other things, that the government did not implement the SDP in the true spirit of the recommendation of the HPC. As such, it could not reduce the regional imbalances expected by the HPC. Considering the decisive role that the SDP can play in redressing interregional and intraregional imbalances, the government has extended the 8–year SDP by four more years from 2015–16 to 2018–19. And it has earmarked Rs. 12,000 Crore for four years (at Rs. 3000 Crore a year). If implemented properly by revising the CDI values and the division-wise and taluk-wise allocations accordingly, it may not be a surprise if the extended 4–year SDP may bring about substantial reduction in regional disparities.

11.4.4. Backward Regions Grant Fund (BRGF)

This is a Central Government programme – based on the principle of affirmative discrimination – introduced in 2007 with a view to enabling backward districts in the country to enter the mainstream development process and thereby promote inclusive development. The Rashtriya Sam Vikas Yojana (RSVY), a plan which was previously administered by the Planning Commission was subsumed into BRGF. In Karnataka, six districts were selected under BRGF. They are: Bidar, Chitradurga,

Davanagere, Kalaburagi (Gulbarga), Raichur and Yadgir. And of the six, four districts belong to NKR and two to SKR. The total amount allocated for 8 years from 2007–08 to 2014–15 for six BRGF districts was 985.78 cr. But the entire amount was not expended; a sum of Rs. 831.63 cr. (84.36 percent) was expended during the 8–year period. Notwithstanding this, the programme could not make significant contribution to the process of reducing regional imbalances.

11.4.5. Hyderabad Karnataka Region Development Board: Article 371 (J)

The Constitutional Amendment of Article 371 by inserting article 371(J), (2nd January 2013) which conferred special status to the most backward Hyderabad Karnataka Region (HKR) in the state, is a milestone in the development of the region comprising the six districts of Ballari, Bidar, Gulbarga, Koppal, Raichur and Yadgir. It is a much sought after demand of the inhabitants of the region. As far as redressal of regional imbalances is concerned, unlike SDP, it is confined to HKR only. One of the important institutional changes that it has brought about is the establishment of a statutory Board called Hyderabad Karnataka Region Development Board (HKRDB). As per the order of the government of Karnataka dated 16th November, 2013, the HKRDB was constituted with 28 members on 23rd January, 2014, and became functional in 2013–14. It is too short a period to evaluate the performance of the Board.

Besides the Board, the other provisions of the Amendment provide reservation in admission to educational institutions, appointments as well as promotions in government service to the natives of this region – both inside and outside the region – are equally important in the development of the region. These provisions have been creating an enabling environment in which the people of the region are not only enabled to acquire capabilities, but also adequate opportunities to use their capabilities to avail the opportunities. Quite a few persons, including students, are benefited from the provision of reservation.

PART FOUR

11.5. CONCLUDING REMARKS

The problem of regional imbalances is not something peculiar to Karnataka; it is a universal phenomenon. What is peculiar about

Karnataka is that the problem, which emerged with the emergence of the enlarged state of Karnataka in 1956, despite several redressal measures, persists in 2016. Why? Is there anything wrong with the metrics that we have been using to measure interregional and intraregional imbalance? Is there anything wrong with the redressal measures that our government has been using from time to time?

As far as the metrics – aggregative as well as disaggregative composite indices and individual indicators – employed by the government to measure development distances in the state are concerned, by and large, they are relatively reliable. Some of the important among them are used in the present exercise, though there are many more methods for measuring imbalances. Among those employed here, the two metrics used by HPCFRRI – CCDI and CDI – give a clear picture of development and deprivation distances respectively among the 175 taluks, 27 districts, 4 divisions and between the 2 regions. From this exercise we come to know: of the 2 regions, NKR lags behind SKR; of the 4 divisions, Gulbarga is the most backward division and Mysore is the least backward division; and the second and third positions go respectively to Bangalore and Belgaum divisions. The HPC study is the first as well as the most comprehensive study (using 35 indicators) to take up disparity analysis down to the taluk level. So, we cannot attribute the failure to wipe out regional imbalances to the metrics employed.

What about the redressal measures? The measures employed to redress spatial disparities are relatively reliable measures. Most of the measures are area-specific – based on the principle of affirmative discrimination – and are aimed at enabling the lagging areas to catch up with the relatively developed areas. These measures did not cover the entire state. For instance, HKADB and its successor HKRDB cover only the 6 districts of HKR (Gulbarga division). But the 8–year SDP – now extended by 4 more years from 2015–16 – covers all the 114 backward taluks in the state (55 of SKR and 59 of NKR). Some of the recommendations, other than SDP, made by the HPC, have much to do with the redressal of regional imbalances.

Even then, we could not make much progress on the redressal front. Some of the reasons could be are:

- In my considered view, the development funds allocated and actually expended were not enough to provide what development economists call "Critical Minimum Effort" or the "Big Push" neccessary for bringing about the qualitative change. The funds were thinly spread across many areas, schemes/projects.

- The SDP, which was expected to transform the situation, was distorted in its implementation. First, it was expected to be implemented in 2003–04 (HPC submitted its Final Report in June 2002) but it was implemented in 2007–08 without revising the indices and the financial requirements. Second, in the very First Year (2007–08) itself, the government, instead of using the allocation formula recommended by the HPC, by using its own formula allocated Rs. 128 Crore less to Gulbarga division – the most backward division. When this deviation was brought its notice, it adhered to HPC formula from 2008–09 onwards. Third, the amounts allocated, often, were not fully released, and the funds released were not fully expended. Those who were in-charge, I think, did not fully own the SDP.

Fourth, effective involvement of the elected representatives has a decisive role in the implementation of redressal measures, particularly of those, who represent lagging regions. This is not happening as far as NKR is concerned. For example, when the position of the Chairman of the High Power Committee for the Implementation of the Recommendations of Dr. D.M. Nanjuandappa Committee fell vacant with the resignation of Mr. Namoshi, the government appointed Mr. Vallyapure, an MLA of HKR, he did not report, it was an opportunity for him to work for the development of his region. He did not. And finally, the citizens who have elected such representatives and particularly the educated electors are equally responsible for such indifference of their representatives. It is said, of course, not wrongly, that the backward people of backward regions are more backward than the backward people of relatively less backward regions.

This, in brief, is the present position of regional imbalances in Karnataka. While formulating and implementing redressal measures, it would be helpful if the government keeps in mind the following suggestions:

- Redressal of regional imbalances needs a well-defined and flexible regional policy. At least now the government should formulate its own regional development policy.
- Responsibility without accountability is of no use in implementing redressal measures as per the time schedule. As it is, nobody is made accountable for the failure of the measures. When profit-driven big business and industrial organizations are talking about Corporate Social Responsibility (CSR), should we not talk about

Administrative Social Responsibility and Accountability (ASRA). I think, we should.

- The focus of the government as well as of the public is on those recommendations of the HPC which have financial implications. There are many other recommendations of the HPC which have bearing on redressal. For instance, the HPC had recommended the establishment of an IIT in Raichur – one of the most backward districts in the state – but, it has been shifted to Dharwad – one of the relatively developed districts, known for its educational infrastructure including Karnatak University and the University of Agricultural Sciences, Fortunately a Central University is established in a village close to Gulbarga city.
- The government should see that the funds are not thinly spread across many areas and many schemes, which would not enable it to provide the critical minimum effort. Required for quantitative and qualitative change. This needs, given the availability of funds, the schemes ought to be prioritized. Of course, it is good politics to please all by thinly spreading the resources, but decidedly, it is bad economics.
- Above all, the implementation committee should see that the funds allocated are fully released, and those released are fully expended in time. And, it should get concurrent evaluation/ mid-term appraisal of schemes done by research institutions, so that corrective measures can be taken, if any deviations are noticed.

In conclusions, I would like to make an appeal to all those officers who are put in-charge of the implementation of redressal measures to consider it their OWN.

REFERENCES

Alono Williaom (1968). *Economic Development and Cultural Change,* 17(1).

Directorate of Census Operations, Bangalore (2001). *Census of India 2001.* Primary Census Abstract. Series 30 Karnataka.

Friedman John and Alons William (*eds.*) (1972). *"Regional Development and Planning: A Reader"*. M.I.T. Press: Cambridge.

Government of Karnataka (2002). Final Report of the High Power Committee for Redressal of Regional Karnataka Imbalances.

Government of Karnataka (2006). Samagra Anki Amhsa: 2006: Department of Public Instructions Sarva Shiksha Abhiyan, Bangalore.

Government of Karnataka (2008). Economic Survey of Karnataka: 2007–08.

Government of Karnataka (2013). State and District Domestic Product 2014–15, DES. Bengaluru.

Government of Karnataka (2014). District Human Development Reports (30 Districts).

Government of Karnataka (2015). Economic Survey of Karnataka: 2014–15.

Hicks, J.R. (1958). *Essays in World Economics*. Oxford: Clarendon Press.

Hirschman, A.O. (1958). *The Strategy of Economic Development USA:* Yale University Press.

Liutz, U. (1962). *Italy: A Study of Economic Development*. London: OUP.

Myrdal, G. (1957). *Economic Theory and Underdeveloped Regions*. Gerald Duckworth.

Seshadri, B. (1991). *Industrializations and Regional Development*. New Delhi: Concept Publishing Company.

Singh Jiwitesh Kumar (1978). *Regional Economics*. Varanasi: Bharati Prakashan.

Williamson, J.G. (1965). "Regional Inequality and the Process of National Development: A Description of Patterns". *Economic Development and Cultural Change*, XIII(4): Part II.

12

Participation in Democratic Decentralized Governance through Grama Sabha: A Case Study from Karnataka

NARAYANA BILLAVA[14] - AND ARUNKUMAR R KULKARNI[15]*

ABSTRACT

Grama Sabha (GS) is the door to see the entire democratic India, and it is an essential component for rural development which can change the fortune of the nation through decision in its meetings. It is a political forum to people in the villages to meet and discuss their problems. The 73rd Constitution Amendment (1993) mandates GS as the constitutionally recognized institute at the grassroot. But the studies revealed that GS meetings have not been found successful in various states. In this context, the present paper tries to present the process of people's participation in Grama Sabha, decision-making, actual role of GS in democratic decentralized governance, and discuss way for strengthening of GS in the future. The paper is based on information collected on Grama Sabha in four selected Grama Panchayats (GPs) in Dharwad district of Karnataka. It reveals that households participation in GS is very less (35%), especially by the weaker sections (SCs and STs) and women. Most (60%) of the people who attended GS felt unsatisfied about its functioning, especially with regard to preparation of developmental plans for the village, selection of beneficiaries, time and date of GS, and poor implementation and monitoring of welfare schemes. It is also unfortunate to know that there is lack of awareness about Modus operandi of conducting GS among the Panchayat officials and GP members. It is found that effective functioning of Grama Sabha mainly depends on leadership quality of

[14] Research Assistant, Abdul Nazir Sab Panchayat Raj Chair, Centre for Multi-disciplinary Development Research (CMDR), Dharwad, Karnataka.

[15] Assistant Professor, Centre for Multi-disciplinary Development Research (CMDR), Dharwad, Karnataka.

**Corresponding author:* E-mail: n.billava@gmail.com; ark.cmdr@gmail.com

Adhyaksha. Awareness among people about GS, convenient time of holding GS, quick responses to the demands of the people and transparency in GP functioning help a lot in making GS successful.

12.1. INTRODUCTION

Article 243A of the Constitution of India describes the composition of Grama Sabha (GS). The same Article (Article 243A) has introduced GS under Karnataka Panchayat Raj Act 1993. As per this Article, GS is the body consisting of all persons registered in the electoral rolls of a village. Thus, GS is a constitutional body as well as an integral part of the concept of a village assembly and it provides a political forum to people in the village to meet and discuss their problems, and gives an opportunity to each and every voter in the jurisdiction of the Grama Panchayat (GP) at the local level to take part in decision-making of decentralized governance, planning and development. Moreover, the GS provides valuable inputs to GP to lead local government effectively, and it also acts as watch dog in the interest of village communities by monitoring the functioning of the GP. GS is the permanent unit in Panchayati Raj system and not constituted for a particular period. GS in Karnataka requires a quorum of 1/10 or minimum100 members of the total GS members (KPR Act 1993: Section 3A). GS provides an opportunity for all community people and marginalized sections (Caste, Gender and Class), to raise their problems and debate on village development issues (Dhavaleshwar and Ali, 2012). The concept of decentralization is generally taken to mean democratic decentralization. In developing countries like India, majority of people are living in the rural areas and people are depending on rural local bodies like Village Panchayat at the lower level and Zilla Panchayat at the upper level than the state and Central Government. GP is the lowest tier in the three-tier Panchayat structure which is nearer to the people, and avails adequate knowledge of local conditions and problems which vary from place to place. Further democratic decentralization increases the opportunities for the popular initiative and participation in the administration and strengthens the democracy.

In Karnataka recently a provision is made for separate women GS (Mahila Grama Sabha) an exclusive platform to discuss women related issues. The GS ensure proper resolution of women related issues. A special GS exclusively for children called "Children Grama Sabha" (Now it's renamed as Children Special Sabha, RDPR Issued Order No. 638–2007) has also been introduced in the Panchayat system, a platform to put children's concerns and forward directly to elected representatives in GS. This GS discusses drinking water facility, construction of toilets and improved access to basic facilities and service in the schools. In addition to these, a special GS is also to be conducted focussing Rashtriya Panchayati Raj Divas (April 24th), Swachh Bharat Mission (October, 2nd), Pradhan Mantri Fasal Bima Yojana (PMFBY), GS on MGNREGA action plan, dealing or coping with drought and any other special GS (as per orders by RDPR/ZP). Moreover, Government of Karnataka amended Karnataka Panchayat Raj Act in 2015, which mentions about Habitation Sabha (Substituted by Act 44 of 2015 w.e.f. 25.02.2016) and Ward Sabha in each ward (like Kerala GS). Thus, many efforts have been made to involve people in the development of village.

12.2. LITERATURE REVIEW

The first Prime Minister of India Pandit Jawaharlal Nehru has said that democracy at the top will not succeed unless it is built on the foundation from below. Diwakar committee in 1963 which was appointed to study the working of Grama Sabha found that the institution of the GS was introduced by statutes as early as in 1947. This committee recommended that, it is necessary to bring the GS into forefront and provide gradual strength to the VP. GS is like a foundation of decentralized democratic system. Scholars (Shivashankar, 2010; Veeresha, 2010) believe that the country has given opportunity for people's participation in the decision- making process in the VP through 73rd Amendment. The studies have revealed that in many states, GS meetings have been conducted in formal manner and people's participation in the decentralized planning process through GS at grassroot level became almost a defunct mechanism (Bhargava and Raphael, 1994; Shivashankar, 2010; Veeresha, 2010). Usually, GS meetings are held at Panchayat headquarters in many states. Therefore, people from distant villages find it difficult to participate in the GS (Mathew, 2000). A study based on field experience from Madhya Pradesh and Rajasthan revealed that many people do not know the dates of the GS meeting fixed by the VP (Choudhury and Jain, 1999; Muraleedharan, 2014). Few studies (Jain, 1999; Oommen, 2009; Shivashankar, 2010) found that GS was not working in true sense, and people had lost faith in the system of GS because of poor attendance, lack of knowledge and skill about the development schemes on the part of the nodal officer, lack of sufficient publicity among members to attend GS, lack of political will, and lack of transparency in recording the minutes of GS. A committee report pointed out that the role of GS/WS (Ward Sabha) is declining in Kerala because of relegation of decentralised planning and development though the state is well known for people's planning and participation (Government of Kerala, 2009).

The idea of GS was accepted by Karnataka in 1985. But with regard its functioning many scholars found that the meetings were not regularly held and peoples' participation was very less (sometime it is less than the quorum of $1/10^{th}$ of voters) (Aziz, 1994; Bhargava and Raphael, 1994; Joshi, 1995; Mathew, 2000; Meenakshisundaram, 1999). Further, the studies pointed out that GS have not being functioning in most parts of Karnataka. Even where they functioned, the attendance was thin and not many marginalized groups (SCs/STs and Women) attended them (Bhargava and Raphael, 1994; Meenakshisundaram, 1999). Lack of awareness among the people, non-seriousness on the part of GP, frequent holding of GSs are some of the main reasons for low participation of public in such meetings (Aziz, 1994; Bhargava and Raphael, 1994). Few studies highlighted that office bearers of the GP were not keen to convene the GS meetings and officials of various departments at the lower level do not attend the GS meetings (Meenakshisundaram, 1999). Further, GS members do not discuss development programmes relating to the village in GS meetings (Meenakshisundaram, 1999; Government of Kerala, 2009).

Decentralised governance in Karnataka has ingredients of both positive and negatives. GS has emerged after a wide process of deliberations. Unless we have a vibrant GS, it is difficult to have empowered and accountable Panchayats (Nambair, 2001). Studies (Roy, 1984; Rathi, 2013) have highlighted that GS gives an opportunity for the persons to directly participate in the decision-making process and play a crucial role in ensuring a transparent and accountable administration. But according to a few other studies people's participation in the decentralized planning process through GS became almost a defunct mechanism (Bhargava and Raphael, 1994; Shivashankar, 2010; Veeresha, 2010).

On the whole, many scholars have revealed that GSs are not working as per the expectations due to several factors. In this context, this paper tries to present the process of people's participation in GS, decision making, actual role in decentralized governance and planning and the ways for strengthening this institution. The analysis is based on primary data collected from four sample GPs (Yarikoppa, Kanakur, Madkihonnihalli and Galagi) in Dharwad district of Karnataka. Within these GPs, 235 households were selected for gathering information on various aspects of GS.

12.3. FINDINGS FROM THE STUDY ON GRAMA SABHA

Legally GS is to be held at GP level once in six months (KPR Act 1993: Section 3A). Further, a special meeting of the GS shall be convened if a request is made by not less than ten percent of the members of the GS with items of agenda specified in such request, and there shall be a minimum of three months period between the two special meetings. The special GS meeting will be called on instructions from government or Zilla Panchayat (ZP) particularly for preparing plans for Mahatma Gandhi National Rural Employment Guarantee Scheme (MGNREGA), Grama Panchayat Development Plan (GPDP), Drought problems Crop Insurance Schemes etc. The functioning of GSs, level of people's participation, the problems faced are discussed in the following paragraphs.

12.3.1. Information on Grama Sabha

People should know well in advance the date, time and venue of GS. This would help them to attend and participate actively in GS. Table 12.1 presents the mode of communication the GPs adopt to inform the residents on GS meetings. The Table reveals that a majority of villagers (about 82%) received information on GS meetings through TomTom and/ or Jatha. Around 18% of villagers come to know about the same through written notices and information by GP members.

Table 12.1: Mode of communication to public on Grama Sabha meetings.

Grama Panchayat	*Tom Tom/Jatha*	*Written notice*	*GP members*
Galagi	84.0	12.0	4.0
Madkihonnihalli	88.9	5.6	5.6
Kanakur	87.5	12.5	–
Yarikoppa	70.8	20.8	8.3
Total	81.9	13.3	4.8

12.3.2. Extent of People's Participation

People's participation in GS not only ensures sustainable development of village but also helps in empowering women and other weaker sections of people. Table 12.2 provides information on the extent of peoples' participation in GSs. It can be seen from the Table that GPs conducted two GS meetings in a year 2010–11. With regard to participation of people in the GSs it varies across the GPs. However, the extent of participation is less than the expected level *i.e.,* less than the quorum of 10%. Further, it is revealed that the GPs took signatures of people who visited their offices in the GS proceedings book/register. Similarly signatures were obtained from the followers of GP members. This is to show that GS had required quorum (1/10 of members or 100 members). The high literacy and active participation of SHG members resulted in higher participation in the GSs in Yarikoppa and Madkihonnihalli GPs. Participation of members by sex reveals that attendance of male members is high compared to females. It is learnt that only the female members of GP, SHG leaders, Anganwadi teachers, Accredited Social Health Activist (ASHA) Workers and women members who wish to get some benefits (like housing, toilet, ration card) attend GS. Among the female members who attended GS, only Anganwadi teachers and Panchayat women members speak relating to their work and benefits to be obtained. This indicates low level of female participation in GSs.

Table 12.2: Details of Grama Sabhas held, people's participation in the selected Grama Panchayats.

Particulars	***Yarikoppa GP***	***Kanakur GP***	***Madkihonnihalli GP***	***Galagi GP***
Number of Grama Sabhas held in a year	2	2	2	2
Members participated (%)	6.8	4.8	6.5	4.4
Percent of male members attended Grama Sabha	43.4	54.5	55.2	75.8
Percent of female members attended Grama Sabha	56.6	39.4	44.8	24.2

***Source*:** Offices of the selected Grama Panchayats.

Discussion with the people in different villages in the selected GPs reveals that most of them have no knowledge about the existence of GS and are being conducted only for the namesake. These meetings are usually conducted when people are busy with their agricultural work and just to avoid their participation. Sincere efforts have not been made to provide information about the date, time, venue and agenda of GS to people. Efforts to motivate people to participate in GSs are also not being made by GP members. Sometimes, the Members of GP themselves prevent the people from participation in GSs as they fear criticism by them on their work, mis-management of funds, etc. All these factors play their role in poor attendance of people in GSs.

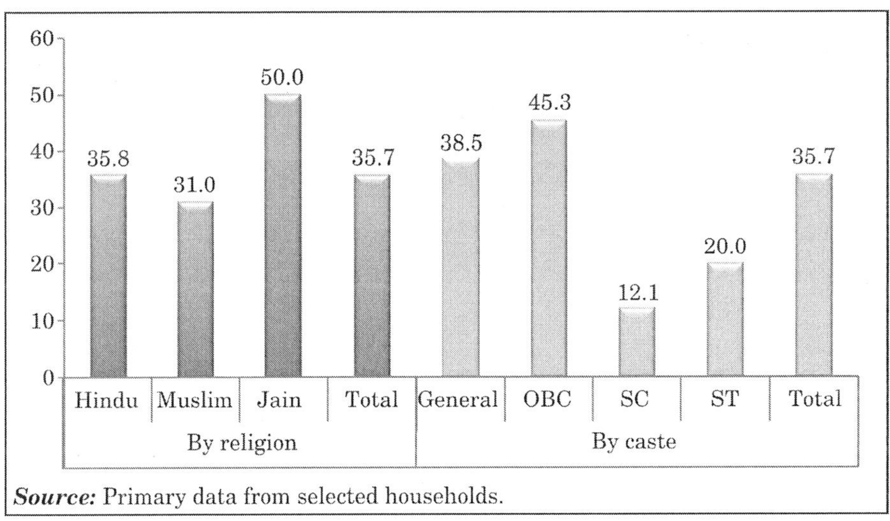

Source: Primary data from selected households.

Fig. 12.1: Participation of households in Grama Sabha by religion and caste.

Fig. 12.1 depicts participation of households in GSs by religion and caste. It may be observed from Fig. 12.1 that 35.8% of Hindu households, 31.0% of Muslims, and 50.0% of Jains participated in GSs. Participation of households according to caste reveals that the other Backward Classes (45.3%) and General (38.5) have participated which is more than the Scheduled Castes (12.1%) and Scheduled Tribes (20.5%). Among the households who attended GS, 86% of them attend all the GSs held in a year. Thus, overall participation of people belonging to the weaker sections is minimal in the GS.

12.3.3. Perceptions of People on Grama Sabha

Fig. 12.2 shows households' perception about functioning of Grama Sabha in the selected GPs. The reveals that on an average around 60% of the households are not satisfied with the functioning of GS conducted by their GP. Satisfaction level is higher (around 70%) among households in Yarikoppa GP which is a developed GP among the selected GPs. In Madkihonnihalli also more number of households are satisfied with the functioning of GS compared to households in the backward GPs of Kanakur (26.1%) and Galagi (33.6%).

Table 12.3 shows reasons for not having good opinion by households about the GSs. It can be seen from the Table that lack of awareness among households about the conduct of GS (59.7%), nature of village politics (52.7%), and inconvenient time (68.1%) are the main reasons for not satisfied about the functioning of GSs. In addition, lack of communication and publicity, unwillingness of the Adhyaksha, Members, and officials to assemble in the GS meeting, and doubts about the power of GS in the minds of the people resulted in not satisfaction of members.

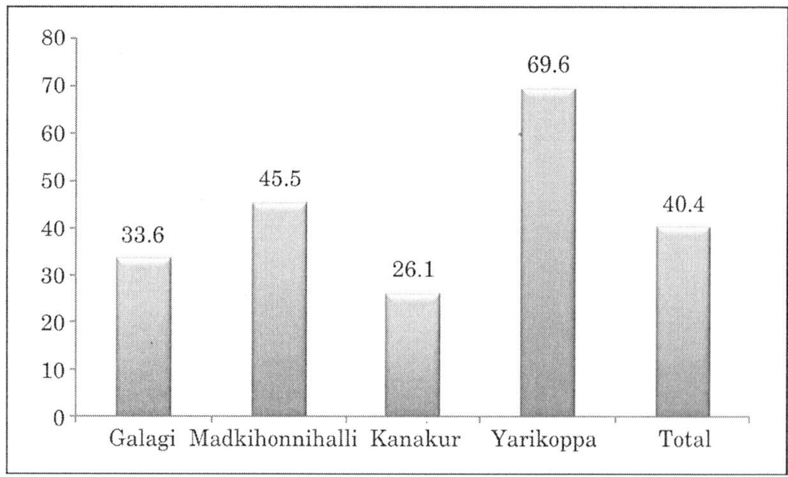

Fig. 12.2: Households level of satisfaction on the functioning of Grama Sabha.

Table 12.3: Reasons for households not satisfied with the working of Grama Sabhas

Reasons for non-satisfaction	*Galagi*	*Madkihon-nihalli*	*Kanakur*	*Yarikoppa*	*Total*
Lack of awareness	70.5	55.6	67.5	45.0	59.7
Village politics	55.0	45.4	60.5	50.0	52.7
Lack of common venue	35.0	30.2	44.5	25.0	33.7
Inconvenient time	75.3	68.6	78.3	50.0	68.1
Lack of communication and publicity	45.6	32.0	54.5	25.0	39.3
Unwillingness of Adhyaksha and officials to convene the meeting	35.5	25.6	43.2	25.0	32.3
Powerlessness of the Grama Sabha	40.0	30.0	45.5	24.0	34.9

12.4. PLANNING AND DECISION-MAKING IN GRAMA SABHAS

GS as stated earlier play an important role in village development. It can bring all the people together to plan and implement programmes for common welfare (Narayanasamy, 1998). GS prepares action plan of the village and approves, it reviews expenditure and income of GP and indentifies beneficiaries of various schemes. Recently, it has been made mandatory for all GPs to prepare action plan for five years which is known as Grama Panchayat Development Plan (GPDP). The Table 12.4 provides information on the issues discussed in the GS meetings. It can be seen from the Table that majority (around 77%) of respondents opined that GP officer and Adhyaksha discussed more about GP schemes and programmes in the GS. Only 44% of respondents opined that decisions are taken in GS concerning to village development, action plan and service delivery. According to respondents majority of the decisions with regard to development are taken in the general body meetings than in the GSs, and Panchayat members are key players when decision are taken by GP.

Table 12.4: Decisions taken in Grama Sabha meetings in the selected Grama Panchayats.

Grama Panchayat	*Galagi*	*Madkihon-nihalli*	*Kanakur*	*Yarikoppa*	*Total*
Preparation of action plan	45.0	57.5	48.0	65.5	54.0
Discussion on GP Schemes/ Programmes	68.5	80.0	73.5	85.5	76.9
Discussion on various sources of GP finance	50	65.7	54.5	70.0	60.1
Decisions taken in GS	35.7	48.0	42.8	52.0	44.6

The members of GS should be satisfied with regard to the functioning of GS. This in turn indicates its usefulness. The Table 12.5 shows the opinion of members of GS on various issues/discussion in the GS. The Table shows that on an average 42.5% of total selected households in four GPs are satisfied with overall role of GS. In Yarikoppa, the level of satisfaction is high because of active participation of members of SHGs and Youth Organizations. Most of the households are not satisfied with level of people participation, preparation of action plan and village plan, efforts by Nodal officer in creating awareness about GS, selection of beneficiaries and Jamabandi.

Table 12.5: Households level of satisfaction on the functioning of GSs (in %).

Particulars	*Galagi*	*Madkihon-nihalli*	*Kanakur*	*Yarikoppa*	*Total*
About people's participation	35.0	45.0	42.0	56.7	44.7
Preparing action plan	46.0	40.4	28.5	60.0	43.7
Village planning	28.0	34.2	26.0	62.3	37.6
Awareness creation by nodel officers	32.3	50.0	36.7	75.0	48.5
Selection of beneficiary	30.6	45.0	21.5	78.6	43.9
Discussion about finance and Jamabandi	25.0	51.0	19.0	52.0	36.8
Overall satisfaction about GS	32.8	44.3	29.0	64.1	42.5

12.4.1. *Grama Sabha – Issues discussed and actions taken*

GPs are primarily responsible for making provision for services and infrastructure in rural areas. Now, this function has been assigned to the GS under section 7 of the Karnataka Panchayat Raj Act, 1993. The issues discussed or activities decided in the GS meetings indicate its importance. Table 12.6 shows the type of issues discussed in the GSs in the selected GPs.

Table 12.6: Major issues discussed in the Grama Sabha meetings in the selected Grama Panchayats.

Particulars	*Yarikoppa*	*Kanakur*	*Madkihon-nihalli*	*Galagi*
Issues discussed in Grama Sabha	1. NREGA 2. Road repair 3. Housing scheme 4. Collection of water tax 5. Creating awareness about latrine facility 6. Others schemes	1. NREGA 2. Lake pitching 3. Housing scheme and beneficiary selection 4. Water shortage 5. Drainage repair 6. Village cleanliness	1. NREGA 2. Repair of old pipelines and maintenance (water leakage from pipes) 3. New pipeline connection 4. Drainage repair	1. NREGA 2. Road repair 3. New pipeline connection households 4. Others new schemes 5. School latrine facility 6. Drainage cleaning
Progress of work after Grama Sabha	Works completed	Incomplete Works	Works completed	Works completed

Table 12.6 reveals that in the GSs, the issues related to employment scheme, water supply and sanitation and employment activities are prominently discussed. The issues relating to planning, finance and Jamabandi are completely neglected. Discussion with villagers reveal that even though the issues related to village development are discussed in GS, they would not be implemented. GP members take their own decisions in general body meetings without considering the suggestions of GS. As majority of issues are not implemented by GP even after discussion in the GSs therefore the people are losing interest in attending GSs. It is reported that GP members do not give attention towards the development of the villages. Moreover the representatives of GPs, especially Adhyakshas, avoid convening of GS meetings just to escape criticism, embarrassment and condemnation from the people.

12.5. CONCLUDING OBSERVATIONS

GS members are lacking knowledge about its very existence and its powers and functions. Systematic efforts are also not being made to create awareness among the public about GS. Lack of information about timing, date and venue of GS are not being given to people well in advance. This results in poor attendance of members, especially weaker sections of the society and women. Active participation of SHGs and Youth organizations ensure active participation of members. During GS, the issues related government programmes, water supply and sanitation and employment generation are mainly discussed. The issues relating to planning, finance and Jamabandi are completely neglected. Most of the issues discussed in GS are not being implemented. Because of all these factors, members are losing interest to participate in GS. To improve this situation, systematic efforts need to be made in the form of creating awareness among people involving SHGs and Youth organizations in every village by GPs. Final selection of beneficiaries for the schemes and programmes need to be finalized in GS itself by taking into consideration the suggestions and comments of its members. This will build confidence in GS and GP leading to more and active participation by the public.

REFERENCES

Aziz Abdul (1994). 'Decentralization: Mandal Panchayat System in Karnataka, National Institute of Rural Development (NIRD), Hyderabad.

Bhargava, B.S. and Raphael, J.C. (1994). 'Working of Grama Sabha in Karnataka: A Study at Micro level'. *Journal of Rural Development, NIRD, Hyderabad*, 13(1): 145–147.

Choudhury, R.C. and Jain, S.P. (*eds.*) (1999). *'Patterns of Decentralised Governance in Rural India', Vol. 1*, National Institute of Rural Development, Hyderabad, India, pp. 1–24.

Dhavaleshwar, C.U. and Ali, S. (2012). A study on people's participation in Grama Sabha and Rural Development in Gulbarga district of Karnataka State". *International Indexed and Referred Research Journal*, IV(39): 25–28.

Government of Kerala (2009). Report of the Committee for Evaluation of Decentralised Planning and Development in Kerala, (M.A. Oommen Committee).

Jain, S.P. (1999). Grama Sabha: Task before the nation. *Kurukshetra*, 48(1): 23.

Joshi, G.V. (1995). Grama Sabha in Karnataka: A non-starter, Kurukshetra, Vol 43 (7): 113-116.

Mathew George (*ed.*) (2000). 'Status of Panchayati Raj in the States and Union Territories of India', Institute of Social Sciences and Concept Publishing Company, New Delhi.

Meenakshisundaram, S.S. (1999). *Grama Sabha: Lessons from Karnataka, Kurukshetra*, 48(1): 59.

Muraleedharan, S. (2014). 'Democratic decentralization and citizenship'. *Economic and Political Weekly*, XLIX(20): 69–74.

Nambiar Malini (2001). Making Grama Sabha work. *Economic and Political Weekly*, 36(33): 3114–3117.

Narayanasamy, S. (1998). Role of Grama Sabha in the New Panchayati Raj System, Kurukshetra, Vol XLVI (7): 11-16.

Rathi Shubhangi (2013). Gandhian Concept of Village Development and India's Development Policy, Bombay Sarvodaya Mandal and Gandhi Research Foundation.

Roy Ramshray (1984). '*Self and Society: A Study in Gandhian Thought*, New Delhi, Sage, p. 123.

Shivashankar, P. (2010). 'Grama Sabha: Challenges before us', *In*: Hasan Ashraful and Prasad Ganesh (*eds.*), ANSSIRD, Mysore, pp. 115–117.

Veeresha Nayakara (2010). 'Functioning of Grama Sabha in Tamil Nadu: A study in selected Village Panchayats in Sriperumbudur Block, Kancheepuram District', *In*: Hasan Ashraful and Prasad Ganesh (*eds.*), ANSSIRD, Mysore, pp. 27–50.

13

Habitation Level Peoples Plan and Its Significance in Tamil Nadu

G. PALANITHURAI[16*]

ABSTRACT

This paper presents an assessment of the Habitation Level Peoples Plan and its Significance in Tamil Nadu. An attempt is made to critically evaluate the objectives of the programme, planning and implementation process, the impact created on the lives of the people. The paper draws insights from a sample of three districts covering Twelve Panchayat Unions (intermediate panchayat) and within these Twelve Grama Panchayats. The findings are based on interaction with officials and the elected representatives of the rural local bodies, focus group discussion with the beneficiaries of the programme, verification of the records / documents at Grama Panchayats, physical verification of the infrastructure created. The study reveals that for the first time in Tamil Nadu, after Independence the remote and neglected hamlets and habitations have benefitted greatly through the THAI programme. Now these villages and in particular the Dalit localities have been provided with regular drinking water supply, electricity connection to the houses, street lights, cement roads, water, shelter and approach roads to burial grounds. The programme has led to the adoption of innovative processes in the planning and implementation. The people belonging to Dalits and other marginalised sections have been participating in the Grama Sabha meetings in a large number. The paper suggests that the innovative ideas adopted need to be sustained, fine-tuned and institutionalized. Funds are channelized to rural local bodies for development through a host of schemes and programmes, the experiences of THAI programme should be guiding spirit.

[16] Professor (Retd), Department of Political Science, Gandhi Gram Rural Institute (Deemed to be University), Dindigul, Tamil Nadu.

**Corresponding author*: E-mail:gpalanithurai@gmail.com

13.1. INTRODUCTION

Tamil Nadu is known for its pro-poor policies, schemes and programmes. From the time of Independence, the political parties in Tamil Nadu which had been in power have developed a pro-poor perspective. Schemes designed and implemented by Government of Tamil Nadu, often, serve as model for other states to follow. Pro-poor focus and intensity of reaching the people at the bottom most rung has been increasing over the years. For instance, it may be Midday Meal (MDM) Scheme or reservation for backward classes or most backward classes, Tamil Nadu is in forefront. The concern for the poor has deepened among the regimes on quite a competitive mode after 1967[1].

Pro-poor schemes have been aplenty in Tamil Nadu[2] and of these 'THAI' (Tamil Nadu Village Habitations Improvement) is the one with most significant intent and impact. The State Government under the AIADMK regime introduced 'THAI' scheme seven years ago *i.e.,* in 2011–12. Even after implementing plethora of schemes for rural upliftment, there are small hamlets and habitations which have never seen proper roads, adequate drinking water, street lights, and electricity in the houses. People, especially the poorest and mostly Dalit women, have to walk for miles to fetch drinking water from the main village. There are villages where the school going boys and girls never saw electricity either in their homes or in the street. Impoverished and aged dalit men and women expose themselves to all sorts of risks if they have to go out in the nights for attending to nature's calls.

In a multi-caste society, dalit women going to the main village to fetch drinking water is (socio-culturally) an unkind task to perform. Communities in the rural areas have not come up to the level of maintaining equality and equity. When a person from the side-line goes to the main village to use the commons, the dignity and self-respect of the person performing that task is always compromised. Commons in the villages are always a bone of contention. However, perhaps, the general impression about Tamil Nadu, especially outside the state is that in every village adequate resources are available; and the resources available are being used equitably by all communities. These kinds of impressions are based on short, cursory visits made by experts who do not have time to get off their cars in order to interact with the rural people. But the reality is different and shocking. Studies have proved time and again[3] that main settlement in most Grama Panchayats (GPs) gets all facilities. The empirical truth underneath this statement can be laid bare, if we probe the question a little deeper: 'who reside in the main villages, and where do the dalits and other poorer sections live?' Those in the main village are well-heeled families whose voice has played a significant role in local decision-making; or dominant caste groups who capture the scheme / programme / facility as their right, as it always has been[4]. The poorer sections remain distanced and away from the visible mains.

The successive governments in the state have made attempts to provide basic facilities to all the hamlets or villages or habitations but they could not reach out to all the habitations due to reasons, *inter alia*, the varying size of the GPs ranging from 3 to 37 habitations. Even the previous government (DMK) made it clear that after implementing the *Anaithu Grama Anna Marumalarchi Thittam* (AGMT) every village ought to have adequate infrastructural facilities for the people to lead a decent human life. AGMT spent rupees twenty five lakh in each Village Panchayat (VP)[5]. Even after implementing that scheme one could see the demands from the people for basic infrastructure facilities[6]. The reality is that in many villages, certain habitations have been neglected constantly while providing facilities[7].

The AIADMK government in the year 2011–12 introduced an innovative rural infrastructure development scheme which is popularly called 'THAI' to address the long felt but unattended demands of the neglected areas and segments. The basic objective of the scheme is to provide minimum infrastructure to the habitations which have remained excluded so far in providing basic infrastructure. The scheme activities have to be planned by the VPs with the active involvement of the stakeholders. The above scheme is being implemented in Tamil Nadu for the past seven years. The basic details and estimated expenditure of the scheme for a period of five years (2011–12 to 2015–16) is given in Tables 13.1 and 13.2.

13.2. OBJECTIVES AND METHODOLOGY OF THE STUDY

This paper broadly analyses the impact of the THAI scheme made in rural areas and on the lives of the people. The analysis made is based on the information from the study report submitted to State Planning Commission. The broad objectives of this paper include: (1) critically analysing the objectives of the scheme; (2) the planning and implementation process followed, and (3) the impact it had made on the life of the people

Table 13.1: Basic details of the habitations and allocated funds.

Sl. no.	*Habitation range*	*No. of village panchayats*	*Total population*	*Average population per village panchayat*	*Allocation per panchayat (Rs. in lakhs)*			*Total requirement (Rs. in crore)*
					Minimum basic	*Additional funds*	*Total funds grant*	
1	Below 5	6241	12534047	2008	20	0	20	1248.20
2	5–15	5434	17392688	3201	20	10	30	1630.20
3	16–25	637	3553429	5578	20	20	40	254.80
4	Above 25	212	1864689	8796	20	30	50	106.00
	Total	12524	35344853	2822	–	–	–	3239.20
	Fund for survey, IEC, preparatory activities and awards							160.80
	Grand Total							3400.00

Source: Computed by author from Government basic data.

Table 13.2: Year-wise details of coverage of VPs, habitations and funds allocated under the THAI scheme.

Sl. no.	*Year*	*No. of village panchayats*	*No. of habitations*	*Allocation (Rs.crore)*
1	2011–12	2,020	25,335	680.00
2	2012–13	2,250	18,581	680.00
3	2013–14	2,500	15,115	680.00
4	2014–15	2,740	12,093	680.00
5	2015–16	3,014	8,270	680.00
	Total	12524	79394	3400.00

Source: Same as in Table 13.1.

Methodology: Impact Assessment Framework

For any impact analysis of rural development projects, people who received benefits out of the scheme in the rural areas are the key stakeholders to be involved right from initiating the planning process to the evaluation of the impact of the scheme[8]. Basically the scheme details have to reach everyone. The stakeholders have to be properly sensitized because they have to participate in all the activities of the scheme from data collection, planning, prioritizing the activities, finalizing the works and carrying out the decided activities. All these steps are necessary steps but they are not sufficient[9]. Bringing them to the mainstream of development and governance activities is not a small task. Rural development schemes and programmes are not meant for the rich, but they are for the poor and the marginalised. These are the people who have always been in their livelihood struggles and they do not have time to participate in all those processes[10]. To make them to participate in the process of planning and implementation of development schemes, they are to be sensitized and facilitated[11]. In the beginning itself ownership has to be built among the stakeholders. Their daily wage has to be compensated or at least a sense has to be created that in equal measure of benefits they are also going to gain by attending the development initiatives and governance initiatives. They have to be involved in planning activities through a process of detailed discourse on development prioritization. Further, they should be involved in implementation and evaluation.

In this process any analysis of evaluation starts with triangulation, photo monitoring, transect walks and personal observation. The whole exercise revolves around the following questions: (a) whether the stakeholders recognize the changes since the inception of the project; (b) whether any learning took place as a result of the scheme among the stakeholders; (c) what are the outcomes of the projects and the schemes in the life of the stakeholders[12].

Stage – I: Informing the stakeholders

Stage – II: Sensitizing them for their participation

Stage – III: Enabling them for their participation in planning

Stage – IV: Their participation in decision making process

Stage – V: Their participation in the process of implementation

Stage – VI: Their participation in evaluation

The framework of impact evaluation of the scheme is given in Chart 13.1.

A combination of methods has been adopted to collect data as it is an empirical study. Detailed one to one interaction has been conducted with officials and the elected representatives of the people in the local bodies. An exhaustive focus group discussion has been conducted with the beneficiaries of the scheme in every Village Panchayat. Apart from the above a thorough verification of the records has been done. Physical verification of the infrastructure created through the scheme has been done. The whole exercise was carried in three districts, covering twelve Panchayat Unions (PUs) and twelve VPs. The VPs were selected for data collection based on the following criteria: (i) range of habitations; (ii) headed by women, SC women, SC and general category of leaders;

(iii) nature of the areas hills, coastal and plain. The details of the selected districts, PUs and VPs is given in Table 13.3.

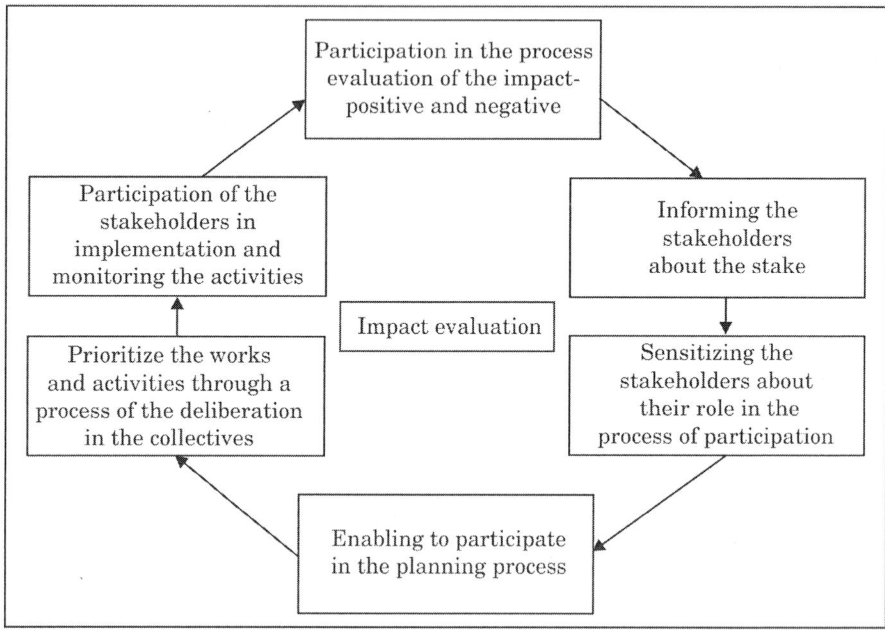

Chart 13.1: Framework of impact evaluation.

Table 13.3: Details of the sample districts, Panchayat Unions and Village Panchayats

Sl. no.	*Districts*	*Panchayat Unions Panchayats*	*Village Panchayats*	*Category of leadership position in Village*
1	Dindigul	Athoor	Ambathurai	General
		Sanarpatti	Sendurai	Women (Gen.)
		Reddiyarchatram	Kasavanampatti	Women (Gen.)
		Kodaikanal	Villpatti*	SC (Gen.)
2	Pudukkottai	Pudukkottai	Vagavasal	General
		Thirumayam	Thulaiyanur	General
		Viralimalai	Viralur	Women (SC)
		Avudaiyarkoil	Mimisal**	Women (Gen.)
3	Villupuram	Marakkanam	Singanur	Women(Gen.)
		Koliyanur	Thennamadevi	Women (SC)
		Kalrayan Hills	Vellimalai*	ST (Gen.)
		Vanur	Bommaiyarpalayam	Women (Gen.)

Note: *Hilly Village Panchayat **Coastal Village Panchayat
Source: Same as in Table 13.1.

The social background of the population of the selected VPs is given in Table 13.4.

Table 13.4: Population details of the sample Village Panchayats (in nos.).

Sl. no.	*Village Panchayat*	*Population*			*Scheduled castes*			*Scheduled tribes*		
		Total	*Male*	*Female*	*Total*	*Male*	*Female*	*Total*	*Male*	*Female*
1.	Ambathurai	9,166	4,560	4,606	2,154	1,078	1,076	–	–	–
2.	Kasavanampatti	4,597	2,331	2,266	759	376	383	–	–	–
3.	Sendurai	15,055	7,635	7,420	1,871	924	947	–	–	–
4.	Villpatti	15,820	7,924	7,896	4,028	2,046	1,982	221	114	107
5.	Vagavasal	3,852	1,956	1,896	790	400	390	4	2	2
6.	Thulaiyanur	5,685	2,845	2,840	1,165	575	590	2	–	2
7.	Viralur	4,090	1,987	2,103	951	471	480	1	–	1
8.	Mimisal	5,482	2,765	2,717	653	314	319	–	–	–
9.	Thennamadevi	2,842	1,446	1,396	1,104	537	567	19	11	8
10.	Singanur	3,255	1,572	1,683	2,496	1,199	1,297	–	–	–
11.	Bommaiyar-palayam	8,266	4,095	4,171	614	295	319	4	2	2
12.	Vellimalai	6,603	3,278	3,325	14	6	8	6,363	3,167	3,196

Source: India Population Census, 2011.

From Table 13.4 one could easily infer that the dalits are the prime beneficiaries in most of the villages. The details of the background of the participants of focus group discussion is provided in Table 13.5.

Before starting the planning process, the officials and elected representatives involved in the plan preparation have been oriented through a training programme. Since the planning and implementation of this scheme have to be done jointly by the elected representatives and the officials both have been trained. A well developed interview schedule has been used for data collection. The tool was prepared by the State Planning Commission. The tool developed by the State Planning Commission is exhaustive. Data collected through this instrument can be used by all and in future also. In such a way the tool has been designed. Preparatory exercises for data collection were done in the villages by mobilizing and sensitizing the people in the process of planning at the habitation level. People have been sensitized in such a way that it is going to help the groups so far neglected in accessing infrastructure facilities through this scheme. Here, it needs to be mentioned that in all the sensitization meetings, the officials unequivocally stressed that this scheme is meant for the habitations

Table 13.5: Background details of the participants of FGD.

Sl. no.	*Village panchayats*	*No. of participants*			*Age group*					*Education*						*Occupation*			
		Male	*Female*	*Total*	*Upto 25*	*26–35*	*36–45*	*46–55*	*56 above*	*Primary*	*Secondary*	*Hr. Sec.*	*College*	*Technical*	*Illiterate*	*Agri.*	*Agri. labour*	*Business*	*Others*
1	Villpatti	9	7	16	1	2	8	4	1	3	2	9	2	0	0	8	5	1	2
2	Sendurai	10	8	18	0	5	7	5	1	6	3	7	1	1	0	10	7	0	1
3	Kasavanampatti	11	3	14	2	4	2	3	3	4	2	3	2	1	1	2	3	1	8
4	Ambathurai	16	2	18	0	4	7	5	2	2	5	7	2	2	0	11	3	1	3
5	Viralur	10	5	15	2	3	7	3	0	5	1	8	0	1	0	7	4	4	0
6	Thulaiyanur	7	4	11	0	2	6	2	1	1	3	5	2	0	0	8	0	0	3
7	Mimisal	8	2	10	0	2	5	1	2	1	3	4	0	1	1	3	1	5	1
8	Vagavasal	6	2	8	0	2	2	3	1	2	2	3	1	0	0	7	0	0	1
9	Singanur	10	7	17	1	5	5	3	3	3	1	5	5	3	0	4	2	0	11
10	Bommaiyarpalayam	8	9	17	1	6	10	0	0	0	3	13	1	0	0	7	0	0	10
11	Thennamadevi	2	28	30	3	21	6	0	0	11	4	13	2	0	0	4	6	0	20
12	Vellimalai	17	13	30	0	10	15	5	0	11	3	12	0	0	4	28	0	0	2
	Total	114	90	204	10	66	80	34	14	49	32	89	18	9	6	99	31	12	62

Source: Same as in Table 13.1

which have been neglected till now in providing basic minimum infrastructure facilities. It raised hope among the hopeless in the remote habitations. People in the main villages also started realizing the implications of exclusion. The officials have played an important role in convincing the people that this scheme is meant for the marginalised.

13.3. IDENTIFICATION OF ACTIVITIES: PLANNING PROCESS

As per the guidelines of THAI scheme, people from the selected hamlets participated in the planning process. The respective VPs collected the basic data from the households and habitations for preparing the development plan. Data collection tools administered in the villages have brought volumes of data with minute details. Some of them are basic. The data collection methods and fields have been designed in such a way that the data can be used in future also. While preparing the plan details of each habitation have been analysed and works have been indentified based on the intensity of need. Technical experts too have helped the VPs to make a thorough analysis of data to determine the works that can be carried out in the habitations. In this process works have been selected not because they are allowed in this scheme but based on the actual requirements of the people in the habitations. Works have been identified and they are prioritized. When the above jobs have been done, care was taken to observe the long term implications. Decisions to identify the works were to be endorsed by a consensus in the Grama Sabha. Another worth mentioning feature of the scheme lies in its flexibility to keep adequate provision for dovetailing the other schemes to be operationalised through a process of convergence, as convergence is a difficult task in rural development activities[13]. VPs being the responsible authority to maintain the assets created through the scheme, it has been mentioned in the scheme that all decisions have to be taken through the Panchayat bodies. By doing so, it has been demonstrated that the areas concentrated by the marginalized population are the integral parts of the village administration and fulfilling the genuine demands of those people is also the prime responsibility of the VPs. They have hitherto been left out in the caste ridden hierarchical village communities. To an outside observer the activities carried out in those habitations, will appear just like routine infrastructure facilities carried out in the villages. There is no innovation on the surface of things. But the process by which the activities have been carried out in the habitations is an eye opener for many since it will create curiosity as to how people of all segments have been involved in the decision-making process. The details of the works carried out in the study villages is given in Tables 13.6 to 13.9.

Table 13.6: Types of work carried out in the habitations –drinking water schemes.

Sl. no.	*Village Panchayats*	*Water supply*							
		Total no. of habitations	*No. of habitations works done*	*New bore-well*	*Mini-power pump*	*Pipe-line extention*	*Hand pump*	*Over head tank*	*Deepening of wells*
1	Sendurai	24	6	3	4	0	0	0	0
2	Ambathurai	11	0	0	0	0	0	0	0
3	Villpatti	26	1	0	0	1	0	0	0
4	Kasavanampatti	11	9	0	4	7	0	0	0
5	Thulaiyanur	29	4	0	5	0	0	0	0
6	Mimisal	10	5	0	0	8	0	0	0
7	Vagavasal	16	6	0	5	1	1	1	0
8	Viralur	18	5	0	6	0	2	0	0
9	Bommaiyarpalayam	4	2	0	2	0	0	0	0
10	Singanur	3	1	0	2	0	0	1	0
11	Thennamadevi	4	1	0	2	0	0	0	0
12	Vellimalai	20	6	0	4	0	0	0	3
	Total	176	46	3	34	17	3	2	3

Source: Author's computation

Table 13.7: Number of street lights provided in the habitations.

Sl. no.	*Village Panchayats*	*Total no. of habitations*	*No. of habitations covered for works*	*Street lights (in no.)*
1.	Sendurai	24	10	75
2.	Ambathurai	11	7	34
3.	Vilpatti	26	8	16
4.	Kasavanampatti	11	6	9
5.	Thulaiyanur	29	8	18
6.	Mimisal	10	3	5
7.	Vagavasal	16	4	32
8.	Viralur	18	3	20
9.	Bommaiyarpalayam	4	2	13
10.	Singanur	3	2	10
11.	Thennamadevi	4	1	4
12.	Vellimalai	20	6	7
	Total	176	60	243

Source: Same as in Table 13.6.

Table 13.8: Number and type of road works implemented in the habitations.

Sl. no.	*Village Panchayats*	*Total no. of habitations*	*No. of habitations covered for works*	*Road*	
				Cement concrete	*WBM and BT*
1.	Sendurai	24	6	6 (6)	0 (0)
2.	Ambathurai	11	6	10 (5)	3 (2)
3.	Villpatti	26	9	10 (9)	19 (1)
4.	Kasavanampatti	11	3	0 (0)	3 (3)
5.	Thulaiyanur	29	13	8 (8)	5 (5)
6.	Mimisal	10	5	2 (2)	3 (3)
7.	Vagavasal	16	4	1 (1)	3 (3)
8.	Viralur	18	5	4 (4)	1 (1)
9.	Bommaiyarpalayam	4	4	7 (4)	1 (1)
10.	Singanur	3	3	3 (3)	0 (0)
11.	Thennamadevi	4	1	0 (0)	1 (1)
12.	Vellimalai	20	9	8 (8)	1 (1)
	Total	176	68	59 (50)	22 (21)

***Note*:** Figures in the parentheses are number of habitations.
Source: Same as in Table 13.6.

Table 13.9: Details of civil works carried out in the habitations.

Sl. no.	*Village panchayats*	*Civil works*							
		Total no. of habitations	*No. of habitations covered for works*	*Facilities in grounds*	*Bathing ghats*	*Threshing floors*	*Retaining walls*	*Culverts*	*Drainages*
1.	Sendurai	24	1	1(1)	0	0	0	0	0
2.	Ambathurai	11	1	1(1)	0	0	0	0	0
3.	Villpatti	26	1	1(1)	0	0	0	0	0
4.	Kasavanampatti	11	1	1(1)	0	0	0	0	0
5.	Thulaiyanur	29	11	1(1)	3	3	2	3	0
6.	Mimisal	10	2	1(1)	0	0	0	1	0
7.	Vagavasal	16	2	1(1)	0	0	1	0	0
8.	Viralur	18	6	6(6)	0	0	0	0	0
9.	Bommaiyarpalayam	4	1	0(0)	0	0	0	3	0
10.	Singanur	3	2	2(2)	0	0	0	0	0
11.	Thennamadevi	4	3	3(3)	0	0	0	0	0
12.	Vellimalai	20	1	1(1)	0	1	0	0	1
	Total	176	32	19(19)	3	4	3	7	1

***Note*:** Figures in the parentheses are number of habitations.
Source: Same as in Table 13.6.

In all 62 water supply related works were executed in the sample villages in 46 habitations. More attention was given to provide mini power pump in 34 places and provision of pipeline extension has been carried out in 17 places.

There are 243 new street lights provided in the sample villages in 60 habitations.

There were 59 cement concrete roads provided in 50 habitations.

22 WBM and BT roads were provided under THAI in 21 habitations.

There are 19 burial grounds in 19 habitations. There are 3 bathing ghats, 4 threshing floors, 3 retaining walls at oorani, 7 culverts and 1 drainage/culvert provided under THAI.

13.4. RESULTS OF THE STUDY

For the first time in Tamil Nadu, after Independence, certain habitations have received regular drinking water supply to fulfill the needs of the households. Their houses have also been connected with electricity. Their streets have been improved through cement concrete roads, street lights have been provided in these areas. The people living in remote habitations had to wait for six decades to get such basic minimum facilities despite the pro-poor nature of the successive state governments. The importance of such a scheme could be realized only by those who have remained deprived of all those facilities so far[14]. For others, this scheme is only an infrastructural facilities creation. If anyone asks about utility, they are generally of multipurpose nature. But they are utilized fully. When their streets are provided with cement concrete roads, these are being used as meeting venue for women self-help groups, and many inhabitants find it comfortable to sleep on the roads. These inhabitants are mostly dalits and for long they have observed the practice of sleeping in the open. When they were asked about the utility of the road, their immediate response was that they sleep comfortably on the cement roads. Moreover, it is a remote area. When their streets get lit, they are being used as playground for small kids. Once the streets used to be dark and dull and people's activities come to an end around six or six thirty in the evening. But now their day's activities continue up to 11pm or 12 in the midnight. It has been narrated by an old man as a stakeholder that life has come to our living places, since the people of those habitations never entertained hope that they will get such facilities. Now it becomes a reality. To them it is unbelievable. Election after election, promises have been made, but nothing materialized. One senior inhabitant exclaimed, now we could not believe our own eyes as what we are seeing. We are now considered as citizens, added another villager. Their sentiments were expressed as, 'someone in our government thought about us'. An old man in one of the Panchayat areas observed, 'when many schemes were being implemented in our villages, our demands had not been considered and all along we were not considered. But now we have not demanded anything but a scheme come to us by crossing many layers of power centre'. It is because of the nature of the scheme 'THAI'. This scheme has given such a protection needed for them[15]. Because local elites always make design to capture programme[16]. It is an unbelievable surprise to many of the elders. Pathway to cremation ground and facilities in the cremation ground were the root cause for many caste conflicts in the villages between dalits and other communities. On many occasions the dalits faced hardship to burry or cremate the dead bodies of the SC communities. All these needs were attended to through this scheme. The plights of the dalits have been lessened and they have been relieved of such worries. Enthused by the activities in their habitations, dalits have started attending the meetings of Grama Sabha in large number as their hopes have been rekindled. When one notices the remote habitations with such infrastructure facilities where dalits are living, one gets the impression that the programme is designed to cater to the needs of the dalits. One cannot measure the joy of the dalit women when they got pipeline for drinking water with borewell and mini pump station very near to their houses. They get enough water supply now. They fetch water whenever they need it. They save time and need not walk miles to fetch water. Unnecessary caste conflicts are also avoided. Because all along they had to walk during odd hours to fetch drinking water from the places where dominant communities were living. Time taken to fetch water has also come down from two hours to few minutes as everything is in their vicinity. When they found new roads, their happiness has increased manifold because previously these were full of wobbling and undulations and now these are smooth and clean. They got the tubelights on the roads which enabled the aged men and women to walk safely.

Till recent times, before the Government of Tamil Nadu evolved this scheme, VPs had received facilities but they did not reach these places because of programme capture culture[17]. Main village would get all such facilities. In the process of planning in the scheme, the involvement of the beneficiaries and others in the VPs resulted in huge mass mobilization while prioritizing the works for the marginalized and the neglected habitations. The Panchayat representatives found it difficult to convince the people of other habitations mostly dominant communities. Addressing equity issue is not an easy task. Very interestingly decisions for providing all basic infrastructure facilities to the Dalit communities have been taken in the Grama Sabha meeting through a discourse. The lengthy deliberations brought a consensus decision. Majority in a multi-caste rural society have come to realize the plight of the marginalized and they have agreed to allow such facilities exclusively to them. It is an encouraging sign in the local governance that social justice and equity issues could be addressed through a deliberative process. Since government officials too participated in the deliberations of the Grama Sabha, they explained about the habitations in the remote areas of Panchayats which have been neglected for a long. In order to provide them the basic facilities, this scheme has been introduced. This kind of official explanations in unequivocal term helped the Panchayats to sensitize the people on social justice and equity issues. Even during prioritizing the works for the neglected areas, the amount is spent only for the feasible and impact making projects. The Panchayats have not spent money as per their will. Since technical team has supported the VPs, the feasibility issue is addressed. Various stakeholders participated in the focus group discussion and endorsed that the money has been spent judiciously in this scheme. Unless it was utilized in addressing a problem, money has not been spent. The following information in the Boxes 13.1 to 13.6 conveys the sentiments and views of the people in beneficiary habitations served under the scheme.

Box 13.1

Our voice is heard at last

Pachamuthu (name changed by the respondent himself) 83 informed that he had seen the British regimes and the governments in independent India. Many things have changed in India. But the living conditions of the Dalits have not changed as much as they expected. He further lamented that "road had come to our Village Panchayat but it failed to come to our habitation, electricity has come to our village, it did not come to our habitation, and water supply had come to our village habitations but it refused to come to our habitations. We led life by nursing the hope that someone will come and hear our plea. Now after sixty years of our independence, this Amma has brought this 'THAI' scheme through which we have seen the electricity in our habitation, we have seen water supply to our habitation and we have seen cement road. It has come. We could not believe our own eyes. We feel that we are part of the society and part of our government". While making observation tears came from his eyes.

Box 13.2

We got benefits and we could use them now through THAI

Sowmya (name changed) has got bicycle from the Government of Tamil Nadu. She used the bicycle on the mud road up to main village to reach her school. She did not have electricity connection in her small house. Later she joined a college and thereby she got a laptop. She could not use the laptop in her house. She used the bicycle and studied up to plus two and now she is in a college. When she interacted with us she made the following observation: "I used to think why our colony is continuously denied of basic facilities such as roads, street lights, electricity connection, and piped water supply. When others are enjoying such facilities in the same village within half a kilometer. Amma enabled me to continue my studies, she further enabled me to learn computer and thereby my confidence level has gone up. I will easily get a job because of the computer knowledge. But now because of the THAI scheme our colony got all those facilities. Thanks to Amma". She did not even mention Chief Minister or J. Jayalalitha.

Box 13.3

Denial is accepted

Gurusamy (name changed) 74 year old, made a comment when we interacted with him on the utility of the scheme. He said that he never heard someone saying that "the Dalits living in the remote area in the same Panchayat are denied their due entitlements. This time the officials made it clear in the Grama Sabha that "this scheme is meant for those people who are denied access to many of the common facilities created for all to lead a decent human life". This statement I valued because over the years nobody came forward to make such a statement at the local level among the members of dominant caste groups. By hearing that statement I gained hope here is a government that works for me and realizes the feelings of the neglected and suppressed all through. Time and again our youth told us that our entitlements have to be claimed honourably. They used to lament on the provisions of the Constitution. We elders always felt that Constitution grants but community at the local level denies our share and entitlements. This scheme has brought a message to all that everyone has got his or her own entitlements. Really one has to be thankful to 'Amma' for her imaginative scheme to reach out to us".Box 13.3

Box 13.4

Community is not communal

While interacting with an official who was involved with scheme, a significant observation was made based on his experience. He said that the community is not communal. "When the scheme was explained to the people of all caste groups, initially many made hue and cry. But when the officials patiently allowed them to express their opinion and argued with them the plight of the neglected segments in the same village in accessing the commons, many realized the plight of the Dalits living in the same village and working for them. What they need is information, deliberation, discourse, and patient hearing. In this scheme, Panchayat, Grama Sabha, line department officials are all involved in planning and prioritizing the works to be executed in the village. People initially resisted and but later they understood through a process of deliberation. At the community level no effort is made to convert the Grama Sabha into deliberative and discourse body rather than keeping it as mute spectators' body".

Box 13.5

Lifelong misery comes to an end

Karupayee (name changed) a farm labourer aged 67, made an observation about this scheme and its implication. "As a Dalit I have to face volley of problems while living in a multi caste Village Panchayat. Being a woman, the problem is compounded and complicated. We are living in a remote area where there is no drinking water facility. When I got married 47 years ago I walked for about four miles to fetch water. Of course at that point of time there was tank meant for it. We were allotted a share from the same tank, from which we had to draw our water. From that day onwards we had been walking at least three kilometers a day to fetch water, we could not get water as it is the last point and water was channelized towards our area after giving water to all other habitations. When we are unable to get adequate water, we have to walk down to main village to fetch water for drinking purposes. While we go there we are treated badly by the elderly conservative women in the main village. Our dignity is always at stake. Now through this scheme we get water at our place as there is a mini pump fixed at our village. At one stroke our fate has been changed. Now within minutes I can get water to my need and quality and at my time. I am thankful to 'Amma' as she felt our miseries".

Box 13.6

Now equality in graveyard

Sukumar (name changed) 43, a Dalit working in a farm as farm labourer said that many a time he witnessed the ordeal that the Dalit families faced in this village while carrying the dead bodies to the cremation ground through a private land. Every time they cross the land of the owner, the Dalit families have to take permission. Granting permission is not regular. The Dalits have been at the mercy of the landlord. But now that problem has been solved by creating a road to reach the cremation ground. Yet another remarkable achievement made through this scheme is providing water facility and a shelter in the cremation ground meant for the Dalits. The above two facilities existed in the cremation ground meant for the dominant castes. But we did not have such facilities. This discrimination was ended by providing the above facilities in the cremation grounds meant for Dalits. Now we find equality at least at the last resting place. This kind of facilities provided to the Dalits made us think of the sensitivity of the government towards the plight of the Dalits. Now our worry is over".

13.5. CONCLUSIONS

"THAI" scheme is unique because of its objective to reach the unreached. Through the process of planning at the Panchayat and keeping the focus on habitation as a planning unit, the apparent neglect of such areas are made visible and people of that VP become sensitive to the issues of exclusion and marginalization. Without looking at the face of the beneficiaries, if one looks at the table it appears nothing more than spending money for laying roads to burial ground, providing street lights, installing drinking water systems which are routine infrastructure facilities. But the noticeable fact is that all the above facilities have been created for the people who have been neglected for the past several years. In every VP money has been spent through a series of development schemes. But certain segments of the society have remained neglected. These neglected segments are the target groups for this scheme. Yet, it is not solely a target oriented scheme. It is both target and process oriented scheme in the sense, that it ensures felt needs of the people are attended to and in this process affected groups are involved at the planning stage. When the planning process was initiated from below, people from all sections and segments have been sensitized on the issues of exclusion. Tamil Nadu is pioneer in addressing the issues of the poor. Innovative pro-poor schemes have been implemented in Tamil Nadu earlier also. It is a model to other states. Likewise this "THAI" scheme is also a pioneering model to address the infrastructural issues of the marginalised.

The experience gained from planning and implementation of scheme will be very useful for introducing integrated development planning as well as for claiming the 14th Finance Commission Awards for Panchayats. The greater participation of the Dalits and other marginalised groups in the Grama Sabha meetings is yet another interesting features one could observe in the process of planning and implementation of the scheme. Now they not only attend Grama Sabha meeting but also any other meeting organised by the Panchayats. If one traces the reasons for such participation one could easily find out that this scheme has given hopes to the hopeless. They have found the benefit, scope and potentials of their participation. They get enormous information from the officials who attend the Grama Sabha meetings. Through their interaction with the officials they get to know the details about facilities and opportunities in other rural development schemes and programmes to improve the conditions of life of the Dalits and other marginalized groups.

This scheme goes a long way in restoring the dignity of people. Women who walked to fetch water for drinking purposes in the main village met with different kinds of unpleasant experiences, the main affront being verbal abuses by the caste Hindus. No doubt water is a common good meant for every household, but the source is in the main village dominated by the caste Hindus. But now they get water in their neighbourhood, which is also a succor to their self-respect and dignity. To cremate their dead, the Dalits had to walk to the cremation ground through the passage across the land of higher caste people. On every occasion they needed to seek permission from the landlord before carrying the dead bodies through their fields. This was a constant source of discomfiture and conflict. By laying separate road to the cremation grounds, their long pending demand has been met. In the same way the Dalits found difficulty in accessing facilities created in the cremation ground meant for the caste Hindus. Cremations during rainy season added to their miseries because, till the completion of the burial work, they had to stand in rains. The shelter created in the cremation ground meant for the caste Hindus cannot be used. They faced similar distress and difficulty in scorching heat during the hot summer days. Now water facilities have been created in the cremation ground meant for the Dalits. It has been a long pending demand but fulfilled through this scheme. The amount spent is not huge. But what the Dalits got through this scheme is the acknowledgement of their right to dignity. Now they feel the self respect of the Dalit poor is intact.

The need of the hour will be to sustain the spirit and enthusiasm with which the scheme has been launched. The first five-year phase has meant a lot for the deprived people not only in terms of the basic facilities but more importantly for the sense of social inclusion which is writ large on the faces of beneficiaries spread across the state. The scheme has introduced innovations in planning and implementations. These innovations need to be sustained, fine-tuned and institutionalized. Funds are channelized to rural local bodies for development through a host of schemes and programmes, the experiences of THAI should be guiding spirit to utilize these resources equitably to fulfill the avowed objective of social justice.

NOTES AND REFERENCES

[1] In 1967 because of shortage of rice in public distribution system and in the open market, the opposition parties made it an election issue which had overthrown the Indian National Congress from power. It was a politics around rice. From 1967 onwards political regimes are sensitive on food especially rice.

[2] At present the central schemes are downsizing. But pro-poor schemes are increasing in Tamil Nadu. For details of the schemes refer to G. Palanithurai, New Panchayati Raj System in Tamil Nadu: Act, Rules and Schemes (in Tamil), Chennai: South Vision (2012).

[3] Palanithurai, G. (2012). Status of Dalits and Dalit Representatives in Rural Local Bodies, New Delhi: Concept Publishing Company.

[4] Bardhan Pranab and Mookherjee Dilip (2000). "Capture and governance at local and national levels". *The American Economic Review*, 90(2): 134–139.

[5] Government of Tamil Nadu, Rural Development Department, Website: *www.tnrd.gov.in*

[6] Service Delivery Study.

[7] Chandra, S. (2006). "Our villages: Ground realities and future prospects", *In*: Singh, Y. P. (*ed.*), New Delhi: Concept. *Indian Village: 2020,* I: 104–110.

[8] Roche, C. (1999). *Impact Assessment for Development Agencies,* Bangalore: Oxfam.

[9] Singh Hoshiar (*ed.*) (1985). Rural Development in India: Evaluative Studies in Policies and Programmes, Jaipur: Printwell.

[10] Scarlelt Epsteni, T., Suryanarayana, A.P. and Thimmegowda, T. (1998). *Village Voices: Forty Years of Rural Transformation in South India,* New Delhi: Sage Publications.

[11] Paul, S. (1987). "*Community Participation in Development Projects*' Discussion Paper No. 6, Washington DC: World Bank.

[12] Singh Katar (2000). *Rural Development,* New Delhi: Sage Publications.
[13] Taori Kamal (2006). "Convergence of delivery system in rural areas", *In:* Singh, Y.P. (*ed.*), New Delhi: Concept Publishing Company. *Indian Village: 2020,* I: 147–150.
[14] Powis Benjamin (2007). *Systems of Capture: Reassessing the Threat of Local Elites*, (Social Development Paper no. 109) Washington DC: World Bank.
[15] World Bank (2011). *Social Protection for a Changing India Vol. II*, New Delhi: World Bank.
[16] Plattean, J.P. (2008). *"Information Distortion, Elite Capture and Task Complexity in Decentralised Development",* Belgium: University of Namur, Centre for Research on The Economics of Development.
[17] Sreedhar, G. and Rajasekhar, D. (2014). *Rural Development in India: Strategies and Processes,* New Delhi: Concept.

14

Decentralisation and Primary Education: Lessons from Sino-Indian Comparativc Study

D. RAJASEKHAR[17]*

ABSTRACT

China and India have pursued decentralization policies to promote school education; but, the approaches followed and outcomes of school education differed across the countries. Against this background, this paper aims to: i) Provide an overview of the decentralization approaches followed in the two countries, and ii) Discuss the outcomes of school education with the help of review of existing literature. The experiences of China and India with decentralisation in education reaffirm the mixed outcomes emanating from implementation of decentralised practices emphasised in the literature. In China, the decentralisation reforms succeeded in resource mobilisation at the local level, improved enrolment rates and reduced student-teacher ratios. However, over devolution of expenditure responsibilities has led to insufficient financing, inadequate provision of educational services and growing inequality. In India, different states have adopted different approaches regarding the management and governance of education as provincial governments were provided with powers to decide what needs to be decentralised in their provinces. The most notable approach is the constitution of parents' committees for facilitating the participation of people in the planning, implementation and monitoring of provision of school education. The educational outcomes differed across the states due to differences in the functioning of peoples' organisations. As far as the outcomes are concerned, there has been good progress in the enrolment rates (especially among girls) in the last two decades – after the introduction of decentralisation

[17] Professor and Head, Centre for Decentralisation and Development, Institute for Social and Economic Change (ISEC), Bangalore, Karnataka.

**Corresponding author:* E-mail: raja@isec.ac.in

reforms. But, much of this progress is to be attributed to government programmes and schemes such as District Primary Education Programme (DPEP), Midday Meal, Education for All Movement and Right to Education Act which not only ensured that there are adequate resources for the development of primary education but were also instrumental in strengthening the decentralisation reforms in India. The experiences of these countries offer some lessons that may be taken into consideration while formulating and implementing decentralisation policies for the education sector in China and India: 1. Decentralisation leads to the improved outcomes through improved governance processes, 2. Accountability is a key mechanism to ensure the quantitative and qualitative reforms regarding education, 3. Accountability is greatly affected by participation and awareness levels of population which in turn is dependent on distribution of literacy and community's socio-economic characteristics. Educational decentralisation policies should therefore be preceded by or concomitant to the policies aiming at ensuring the above, 4. Sufficient resources at the disposal of local implementing authorities and financial autonomy are crucial for implementing the reforms, and 5. A clear statement and division of responsibilities is important to avoid later confusions among different levels of local government in the implementation.

14.1. INTRODUCTION

India is often compared with China in studies on progress of education (Dreze and Loh, 1995; Acharya *et al.*, 2001; Rao *et al.*, 2003; Kingdon, 2007; Goldman *et al.*, 2008). Some papers such as Kingdon (2007) have provided a comparative perspective on education in India and China as background for analysing the factors that influenced the progress of education in India, while others (such as Dreze and Loh, 1995; Rao *et al.*, 2003; Acharya *et al.*, 2001; Goldman *et al.*, 2008) have undertaken an in-depth comparative analysis of human resource development and/or education in these two countries. Such an analysis is justified on the grounds that a comparison of the two countries which faced similar challenges in 1940s and which have taken up different routes[18] in addressing these challenges (Dreze and Loh, 1995: 2868) will yield

[18] But, they also shared three important features in their quest for having educated and modernized societies. First, the National Leaders (Nehru in India and Den Xiaoping in China) recognized education as an integral part of the economic development. Second, the elitist tradition in education has influenced both the countries to focus on higher education. Third, as both the countries were influenced by the Soviet Union, the curriculum adopted by India and China focused on science and technology (Goldman *et al.*, 2008).

meaningful results. Rao *et al.* (2003: 154–155) provide the following reasons why India-China comparative study on education is of significance when it comes to drawing lessons. First, it allows the social scientists to have a historical perspective on the link between the state policy and primary schooling given that both the countries have had similar status on primary school enrolment in 1940s and, subsequently, the different political transitions had different results in educational outcomes. Second, a Sino-Indian comparative analysis enables an evaluation of strategies pursued to promote primary education in multilingual, vast countries characterised by diversity and disparity in economic resources.

The studies comparing the educational progress in India and China have focused on a number of factors to explain the differences in educational outcomes such as the the role of state (Acharya *et al.*, 2001), policy implementation links, cultural belief systems, teaching and learning processes and the physical condition of schools (Rao *et al.*, 2003). Some of the studies (Acharya *et al.,* 2001; Goldman *et al.*, 2008) have touched upon the role of decentralisation; but, they have only made a passing mention. In this paper, we aim to discuss the importance of decentralisation in explaining the progress of school education across the two countries.

The main objectives of the paper are: (i) to provide an overview of the decentralization approaches followed in the two countries, and (ii) discuss the outcomes of school education. We will be mainly depending on the existing studies for such a comparative study. It is hoped that such a comparative analysis will provide lessons for improving school education in both the countries.

The paper is presented in four sections. Following the introduction, we will provide a brief discussion on the need for decentralization in the delivery of basic education. In Section 3, the progress in the primary education, an overview of decentralization approaches followed and outcomes achieved in China and India, respectively, are presented. In the final section, the lessons emerging from the comparative study are brought out.

14.2. NEED FOR DECENTRALISATION IN THE DELIVERY OF BASIC EDUCATION

Poor educational output is a persistent problem even after concerted and collective efforts made in this direction since the declaration of

Millennium Development Goals. United Nations (2014) indicates that although developing countries have made considerable progress in achieving the target of universal primary education, 58 million children in the primary schooling age-group are out of school. Globally, high dropout rates remain a big challenge and more than one in every four children entering primary school in developing countries is likely to dropout and that global number of illiterates remains high despite rising literacy rates. The quality of education imparted is also poor. Weak learning outcomes are a characteristic feature of the developing countries where children learn much less than what is to be imparted as per the curriculum. As a result, literacy and numeracy skills are poor even among children completing primary education. Besides this, lack (and/ or inadequate supply) of basic school equipment, poor infrastructure, and the quality and availability of teachers at schools are common concerns shared by the developing countries. The picture is somewhat identical for the secondary education as well. This is disturbing considering the importance of education for human, social and economic development.

Governance and management related issues are one of the associated factors with such poor educational outputs. Access, accountability, efficiency and equity affect the quantity and quality of education to a great deal. Decentralisation is often presented as a promising policy option to overcome these problems and thereby improve educational outputs. Moreover in the case of provision of public services like education, decentralisation allows quicker identification of problems and offers more appropriate solutions to them (Machado, 2013). The channels through which decentralisation is supposed to offer better results mainly include: (i) local knowledge leading to responsiveness; (ii) participation giving way to representation, a sense of ownership and accountability; (iii) local competitiveness enhancing the chances of provision of better quality of services, and (iv) the mobilization of resources at the local level. Local governments have the information and incentive to allocate the resources according to the local preferences and hence leading to responsiveness. This improves the quality of expenditure and maximizes its impact leading ultimately to the greater use of services by the people (Faguet and Sanchez, 2009). These processes, theoretically inherent in the concept of decentralisation, are discussed by Serrano and Llop (2012). According to them, the reasons why governments decide to initiate decentralisation process around education are:

> '...seeking improvements in efficiency, improvements in financing and redistribute power to decision-making bodies with better

knowledge of educational needs. The efficiency goal is argued on the basis that a centralised system is often characterised by having a high bureaucratic burden thus incurring losses of resources and time. By decentralizing decisions, they are accelerated and at the same time, better information is available to run. The efficient allocation of resources by subnational governments allows to adjust better of the allocations in education as opposed to large national budgets that are not always allocated efficiently. On the other hand, the redistribution of decision-making is seen as a way to include the less weighted groups giving better facilities in attending their needs' (Serrano and Llop, 2012: 5).

Fiske (1996: 12–24) examined the question of why decentralisation was initiated to provide educational services in a number of countries. He concludes that decentralisation 'will improve the quality of teaching and learning by locating decisions closer to the point at which they must be carried out and by energising teachers and administrators to do a better job' (Fiske, 1996: 24).

The above have influenced many countries positively to adopt decentralisation as their preferred policy option in various sectors, including the delivery of educational services. It was noted that most of the countries have been experimenting with one or the other form of decentralisation since the late 1990s (Manor, 1999; Channa and Faguet, 2012).

However, recent literature also suggests that decentralisation may not always lead to the improved level of services, and that factors other than decentralisation determine the expected outcomes (Brosio, 2014). This is exemplified by the country cases[19] that portray rather a mixed picture (Rajasekhar and Upadhyay, 2015).

It is in this context that this paper seeks to analyse the experiences of India and China with regard to decentralisation in the area of education with the objective of understanding and identifying lessons

[19] A number of empirical studies on decentralisation and education (Faguet and Sanchez, 2009; Mahal *et al.*, 2000; Yoem, Acedo and Utomo, 2002; Yolcu, 2011; Machado, 2013; Brosio, 2014; Shen, Zhao and Zou, 2014) discuss and analyze the experiences of countries with educational decentralisation either individually or in comparison to other countries. A review of these studies and analysis suggests that educational decentralisation has not led to uniform outcomes throughout. While decentralised governance has resulted in an improvement in certain areas, the results in others have not been so promising.

for improving education in both the countries. It must be however noted that there is considerable diversity in both the countries, and the role of decentralisation is to be looked at together with various other socio-cultural-economic factors. The issues relating to such diversity are incorporated into the analysis where they are relevant. The scope of the paper is limited to only primary education. It is to be noted that primary education is referred to primary (7 to 11 years of age) and junior secondary (12 to 14 years of age) in China, and primary (6 to 10 years) and upper primary (11 to 13 years) in India. Decentralisation is taken as transfer of powers, functionaries and finances to the local government. In other words, when powers, functionaries and finances are transferred to local government for the provision of primary education then it is referred to as decentralisation in education.

14.3. DECENTRALISATION, EDUCATIONAL GOVERNANCE AND OUTPUTS IN CHINA AND INDIA

The meaning of the term 'decentralisation' was different to different people in different times. The reason for this is probably the multidisciplinary application of the concept which has resulted in attributing various shades of meaning depending on the context in which it was discussed. However, it is commonly understood that decentralisation is the transfer of functions, functionaries and finances from the centre towards the periphery, though the content and pattern of this transfer may vary. Based on this content and pattern of transfer, decentralisation may take many forms. Deconcentration, delegation, devolution and privatization are the most commonly discussed forms of decentralisation (Rondinelli, 1983) that are followed to apply decentralisation in practice. Among these forms, deconcentration is considered as the weakest and devolution as the best[20]. A review of experiences of different countries (Rajasekhar and Upadhyay, 2015) shows that decentralisation in education has largely been pursued as a part of the overall decentralisation strategy. We will now examine the experience of China and India in the field of primary education. In this section, we will first provide an overview of policies relating to the promotion of primary education, decentralisation approaches followed in each country and a brief discussion on outcomes.

[20] However recent literature indicates that all the forms are complementary to each other.

14.4. CHINA: DEVELOPMENT OF PRIMARY EDUCATION

When the People's Republic of China was formed in 1949, the government made efforts to bring basic education to the masses in the first one-and-half decades as the literacy rate was only 20 percent in 1950. At the same time, importance was also given to higher education so that 'governing elite' could be prepared. There was rapid growth of primary education until 1958, and the net enrolment rate increased from 25 percent in 1949 to 62 percent in 1957 (Acharya *et al.*, 2001; 239). But, there was continuous decline in primary education thereafter on account of economic crisis resulting from the Great Leap Forward[21] (Goldman *et al.,* 2008).

During the period of Great Cultural Revolution (1966–1976), Mao Zedong believed that the educational system was creating a new elite class that may hinder the progress towards the socialist path of development. A number of reforms were therefore initiated to bring far reaching changes in the educational system. Surowsky (2000), in his essay on the History of the Educational System of China, concludes that the period of the Cultural Revolution was a very disruptive not only for the Chinese society but also for the education. The educational infrastructure was destroyed as a result of revolutionary struggles, and students suffered because of watered-down or non-existent curriculum. According to him, the only gain was the spread of elementary education to a large proportion of school-aged children because of agricultural collectivisation which allowed for the creation of a number of 'commune schools', overseen directly by the collective rather than by higher-level agencies. However, such a spread of elementary education was at the expense of quality.

With the rise of Deng Xiaoping in 1978, the educational policies were reverted to those that were initiated during the early 1960s. The process of regularisation was resumed. In this process, academic standards were reintroduced at all the academic levels. The policies during the period after 1976 emphasised quality rather than quantity in the delivery of educational services. The school system was expanded to include vocational or work-study schools so that those children who were not meeting the standards could pursue vocational education.

[21]This was an economic and social campaign by the Communist Party of China during 1958 to 1961. Led by Mao Zedong, the campaign aimed to rapidly transform the country from an agrarian economy into socialist society through rapid industrialization and collectivization.

This, however, led to a debate whether universal basic education will ever be achieved. Partly in response to this debate, a compulsory nine-year (elementary and junior secondary) educational policy was introduced from 1978 onwards (Surowsky, 2000).

14.4.1. Decentralisation Reforms

Decentralisation reforms were introduced from the viewpoint of resource mobilisation. The compulsory basic education was considered to be ambitious given the socio economic realities of China at that time and the weak financial base for education. This was particularly so for the basic education which had the largest enrolment of 173 million in 1985. Tsang (1996; 424–5) argues that as the financial resources needed to implement the compulsory education policy were substantial and the barriers in the less developed regions (in land and other poorer areas) were severe, the government has initiated financial reforms. These reforms also became necessary from the viewpoint of public finance reforms considered key for the success of economic reforms pushed by Deng Xiaoping. A key strategy was the decentralisation of decision-making powers and financial responsibilities from the central government to provincial and local governments. Financial reform in education was considered as key strategy in the overall decentralisation strategy of public finance.

Before the reforms, public finance was very much centralised (Tsang, 1996). From 1982, a multi-level public financing system, in which each level of government was responsible for its own finances, was created. Three elements of this system were: "1) defining the tax base and financial responsibilities for each level of government, 2) providing decision-making power and autonomy to each level of government, and 3) specifying intergovernmental fiscal relationship (in fixed amount of subsidy or surplus in a five-year period" (Tsang, 1996: 424).

In so far as the delivery of educational services was concerned, two defining characteristics of the financial reform was decentralisation in financing structure and diversification in financial resources for education. For the provision of education, local governments are responsible for basic education and financing is diversified with budget allocations constituting just over half of aggregate spending. The central government retains its role of policy maker and planner for overall education. The provinces are responsible for making overall development plan including inspection, determining operational standards and offering assistance to counties to help them meet the recurrent expenditure on education. Cities or districts in large cities implement compulsory education in urban areas and counties are responsible for rural areas.

As a consequence of decentralisation reforms, China transformed into a highly decentralised country in terms of its administrative structure and fiscal arrangements for the delivery of important services including education. This has been vertically divided into five levels, each responsible to the level immediately above in the vertical structure. Apart from the central level, sub-national governments are organised into four level hierarchical systems. There are 33 provincial-level units comprising of provinces, autonomous regions, metropolitan areas and special districts. Sub-provincial level consists of prefectures and municipalities at the prefecture level, counties, autonomous counties and cities at the county level and towns and villages at the bottom level. Governments at the township level serve as the basic administrative unit in the vast countryside whereas village governments, though providing public services, are treated more as community units rather than the government organs (Shen, Zhao and Zou, 2014: 137). Fiscal arrangements also correspond to the administrative structure and have five levels accordingly.

14.4.2. Outcomes of Financial Reforms

The financial reforms have stepped up the resource mobilisation at the local level. The contribution of 'budgetary allocation[22],to total funding on primary and general-secondary education declined from 78.8 percent in 1986 to 60.9 percent in 1992, while that of extra-budgetary sources (surcharges/levies, social contributions, school-generated income and school fees) increased from 21.2 to 39.1 percent during the same period (Tsang, 1996; Table 2 on page 431). This is further corroborated by Zhang and Kanbur (2005). After compiling the data on sources of education expenditure for the period 1990–1998, they note that the government's share has declined from 64.6 percent in 1990 to 53.1

[22] Two sources constitute the budgetary allocation; i) allocation from the own budget of the government (financed from own tax base), and ii) categorical grants in education from higher levels of governments. The former is primarily used for the expenditure on personnel; the excess fund, if any, can be used for non-personnel inputs and school repairs. The latter is specific-purpose grant that can be used for personnel, non-personnel or capital inputs.

percent in 1998. During the same period, the share of tuition and incidental fees (out-of pocket expenditure) increased from 2.3 to 12.5 percent (*ibid*). By 2003, the sub-provincial government has met 77.2 percent of the total public expenditure on education, while the central and provincial governments have met 8.2 percent and 14.6 percent, respectively (Shen, Zhao and Zou, 2014: 139).

China witnessed considerable progress in the spread of primary education after decentralisation reforms were introduced. The data compiled by Zhang and Kanbur (2005: 191) show that the primary school enrolment has increased significantly after the initiation of decentralisation reforms. Their data show that the primary school enrolment rate has increased from 49.2 percent in 1952 to 93 percent in 1979 and to 98.9 percent in 1998. The quality of education (measured in terms of primary school graduates entering secondary schools) has also improved from 44.2 percent in 1957 to 94.3 percent in 1998. The ratio of students to teachers in primary schools declined from 35.6 in 1952 to 22 in 1990; but again went up in the decade of 1990s. The number of students per teacher was 24 in 1998 (*ibid*).

However the responsibilities of counties and townships are not clearly defined and practically townships bear most of the burden of financing responsibilities even in poor counties. This has led to a greater demand on local resources and local administrative capacity. The data for 2003 on education expenditure by various levels of government reveal that there was financial burden at the local level (Shen, Zhao and Zou, 2014: 141). In 2003, sub-national governments had been responsible for more than 90 percent of budgetary expenditure on education with over 50 percent coming from the county and township levels. In particular, county governments have contributed more than 40 percent of the overall government education expenditure. Hence, education comes as the single most important social service provided by counties and townships. To reduce the inequality in financing and service provision, earmarked grants are provided but this was insufficient to fulfil their needs.

The problem of vertical fiscal imbalance[23] has intensified the problem. The centralised revenue and devolved expenditures at each level at the expense of subordinate level has resulted in a situation where the lowest level of government was incapable of financing the public services

[23] We have heard that this problem has been of late addressed; but, we do not as yet know the impact of this.

including education. This has in turn resulted in low investment in education; Shen, Zhao and Zou (2014: 146) show that education expenditure as percentage of GDP in China was lower than that in South and East Asia and India. Hence fiscal decentralisation has negatively impacted the budget on education as a share of total government spending[24] (Zheng, 2008 as quoted in Wang, Zheng and Zhao, 2011).

Further, the horizontal disparity among regions and within regions has led to inadequate spending towards education in poorer regions due to low economic development of these regions leading to low quality of education. This has severely affected the national goal of universalisation of nine years of compulsory education among school-aged and literacy among adult population below 20 years. This has been particularly the case in poorer regions which are not able to provide quality education to its population due to financial burden. Until 2002, 372 counties were unsuccessful in achieving the national target. Disparity in access-educational attainment (Dahlman, Zeng and Wang, 2008 as quoted in Wang, Zheng and Zhao, 2011), education spending and quality of services is substantial in rural-urban and coastal-inland regions also. Data show that urban areas spent 84 percent more on primary education and 69 percent more on junior secondary education than the rural areas. Coastal areas spent 71 percent on primary education and 75 percent on junior secondary education more than inland areas (Tsang and Ding, 2005 as quoted in Shen, Zhao and Zou, 2014). There is, therefore, a large gap between expenditure and revenue assignments. Weak fiscal transfers have made the decentralised education system inefficient and ineffective in ensuring the quality services and have passed the financial burden to the parents.

This has resulted in regional inequalities in the spread of primary education. Zhang and Kanbur (2005), who have undertaken a detailed analysis on education inequality in China, conclude that the illiteracy rate has steadily declined over a period of time, thus suggesting that the nine-year compulsory education has been successful. However, rural-urban and gender-gaps could be seen in the spread of literacy. The illiteracy rate in rural areas was double to that in urban areas. Likewise, the illiteracy rate among females was more than double to that among

[24]This is notable because, as compared to India, East and South Asia, Latin America, United States and United Kingdom, China has the lowest spending of its GDP on education (Shen, Zhao and Zou, 2014).

men; this indicates gender bias against girls. The situation in inland areas was worse (Zhang and Kanbur, 2005: 196–197).

Regional inequality in the provision of primary and secondary education was analysed for the period 1950 to 2000 by Zhang and Kanbur (2005: 199–200). Gini coefficients of student/teacher ratios in primary and secondary schools show a similar pattern except during the cultural revolution period (1966–1976) when the secondary schools were disrupted. The regional inequality in the provision of public education increased from the late 1970s onwards, thus suggesting that the decentralisation reforms have resulted in regional inequality. Zhang and Kanbur (2005: 201) provide the following reasons why decentralisation has contributed to regional inequality. First, the increasing fiscal decentralisation has reduced the redistributive power of the central government. The decentralised governments, especially those in poor regions with insufficient own revenue, have gradually withdrawn from the role of ensuring quality in the delivery of educational services. Second, investment on public infrastructure in rural areas became difficult due to weak governance at the village level. Third, the local government was not as successful in the mobilisation of local manpower for public works as it was during the planned era. This was because in the market economy, people were not willing to render free services as they expected that their labour must adequately be compensated.

Thus, over devolution of expenditure responsibilities has led to insufficient financing and provision for core public services like education and health and growing inequality across the country owing to the absence of a national common standard and growing regional development disparities (Shen, Zhao and Zou, 2014).

14.5. INDIA: POLICIES RELATING TO PRIMARY EDUCATION IN INDIA

As compared to China, the development of education in India was characterised by relative stability. The education system that India inherited from the British in 1947 was well developed. The policies pursued in India soon after the independence focused on higher and secondary education. There was rapid, unplanned and uncontrolled expansion of higher and secondary education on account of policy thrust and funding support by the government as it was believed that this type of educational system was needed for the creation of scientific, technical and other manpower for the planned economy. The primary education continued to be neglected; as a result, the problem of mass illiteracy continued.

In order to address the problem of uneven development in the different levels of education, a commission under the chairmanship of D.C. Kothari was appointed in 1964 to formulate policies to address this problem. The Commission recommended (in 1966) government-provided free and compulsory education for all the children up to the age of 14 years (Ghosh, 2000: 179–180). However, the resources necessary for the implementation of this recommendation were not allocated. As a result, although the provision of free education existed, the problem of low enrolment rate and high dropout rates persisted due to a number of factors including socio-cultural-economic factors.

The National Policy on Education, announced in 1986, called for stepping up of financial and organisational support to the educational system so that it could improve access to education among women, those belonging to disadvantaged groups and rural dwellers. For the first time the importance of primary education was realised, and a number of initiatives were started to improve the enrolment as well as the quality in education. These initiatives aimed to: i) improve the human and physical resources available in primary schools (in 1987–88); ii) create a resource for the continuous upgrading of teachers' knowledge and competence (in 1987); iii) provide a cooked hot meal every day for children in the government primary schools to improve incentives for enrolment (since 1995); iv) emphasize the decentralised planning and management, improved teaching and learning materials, and school effectiveness (since 1993), and v) achieve universal primary education under the Education for All Movement through micro-planning and school-mapping exercises, bridging gender and social gaps (since 2000). More importantly, Right to Education Act was passed in 2009 and came into effect from 2010 onwards. The Act aims to provide free and compulsory elementary education for the children in the age group of 6–14 years. For the first time in the history of educational development in India the children could access education as legal entitlement.

14.5.1. Decentralisation Initiatives

The decentralisation of education in India took a formal shape in the form of 73rd and 74th Constitutional Amendments in 1992. This provided for the setting up of local bodies (Panchayats), uniformly throughout the country[25], at village, block and district levels (village being the most basic unit), and also in urban areas through democratic process of election and for delineation of their functions and responsibilities. Regarding education, Panchayat Raj Institutions were assigned the responsibility of primary and secondary education, technical training and vocational education, adult and non-formal education[26]. A division of responsibilities regarding education among local bodies at different levels is also recommended in various sections of Panchayati Raj Act as follows:

- ***Grama panchayat*** is given the responsibility of providing education through primary and middle schools, of creating awareness among the people and ensuring enrolment of all the children in primary school, and of construction and maintenance of hostels.
- ***Panchayats at block level*** are supposed to promote primary and secondary education, construct and maintain school buildings and provide for education for working children.
- ***Panchayats at district level*** have a role in construction of roads connecting all the schools and colleges in the district, construct and maintain primary and secondary schools and hostels, construction and maintenance of schools and hostels for scheduled caste, scheduled tribes and other backward class students, provision of scholarship, free text books, teaching and learning materials for such groups.

The core of educational decentralisation consists of planning, management, control, evaluation and adequate autonomy on revenue and expenditure decisions. It is to be noted, however, that the different states in India, in pursuance of the Act, have adopted different approaches regarding the management and governance of education. For example, in Bihar, responsibilities of the Panchayats regarding education are limited to the construction and management of the schools.

[25] Panchayats existed and were functioning even before 1992. However, setting up of these Panchayats was not a mandate; states were directed, not obliged for setting up Panchayats at local level. Hence, the structure of Panchayats also varied across the states. The Amendments provided for a uniform structure of Panchayats to be followed by all the states mandatorily.

[26] Eleventh Schedule of Constitution enumerates 29 functions to be taken up by the Panchayats which also includes above-mentioned functions regarding education. However the devolution of these functions is left to the states and there is variation across the states with respect to devolution of these functions.

In Uttar Pradesh, the roles and responsibilities of local bodies are clearly defined; but their implementation status is questionable; Kerala has devolved important functions like supervision of routine school functions including the performance of teaching and non-teaching staff, offering assistance regarding disciplinary action against such staff if needed and monitoring the existence of adequate staff at the beginning of academic year. The state has also devolved 40 percent of its budget to Panchayats for developmental plans including education which is not the case with many other states. Karnataka has devolved the teacher recruitments to the block level and several other such variations can be seen across the states (Govinda and Bandopadhyay, 2010).

14.5.2 People's Participation in School Management

Community involvement and participation has been a professed goal of education decentralisation in India since beginning. Following the National Education Policy, 1986, there was a significant move to involve the community in the provision of education services. Almost all the states, through government orders, have established Village Education Committee (VEC) that includes parents, community members and teachers. In some states like Karnataka, School Development and Monitoring Committee (SDMC) was established as a powerful decision-making institution at the school level with an outreach to the parents through parents' council (Govinda and Bandopadhyay, 2010). Further, the Central Advisory Board of Education, 1993, has also recommended setting up of village education committee at village level and education committee at the block level as part of the Panchayat system itself (Mukhopadhyay, Ramkumar and Vasavi, 2009). It is notable that in some states VECs are also responsible for mobilization and utilization of funds available from government and other sources. Under the Education for All Movement, VECs are credited with the responsibilities of deciding, in consultation with school authorities, how the funds will be used for the development of the school. Instances of their involvement in monitoring the attendance of teachers and students, volunteer teaching and teaching learning materials preparation have been there (Ramachadran, 2001 as quoted in Govinda and Bandopadhyay, 2010). Similarly SDMCs are supposed to be engaged in the management of school, ensuring enrolment of children, supervising student and teachers' attendance, community mobilization and help in ensuring the quality of education.

However, these constitutional, structural and legal arrangements have not led to the active participation, increased accountability or improved learning outcomes in most of the cases. The involvement of Panchayats has been minimal with their engagement confined mainly to construction and maintenance of school buildings. The lowest tier of the Panchayats had negligible say in educational matters of local schools. Lack of clarity and information-awareness about their roles and responsibilities, financial dependence in the absence of adequate revenue generating powers, periodic alterations and functional instability and political co-option, elite capture, have been among the major reasons for low involvement of Panchayats in educational governance (Fiske, 1996; Govinda and Bandopadhyay, 2010; Mukhopadhyay, Ramkumar and Vasavi, 2009). As far as the participation of community is concerned, this also has been low and has often been limited to contributions in cash or kind (Govinda and Bandopadhyay, 2010). Even in states like Kerala, VECs and other institutional structures for community participation have not taken root and are characterised by lack of acceptance among stakeholders (Mukundan and Bray, 2004). The study of Ramachandran (2002) as quoted by Govinda and Bandopadhyay (2010), suggests 'the VECs either do not function or seem to function with mechanical intensity rather than a genuine sense of participation and commitment'. As in the case of Brazil and Turkey, factors like poverty, inequality, illiteracy have been identified as impediments for the participation of marginalised (Mukhopadhyay, Ramkumar and Vasavi, 2009; Govinda and Bandopadhyay, 2010).

In this regard, Mukhopadhyay, Ramkumar and Vasavi (2009: 26) emphasise that:

> 'Although cases of positive contribution and engagement exist even among the most disenfranchised communities, the ability of many marginalised and non-literate communities to be able to contest forms of education exclusion, dysfunctional schools and errant teachers remains limited. Cultural barriers, such as inability to engage with upper caste and traditional elite, the culture of political and social subordination etc., limit the capacity of these processes and structures. The need to enable women, members of minority and disadvantaged groups to access these structures and become active participants in the process still remains a challenge'.

Lower participation causes low accountability of teachers and thereby low results as far as learning outcomes are concerned. Pandey, Goyal and Sundararaman (2008) in their study of three states of Uttar Pradesh,

Madhya Pradesh and Karnataka found that teachers may not be accountable because the community does not have the capacity to hold them accountable as parent members of VEC are not participating in their oversight capacity. The learning outcomes which were found to be low in Uttar Pradesh and Madhya Pradesh and higher in Karnataka also mirror the lower participation and lower accountability of teachers. Karnataka data show that the members of SDMCs have received training on their roles and responsibilities and are aware on this as compared to their counterparts in Uttar Pradesh and Madhya Pradesh. Similarly, the proportion of teachers present in the schools and engaged in teaching is higher in Karnataka. Though other factors such as child's socio-economic background may be influencing their learning, teachers' engagement in teaching and teachers' attendance in Karnataka is found to be significantly and consistently associated with higher scores. The example of Himachal Pradesh also indicates that with the active involvement of Mother Teacher Associations, the attendance and performance of children has improved. Further this helps in increasing the participation and enrolment of girls and making the school environment more gender friendly (Govinda and Bandopadhyay, 2010).

Primary school enrolment in India has been a success story. The enrolment rates have crossed 96 percent after 2009. Notable feature is that the proportion of girls in the new students joining in the school during period 2007 to 2013 was 56 percent. This implies that the decades-long problem of gender disparity in the enrolment is being addressed. There has also been an improvement to the infrastructure; there are now 1.4 million schools and 7.7 million teachers. This means that 98 percent of villages have a primary school (class I-V) within one kilometer and 92 percent have an upper primary school (class VI-VIII) within a three-kilometer walking distance. However, dropout rates continue to be high. In India as a whole, 29 percent of children drop out before completing five years of primary school, and 43 percent before finishing upper primary school. High school completion is only 42 percent. There are also problems of teacher shortage, and lack of infrastructure in the schools.

14.6. CONCLUSIONS

This paper has reviewed the studies on decentralisation and education in India and China with an objective of providing an overview of decentralization approaches followed in these countries. The paper first provided a background on problems of poor educational outcomes and how decentralisation is helpful in addressing these problems. After discussing the concept of decentralisation in brief, the policies to promote primary education, decentralization reforms in the provision of education and outcomes in China and India are provided. The experiences of China and India with decentralisation in education reaffirm the mixed outcomes emanating from implementation of decentralised practices emphasised in the literature.

In China, local governments are responsible for basic education and financing is diversified. The central government retains its role of policy maker and planner for overall education. The provinces are responsible for making overall development plan including inspection, determining operational standards and offering assistance to counties to help them meet the recurrent expenditure on education. Cities (or districts in large cities) implement compulsory education in urban areas and counties are responsible for rural areas. The decentralisation reforms succeeded in resource mobilisation at the local level, improved enrolment rates and reduced student-teacher ratios. However, over devolution of expenditure responsibilities has led to insufficient financing,inadequate provision of educational services and growing inequality.

In India, the Constitution provides for setting up of local elected bodies at different levels in both rural and urban areas through democratic process of election and delineation of their functions and responsibilities. It also assigns the responsibilities of school education to the elected bodies at the district, sub-district and local levels. It is to be noted, however, that the different states in India have adopted different approaches regarding the management and governance of education as provincial governments were provided with powers to decide what needs to be decentralised in their provinces. The most notable approach is the constitution of parents' committees for facilitating the participation of people in the planning, implementation and monitoring of provision of school education. The educational outcomes differed across the states due to differences in the functioning of peoples' organisations. As far as the outcomes are concerned, there has been good progress in the enrolment rates (especially among girls) in the last two decades – after the introduction of decentralisation reforms. But, much of this progress is to be attributed to some government programmes and schemes such District Primary Education Programme (DPEP), Midday Meal, Education for All Movement and Right to Education Act which not only ensured that there are adequate resources for the development of primary education but have also been instrumental in strengthening the decentralisation reforms in India. For instance, DPEP emphasised on the district level perspective and formulation of district level annual work plans, while Education for All Movement located the planning at the village level.

The cases of China and India suggest that the decentralisation reforms in education have been initiated with motives other than pursuance of democratic and participatory ideals. In China, the decentralisation in education was initiated to address the problem of inadequate finances for the promotion of primary education. Studies therefore argue that extreme level of expenditure decentralisation with little revenue decentralisation indicates that the motive was to offload the financial burden of central government through decentralisation reforms in the country, though efficiency arguments are often presented as a rationale. In India, it is argued that, pressure from international community has led decentralise its educational management and governance.

A review of the structure of decentralised education system in these two countries shows that all the levels (central, provincial and local) of the government share authority over different functions regarding provision of education. In India, states retain their dominance in educational governance and management, though they were directed to devolve their powers to the local bodies. As a result the local government is marginalised in so far as the governance and management of schools is concerned.

Financial devolution is something which characterises the decentralisation reforms in China. Local governments have succeeded in the mobilisation of local resources and enjoy decision-making powers. However, the expenditure decentralisation without concomitant revenue decentralisation has resulted in the inequality of education. In India, on the other hand, the vision of the constitutional amendment on decentralisation is not translated at the local level in so far as the education is concerned. Hence, local government does not have powers, control over the staff and finances earmarked for the development of education. The only form of decentralisation is the role given to the community in the management of schools. As participation is central to the idea of decentralisation, participatory committees are being constituted as a component of the decentralisation reforms. With the active involvement of these committees, enrolment has improved in states like Himachal Pradesh and learning outcomes were recorded to be higher in Karnataka that could secure participation from parents through parents committees. However, these committees are in general weak institutions with limited voice in decision-making or functioning. They are also captured by the elite. This has also resulted in inequality in the spread of education. Thus, in both the countries, decentralisation reforms have resulted in inequality in the spread of primary education; but, the mechanisms were different.

Although a thorough analysis of the impact of decentralisation on outcomes is difficult, the paper offers some indications. Financial dependency of local governments seems to a major factor. In the absence of adequate financial devolution to local governments in India, they did not play significant role in the promotion of primary education. On the other hand, China could not ensure the access and quality of education even after devolution. Here, the expenditure decentralisation did not coincide with revenue decentralisation which left the local governments with little resources to deal with its educational expenditures. Besides, this also suggests that total lack of central intervention without any common guidelines may also be detrimental. These findings correspond closely to the conceptual description of decentralisation that suggests that community characteristics, local capacity, training and sensitization of local as well as provincial-national officials and a long experience with democracy determine the outcomes to a great extent.

The experiences of these countries offer some lessons that may be taken into consideration while formulating and implementing decentralisation policies for the education sector in China and India:

1. Decentralisation leads to the improved outcomes through improved governance processes.
2. Efficiency and effectiveness in service provision is improved when the service providers, be it the local government or the schools are held accountable for results (Gershberg, 2005). Accountability is a key mechanism to ensure the quantitative and qualitative reforms regarding education.
3. Accountability is greatly affected by participation and awareness levels of population which in turn is dependent on distribution of literacy and community's socio-economic characteristics. Therefore it is suggestible educational decentralisation policies should be preceded by or concomitant to the policies aiming at ensuring the above.

4. Sufficient resources at the disposal of local implementing authorities and financial autonomy are crucial for implementing the reforms.
5. A clear statement and division of responsibilities is important to avoid later confusions among different levels in the implementation
6. Awareness generation regarding roles and responsibilities at each level of implementation and in community is very important to actualise the potential of decentralised education reforms.
7. Certain level of central government intervention in terms of setting the common minimum standards and broad guidelines is instrumental in dealing with regional disparity which may increase by localization.

REFERENCES

Acharya Alka, Baru Rama, V. and Nambisan Geetha, B. (2001). The State and Human Development. *In:* Deshpande, G.P. and Acharya Alka (*eds.*). *Crossing a Bridge of Dreams: Fifty Years of India and China*. New Delhi: Tulika.

Brosio, G. (2014). 'Improving service delivery through decentralization: A challenge for Asia', *ADB Economics Working Paper Series, No. 389*.

Channa, A. and Faguet, J.P. (2012). 'Decentralization of health and education in developing countries: A quality-adjusted review of the empirical literature', *Economic Organisation and Public Policy Discussion Papers,* EOPP 38. STICERD, London School of Economics, London, UK.

Dreze Jean and Loh Jackie (1995). Literacy in India and China. *Economic and Political Weekly*, 30(15): 2868–2878.

Faguet, J.P. and Sanchez, F. 2009. 'Decentralization and access to social services in Colombia', CAF Working Paper No. 2009/01.

Fiske, E.B. (1996). *Decentralization of Education Politics and Consensus.* World Bank. Washington, D.C.

Gershberg, I.A. (2005). *Towards education decentralization strategy for Turkey: Guideposts from international experience*. World Bank, Washington, D.C.

Ghosh Suresh Chandra (2000). *The History of Education in Modern India: 1757–1998*. New Delhi: Orient Longman.

Goldman Charles, A., Kumar Krishna, B. and Liu Ying (2008). *Education and the Asian Surge: A Comparison of the Education Systems in India and China*. Occasional Paper, Centre for Asia Pacific Policy, International Programs at RAND.

Govinda, R. and Bandopadhyay, M. (2010). Changing framework for local governance and community participation in elementary education in India. Create Research Monograph No. 35.

Kingdon Geeta Gandhi (2007). The progress of school education in India. GPRG-WPS-071, Global Poverty Research Group (*www.gprg.org/pubs/workingpapers/pdfs/gprg-wps-071.pdf accessed on October 1, 2015*).

Machado, F.V.P. (2013). '*Decentralization and Accountability: The Curse of Local Underdevelopment*', IDB Working Paper Series, No. IDB-WP-397.

Mahal Ajay, Srivastava Vivek and Sanan Deepak (2000). *'Decentralization and Public Sector Delivery of Health and Education Services: The Indian Experience'*, ZEF Discussion Papers on Development Policy, No. 20.

Manor James (1999). *The Political Economy of Democratic Decentralisation*. The World Bank: Washington D.C.

Mukhopadhyay, R., Ramkumar, N. and Vasavi, A.R. (2009). *Management of Elementary Education Structures and Strategies*, New Delhi: National University of Educational Planning and Administration.

Mukundan, M.V. and Bray, M. (2004). The decentralisation of education in Kerala state, India: Rhetoric and reality. *International Review of Education*, 50: 223–243.

Pandey Priyanka, Goyal Sangeeta and Sundararaman Venkatesh (2008). *'Public Participation, Teacher Accountability and School Outcomes'*, World Bank Policy Research Paper No. 4777.

Rajasekhar, D. and Upadhyay, M. (2015). 'Decentralization and people's participation in educational governance', *In:* Singh Avinash (*ed.*), *People's participation and decentralized educational governance: Policy reforms and programme practices,* Routledge: New Delhi (forthcoming).

Rao Nirmala, Kai-Ming Cheng and Narain Kirti (2003). Primary schooling in China and India: Understanding how socio-contextual factors moderate the role of the State. *International Review of Education*, 49(1–2): 153–176.

Rondinelli Dennis, A. (1983). Implementing decentralization programmes in Asia: A comparative analysis. *Public Administration and Development*, 3: 181–207.

Serrano, Luis Diaz and Llop, Enric Meix (2012). 'Do fiscal and political decentralization raise student's performance ? A cross country analysis', IZA Discussion Paper No. 6722.

Shen Chunli, Zhao Xiaojun and Zou Heng-fu (2014). *'Fiscal decentralization and public service provision in China'*. *Annals of Economics and Finance*, 15(1): 135–160.

Surowski, David B. (2000). *History of the Educational System of China*. An essay commissioned by Projects for *International Education Research*. *https://www.math.ksu.edu/~dbski/writings/history.html* (accessed on October 4, 2015).

Tsang Mun, C. (1996). *Financial reforms of basic education in China*. *In*: *Economics of Education Review,* 15(4): 423–444.

United Nations (2014). The Millennium Development Goals Report, United Nations, New York. *http://www.un.org/millenniumgoals/2014%20MDG%20report/MDG%202014%20English%20web.pdf (accessed on May 5, 2015)*.

Wang, W., Zheng, X. and Zhao, Z. (2011). 'Fiscal reform and public education spending: A quasi-natural experiment of fiscal decentralization in China'. *Publius: The Journal of Federalism*, 42(2): 334–56.

Yoem, M., Acedo, C. and Utomo, E. (2002). 'The reform of secondary education in Indonesia during the 1990s: Basic education expansion and quality improvement through curriculum decentralization'. *Asia Public Education Review*, 3(1): 56–68.

Yolcu, H. (2011). 'Decentralization of education and strengthening the participation of parents in school administration in Turkey: What has changed?' *Educational Sciences: Theory and Practice*, 11(3): 1243–51.

Zhang Xiaobo and Kanbur Ravi (2005). Spatial inequality in education and health care in China. *In*: *China Economic Review*, 16: 189–204.

15

Poverty Reduction through Panchayats: Evidence from the Field

R. MANJULA[27]*

ABSTRACT

Community participation through democratic decentralisation is suggested as it brings in qualitative governance processes. The theoretical linkages between decentralisation and poverty reduction have been well established in the literature. On this theoretical premise, the paper explores the links between poverty reduction and the implementation of public works programme (Mahatma Gandhi National Rural Employment Guarantee Scheme – (MGNREGS) through decentralised government. MGNREGS, which is being implemented by the Grama Panchayats, is expected to provide better livelihood security to the rural households especially those who are dependent on wage labour. With the help of primary data collected from the sample households spread across several Grama Panchayats from developed and backward taluks of Ballari district in Karnataka, the paper aims to analyse the impact of MGNREGS on poverty reduction. The paper finds that the proportion of households crossing poverty line with MGNREGS earnings was only 5.1 percent in Ballari taluk and 3.8 percent in Kudligi taluk. This shows that the impact was low in general, but comparatively lower in the backward taluk of Kudligi. This negates the general expectation that the decentralised governance will be more effective in backward region. Secondly, although MGNREGS did contribute to the poverty reduction, the contribution is not sufficient to lift the ultra poor households above the poverty line. However, there was a positive impact on those households who are bordering on poverty line. If notional income from MGNREGS, with an assumption that the households obtained full employment of 100 days, is included in the monthly per capita income of the poor households, one can see a considerable

[27] Assistant Professor, Centre for Decentralisation and Development, Institute for Social and Economic Change (ISEC), Bengaluru, Karnataka.

**Corresponding author:* E-mail: manjula@isec.ac.in

decline in the proportion of poor among sample households. The paper concludes that if MGNREGS was properly implemented more number of poor households would have come out of the poverty.

15.1. INTRODUCTION

Decentralisation means transfer of powers, finances and functionaries from the higher levels of government to local government. The need for greater decentralisation for effective implementation of wage employment programme or poverty alleviation programmes has been pressed from several quarters such as academia, donor agencies and civil society organisations. Accordingly, decentralised governance has not only been introduced for an improvement in the public service delivery but also for the effective implementation of poverty alleviation or wage employment programmes in a developing country like India. Given the failure of the state for effective implementation of poverty alleviation programmes in rural and urban areas, community participation through democratic decentralisation is recommended not only to bring qualitative governance processes (participation, accountability and transparency) but also to achieve effective, equitable and sustainable development outcomes.

It is widely believed that decentralisation results in poverty reduction (Jutting *et al.,* 2005). In literature, the need for decentralisation has been argued from the viewpoint of providing right incentives for incorporating the needs and preferences of the people in the planning, implementation and monitoring. Given that the proximity of the people to the local government, people will be involved in the preparation of planning for development activities. The elected leaders have incentives to incorporate the needs and preferences of the people in the decentralisation plan. In the specific context of wage employment programmes, since the Grama Panchayat is expected to prepare a shelf of projects it may find it easy and convenient to involve people in the plan preparation. Elected leaders have incentive to incorporate the needs and preferences of people as this means that they are addressing the needs to their constituency (Crook and Sverrisson, 2001; Blair, 2000; Crook and Manor, 1998; Manor, 1999; Rondinelli *et al.*, 1989; Kulipossa, 2004).

The second viewpoint relates to information. Asymmetric information is a serious problem in any attempt to intervene for development and the delivery of services. A centralised authority does not have an unlimited ability to collect information and monitor agents. Decentralised government is in a better position to obtain information on resource endowments, technology and fiscal capacity at the local level. The powers should be, therefore, transferred to the lowest possible level and decision making should be under the direct control of the citizens. This point is specifically relevant in the context of wage employment programmes. As compared to the central government, the decentralised government (and elected political leaders) will be well aware that who among those belonging to disadvantaged groups need wage employment, when they are in need and so on. It also has better information on what works will be more useful to the village economy.

The third relates to democratisation and participation. The participation of citizens is expected to lead to good development outcomes – effectiveness, equity and sustainability. If people participate right from the planning stage, they will also be showing more interest on effective implementation of wage employment works, ensuring equity in the distribution of benefits and sustaining the rural assets (Rondinelli, 1983; Kulipossa, 2004; Sharma, 2006).

However, decentralisation is not a solution for all the problems faced at the villages in the developing countries. The literature cautions the enthusiasts that there could be dangers of decentralisation (Prud'homme, 1995; Tanzi, 1995). Prud'homme (1995: 202–13) notes that decentralisation can increase disparities, jeopardise stability, undermine efficiency and lead to corruption.

Another important issue is the role played by the elected leaders. In the local government (Grama Panchayats), the elected representatives can act as a bridge between the local government and the people. The affirmative action would ensure the representation of different sections of the society as elected members of the local government. These elected representatives will have incentives to represent the needs and preferences of the people belonging to different community. However, elite capture is one of the problems associated in the decentralised governance if there is no information on the scheme among the intended beneficiaries, if they are not empowered and if other conditions are not incorporated (Lakha, Rajasekhar and Manjula, 2015; Rajasekhar, Babu and Manjula, 2018).

Against this background, this paper examines the role of Grama Panchayats in the implementation of poverty alleviation programmes and their role in the reduction of poverty by taking Mahatma Gandhi National Rural Employment Guarantee Scheme (MGNREGS) as poverty alleviation programme in two taluks of Ballari district. While Ballari taluk is the developed, Kudligi is the backward taluk. The primary data were collected from over 500 persons, who had worked in MGNREGS as per official records, spread across 38 randomly selected Grama Panchayats. The methodology adopted was to select a village from each GP on the basis of probability proportional to wages to total expenditure on MGNREGS in the village. From each of the selected villages, two works were selected with probability proportional to the earned MGNREG wages in the work. From each work, eight job cards were randomly selected. Where there are eight or fewer job cards in the work muster rolls for 2010–11, all job cards are drawn. From each selected job card, a worker name was drawn only from those workers on the job cards who have worked on the selected work in 2010–11. In all, data were collected from 533 households covering 38 villages.

15.2. ROLE OF PANCHAYATS IN MGNREGS IMPLEMENTATION

The Mahatma Gandhi National Rural Employment Guarantee Scheme (MGNREGS) is based on the Act passed in 2005. This Act was a landmark legislation to ensure livelihood security for the rural poor as a statutory legal right. The legal right to work is new compared to past provisions for employment guarantee and poverty alleviation. MGNREGS provides for 100 days of guaranteed wage employment to every rural household whose adult members volunteer to do unskilled manual work. The scheme, besides providing a social safety net[28] for the poor and vulnerable groups, seeks to revitalize the rural economy, facilitate investment in local public goods and empower the poor in the process. The thrust of the scheme is the creation of sustainable livelihood activities by rejuvenating the natural resource base of the rural economy and creating community assets that will eventually make wage employment programmes redundant and alleviate chronic poverty in rural India. Minimum wages, unemployment allowance, gender-sensitivity, participatory democracy, transparency and accountability form key components within the overall framework of the scheme.

[28] The social safety net is incorporated in the Act by means of the provision for payment of unemployment allowance if the government fails to provide employment within 15 days of the demand for work being articulated through an application for employment. The Act provides important safeguards at each stage of the scheme, including compensation in case of delayed payment. The safety net can alternately be understood in terms of the constitutional obligation to provide employment on demand, a vital measure to prevent distress migration.

The worldwide attention to MGNREGS is also because of the potential that the scheme has for democratization at the local level. Local government, especially Grama Panchayats, is central to the implementation of the MGNREGS. In order to ensure greater decentralization and democratization, GPs are assigned the role of principal implementing agency with Grama Sabha and GP placed at the heart of the implementation process.

The *Grama Sabha* is responsible for recommending works to be taken up and conducting bi-annual social audits of all works within the GP jurisdiction. Grama Sabha meeting is to be convened following commencement of the MGNREG Act in the district to inform people about the provisions of the Act, mobilize applications for registering households and verify the same. This forum is also to be used for informing people about implementation of the scheme and communicating the progress of the works taken under the scheme. The Grama Sabha is to monitor execution of works within the jurisdiction of the GP, registration and issue of job cards, payment of wages and employment provided to each applicant. It is also responsible for constituting the Vigilance and Monitoring Committee for a period of one year and ensuring adequate representation of women and SCs/STs in the committee.

The GP is given wide-ranging responsibilities, as mentioned in the operational guidelines of MGNREGS (GoI 2008 and 2013) that include:

i) Preparing a development plan, based on Grama Sabhas' recommendations, forwarding the same to the district government for preliminary scrutiny and approval. This plan, consisting of a shelf of projects arranged priority-wise, should be ready before the commencement of the year in which the works are to be executed.
ii) Receiving applications for registration, verifying the same within 15 days of application and completing registration.
iii) Issuing job cards within 15 days of registration, updating the same regularly, communicating additions and deletions to the programme officer.
iv) Receiving applications for employment. Issuing dated receipts following such application.
v) Allotting employment within 15 days of application, informing the district government in case of inter-GP works.

vi) Executing a minimum of 50 percent of works (in terms of costs) as an implementing agency and providing sanction to commence works.

vii) Ensuring a minimum wage-material ratio of 60:40.

viii) Paying wages on a pre-determined date, preferably at the GP; responsibility of opening bank accounts for workers may also be involved if the banking system is used for making payments[29].

ix) Maintaining records including the muster Roll, besides standard paper work. Maintenance of muster rolls is important due to the GP's role as an implementing agency as well as to enable data coordination and inspection of records.

x) Management of funds is also the responsibility of GP. The GP shall have a single bank account for MGNREGS funds to be operated by the President and Secretary of GP. Prior approval of the expenditure is required, details of the same have to be presented at GP meetings and made available for social audit. The GP also has to apply for additional funds to the district government when 60 percent of allocated funds have been utilized.

xi) Convening the Grama Sabha for social audit.

xii) Monitoring the implementation of programme at the village level and works undertaken by other Implementing Agencies[30], maintenance of the muster rolls and wage paid by them.

xiii) Documents, records and accounts pertaining to the MGNREGS must be made available for public scrutiny and actively displayed at the GP premises.

xiv) 'Employment Guarantee Day' must be observed on a particular day of the week in every GP to facilitate processing of applications, payment of wages and unemployment allowance, if any, allocation of work and active disclosure of information regarding the scheme.

---

[29] Payment of wages must be made in public at Grama Sabha meetings or at the worksite to ensure transparency. However, the Operational Guidelines advocate 'separation of payment agencies from implementing agencies' by making payments through Post Offices or Banks, as this method is efficient and transparent. If payments are made through Banks, the accounts have to be opened by GPs or Banks on behalf of workers.

[30] As per MGNREGS Operational Guidelines (2008:29): 'The other Implementing Agencies can be Intermediate and District Panchayats, line departments of the Government, Public Sector Undertakings of the Central and State Governments, Cooperative Societies with a majority shareholding by the Central and State Governments, and reputed NGOs having a proven track record of performance. Self-Help groups may also be considered as possible Implementing Agencies'.

In its dual role as principal authority for planning and implementation at the village level and implementing agency for executing the works not less than 50 percent of budget, the GP has greater responsibility with regard to the MGNREGS.

Above the GP level, the burden of implementation is sparsely distributed and progressively decreases. The Programme Officer in the Zilla Panchayat is entrusted with substantial responsibilities ranging from preparing Block level plans, coordinating with the GP and the District Programme Coordinator, supervising and monitoring various works, redressing grievances, payment of wages and overseeing the functioning of the Grama Sabha. The Programme Officer is accountable to the District Programme Coordinator.

The District Programme Coordinator is responsible for overall implementation at the district level, preparation of the District Plan and Labour Budget and coordinating with the Programme Officer and State Government agencies. The responsibilities of state government include provision of training, budget provisioning, setting up the State Employment Guarantee Council, reviewing and monitoring the scheme, and disseminating information lie with the State Government. A similar advisory role is played by the Central Government.

15.3. SHARE OF MGNREGS EARNINGS TO TOTAL INCOME

In order to assess the contribution of MGNREGS in the poverty reduction it is important to assess the share of income from the scheme to total income. However, before we do that, a brief description of the sample households is provided below. Exactly 43 percent of the sample households belonged to SC/ST community. Ballari taluk has relatively higher proportion of SC/ST households. Sixty percent of the sample households lived in their own houses, while the rest lived in government provided homes. Over 75 percent of the sample households possessed Below Poverty Line (BPL) ration cards, while nearly 50 percent of them stated that their principal occupation was wage labour either in agriculture or non-agriculture. The proportion of landless households is about 28 percent and about one-third of the sample households owned less than 2.5 acres of land. The proportion of households owning more than 5 acres of land is only around 15 percent. This suggests that most of the sample households are poor.

Let us undertake an analysis of the poverty status of the worked households. The poverty line as mentioned by the Planning Commission was Rs. 902 of monthly per capita expenditure for rural Karnataka during 2011–12. Since we do not have data on consumption, we have taken income as proxy and worked out Monthly Per Capita Income (MPCI) (Fig. 15.1). Expectedly, the sample households from backward taluk were relatively poorer than those from the developed taluk. About one-third of households from Kudligi taluk were living below the poverty line with less than Rs. 902 of monthly per capita income, while the corresponding figure for Ballari taluk was about 22 percent. The proportion of households earning monthly per capita income of more than Rs. 2,250 was comparatively high in developed taluk.

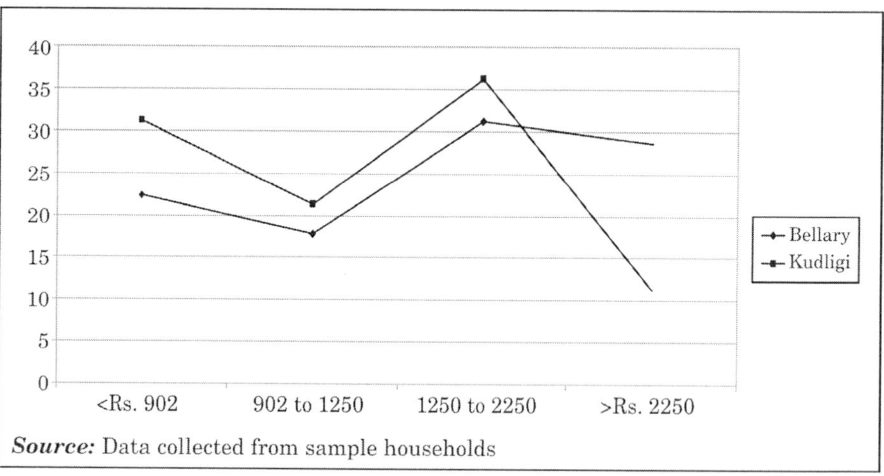

Fig. 15.1: Monthly per capita income (Rs.) of the participating households (2010–11).

Having presented the poverty status of the sample households, let us turn to the annual wage income obtained by way of participating in MGNREGS. About 26 percent of households from Ballari earned less than Rs. 1,000 per annum from MGNREGS, while the corresponding figure for Kudligi taluk is only 18.8 percent (Table 15.1). One striking point is that most of the households have earned the wages either between Rs. 1,000 and Rs. 2,000 or between Rs. 2,000 and Rs. 4,000. Notably, households' earning more than Rs. 6,000 was relatively high in the backward taluk.

The share of MGNREGS earnings in the total income ranged from zero to a maximum of 28 percent among the sample households that have taken part in MGNREGS. The distribution of sample households by proportion of MGNREGS earnings to total income is provided in Table 15.2. For most of the households, irrespective of taluks, the share

Table 15.1: Distribution of participant households (%) by annual earnings from MGNREGS (2010–11).

Taluk	*Annual earnings (Rs.) from MGNREGS*							
	0	***<= Rs. 500***	***Rs. 500–1000***	***Rs. 1000–2000***	***Rs. 2000–4000***	***Rs. 4000–6000***	***>Rs. 6000***	***Total (nos.)***
Ballari	10.8	13.4	12.7	16.6	24.2	12.1	10.2	157
Kudligi	12.5	7.5	11.3	15.0	27.5	10.0	16.3	80
Total	11.4	11.4	12.2	16.0	25.3	11.4	12.2	237

Source: Data collected from sample households.

of the MGNREGS earnings to total income was less than five percent. Only in about 11 percent of the households from backward taluk, the proportion of MGNREGS earnings was more than 10 percent.

Table 15.2: Distribution of participant households (%) by proportion of MGNREGS earnings to total household income.

Taluk	*Proportion of MGNREGS earnings to total income*				
	0%	*< = 5%*	*5–10%*	*>10%*	***Total (nos.)***
Ballari	10.8	72.0	12.7	4.5	157
Kudligi	12.5	56.3	20.0	11.3	80
Both the taluks	11.4	66.7	15.2	6.8	237

Source: Data collected from sample households.

From the above discussion, one important conclusion that can be drawn is that the wage income from MGNREGS did not constitute a large share in the total income of the households. In general, the average income earned by the households working in MGNREGS was not substantial amount. However, there are differences across the taluks in terms of contribution of MGNREGS wages to total income. Hence, an attempt is made to find out the impact of MGNREGS earnings on the poverty, and the extent to which the earnings from MGNREGS helped the poor households to cross the poverty threshold.

15.4. IMPACT OF MGNREGS ON POVERTY

The comparison between the monthly per capita income with and without MGNREGS earnings is presented in Table 15.3. As stated earlier, the households whose MPCI was less than Rs. 902 can be classified as poor households. Of them, the households whose income is even lesser (around Rs. 600) can be called as 'ultra poor' households.

Now the question is whether earning from MGNREGS has helped these ultra poor and poor households to move out of the poverty?

Table 15.3: Distribution of participant households (%) by MPCI with and without MGNREGS earnings and taluks.

MPCI (Rs.) after including MGNREGS earnings	*MPCI (Rs.) without MGNREGS earnings*					
	<= Rs. 600	*Rs. 600 to 902*	*Rs. 902 to 1,250*	*Rs. 1,250 to 2,250*	*>Rs. 2,250*	*Total*
			Ballari			
< = Rs. 600	100.0	0.0	0.0	0.0	0.0	12.7
Rs. 600 to 902	0.0	73.3	0.0	0.0	0.0	14.0
Rs. 902 to 1,250	0.0	23.3	92.0	0.0	0.0	19.1
Rs. 1,250 to 2,250	0.0	3.3	8.0	93.8	0.0	30.6
>Rs. 2,250	0.0	0.0	0.0	6.3	100.0	23.6
Total	12.7	19.1	15.9	30.6	21.7	100.0 (157)
			Kudligi			
< = Rs. 600	84.6	0.0	0.0	0.0	0.0	13.8
Rs. 600 to 902	15.4	82.4	0.0	0.0	0.0	20.0
Rs. 902 to 1,250	0.0	17.6	86.7	0.0	0.0	20.0
Rs. 1,250 to 2,250	0.0	0.0	13.3	96.6	0.0	37.5
>Rs. 2,250	0.0	0.0	0.0	3.4	100.0	8.8
Total	16.3	21.3	18.8	36.3	7.5	100.0 (80)

Source: Data collected from sample households.

As can be seen, 12.7 percent of the ultra poor households in Ballari continue to be ultra poor households even after including earning from MGNREGS. This means that MGNREGS did not contribute to the upward mobility of ultra poor in this taluk. However, the situation was slightly different in the case of Kudligi taluk. There was a positive impact on MPCI in the case of 15.4 percent of ultra poor households; however, the impact did not result in ensuring that these ultra poor households move out of poverty.

It is heartening to note that the MGNREGS earnings has helped some the poor households, who were in the borderline (income ranging Rs. 600 to Rs. 902) from the both the taluks to come out of poverty. About 23 percent in Ballari and 17.6 percent of poor households in Kudligi have moved up to the next stratum of the income category *i.e.,*

Rs. 902 to 1,250. This means that the wages earned from working in MGNREGS have contributed to an increase in the income of the poor households, and in the process, lifting them from the poverty. In fact, about 3 percent of poor households in Ballari have managed to move up to Rs. 1,250 to Rs. 2,250 income category.

To summarise, the proportion of poor households comes down from 19.1 percent to 14 percent once the earnings of MGNREGS are included in the household monthly per capita income in developed taluk (Table 15.4). The corresponding figure for backward taluk is relatively low, *i.e.,* from 21.3 percent to 20 percent. Overall, nearly 5 percent of the households belonging to 'ultra poor' and 'poor' categories from both the taluks have crossed the poverty line with the help of MGNREGS wage income (Table 15.4). While there is no impact of MGNREGS on ultra poor households in the developed taluk, marginal impact could be seen on ultra poor households in the backward taluk. Overall, the impact of MGNREGS on poverty was relatively lower among the ultra poor and poor households in backward taluk as compared to those in the developed taluk.

Table 15.4: Mobility of participant households with MGNREGS income.

Monthly per capita income category (in Rs.)	***Ballari***		***Kudligi***		***Both***	
	Without Mgnregs	***With Mgnregs***	***Without Mgnregs***	***With Mgnregs***	***Without Mgnregs***	***With Mgnregs***
<=Rs. 600	12.7	12.7	**16.3**	**13.8**	**13.9**	**13.1**
Rs. 600 to 902	**19.1**	**14.0**	**21.3**	**20.0**	**19.8**	**16.0**
Rs. 902 to 1,250	15.9	19.1	18.8	20.0	16.9	19.4
Rs. 1,250 to 2,250	30.6	30.6	36.3	37.5	32.5	32.9
>Rs. 2,250	21.7	23.6	7.5	8.8	16.9	18.6
Total	157		80		237	

Source: Data collected from sample households.

The overall impact on the poverty of households is summarised in Table 15.5. The proportion of poor was 31.8 percent in Ballari, while it was comparatively high in Kudligi taluk (37.5 percent). The poverty of these poor households comes down when the actual earnings from MGNREGS are taken into account. In other words, the actual amount earned by working in MGNREGS has contributed to the decline of poverty in about 5 percent of households from Ballari district and in 3.8 percent of households in Kudligi.

Table 15.5: Proportion of the poor moving out of poverty with MGNREGS income.

	Ballari	*Kudligi*	*Overall*
% of poor initially	31.8	37.5	33.8
% of poor after including their actual MGNREGS earnings	26.8	33.8	29.1
% of poor moved out of poverty	5.1	3.8	4.6
% of poor after including notional MGNREGS earnings (full 100 days of employment)	15.3	13.8	14.8
% of poor who would have moved out of poverty	16.5	23.7	19.0

However, the impact of MGNREGS on poverty would have been much more pronounced if the MGNREGS was implemented well by ensuring that all the households who had demanded for work were given full 100 days of work. Notional income from MGNREGS has been arrived at with an assumption that the households obtained full employment of 100 days. When the notional earning from MGNREGS is included in the MPCI of the poor households, one can see a considerable decline in the proportion of poor (Table 15.5). Thus, if MGNREGS has been properly implemented more number of poor households would have escaped from the poverty.

15.5. CONCLUSIONS

MGNREGS did make a contribution to the household income, but it was not large enough for ultra poor to reach to the threshold level of poverty line. The analysis on the extent to which MGNREGS alleviated poverty among households revealed that the proportion of households crossing poverty line with MGNREGS earnings was 5.1 percent in Ballari taluk as compared to 3.8 percent in Kudligi. We also found that the impact of MGNREGS would have been much more pronounced if the scheme was implemented well by ensuring that all the households demanding for work were given full 100 days of work. If notional income from MGNREGS, with an assumption that the households obtained full employment of 100 days, is included in the monthly per capita income of the poor households, there would have been considerable decline in the proportion of poor among sample households. Thus, if MGNREGS has been properly implemented more number of poor households would have escaped from the poverty.

ACKNOWLEDGEMENTS

I am grateful to Prof. D. Rajasekhar for his critical and valuable comments on an earlier draft of this paper. I am also thankful to Prof. B.K. Tulasimala and Prof. M. Devendra Babu for their comments and suggestions.

REFERENCES

Blair Harry (2000). "Participation and accountability at the periphery: Democratic local governance in six countries". *World Development*, 28(1): 21–39.

Crook, Richard C. and Manor James Manor (1998). *Democracy and Decentralisation in South Asia and West Africa*. Cambridge: Cambridge University Press.

Crook, Richard C. and Sverrisson, Alan Sturla (2001). "Decentralisation and poverty alleviation in developing countries: A comparative analysis or, is West Bengal unique?" IDS Working Paper 130. Brighton: Institute of Development Studies.

Government of India (GoI) (2008). The National Rural Employment Guarantee Act 2005 (NREGA), Operational Guidelines 2008 (3rd edition), Ministry of Rural Development, Government of India, New Delhi.

Government of India (GoI) (2013). The National Rural Employment Guarantee Act 2005 (NREGA), Operational Guidelines 2013 (4th edition), Ministry of Rural Development, Government of India, New Delhi.

Johannes Jutting, Corsi Elena and Stockmayer Albrecht (2005). Decentralisation and Poverty Reduction, Policy Insights No.5, OECD Development Centre.

Kulipossa (2004). 'Decentralization and democracy in developing countries: An overview'. *Development in Practice*, 14(6): 768–779.

Lakha Salim, Rajasekhar, D. and Manjula, R. (2015). Collusion, cooption and capture: Social accountability and social audits in Karnataka, India. *Oxford Development Studies*, 43(3): 330–348.

Manor James (1999). *The Political Economy of Democratic Decentralisation*. Directions in Development Series. Washington DC: World Bank.

Prud'homme Rémy (1995). 'The dangers of decentralization'. *The World Bank Research Observer*, 10(2).

Rajasekhar, D., Devendra, Babu M. and Manjula, R. (2018). *Decentralised Governance, Development Programmes and Elite Capture*, Springer, Nature Singapore.

Rondinelli, Dennis A. (1983). Implementing decentralisation programmes in Asia: A comparative analysis. *Public Administration and Development*, 3.: 181–207.

Rondinelli Dennis, McCullough, J.S. and Johnson, R.W. (1989). "Analyzing decentralization policies in developing countries: A political economy framework". *Development and Change*, 20(1): 57–87.

Sharma, C.K. (2006). 'Decentralization dilemma: Measuring the degree and evaluating the outcomes'. *The Indian Journal of Political Science*, 67(1): 49–64.

Tanzi Vitto (1995). 'Fiscal federalism and decentralization: A review of some efficiency and macroeconomic aspects'. *In*: *Annual World Bank Conference on Development Economics, (eds.)* Bruno Michael and Pleskovic Boris. Washington D.C: The World Bank.

16

Dysfunctional School Development and Monitoring Committees: A Critical Appraisal in Lambani Thandas of Karnataka

PRADEEP RAMAVATH J.[31]*

ABSTRACT

National policy on education of 1986 visualized direct community involvement in the management and monitoring of school development activities through decentralised educational governance framework. Article 21A of Indian Constitution mandates state to guarantee 'elementary education' as an important fundamental socio-cultural right of children aged between 6–14 years. This important Constitutional responsibility when read along with article 273G and Eleventh Schedule visualizes maneuvering decentralised governance mechanism in elementary education through Grama Panchayats. Systematic co-option efforts to create parallel institutions in 'decentralized governance framework' with the establishment of school development and monitoring committees by centralized executive order is an unintended effort by educational bureaucracy to delink Panchayats from mandated constitutional responsibility. Unplanned fund disbursal by Sarva Shiksha Abhiyan and recent confusions created by 'right to education act of 2009' on the roles and responsibilities of individuals, authorities, institutions etc., are seen as some of the common reasons for disfunctioning of school development and monitoring committees in Lambani Thandas of Karnataka. Critical appraisal of these committees using institutional ethnography has helped to probe more on the inability of these badly engineered 'pseudo decentralized structures' in performing the roles and responsibilities prescribed to them by educational bureaucracy. Thus proposed paper is administered to incorporate on the challenges and issues related to incorrect visualisation

[31] Assistant Professor, National Law School of India University, Bengaluru, Karnataka.

**Corresponding author:* E-mail: pradeep.ramavath@gmail.com

of equitable quality elementary education to disadvantaged Lambani communities through constitutionally decentralised institutional structure and processes.

16.1. INTRODUCTION

The focus of the paper is on dysfunctional School Development and Monitoring Committees (SDMCs) in *Lambani thandas*[i] of Karnataka. Delinking SDMCs from Panchayats and creating toothless governance mechanism through co-option is a challenge to the constitutional aspirations. Issues of non-participation, misutilization of state's resources makes one to critically question on the need for such a ritualistic decentralized governance mechanism in elementary education. Most of the SDMCs in *Lambani thandas* exists in school registers and perform their functions on school records; they are dictated by the power-centers at both school and community. Arguments for voicelessness and disfunctioning of SDMCs are based on the field studies conducted in sixteen *Lambani thandas* located in four educational districts of Karnataka[33].

16.2. CENTRALIZED EDUCATIONAL DECENTRALIZATION

Indian state has chosen 'education' as one of the socio-economic tool to provide equity for marginalized communities. Decentralized systems and spaces designed to involve marginalized section of people in educational governance needed a long term vision and perspective. Educational interventions for the marginalized sections through decentralization framework suffers from political and administrative malfunctioning syndrome. True decentralization in Education is not possible without the active participation of local communities (Menon, 1998). Several studies (Davies and Lynn *et al.*, 2003; Carney *et al.*, 2007; DPEP, 1999; PPU and NLSIU, 2004), have suggested that an overall improvement in the school system and its delivery depend on

[i] Thandas are the hamlets inhabited exclusively by Lambanis. Administratively a Thanda refers to a hamlet with a small number of population (around 100 households) *vis-à-vis* 'village'. Each Thanda is considered a part of a nearby village, although the two habitations could be distant from each other.

[33] Shimoga, Davanagere, Chitradurga and Bellary districts are selected for the study, pseudonyms are used to represent the names of Thandas and respondents, and author deserves complete right to disclose the names of Thandas if required for essential education related development interventions.

effective 'community participation'. It helps in building a sense of ownership. In fact, lack of community participation in terms of active parent-teacher interaction is a serious impediment to effective functioning of schools in backward areas of the country.

Decentralized planning and management of elementary education was a goal set by National Policy on Education of 1986. Policy visualized direct community involvement in the form of Village Education Committees (VECs) for management of elementary education. Alternatively same decentralization process is also viewed as part of liberation rhetoric (Govinda and Diwan, 2003).

In India educational decentralization became a synonym for community participation in schooling processes, even though other forms and types of decentralization practices existed in practice. Hence focus of educational decentralization canvas in India was on the community participation dimension, particularly on constitution of committees for management of education at community level. None were actually bothered about their longterm impact. Everyone was busy in creating educational committees on a programmatic approach. Most of the initiatives towards formation of school committees were designed and operationalised through international aid strategies; hence it was liberation rhetoric and not a true aspiration of local community. In local contexts social structures and their composition notably manipulated the constitution and functioning of education committees in rural India, most villagers were uninformed about existence of VECs during operationalisation of World Bank funded District Primary Education Programme (DPEP). Lack of awareness among VEC members about their roles and functions, time constraint, social structure, illiteracy, lack of communication, irregular capacity building etc., were causes of disfunctioning of VECs during DPEP days (Bhattacharya, 2001). Major concern was with respect to lower involvement of parents from disadvantaged backgrounds in parent-teacher meetings and their severe under-representation in the education committees (Prathichi, 2002).

After the commencement of Sarva Shiksha Abhiyan (SSA) as flagship programme of central government for development of school education, most of the programmes of DPEP were merged in larger SSA framework. It was mandated in SSA framework about the responsibility of governments at local, state and national level to work in decentralized governance framework to provide facilities on a priority basis for poor and marginalized sections with more attention to (SCs) and Scheduled Tribes (STs). Set of reforms as envisaged in SSA such as improvement in curriculum, teachers, management, school environment, supervision and learners' assessment etc., became key strategies for mainstreaming disadvantaged communities, but these reforms were not contextualized and redesigned to suit the local needs. Presently SSA scheme is facing severe challenge of translating the big visions into little details, state governments are noticed to be unconcerned about the intricacies of the programme, and no one is interested to enforce neither the standards as they exist nor trying to innovate better implementation strategies. SSA has only enabled pumping of more money down a very leaky pipe (Nilekani, 2008).

Contribution of community is not up to the mark as perceived in mission of SSA; basic foundation for achievement of SSA is community participation but necessary initial step creation of community awareness of SSA was not followed at the right time. In many ways SSA tries to continue previous legacy of disconnecting school from community. Further, absence of PRI leaders on the governing council or on the executive committee of SSA society strongly gives the message about recentralization of educational decentralization process.

16.3. DYSFUNCTIONAL DESIGN OF SDMCs[ii] IN KARNATAKA

Task Force report by Raja Ramanna Committee (2000) acted as precursor for conceptualization of present day SDMCs. During initial days it was believed that legal and administrative framework of SDMCs would be derived from Karnataka Panchayat Raj Act 1993, but several versions of executive orders from education secretariat (SDMC bye laws of 2001 and 2006) became unquestioned biblical texts on which SDMCs became operational replacing earlier existing VECs. Uniformity was ensured on the composition, objectives, duties, and responsibilities, procedures relating to their roles, functions and responsibilities. On the surface SDMCs looked like democratic institutions deriving their powers from Civic Amenities Committees (CAC) of Panchayat Raj Institutions (PRIs). Powers were delegated to school head teacher who is also secretary of the SDMC; s/he acted as supreme authority taking decisions on behalf

[ii] In 2001, School Development and Monitoring Committees (SDMCs) replaced the Village Education Committees (VECs) in Karnataka. An SDMC has three year term. SDMCs comprise nine elected parent members, four ex-officio members and six nominated members (including students) to ensure parental and community involvement and participation in the day to day activities of schools. A committee meets once a month to review the functioning of the school.

of SDMC members. No PRI members were seen taking part at SDMC meetings and proceedings. This was very problematic as SDMCs found not sharing their school development plans, which had adverse repercussions on the entire educational planning cycle (IRMA, 2009: 18). Further absence of local participation in SDMCs has lead to phenomenon of 'elite capture', unjust distributional outcomes and initiatives without long term plans, thus failing to achieve expected developmental goals in an efficient manner (Kumar, 2006).

16.4. LAMBANI THANDAS OF KARNATAKA

Lambanis[iii] are culturally unique tribes migrated from Rajasthan and settled in different parts of Karnataka. According to 2001 census their total population was 1.1 million which comprised of 12% scheduled caste population of the state; their literacy rate is just 32.26%. Majority of the Lambanis are landless laborers and depend on wage employment, forest produces for their survival, but in recent times there has been increased land ownership among them, further government employment schemes also have helped them to some extent.

The *Lambani thandas* are the hamlets inhabited exclusively by *Lambanis,* administratively a *thanda* refers to a hamlet with a small number of population (around 100 households) *vis-à-vis* 'village'. Each *thanda* is considered to be part of a nearby village, although the two habitations could be distant from each other. In all districts *Lambanis* have settled down in *thandas* isolated from main village. The number of *thandas* as well as their population varies substantially from district to district. There are more than 3000 such *thandas* are there on official records, only 300 have been converted into revenue villages. *Thandas* are characterized by lack of basic facilities like provision for health, education and water facilities. These *thandas* are concentrated in the

[iii]The Lambanis (also Banjari, Bangala, Banjori, Banjuri, Brinjari, Lamani, Lamadi, Lambani, Labhani, Lambara, Lavani, Lemadi, Lumadale, Labhani Muka, Gohar-Herkeri, Goola, Gurmarti, Gormati, Kora, Sugali, Sukali, Tanda, Vanjari, Wanji) are a community in India spread in Andhra Pradesh, Karnataka, Maharashtra, Madhya Pradesh, Rajasthan and other states of India. About half their number speaks Lambadi, one of the Rajasthani dialects of Hindustani, while others are native speakers of Hindi, Telugu and other languages dominant in their respective areas of settlement. They are a Scheduled Tribe in Andhra Pradesh (where they are listed as Sugali) and Orissa, a Scheduled Caste in Karnataka, Haryana, Punjab, and Himachal Pradesh. Banjara Thandas are the habitations in the State of Karnataka Dominated by Banjaras.

districts of Bijapur, Shimoga, Chitradurga, Raichur, Bellary, Dharwad, Davanagere and Gulbarga. Few *thandas* are also found in the rural districts of Mysore, Bangalore, Chamarajanagar, Hassan and Ramanagara.

The process of schooling among *Lambani* community is of very recent phenomenon. 80% of the students who are in schools from Lambani community are first generation learners. *Lambani thandas* are having very low literacy rate compared to the main revenue villages. Education is the most neglected part in *Lambani* community.

16.5. DYSFUNCTIONAL SDMCs IN LAMBANI THANDAS

Interpretations regarding disfunctioning of SDMCs in *Lambani thandas* are derived from the analysis of their guidelines, composition, method of functioning, activities carried out in previous financial years in their respective socio-economical and political context. Further role played by SDMCs in – universalisation, educational processes and extra-educational politics helped to probe more on efficacy of SDMCs in *Lambani thandas.* Issues relating to role of SDMCs in stratification processes needs more in-depth understanding of larger societal reproduction processes mediated by caste, gender and class issues. Thus present analysis is a brief insight on the existence of SDMCs in *Lambani thandas* and thoughts on their sustainability in constitutionally mandated decentralization framework.

16.6. STATE GUIDELINES 'RHETORIC *VERSUS* REALITY'

Notification issued by education secretariat during 2006 acts as model bye-law to be followed by each school for the formation of SDMCs. This is very important document which gives guidelines for schools regarding constitution of SDMC, defined roles, functions, responsibilities of the members along with the method of election of members of The SDMCs. Nearly 87% of the schools in *thandas* reported that they don't have circular *('Suttole')* which provides clear information on SDMC formation and meetings, on the rights, duties, responsibilities of SDMC members and sub-committees, and on other related issues. Remaining 13% of the schools even though had a copy of circular are not aware of basic information about the formation of SDMCs as mandated in the circular. Only person who knew something about existence of the circular was school head teacher! Thus in the sample *thandas* 68% most essential literatures were not present for the effective functioning of SDMCs;

similarly 68% of schools do not have all required literature as prescribed by SSA. This problem has been ascribed to non cooperation of Block Resource Coordinators (BRCs) and Cluster Resource Coordinators (CRCs) in timely delivery of resource materials to schools. But, BRCs and CRCs blame block and district authorities for delay in supply of these literatures.

16.7. SCAPEGOATING PAPER TIGERS

75% of the members of SDMC in *Lambani thanda* were selected by influential political leaders in *thanda* or main revenue village. These political leaders are close associates of Grama Panchayats members and MLAs. 25% said they have been selected by the head teacher of the school. No one remember about election conducted in school for SDMC or any gathering of parent council. During the discussion head teacher blamed community for distancing itself from the school activities and on the other end SDMC members blamed head teacher for keeping them away and uninformed about the school matters. But on SDMC records attendance of the members is shown though proxy signatures. 80% of the SDMC members in the selected *Lambani thandas* are illiterate and hence not interested in reading the meeting proceedings.

16.8. FORCED HELPLESSNESS

School quality inputs such as contribution of SDMCs for the development of schools in *thandas* are largely dependent on different structural characteristics such as caste and class dynamics. In most of *Lambani thandas* teachers belonged to upper caste; these teachers never see value of parents' participation in school governance. Listening to the opinions of members from *Lambani* community by head teacher is not encouraged by fellow teachers. No one from the community are supposed to ask about teachers' absenteeism. SDMC president *Sankra Naik* in *Venkateshpur Thanda* says "Sir, how can I question the head teacher who is from upper caste community, he only has selected me as president of this SDMC, we work in his field as wage laborers, we don't know much about the quality of his teaching, but he ensures midday meal for our children even during his absence". This state of learnt helplessness of parents and members of SDMCs is a serious problem to be considered in most of the *Lambani thandas.* Power relationship existing between elected SDMC member and head teacher plays a critical role in determining the regularity of teachers in school. Irregularity of teachers is a major issue in degradation of quality in *Lambani thandas*. Few teachers even after coming to the schools were seen busy in preparing for competitive exams[iv] they ask senior children to take care of younger siblings.

16.9. EDUCATIONAL PROCESSES AND SDMCs

SDMCs in *thandas* are totally ignorant on their roles in helping schools for enrolment and retention drives. None remember participating in any such drives; they say it is the wish of parents to send their children either to school or send them to wage earning. They feel midday meal programme has helped in enrolling more children to schools. 50% schools have recipe in midday meal decided by few community volunteers. 62% schools have mother volunteers in midday meal programme. Attendance among the *Lambani* students is generally low during sowing season as children go to field in helping their parents. SDMC has no opinion on these issues of low attendance and retention of the students.

It is clearly evident from the interactions and school records about focus of SDMCs towards civil construction works. 100% of the presidents and Grama Panchayat members said that, the major activity has been supervision of civil works. 43% of the presidents and less than 12% of members reported that they are involved with SDMCs in resource mobilization for the school. Efforts made by the SDMCs have been relatively weak in the areas of motivating teachers and extending school benefits to concerned beneficiaries, ensuring 220 working days etc.

16.10. EXTRA EDUCATIONAL POLITICS

State of confusion prevails regarding the pattern of formation of SDMCs at school level. Some of youths in *thanda* said that, those who support local MLA have higher chance of being selected as SDMC president. When asked about the election most of them said they were hardly aware of any such election took place at schools, even the SDMC presidents agreed on this critical issue and said one needs to have good political influence to be selected for the position of SDMC president as it involves good amount of 'money transaction'. The issue of empowerment

[iv] Teachers consider their position as very inferior job, they say if they get selected as exercise inspectors, Panchayat Development Officers (PDOs) etc., will help them to increase the status in society. In most of the visited schools teachers were busy preparing for PDO examination.

and involvement of women in SDMC structures in *Lambani thandas* showed very poor participation from women members in the decision making process.

16.11. CONCLUSIONS

Exhorting reluctant community members to take active interest in educational needs of their children demands for a holistic and long term strategy. Suboptimal and short term solutions such as formation of SDMCs without situating them in a larger societal context is a serious mistake committed by educational bureaucracy in *Lambani thandas*. Present SDMCs in *Lambani thandas* do not owe their existence with larger PRI governance mechanism; on the other hand PRIs see these SDMCs as agglomeration of voiceless parent community. SDMCs are puppets in the hands of head teacher and other higher level of educational bureaucracy. They are created as symbolic institutions representing democratic principles in school governance mechanism and help educational administrative machineries to spend resources channelized by SSA. The impact made by SDMCs is a larger question to be addressed but, the mere existence of these improperly conceived pseudo-participatory structures are problematic to the educational system as they do not have any positive benefits either.

REFERENCES

Bhattacharaya, S. (2001). Functioning of Village Education Committee- A Study of Selected VEC's in Ghunchua Cluster of Morigaon District, Assam. Unpublished Dissertation. New Delhi.NUEPA.

Carney, S., Bista, M. and Agergaard, J. (2007). Empowering the "Local" through education, exploring community managed schooling in Nepal. *Oxford Review of Education*, 33(5): 611–628.

Circular, Karnataka Government Public Education Department Commissioner office Dated 13/06/2001 regarding the SDMCs.

Davis *et al.* (2003). Education decentralization in Malawi: A study of process. *Compare*, 33(2): 139–154.

Government of Karnataka (2006). Education Secretariat- Notification No. ED 122 PBS 2004. Bangalore dated 14–06–2006.

Govinda, R. and Diwan, R. (*eds.*) (2003). *Community Participation and Empowerment in Primary Education*. New Delhi. Sage Publications.

IRMA (2010). State of Panchayats Report 2008–09. Indian Management Research Institute. Anand.

Kumar, V.A (2006–2007). Popular participation in primary education in Rural Karnataka and Andhra Pradesh. *Journal of Karnataka Studies*, 3(2) and 4(1): 71–85.

Menon, P. (1998). Functioning of village education committees: A study of selected VECs in Haryana. New Delhi, NIEPA.
MHRD (1992). National Policy of Education 1986– POA.
MHRD (1999). A study on community mobilization and empowerment for universalisation of elementary education- A synthesis report DPEP.
Nilekani, N. (2008). *Imagining India*. Penguin Group, New Delhi.
PPU and NLSIU (2004). School development and monitoring committee- Research report. Government of Karnataka. Bangalore.
Sarva Shiksha Abhiyan (2011). Framework for implementation, MHRD.
The Pratichi Education Report (2002). *The Delivery of Primary Education: A Study in West Bengal.* Mumbai, Pratichi (India) Trust.

Subject Index

M

N

O

P

Q

R

S